Praise for

The Resilience Imperative

At last, a comprehensive, hands-on guide to all the viable cooperative community-building options inherent in the great transition to cleaner, greener, more equitable economies.

—Hazel Henderson, D.Sc. Hon., FRSA, author, futurist,
and president, Ethical Markets Media

Resilience is the watchword for our dawning era of economic and environmental instability.... *The Resilience Imperative* is exactly what's needed to get us moving in the right direction.

—Richard Heinberg, author, *The End of Growth*, Senior Fellow, Post Carbon Institute

Exceptionally valuable—in vision, in strategic understanding, in concrete ways to build forward. A handbook for a morally meaningful and sustainable future!

—Gar Alperovitz, author of *America Beyond Capitalism*, and
Lionel R. Bauman Professor of Political Economy, University of Maryland

There are books that describe the desirability of a good society and others the feasibility – *The Resilience Imperative* is unique in that it achieves both. It does so by unifying means and ends. It's a book you should read and then go away and do.

—Neal Lawson, Chair of Compass UK and author of *All Consuming*

The Resilience Imperative tells us that it is ok to dream in the daytime. The authors are practical pioneers with an unrivalled track record of co-operative innovation. In this book, they show how they have done it.

—Ed Mayo, Secretary General of Co-operatives UK

This book is a beacon of hope. It sets out so clearly why 'business as usual' is disastrous for both us and the planet, and spells out the necessary solutions. It then goes much further by demonstrating brilliantly the many positive changes that are already happening and which point the way to a resilient, fair and flourishing future. It ends by challenging each of us to look at what we are going to do personally to advance the Great Transition. This is a primer for life and how to live it.

—Stewart Wallis, Executive Director, new economics foundation UK

The Resilience Imperative offers practical innovations for individuals and communities to help transition to a more humane steady-state economy. Realistic, accessible and uplifting, it is an important contribution to contemporary debates about our global future.

—Ann Pettifor, Director of PRIME Economics and
author of *The Coming First World Debt Crisis*

The Resilience Imperative is one of the most compelling books available in pointing the way to a necessary, new way of living with respect in Creation. If there is one book to read, this is it.
—Very Rev. Dr. Bill Phipps, moderator, United Church of Canada 1997-2000, chair of Faith and the Common Good

A remarkable book, as far-ranging as it is deep, informed both by historical precedents and emerging innovations. Those of us working in nonprofit finance in the United States will benefit enormously from [the authors'] perspective.
—Clifford Rosenthal, President and CEO, National Federation of Community Development Credit Unions USA

Lewis and Conaty chart, with practical examples, the robust alternative of co-operative forms of enterprise which work for the benefit of all rather than the enrichment of the few....it is an essential read.
—David A Rodgers, President, International Co-operative Alliance Housing Sector Organisation

If you, like me, are searching for something practical and inspiring to counter and replace the social and economic destruction towards which this world seems rushing. *The Resilience Imperative* is your book. Grab it, read it, think about how you and your friends can use it.
—Stewart E. Perry, author *Communities on the Way: Rebuilding Local Economies in the United States and Canada*

What is exceptional about *The Resilience Imperative* is that the persuasiveness of its arguments is enhanced by the incredible range of practical examples which show both what needs to be done, and the arguments and policies required to ensure these beacons can be replicated to become the norm. It will be an invaluable resource and I'm sure much used by countless activists to put illustrative flesh on their campaign goals.
—Colin Hines, Convener UK Green New Deal group

The Resilience Imperative is a most welcome and timely contribution to the field of sustainability studies, offering both policy makers and practitioners a wealth of ideas to guide the rethinking – and reforming –of the capitalist paradigm.
—John Restakis, Executive Director, BC Co-operative Association, and author of *Humanizing the Economy: Co-operatives in the Age of Capital*

[The authors'] practical solutions to enhance democracy are signposts for a cultural shift to solidarity, co-operation and sufficiency, offering a future rich with possibilities. The challenge shared by all of us is to build momentum for that shift. *The Resilience Imperative* makes a vital contribution to those urgent efforts.
—Michael Toye, Executive Director, Canadian Community Economic Development Network

THE RESILIENCE IMPERATIVE

COOPERATIVE TRANSITIONS
TO A STEADY-STATE ECONOMY

··

Michael Lewis *and* Pat Conaty

new society
PUBLISHERS

Cover design by Diane McIntosh.

Printed in Canada. First printing April 2012.

New Society Publishers acknowledges the support of the Government of Canada through the Book Publishing Industry Development Program (BPIDP) for our publishing activities.

Paperback ISBN: 978-0-86571-707-7
Ebook ISBN 978-1-55092-505-0

Inquiries regarding requests to reprint all or part of *The Resilience Imperative* should be addressed to New Society Publishers at the address below.

To order directly from the publishers, please call toll-free (North America) 1-800-567-6772, or order online at www.newsociety.com

Any other inquiries can be directed by mail to:

New Society Publishers
P.O. Box 189, Gabriola Island, BC V0R 1X0, Canada (250) 247-9737

Library and Archives Canada Cataloguing in Publication

Lewis, Mike, 1952-
    The resilience imperative : cooperative transitions to a steady-state economy / Michael Lewis and Pat Conaty.

Includes bibliographical references and index.
ISBN 978-0-86571-707-7

    1. Sustainable development. 2. Sustainable development--Case studies.
3. Cooperative societies--Case studies. 4. Environmental economics. 5. Social change--Economic aspects. I. Conaty, Pat II. Title.

HC79.E5L49 2012   338.9'27   C2012-901825-2

New Society Publishers' mission is to publish books that contribute in fundamental ways to building an ecologically sustainable and just society, and to do so with the least possible impact on the environment, in a manner that models this vision. We are committed to doing this not just through education, but through action. The interior pages of our bound books are printed on Forest Stewardship Council®-registered acid-free paper that is 100% post-consumer recycled (**100% old growth forest-free**), processed chlorine free, and printed with vegetable-based, low-VOC inks, with covers produced using FSC®-registered stock. New Society also works to reduce its carbon footprint, and purchases carbon offsets based on an annual audit to ensure a carbon neutral footprint. For further information, or to browse our full list of books and purchase securely, visit our website at: www.newsociety.com

new society
PUBLISHERS

MIX
Paper from
responsible sources
FSC® C016245

Contents

Acknowledgments

First and foremost we wish to acknowledge that our efforts have been inspired and informed by the brilliance and thoughtfulness of many, many people who have grappled with how to shape a more fair, just and sustainable human civilization. We have had the privilege of internalizing some of their profound insights and wisdom as we wrote this book. You will see their names and citations throughout.

Second, we are blessed in our lives with a wide range of colleagues in Canada, Britain, Ireland, the UK, the US, Sweden, Italy, Spain, Germany and Latin America whose commitment to 'figuring out' generative and practical means to navigate a way through the 21st century have contributed so much to our thinking.

Third, we would especially like to thank Shann Turnbull, Cliff Rosenthal, John Emmeus Davis, David Rodgers, Oscar Kjellberg, Naomi Kingsley, Michael King, Margrit Kennedy, Lana Hersak and Margie Mendell for checking and helping us revise key chapters. We also thank Audrey McClellan, our able editor who facilitated a relatively pain-free process of revision that led to a much better text. And, of course we wish to personally thank Ingrid Witvoet, the Chief Editor of New Society Publishers. Within two days of receiving a draft table of contents and chapter she enthusiastically expressed her interest and two weeks later this volume was approved for publication. We were happily stunned.

Fourth, as co-authors we acknowledge each other. Without the two of us cooperating, contending, collaborating, learning and writing together, this attempt to connect some of the dots important to taking up the resilience imperative would not have been possible. We profoundly extend our thanks to each other.

Fifth, we acknowledge all those that have shaped us and those that have accompanied us on this journey the last four years of researching and writing. We particularly thank the BC – Alberta Social Economy Research Alliance, who provided some important supports for both writers, and their funders, the Social Science and Humanities Research Council. The Canadian Centre for Community Renewal staff have been very patient and supportive, particularly Don McNair who immensely improved the quality of our efforts through his editing and graphics and without whom we would not have met our deadlines.

Finally, we could not have started nor completed this book without the inspiration and patience of our partners, children and grandkids. Their support and encouragement helped us go the distance.

CHAPTER 1

Resilience: The 21st - Century Imperative

*We cannot solve our problems with the same thinking
we used when we created them.*
— Albert Einstein

Our job is to make hope more concrete and despair less convincing.
— Anonymous Welsh poet

*Another world is not only possible, she is on her way.
On a quiet day, I can hear her breathing.*
— Arundhati Roy

HUMANS FACE PROFOUND CHALLENGES over the next century — climate change, peak oil, a growth-addicted global financial system, gross inequity. Simply tweaking the way we do things will not be enough to help us muddle through. "Business as usual" is a perilous option bound to drive our species onto the proverbial rocks. We should not expect to survive with any kind of dignity if we continue what we are doing. Rather, we must radically shift the way we see, think, and act in relation to each other and the planet.

It has likely never been so important, or possible, for humans to contemplate the possibility of our own demise. From the individual to the household, from the local to the global, achieving a timely, deep, and fair reduction in the use of fossil fuels is so compellingly important it deserves to be seen as the "great moral cause of our times," as Al Gore describes it.

"Tinkering with the status quo or embracing false positives will only slow the devastation, not prevent it." This is the view of the laureates of the Right Livelihood Awards (an alternative to the Nobel Prize designed to recognize individuals and organizations forging concrete and replicable solutions to vexing human problems). These laureates, like many other people across the globe, are adopting an increasingly urgent tone in their declarations: "We want to awake the world to the fact that now is our last chance to decide: Do we risk collapse through business as usual? Or do we have the wisdom and courage to radically shift our paradigm in favour of a secured common future?"

The answer to these questions may well be known within a generation, two at the most. In the meantime, there is much to do. Our actions, or our failure to act, will draw lines that bend the curve of history. Yesterday's sketches need not predestine the outcome of the human story on this planet. Our species has proven itself resilient in the past. We can adapt. We can make shifts. The question is whether we can do so on the scale and at the pace required to change the current trajectory.

Navigating the SEE Change: The Pedagogy of Transition

In this book we argue for a transformative re-evolution away from a global growth economy fed by fossil fuels toward more local and resilient economies. We also suggest a route to get there, a four-part methodology we have called SEE Change (SEE = Social, Ecological, Economic).

First, SEE Change requires that we SEE our planet and our place in it differently. We must redefine our field of vision, broaden our understanding of the context and challenges we face, and open our eyes to new ways of meeting our basic needs. The steadfast pursuit of economic growth is seldom questioned in our culture, and gross domestic product (GDP) remains a dominant measure of our well-being, but we question this viewpoint, deeply. Our purpose is to make a modest contribution to advancing what John Stuart Mill, in *Principles of Political Economy*, positively proposed as a future "stationary state economy," a possibility also contemplated by John Maynard Keynes in his 1930 essay "Economic Possibilities for Our Grandchildren." Such a venture may seem an apostasy to many. We beg to differ.

Second, we must SEEK strategic pathways through which to bring into balance our relationships with each other and with the earth. This is the "Great Transition" Kenneth Boulding so compellingly set out as a prerequisite to sustainability 50 years ago in *The Meaning of the Twentieth Century*. It is anything but simple. The profound imbalance caused by unfettered economic growth can render us immobile, even if we do begin to SEE the world differently. It all seems so overwhelmingly difficult, so challenging, hopeless even, given the depth of our dependence on fossil fuels and addiction to economic growth. How do we even begin to begin?

Difficult? Yes. Challenging? Unquestionably! But hopeless? Not in our view. The innovations we present in this book — a mere sample of the creative action being taken across the globe — serve to reduce our timidity. True, they are not solutions in and of themselves. Instead, like trailblazers' marks, they serve to guide and inspire us as we build paths to a future in which our needs for finance, shelter, energy, and food are met on a more local and regional basis. Moreover, when we see how these innovations interconnect, new possibilities emerge for scaling up and spreading innovation.

Third, we must SHARE what we are learning, spreading the knowledge far and wide. Inspiring others with concrete evidence of the possibilities for SEE Change at the local and global levels is a constant task in the pedagogy of transition. Billions of us are hungry for alternatives to spending our lives on an economic treadmill that seems to be running faster and faster, at a steeper angle, as we struggle to stay where we are.

However, those who have a vested interest in the status quo will greet our suggestions with derision, contention, and vigorous resistance, which means we must SECURE the paths we cut through the hubris of our 21st-century predicament. We are at an unprecedented juncture of human history, where past assumptions are being challenged to the core. Many remain powerfully attached to the assumption that self-interested, profit-driven economic growth will produce the greatest public good. Economic and political elites are not inclined to SEE the world any differently than they currently do, though, happily, exceptions are becoming more apparent. Even so, it is absolutely necessary to build local, regional, national, and global strategies to secure the transition road as we travel it.

Unprecedented Volatility: A Sign of the Times

Uncertainty, stress, variation, and diverse challenges have been constants during our 200,000-year stint on our 4-billion-year-old planet. Our interaction with the wondrous multitude of ecosystems from which we evolved has defined us as a species. Our capacity to learn, innovate, and adapt developed within nature's womb, and our diverse cultures took root there. Our lives have been imbued with meaning derived from the place we inhabit on the planet and our imaginings of how we came to be here. This is the heart of the human story, a story that reveals us to be resilient creatures.

That resilience will be sorely tested this century and beyond. The gentle curve of time that shaped our social, economic, and cultural evolution was like a slow-motion film in comparison to the explosive period of volatile change that burst upon us in the 20th century. We were hunter gathers for 95 percent of our existence. Growing food has occupied but 5 percent of our time on the planet, and the industrial revolution is so infinitesimal as to be irrelevant in evolutionary terms. Yet since the mid-19th century, when we began the commercial exploitation of oil, that powerful store of

Fig 1.1: *Volatile road.* Source: © Skypixel | Dreamstime.com

ancient sunlight nature deposited over hundreds of millions of years, we have extended human influence over the planet so completely that both ourselves and the planet have forever been altered. Our ingenious capacity for innovation has unwittingly unleashed changes that put the ecosystems we depend on at risk, and has thus endangered our own and other species.

Consider the merits of the following points, whether they resonate or not.

- ✓ We evolved in a relatively stable planetary climate. Today we have an increasingly volatile climate due to our burning of fossil fuels.
- ✓ We depended on the sun for our energy virtually our entire history. Today we depend on non-renewable fossil fuels, the most powerful and flexible energy source on the planet.
- ✓ Money as we know it is a recent invention. Originally it was a means of exchange. Today its pursuit has become an end in itself. Its acquisition and use is a central preoccupation for billions of us.
- ✓ The consequences flowing from this entangled trinity are erupting all around, thrusting us into an unprecedented era of volatility.

Let's take a look at some of the evidence.

Fossil Fuels and Climate Change

The 2007 reports of the Intergovernmental Panel on Climate Change (IPCC) did not mince words. One thousand scientists from around the world declared that climate change is real and that the time for avoiding cata-strophic consequences is short. Since then, their predictions of the rate of climate change have proven conservative. In early 2009, James Lovelock, in *The Vanishing Face of Gaia*, noted that the single most important indicator of climate change, the rise in sea level, had already outpaced the IPCC 2100 projection of 18 to 59 centimeters by 1.6 times. The latest evidence from the eight-nation Arctic Assessment and Monitoring Program is even more alarming. In 2011 the AAMP projected sea levels could rise by as much as 1.6 meters by the end of this century.

The amount of carbon in the atmosphere is also increasing. Currently, the ratio stands at 390 parts per million (ppm) as measured by the Mauna Loa Observatory, a leading center for atmospheric carbon measurement. James Hansen, head of NASA's Goddard Institute for Space Studies, sug-gests that if we wish to keep a planet similar to the one on which civilization developed, we should aim to reduce the ratio to 350 ppm. But given the prognosis for economic growth completed by the US Energy Information Administration in May 2009, carbon emissions can be expected to increase from 29 billion metric tons (2006) to 40.4 billion in 2030. In short, we are going in precisely the wrong direction.

The increase in carbon emissions has not been perfectly linear. The 2008 recession was good news in terms of carbon containment. The International Energy Agency projected a 3 percent decline in carbon emissions in 2009 — three-quarters from a slowdown in industrial activity due to the finan-cial crisis, and one-quarter from growth in the use of renewable energy and nuclear power. The actual result was not quite so dramatic; recession drove emissions down 1.9 percent. Depressingly, in May 2011 the same agency reported the carbon results of the global economic recovery underway: car-bon emissions increased by 5.9 percent in 2010, the largest annual increase in human history. Three-quarters of that increase came from the emerging economies of China and India.

Carbon emissions have fallen three other times in the last 40 years. The first drop occurred during the oil crises of the early 1970s. At that time, the price of oil more than doubled, forcing many industries to contract or close. Emissions fell again in the early 1990s with the economic collapse of the Soviet Union. Russian industrial output plummeted, coal mines closed, and people could not afford to heat their homes. Carbon emissions fell 0.3 per-cent in 1998, due in part to greater energy efficiency, but, alas, the main cause was Britain and Germany switching from coal to gas and China reducing its subsidies to the coal industry.

Apart from these anomalies, carbon emissions have increased an aver-age of roughly 3 percent a year since 1950, and our reliance on fossil fuels is projected to increase 22 percent by 2025, from 85 million to 101 million barrels of oil per day.

Whether we will reach such a level of consumption is questionable. Many politicians, military analysts, investment bankers, geologists, and industry experts have presented detailed and persuasive evidence that while demand for oil may be increasing, oil discovery and oil reserves are in decline. Many assert that oil production has already reached its peak.

On the climate change front, this may seem like good news. Could a fall in the accessibility and affordability of fossil fuels bring carbon emissions under control? Recent research suggests this may be the case. The aforementioned Goddard Institute has examined several scenarios and reports that carbon dioxide in the atmosphere could be kept below 450 ppm — the level scientists view as the tipping point for uncontrollable climate change. We simply must stop burning coal by 2050. They contend there is not enough oil and gas to take us over the 450 ppm mark. While this is still a long way from the target of 350 ppm, it suggests that the consequences of climate change may be somewhat less severe. However, China is opening a new coal-fired power station every week, so it's questionable whether we can achieve the desired reduction in coal use. And as oil costs rise, corporations plan to build more than 200 new coal-fired plants in North America and Europe, increasing the level of use for that resource as well.

Fig. 1.2: *Coal plants must be shut down if we are to avoid reaching an atmospheric carbon-dioxide level of 450 ppm, which scientists view as the point of no return for climate change.*
Source: © Jjayo | Dreamstime.com

Fossil Fuels and Global Finance

Less of a consolation is the rise in the cost of living that we all can expect as the global demand for oil goes steadily upward and its supply goes steadily downward. In its 2008 annual report, the International Energy Agency stated that production from the world's mature oil fields was declining by 6.7 percent annually. More and more wells are drilled every year, yielding smaller and smaller volumes.

To be sure, the trajectory of oil prices is not linear. In July 2008, prices peaked at $147 per barrel, leading to food riots in Morocco, Yemen, Senegal, Uzbekistan, Indonesia, Mexico, and Mauritania. Prices fell to just $34 by the end of 2008, then doubled again by March 2009. In the midst of the recent financial crisis, the deepest recession since the 1930s, the demand for oil declined by 3.5 million barrels per day. Still, by March 2012, prices were back up over $106. Jeff Rubin, former chief economist with world markets at the Canadian Imperial Bank of Commerce, predicted in 2009 a price of $225 per barrel by 2012.

Rubin's prediction seems doubtful as this book goes to press: the prospects of debt defaults in Europe could propel us into another slide, not unlike that of 2008, as demand declines. Nevertheless, Rubin is not alone in his projection of the general trend. More and more analysts consider the delays that recession has brought to the exploration and development of new oil projects a virtual guarantee of higher prices. There is also a growing consensus that over half the global endowment of oil has already been consumed. Couple that with the exponential increase in China's and India's demand for oil and the inability of oil-exporting countries to increase production, and there are literally barrels of uncertainties. It is almost certain that oil prices, already volatile, will continue their upward rise.

It is important to note that there are serious counterarguments to parts of this analysis. A major one is that rising oil prices will trigger new innovation. Development of new supplies, the reworking of existing wells, and the exploitation of oil shale and oil sands are all well underway. Pricing drives profit margins, which in turn drive investment. True; this is the way things work. Unfortunately, rising oil prices also trigger recession. Five of the last six recessions corresponded with a spike in the price of oil, a crucial connection that receives scant attention outside of a few think tanks that take peak oil seriously.

A big problem in this discussion of the price-innovation relationship is that it does not account for a lot of costs. What are the costs of the pollution and carbon emanating from the Alberta oil sands, or the costs of the huge volume of water required in a province projected to have severe water problems this century. What of the poisoned groundwater created by the exploding gas shale practices across North America? And who in industry and policy circles is admitting publically the vast amounts of energy it takes to get one unit of energy from such sources?

If these costs are not considered part of the real price, investment decisions are skewed to more of the same — more investment to find fossil fuels farther afield or to develop known sources that have been inaccessible. This drives up carbon emissions when what we need is pricing that reduces fossil fuel use and redirects investment into clean energy. Until we have pricing that reflects the true costs, there is a huge brake on long-term investment flowing into the alternatives. The perceived financial risk is too high because the cost of fossil fuel is artifically low. Thus we are left with wild swings in the price of oil, which feed economic volatility, neutering our capacity for a generative movement toward a steady-state economy.

However, oil prices are not the only source of financial uncertainty. It may well be the mystifying world of money and global finance that is the biggest source of volatility.

Money and Meltdowns

Just how volatile the financial markets have become is dramatically depicted in Table 1.1. Note, only one of the 23 financial crises listed occurred before 1970 — that was the Great Depression of the 1930s. The other 22 took place between 1970 and 1998, a mere 28 years. Twenty of them occurred since 1982, an average of 1.25 every year for 16 years.

The obvious question is why was the period from 1933 to 1970 so financially stable when it was such a volatile period in so many ways? The answer is pretty simple: Interest rates were kept strictly regulated at a low level.

Table 1.1 Selected episodes of financial instability (1933–98)	
1933 Great Depression (USA)	1990 CP Crisis (Sweden)
1970 Penn Central (USA)	Banking Crisis (Norway)
1973 Secondary Banks (UK)	1991 Banking Crisis (Finland)
1974 Herstatt (Germany)	Banking Crisis (Sweden)
1982 Debt Crisis (LDC)	1992 Banking Crisis (Japan)
1984 Continental Illinois (USA)	Bond Market Collapse (Europe)
1985 Regional Banks (Canada)	1993 Exit from European Exchange
1986 Market Collapse (France)	Rate Mechanism (UK)
Mid-80s Thrift Crisis (USA)	1994 Bond Market Reversal
1987 Stock Market Crash	Mexican Crisis
1989 Junk Bond Market (USA)	1997 Asian Crisis
Banking Problems (Australia)	1998 Russian Crisis

Note: LDC refers to "lesser-developed countries."

Geoff Tily, a post-Keynesian economist, provides the evidence in his 2010 book *Keynes Betrayed*. What his analysis shows is the relative stability of heavily regulated periods compared to deregulated periods:

- High cost of capital during the 1920s
- Capital cost reduced during the 1930s through the Second World War
- A sustained period of low-cost capital between 1945 and the early 1970s
- A period of negative real interest rates in Britain in the 1970s
- An era of high-cost capital from the 1980s into the late 1990s
- A brief period of low-cost capital from the end of the 1990s into the early 2000s

As the cost of capital increases, so too does debt. The common feature underlying each of these financial crises is debt accumulation.

In 1992, an economist named Hyman Minsky predicted the financial collapse of 2008. So accurate was his forecast that central bankers around the world grudgingly acknowledge what has become known in these rarefied circles as the "Minsky moment." In his 1992 paper "The Financial Instability Hypothesis," he compared financial markets to addicted gamblers: they follow their own casino logic and chronically surge out of control. In his view, unless they are strictly regulated, financial markets are intrinsically unstable. Minsky argued that, as economies go into a boom, corporations rake in so much money it exceeds the sums needed to pay off their debt. Flush with cash, the job of corporate investment managers is clear — figure out ways to use money to make more. Unless arrested by government intervention, they invent and employ increasingly risky methods to do so. The inevitable result is a crisis in the financial system and the risk of collapse. This is what happened in the Great Depression. It is also what happened in the subprime mortgage crisis that blew up the global financial system in 2008 (Figure 1.3).

The story of two Bolivian sisters, friends of one of the authors, illustrates well the risks to average folks inherent in a deregulated financial system. The two entered the United States illegally in 2000, settling with their husbands and children near Washington DC. For years they had run their own microbusiness in La Paz, working 18 hours a day. Now they found work as cake decorators, rapidly becoming prized employees for their artistry and efficiency, though as illegal aliens they were underpaid. To make ends meet they worked 7 days a week, 16 hours per day. Their "day off" was an 8-hour shift.

Less than a year after their arrival, President Bill Clinton granted an amnesty to illegal immigrants. With a deep sigh of relief, the two families

Fig. 1.3: *US mortgage lenders filed a record 3.8 million foreclosures in 2010, up 2 percent from 2009, and an increase of 23 percent from 2008. In 2011 the number of foreclosures declined, but they are poised to rise to a projected 3.5 million in 2012. That is a lot of displaced people who no longer "Occupy" what they once called home. And the banks are selling the houses off for much less than what is owed.* Source: © Mike_kiev | Dreamstime.com. (Statistics from the RealtyTrac.com website. Projections for 2012 are from the Future Tense website, www.ftense.com/2012/01/foreclosure-filings-to-surge-in-2012.html).

set out to secure what they believed to be their passport to getting ahead, the coveted green card. It arrived in 2004, along with a hike in wages. Realizing the dream of owning their homes seemed the logical next step. Housing prices continued to rise, and if they did not get in the market now, they would not be able to afford it. Why not pay more now and benefit from the uplift in the market?

Somehow they managed to secure a loan. Their payments were $3,000 per month, $1,000 more than the rent they paid previously. It worked for a while...until their husbands' work became more irregular. Then it became impossible to keep up with the bills. One of the sisters started looking at options for refinancing to reduce her monthly payments to $2,400. She met a mortgage broker who put together a deal that would see her pay $2,600 per month for six months, after which it would fall to $2,400. Unfortunately she had neither the time nor the money to pay a lawyer to review the agreement. After two years the payments rose from $2,400 to $3,700, and two years after that they rose to $4,700. These increases became impossible and as missed payments mounted, there was no choice but to walk away.

The common term for such practices is "predatory lending." It is an apt description. Here is how it works. Once the two women signed the broker's agreement, he sold the mortgage to Country Wide Mortgages, got his take, and was out of the picture. Country Wide Mortgages then bundled up the two sisters' mortgages with hundreds of others and sold them as a package to an investment bank. In turn, the bank wired together thousands of these bundles, readying them for sale on the international market as a type of derivative called a mortgage-backed security. The theory is that by pooling so many mortgages, risk is reduced. To prepare them for sale in the global market, the bank paid for insurance from a financial giant like AIG. Last but not least, the bank paid to have a security rating agency like Standard and Poor assess the risk. Triple A ratings were the standard result, the best guarantee available to persuade investors of all kinds that this was a high-yield investment with moderate risk. After all, the derivative consisted of real mortgages backed by a piece of America. It was now ready to peddle across the globe. People saving for their retirement, pension funds, corporations, banks, governments — customers of all kinds unwittingly assumed they were making a prudent but relatively lucrative investment.

The systemic flaws began to show up as the predatory terms of subprime mortgages hit unsuspecting householders. Like the two Bolivian sisters, they were forced to walk away. This exodus became a tsunami when in 2006 the prime rate of interest almost doubled overnight, jumping from 2.5 to 4.5 percent. Hundreds of thousands abandoned their homes. Housing prices plummeted. The security of millions more declined as the market values of houses sank below the value of the mortgage they carried. Credit started crunching and foreclosures started mounting. When investors across the globe smelled the rot, they bailed out, flushing the "value" of derivatives down the toilet as if they were no more than flimsy bathroom tissue. The collapse ricocheted across the world, hurting everyone from two hard-working sisters in Virginia to small and large investors. This is the Minsky moment. The asset inflation stops, prices take a nosedive, and the bubble bursts.

Iconic billionaire investor Warren Buffett was among a very few in his profession to warn shareholders that derivatives were ticking time bombs. In his Berkshire Hathaway annual report of 2002 he wrote: "These instruments will almost certainly multiply in variety and number until some event makes their toxicity clear. Central banks and governments have so far found no effective way to control or even monitor, the risks posed by these contracts. In my view derivatives are financial weapons of mass destruction, carrying dangers that, while now latent, are potentially lethal."

Paul Mason, economics editor at the BBC, adds some perspective and texture to the bursting bubble of the Minsksy moment. In the 1990s a series of legislative moves in the United States virtually freed the American financial system from its regulatory tether. The repeal of the Great Depression-era Glass–Steagall Act, which had placed strict regulatory controls on the banks, was most significant. Banks became free to merge with insurance companies and could lend in any US state, and of critical importance to the Wall Street lobby, derivatives were exempted from any regulation whatsoever.

This paved the way for the speculative DotCom boom in 1997, a bubble that burst just after the bombing of the World Trade Center towers. In his book *Meltdown,* Mason describes how economic decline ensued, aided and abetted by the corruption of Enron and others caught either illegally manipulating share prices by hiding debt and losses in offshore companies to protect share value or hiding profits to avoid taxes. The problem became how to jump-start economic growth.

Alan Greenspan, head of the US Federal Reserve slashed the bank prime rates to 1 percent, which created a flood of cheap mortgage credit in the housing market. The stage was set for what became the subprime fever. When this bubble showed signs of bursting, speculative capital started to shift into oil, food, and other commodities. And after Lehman Brothers, one of the leading derivative peddlers, collapsed, the walls came tumbling down.

The problems are far from over. Bank exposure to the fiscal crisis in Ireland, Greece, Spain, Portugal, and Italy — a crisis caused in large part by the recklessness of the banks themselves — is threatening the so-called eurozone, as taxpayers in other countries of Europe are being called on to shore up governments in danger of defaulting on "their" debt. A second-stage financial crisis is upon us as this book is being completed. Mervyn King, governor of the Bank of England, has noted that the heavy exposure of German, French, US, and UK banks to a Greek default could well add another crisis to the list set out in Table 1.1.

When viewed from the vantage point of ordinary people, the impacts of wholesale deregulation are enormous. Mason shows that during the period when banks were strictly regulated, the income of the poorest 20 percent of Americans rose (post 1940) by 116 percent. The income share of the richest 1 percent fell. Their 20 percent capture of all income in 1929 was halved in the matter of a few years. However, once deregulation started in the mid-1970s, it was not many years before once again the level of inequality shot up; the richest 1 percent once again commanded almost 20 percent of the

"Some day, dear child, you will learn that life is full of mysterious cycles. Sometimes, the rich get richer, and the poor, poorer. Sometimes the rich get richer, and the poor remain the same."

national income. Meanwhile, the income of the poorest 20 percent rose infinitesimally; for men, by 2009 their income had actually declined over the previous 30 years. Not surprisingly, personal household debt doubled in the same period.

Edifying, is it not? When interest rates were kept low by government, the poor got richer and the rich got poorer. When government got out of way and the free market was unleashed, once again the rich got richer and the poor got poorer.

All of this becomes even more troubling when one sees how the financial sector has swollen out of all proportion to the real economy. In 1980, the size of the world's financial assets was equivalent to global GDP; in 2008, total financial assets were three times global GDP. In the 1960s, financial organizations accounted for 14 percent of corporate profits; by 2008 that had risen to 39 percent, further evidence that investment in the real economy is being abandoned in favour of speculative investment in the casino economy. In 2007, according to Paul Mason, UK pensioners had 30 percent of their pensions invested in speculative hedge funds, up from 5 percent just six years earlier. (We'll take a closer look at this development in Chapter 11.)

One wonders if this capture of wealth by a tiny fraction of the population is at the heart of Nelson Mandela's condemnatory lament, quoted in the United Nations Development Programme's 2005 *Human Development Report*: "Massive poverty and obscene inequality are such terrible scourges of our times — times in which the world boasts breathtaking advances in science, technology, industry and wealth accumulation — that they have to rank alongside slavery and apartheid as social ills."

In a century of volatility whipped up by climate change, peak oil, and a global financial system gone awry, it is little wonder that the way forward appears murky. What seems more certain is that there is a connection between impoverishment of the many, unwarranted enrichment of the few, and a planet groaning under the weight of it all.

Progress and Growth: Navigating through the Rearview Mirror

With this unholy trinity of climate change, peak oil, and the casino economy framing our future options, it is easy to understand why it is so hard to see the world afresh. Especially when it seems so much of the discourse of elites and average citizens alike is embedded in well-honed myths and unexamined assumptions. It is as if we are driving toward the future with our eyes locked on a magical rearview mirror. However we tilt the mirror, and wherever we drive, comforting images of "progress" remain in view, locked in by a century of dazzling technological and economic achievement. Material goods, life spans, and beauty-enhancing refits appear to multiply endlessly into the future.

However, if humans had not learned how to harness oil and manipulate it in various ways, life as we know it today would be unimaginable. Modern transportation would not exist. Plastics would not exist. Pesticides, synthetic fertilizers, and all manner of fuel-driven agricultural and irrigation implements would not exist. Our population would not have exploded to 7 billion, a 600 percent increase in 150 years. The dramatic economic growth we have experienced would not have occurred.

Over most of human history, economic growth has been negligible. For millennia, we depended wholly on direct sunlight for the energy needed to meet our everyday needs. We lived in a steady-state economy.

Yet today, in the face of overwhelming evidence to the contrary, many remain adamant that things will continue to unfold as they have over the last six generations. The aforementioned analysts at the US Energy Information Administration have calmly projected a 22 percent increase in demand for fossil fuel and a 40 percent increase in carbon emissions over the next 15 to 20 years. Would one not expect them to point out the problems inherent in this tidy, linear progression from the past into the future? Might they be fearful of setting off widespread alarm about the disastrous consequences of such developments for the environment and humanity? Or might it be that economic growth is so powerful a paradigm in our culture that challenging it is viewed as dangerous terrain? Might we be so captivated by our material abundance, ever-expanding consumption choices, and extended life spans that we are anaesthetized to the costs that underlie our addictive attachment to the benefits of "progress" and "prosperity"?

We are enamoured, rightly so in many ways, with the benefits stemming from remarkable discoveries, knowledge, and advancement that have accompanied the last 200 years. Given this remarkable track record, why would we not expect that human ingenuity, scientific knowledge, technological invention, and the ample natural endowment of an entire planet would not deliver the goods well into the future?

So powerful is this vision that even those who reject the happy unfolding of endless progress have difficulty imagining a future without economic growth. Given our entanglement in the global economic system, the idea of staging a strategic retreat to a low carbon, steady-state economy is enormously difficult to grasp.

In part, what impedes our breaking out of the box is the conviction that economic growth and prosperity are synonymous — too many believe that we can't have one without the other. Tim Jackson and his colleagues on the UK Sustainable Development Commission worked long and hard to disentangle the concepts. In their report "Prosperity without Growth," they do so by redefining prosperity, the popularly accepted outcome of growth:

> Prosperity transcends material concerns. It resides in the quality of our lives and in the health and happiness of our families. It is present in the strength of our relationships and our trust in the community. It is evidenced by our satisfaction at work and our sense of shared meaning and purpose. It hangs on our potential to participate fully in the life of society. Prosperity consists in our ability to flourish as human beings — within the ecological limits of a finite planet.

Jackson and his colleagues also presented a new vision of governance. To refocus the economy and society on that vision of prosperity, government must accomplish three key tasks. It must

- develop "a new macro-economics for sustainability...that does not rely for its stability on relentless growth and expanding material throughput";
- "provide creative opportunities for people to flourish," free of the damaging dynamic of consumerism; and
- "establish clear resource and environmental limits on economic activity and develop policies to achieve them."

Why don't others, inside and outside government, consider these policy options? Jackson's answer to this question is revealing. He pinpoints the fear that makes it so difficult for people to imagine transition. For most, the only alternative to growth is economic collapse: "The modern economy is structurally reliant on economic growth for its stability. When growth falters... politicians panic. Businesses struggle to survive. People lose their jobs and sometimes their homes. A spiral of recession looms. Questioning growth is deemed to be the act of lunatics, idealists and revolutionaries. But question it we must."

So why not simply decouple economic growth from environmental damage? Rather than stop growth, we could green the economy by consuming less energy per unit of production, with better containment of carbon, etc. "That's certainly the most common answer," replies Jackson,

> that we de-couple, that we just continually keep growing the economy but make everything much more efficient in order to reduce its material impact. The evidence in our report is very strong that this just isn't working...globally many of the most important resource trends are going in the wrong direction. Actually, far from decoupling, we're intensifying resource use associated with economic output, so whatever else we say about de-coupling, we have to say, "It ain't working right now." And it doesn't show any signs of working unless we really confront what's going on within the economic system itself.

Is it possible for the beneficiaries of 150 years of fossil-fuel-fed economic growth to transcend their own culture? Unfettered markets, trade, and capital flow, and the primacy of private property have become powerful motifs. They are promoted as the economic guarantors of individual freedom and security. Is it possible for those who cling to such views to SEE the world differently?

Maybe. There are signs popping up in the most unexpected places. Perhaps the most intriguing example is provided by Alan Greenspan, former chairman of the US Federal Reserve Board and a guru of the free marketers. The collapse of the global financial system in 2008 shook him to the core, as his testimony that year before a congressional committee reveals. Greenspan's exchange with Congressman Harry Waxman on 23 October 2008, tells the story well.

Congressman Harry Waxman: This is your statement [quoting from Greenspan] — "I do have an ideology. My judgment is that free, competitive markets are by far the unrivalled way to organize economies. We have tried regulation, none meaningfully worked." That was your quote. You had the authority to prevent irresponsible lending practices that led to the subprime mortgage crisis. You were advised to do so by many others. And now the whole economy is paying the price. Do you feel that your ideology pushed you to make decisions you wish you did not make?

Greenspan: ... What I am saying to you is, yes, I found a flaw. I don't know how significant or permanent it is, but I have been very distressed by that fact.

Waxman: You found a flaw?

Greenspan: I found a flaw in the model I perceived is the critical functioning structure that defines how the world works, so to speak.

Waxman: In other words, you found that your view of the world, your ideology, was not right, it was not working.

Greenspan: Precisely. That is precisely the reason I was shocked, because I had been going for 40 years or more with very considerable evidence that this was working exceptionally well.

Fig. 1.5: *Former US Federal Reserve chairman Alan Greenspan waits to testify before the House Committee on Oversight and Government Reform on the roles and responsibilities of federal regulators in the current financial crisis, 23 October 2008.* Source: TIM SLOAN/AFP/ Getty Images.

A flaw indeed! Still, one has to wonder. Now that Greenspan's core beliefs have been so rudely unmasked, will he change? Would average citizens change? Or would we be paralyzed by fear and uncertainty? Raj Patel, author of *The Value of Nothing*, holds the latter view. He believes "it would be too big a shock to have the fundamentals of policy in both government and the economy proved wrong, and to have nothing with which to replace them."

Another Way? Five Exit Ramps

To address this dilemma — the desire to change paralyzed by the fear of change — we set out in the balance of the chapter some key concepts and strategies that can help us SEE our world and our place in it afresh: strengthening our resilience, reclaiming the commons, reinventing democracy, constructing a social solidarity economy, and putting a price on the services nature provides to humans so we might awaken to the real costs of our current profligacy. Think of them as "exit ramps" from the crumbling economic ideology of the industrial age that will take us to the more fruitful and effective paths of a steady-state economy. We will refer to them throughout the book as we examine what is possible when we muster the courage and the confidence to face reality head on.

Resilience: Strengthening Our Capacity to Adapt

In science, resilience is defined as "the amount of change a system can undergo (its capacity to absorb disturbance) and essentially retain the same functions, structure and feedbacks." For nearly four decades, scientists have been studying the resilience of ecosystems. The degradation of ecosystems by human-induced stresses became more evident over this time and really took off as a field of study after the publication of *Panarchy*, by Lance Gunderson and Buzz Holling, in 2001. Interest in and research into resilience applications to the social-economic-ecological challenges we face have exploded across the globe since then.

When the first global ecosystem assessment was completed (the Millennium EcoSystem Assessment in 2005), it found that 60 percent of the planet's ecosystems were being degraded or used unsustainably. These findings dramatically illustrate the importance of restoring and maintaining resilience. Degraded ecosystems reach a critical threshold or "tipping point," at which point they may rapidly and dramatically change. Life-giving services are lost in the process — fresh water or air quality, for example, or the natural capacity to sustain fisheries, regulate climate, and control pests.

Our treatment of natural resources as a commodity for profit with little reference to the implications for ecosystem health is responsible for the growing risk that tipping points will be reached. When we maximize yields at the lowest cost — whether the crop is timber from the forest or soil-damaging monocultures of grains or vegetables; whether we are emptying aquifers by "mining" water or burning coal to produce cheap electricity — our singular interest in production and narrow definition of productivity are out of sync with nature.

The study of resilience in ecosystems has revealed how the activities of human beings are now so dominant across the landscape that ecosystem health cannot be discussed without reference to our species. Resilience scientists talk about social-ecological systems, suggesting that the well-being of both are inextricably linked and interdependent. Resilience principles are also increasingly being used to examine human systems and organizations, the theory being that if we are to restore ecological resilience, we need to align our way of living within the boundaries of nature. These ideas feed a rapidly growing field of scholarship focused on determining how we might do this in communities and regions as well as entire sectors of the economy, such as finance and public services. Given the challenges we face, it seems a timely field of enquiry.

Throughout this book we use seven key resilience principles as a lens through which to examine a wide range of innovations relevant to navigating the transition to a steady-state economy. Living as we do in a context where human vulnerability to multiple stresses is increasing, it is more important than ever to strengthen community resilience. Our capacity to both mitigate and adapt to the disruptive implications of climate change, peak oil, and ecosystem decline ultimately depends on it. As Thomas Homer-Dixon wrote in *The Upside of Down,* "If we want to thrive, we need to move from a growth imperative to a resilience imperative." Economic growth "must not be at the expense of the overarching principle of resilience, so needed for any coming transformation of human civilization."

The seven principles of resilience that guide our reflections in this book are set out here and in Figure 1.6.

- *Diversity: A resilient world would promote and sustain diversity in all forms (biological, landscape, social, and economic).* Diversity is a major source of future options and thus of a system's capacity to respond to change and disturbance in different ways. Resilient systems would celebrate and encourage diversity. They would both offset and complement the current trend toward homogenizing the world. They would encourage multiple uses of land and other resources.
- *Modularity: A resilient world would be made up of components that can operate and be modified independently of the rest.* In resilient systems,

everything is not necessarily connected to everything else. Overly connected systems are susceptible to shocks that are rapidly transmitted throughout the system. The recent global financial crisis is an excellent example. The modularity of a resilient system enables it to mitigate or absorb the repercussions of disaster.

- *Social Capital: A resilient world would promote trust, well-developed social networks, and leadership.* The resilience of social-ecological systems is rooted in the capacity of people to respond effectively to challenges together, not singly. In other words, trust, strong networks, and leadership are critically important.

- *Innovation: A resilient world would place an emphasis on learning, experimentation, locally developed rules, and embracing change.* Resisting change is counterproductive in a resilient system. Instead, by offering help to those who are willing to change, the system fosters innovation. When events begin to erode rigid connections and behaviors, innovation opens up new opportunities and resources for creative adaptation.

- *Overlap: A resilient world would have institutions whose governing structures include "redundancy." It would also have a mix of overlapping common and private property rights, increasing access to land.* Redundancy in institutions increases the diversity of responses possible in the face of disturbance and crisis. As a result, overall flexibility and the effectiveness of adaptation increase. By contrast, top-down, centralized, "efficient" structures with no redundancy tend to fail when faced with change outside the scope of their mandate. In short, messy is better than streamlined. Similarly, exclusive private property rights are at the heart of many strategies of resource use. Resilience increases when wider access and a mix of common and private property rights compromise this exclusivity.

- *Tight Feedback Loops: A resilient world would possess tight feedback loops (but not too tight).* Feedback loops refer to the communication flow within a system. Information about the impact of a particular process or event is returned to the system to enable it to correct itself next time. Resilience in a social-ecological system is characterized by focused effort to maintain, or tighten, the strength of feedbacks. They allow us to detect thresholds before we cross them.

- *Ecosystem Services: A resilient world would consider and assess all the ecosystem services that the market economy currently disregards.* The market economy does not price services emanating from the earth and its ecosystems (e.g., pollination, water purification, nutrient

Fig. 1.6:
Seven principles of resilience.

cycling, and many others identified in the Millennium Ecosystem Assessment). These ecosystems are therefore not valued within the narrow cost-benefit analysis characteristic of resource development. Such pricing is critical in order to estimate cumulative impacts on different scales and time horizons, and to assess the effect that a development will have on the integrity of ecosystem services.

Reflection on these principles of resilience yields the following four broad strategies we need to take seriously as we SEEK pathways to a low-carbon, steady-state economy.

Reclaiming the Commons

When one looks far back into human history, private property and commercial markets rarely existed. Where they did, they were of marginal importance to the everyday functioning of human beings. Historically, the "commons" were the lands and waters that provided people in their vicinity with the means of living. The rules and norms that have regulated access to and use of the commons, their management, and the sharing of surplus have differed from time to time and place to place across the globe. Indeed, they still differ today in those places where commons continue to exist.

As is revealed in the next chapter, the enclosure of the commons — or, in plain language, the privatization of what was once the domain of commoners — has been underway for five centuries. The commoners have fought this, and their resistance has been promising and energetic, but more often than not they have been defeated or deflected. In each century the appetite of those doing the enclosing seems to have become more voracious. The capture of the "ownership" and/or exclusive control of land and resources by private individuals or corporations seems to whet the appetite for more and more. In the process, complex local systems for managing resources for everyone's long-term benefit have been destroyed, and private property and associated rights have become sanctified. Now we must ask whether the enclosure of the commons, wrapped in the sacred status afforded private property, is leading us to the promised land — or could it be placing the social and ecological security of all of us, human and otherwise, at severe risk?

Privatizing the planet's resources received powerful support from a paper written in 1968 by microbiologist Garret Hardin, "The Tragedy of the Commons." His central question was simple: What happens when individuals compete for a scarce resource? His simplistic conclusion was that, "when faced with a scarce resource, people will be overrun by their own selfish desires to consume it, even if they know that they're destroying it in the process." In short, although he cited no supporting evidence, Hardin claimed that individuals destroy the common good in the pursuit of their selfish desires. (He made no reference to the destruction of much of the world's commons through transfer to private ownership and control.)

There is a fascinating irony here. Ayn Rand, author of *The Virtue of Selfishness: A Concept of Egoism*, whose acolytes include Alan Greenspan, proposed that an individual's pursuit of selfish desires is the route to advancing the common good. Is Rand right and Hardin wrong or vice versa? Could both be right — or both wrong?

Consider fisheries, the most cited example of the "tragedy of the commons." According to Hardin, each fisher is motivated to maximize his catch, regardless of the environment. Eventually the resource collapses. At first glance, the decline in world fisheries would appear to confirm Hardin's analysis. However, when one digs deeper, things look different. Pakistan's rich fishery has supported tens of thousands of small-scale fishers and their communities for centuries. Yet in the last ten years, the Pakistani Fisherfolk Forum (PFF) has reported a 70 to 80 percent drop in their harvest — and with that drop, a growing hunger, indebtedness, and poverty in their villages along the Arabian coast. Why is this happening? Is it because the commons is being overrun?

In 2001 the military rulers in Pakistan, eager to increase export earnings, permitted foreign trawlers to fish within 12 miles of the coast instead of the former limit of 35 miles. The 12-mile zone is reserved for locals, at least in theory. In fact, international joint ventures flout the rules by flying Pakistani flags. Meanwhile, the real locals complain that their interests have been compromised in the interests of government graft. Locals also complain that industrial trawlers working 24 hours a day with nets stretching three kilometres not only destroy the resource but also waste it. In his book *The Value of Nothing*, Raj Patel wrote, "According to the PFF, only 10% of the trawlers' catch has any value on the international market, and the other 90% is thrown away. It sounds high, but internationally, even factoring in some of the best-regulated global fisheries, by-catch makes up some 40% of all marine catches."

In this case it seems the commons are being not so much overrun as taken over. The local people's sustainable use of the resource has been displaced by the marriage of profit-seeking capital and ecologically destructive technology. This is enclosure at work in the modern day.

There are inspiring, if rare, examples of local commoners reclaiming their fisheries. In Chile, industrial trawling was banned in the 1960s due to resource concerns and in order to protect inshore fishers. At first the Chilean government instituted a quota system, allocating a portion of the catch to individual fishers. It did not work. In its place, the government and fishers' organizations up and down the coast together developed a system of territorial use rights. Describing the process, Patel wrote: "Fishing villages and fishers' organizations were awarded collective rights over specific traditional fishing grounds that they'd known and fished for generations. Enforcement was devolved to local fisher people's unions. It worked: The fisheries recovered."

Elinor Ostrom, winner of the 2009 Nobel Prize in Economics, gave added weight to the wisdom of reclaiming the commons. In its citation, the Nobel Committee observed that her work on common pool resources shows how "forests, fisheries, oil fields or grazing lands can be managed successfully by the people who use them, rather than by governments or private companies." Ostrom's research elevates the strategic importance of supporting the development of self-organizing and -governing forms of collective action:

> The sheer variety of cultural and biological adaptations to diverse ecological conditions is so great that I am willing to make the following assertion: Any single, comprehensive set of formal laws intended to govern a large expanse of territory containing diverse ecological niches is bound to fail in many of the areas where it is applied. Improving the abilities of those directly engaged in the particulars of their local conditions

to organise themselves in deeply nested enterprises is potentially a more successful strategy for solving resource problems than attempting to implement idealized, theoretically optimal institutional arrangements. There is plenty that national government officials can do to help a self-governing society.

We will revisit the story of the commons, its enclosure, and the commoners' push back in the chapters that follow. Reclaiming the commons is a vital component in strengthening the resilience of the communities and regions in which we live. The silos created by exclusive private property rights must be broken down. And the relevance of an agenda to reclaim the commons is not restricted to land and natural resources. Indeed, given the modern power of the volatile trinity of carbon, oil, and capital, the 21st-century struggle for the commons and the common good cannot but include capital, our workplaces, and the biosphere we all depend on. Our access to and management of the commons must be redesigned through a mix of common and private property rights. In short, we must reunite the "I and the We," and reject the life-damaging ways in which both Hardin and Rand defined the world.

Reinventing Democracy

What makes mass society so difficult to bear is not the number of people involved, but the fact that the world between them has lost its power to gather them together...and to separate them.

— Hannah Arendt, *The Human Condition*

Enclosure of the commons robs people of the means to sustain themselves where they live. In the process, the role of local people in local governance is destroyed. There is no commons for them to manage. Private owners — today primarily corporations — continuously call for the rules of the game to be rewritten in their favour, their rationale being that the benefits will trickle down to the rest of us. Privatization and constant pressure to shape public policy to corporate ends not only redirect the benefits of the commons but are also a profound assault on participatory democracy.

Alexis de Tocqueville developed the theory of associative democracy in the 1830s, based on his in-depth study of the democratic mutual aid spirit he found in America. In *Democracy in America* he argued that government and citizens should be wary of the state replacing "independent associational life" — what today we often refer to as civil society. Tocqueville believed economic freedom fostered greed, which in turn engendered political apathy, excessive individualism, and passive reliance on the state.

It is easy to see the time coming in which men will be less and less able to produce, by each alone, the commonest bare necessities. The tasks of government must therefore perpetually increase, and its efforts to cope with them must spread its net wider. The more government takes the place of associations, the more will individuals lose the idea of forming associations and need the government to come to their help. This is a vicious cycle of cause and effect.

A current civil society argument, one that is gaining force, states that reclaiming the commons is inseparable from reinventing and extending the scope of democratic participation and control. If Ostrom is right, then centralized, distant, and locally unaccountable power cannot accomplish the transition to low-carbon, ecologically sustainable communities. What's more, in the age of climate change and peak oil, resilience requires a quality of social capital — trust, collaboration, cooperation, and leadership — rooted in the places where people live.

Like other aspects of transition, the reinvention of democracy is not simple. To start, we must contend with the assertion that "the economy produces people." As Sam Bowles and Herbert Gintis wrote in *Democracy and Capitalism* in 1986, "The experience of individuals as economic actors is a major determinant of their personal capacities, attitudes, choices, interpersonal relations, and social philosophies. Individuals develop their needs, powers, capacities, consciousness, and personal attributes partly through the way they go about transforming and appropriating their natural environment. Moreover, individuals and groups regulate their own development in part to the extent that they succeed in controlling their own labour."

Historically, enclosure has removed most people's capacity to control their own labor. Our choices today involve what to consume and how to capture personal economic benefits from renting out our labor. The more "marketable" we are, and the more competitive we are in the labor market, the more personal consumption we can enjoy. If we can extract sufficient wages to save for a down payment and qualify for a mortgage, we might buy a home to help build our personal wealth.

The narrowing of our economic choices, combined with the concentration of capital and the limited role of most workers in production, have consequences that are, as Bowles and Gintis put it, "intended and unintended," and "antithetical to the development of democratic culture."

True, we participate in representative government, where our "individual" vote is sought in order to confer "collective" power and authority.

But does this constitute democratic governance? Is this the limit of the democratic values we aspire to? In the political contest, where the winners mediate their mandate through the powers vested in the state, the choices on our menu are reduced to two: "the conservative reliance on the market and the social democratic disposition toward an enlarged state." There is a deep historical legacy of resistance to this limited menu for citizens, which will be revealed in Chapter 2.

The concept of associative democracy is a bridge across the increasingly misleading solitudes favouring either the market or the state. Thus, our organizing and institutional challenge is to govern ourselves in such a way that we have the capacity to reweave our economies on a more local basis while building our resilience.

We are at a juncture of unprecedented dependence on a globalized and centralized system of production, communication, and transport. This system is highly vulnerable to disruptions arising from declining oil supplies and increasing climate change. Our world is going to become much smaller as the pressure begins to fray global supply chains. The logical response to the multiple challenges flowing from this forecast is to place authority and financial resources as close to where people live as possible, realizing that there are always different scales related to function to be considered. The European Union has used the Catholic social doctrine of subsidiarity as one means to figure out how to distribute functions between federal, national, and regional levels. Its basic thesis, described by Paul Hirst in *Associative Democracy*, is that any "function should be performed at the lowest level consistent with competent administration."

However, this is not just a call for devolving power from one level of government to another, though devolution of public powers has a role to play. Rather, we imagine that self-governing associations will evolve into the "primary means of democratic governance of economic and social affairs." Ceding selected state functions to such associations, and creating public mechanisms to finance them, could remove from centralized bureaucracies those functions beyond their level of competence, while providing the potential for a much greater level of citizen engagement and accountability. Enabling democratic associations to expand the resources and tools available to address the challenges of transition is a key objective. As we will see, this can be achieved by mobilizing local and regional financial tools and shaping markets and production relevant to meeting basic needs (for such items as food and energy) in a more resilient manner.

This is a far cry from the classic liberal democratic assumption that democratic government is based on accountability to the individual citizen. Indeed, the outlines of associative democracy might evoke derision from some, who charge that it is stripping representative democracy of its right to govern based on the consent of the governed. Such arguments are weak, especially when, as Hirst points out, the "bulk of economic affairs are controlled by large privately-owned corporations, and the great bulk of social affairs are controlled by state bureaucracies." Increasing the space in which local and regional associations exert significant democratic influence over economic and social functions advances democratic participation and ownership of the responsibilities of citizenship.

Not surprisingly, there is resistance. When citizen-based movements and associations present their interests to government, they often find themselves defined by the powers that be as "interest groups" whose demands and suggestions must be discreetly managed. This denigration of voice beyond a periodic vote makes no sense given the challenges we face. It is a narrow conception of political action that is not only discouraging to people acting meaningfully where they live but is also increasingly unacceptable, as evidenced by the Occupy movement's impatience with the ways present and future generations are being compromised by unaccountable wealth and power.

Resilience thinking requires us to expand our democratic repertoires and decentralize authority to act more powerfully. We need to multiply the ways and means by which people can experiment, participate, and extend their collective capacity to become more self-reliant.

Why? There are at least three reasons.

- Participation in self-government and self-management is a form of democratic learning. It is a means of increasing social capital. It is also a prerequisite for enlarging the capacity for community and collective action.
- "The isolated individual — as a voter or as a buyer of commodities — is relatively powerless to resist the claims of the state." As we can see in the example of the Chilean fishers associations, the individual can be greatly empowered by what Bowles and Gintis describe as "the availability of a rich selection of collective forms of democratic social action not beholden to the state." This is a form of collective liberty that extends democracy and increases community resilience and self-reliance.
- Extending democracy requires "at least a minimal identification of the citizen with public life and some notion of collective interest." Philosopher Charles Taylor said it well in his study of Hegel: "What modern society needs...is a ground for differentiation, meaningful to the people concerned, but which at the same time does not set

the partial communities against each other, but rather knits them together in a larger whole."

The political wasteland that now stretches between the individual and the state can disempower and depoliticize us. Decentralized, more autonomous communities are a strategic resource for transition. They are also an end in themselves, no less vital than the recovery of our capacity to value human dignity in our public discourse and in our daily lives. Much in this book testifies to the effectiveness and resilience of democratic decentralism as a key transition strategy.

Constructing a Social Solidarity Economy

Collaboration, cooperation and coordination among citizens and stakeholders inhabiting any social-ecological system is a fundamental pre-requisite to restoring ecosystems in danger of collapse and maintaining ecosystems that are relatively healthy.

— Brian Walker, *Resilience Thinking*

We have already indicated that an ideology based on selfishness, competition, and endless growth is colliding with ecological limits. Further, we have argued that reclaiming the commons and extending democratic values and practices are two strategies that are crucial to the SEE Change. Embedded in all these propositions is the notion of "solidarity," between each other and with the earth. Neo-conservatives may well jump on this word as evidence of a far-left plot. It is not. Indeed, some of the best of conservative philosophy recognizes the virtue of conservation, thriftiness, and mutual aid rooted in community self-reliance. We choose to elevate solidarity as a multidimensional concept, common to all aspects of resilience and imbued with the qualities and strategies we need to propel us out of the privatized, consumption-oriented world in which so many of us find ourselves.

The "social solidarity economy" is both a concept and an emerging movement. It recasts a set of ideas and several fields of practice whose origins lie in unmet human needs — for example, the cooperative movement, community economic development, economic democracy, community land trusts, community development finance, trade unions, credit unions, fair-trade and non-profit associations, and charities. All can be traced to people, communities, and regions marginalized by ideology, market failure, or the inadequacy of public policy, or by all three.

The organizations and initiatives launched in defense of these people and places also go by several names — civil society, the third sector, or the social economy all describe the terrain they occupy. Central to their activity is the reinsertion of social purpose, mutual aid, and self-help into the economy. These practices are all expressions of "reciprocity." In contrast to the likes of Greenspan and other free-market ideologues, social economists argue that reciprocity should be the central economic principle that shapes the management of markets, trade, and capital. From the standpoint of reciprocity, community and societal benefit is a fundamental component of a broader socio-economic calculus. The diversity of the commons is valued over and above the homogeneity of the global market place. John Pearce applied the term "third system" to encompass this arena. Figure 1.7 shows how it includes the voluntary sector, a range of associations, the family economy, and the social economy.

Conceptually and practically, the third system forms only one part of the economy. The first system is private and profit-oriented, what people normally refer to as the "private sector." It includes everything from micro-businesses to multinational corporations. The second system, which also extends from the local to the global, is concerned with the planned provision and distribution of public goods and services, usually through some kind of government authority. The boundaries between these three systems, while permeable, remain conceptually distinct. They are set apart by their different interests, which are expressed through how they are owned, how they are controlled, and their purpose.

Within the third system, the social economy distinguishes itself by earning all or part of its income from the market and infusing its economic activities with social purpose. Through social and cooperative enterprises of various types, the interests of poor, immigrant, worker, and women's groups are explicitly recognized and integrated into production settings. The social economy, you might say, is the economic expression of civil society's social consciousness.

There are different perspectives on the role of the social economy in social change. Reformists generally seek more resources for disempowered constituencies. To make this happen, they also strive to ensure the social economy (the two lower left wedges in Figure 1.7) attains equal standing with the state and the market. A more radical perspective holds the social economy to be a transformative strategy. Pearce described it as a "construction site" upon which to build strategies, tools, and institutions that can challenge the hegemony of free-market values in the first and second systems. Advocates of this perspective see their role as "socializing" the first and second systems with the values of justice, inclusion, balance, diversity, and ecological sustainability; with the principle of reciprocity; and with the practices of self-help, mutual aid, and democracy.

Nevertheless, the private system continues to dominate. It exercises much of its power to improve the prospects for profit. It has major influence on the second system, continuously striving to make public policy, finance, and personnel recognize how public good is attained through private gain. Within this context, the possibility that the third system alone could disturb the hegemony of free-market values seems slight. It simply lacks the political and cultural influence at this time, although it is growing.

Compare this with the conceptual cloth from which the social solidarity economy is cut. Instead of having relatively distinct boundaries between the three systems, the solidarity economy, as depicted in Figure 1.8, cuts across

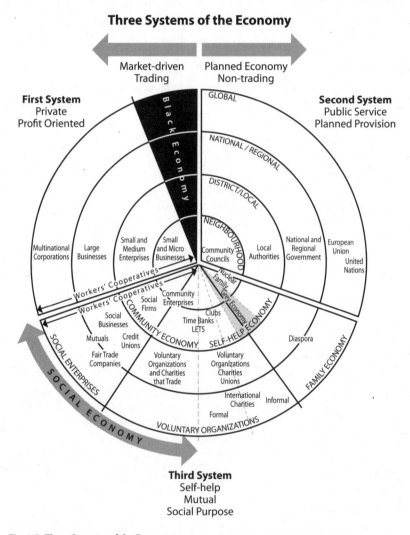

Fig. 1.7: *Three Systems of the Economy.* Source: John Pearce, Social Enterprise in Anytown

The Solidarity Economy — An Emerging Movement

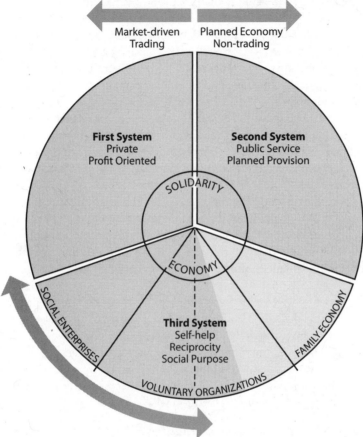

Fig. 1.8: *Solidarity Economy.* Source: John Pearce, Social Enterprise in Anytown.

all three systems. While currently the circle at which they intersect may be small, its implications are huge.

The solidarity economy represents a provocative assault on the view that selfishness is imprinted deep in our economic DNA. In all three systems there are people, organizations, businesses, and governments that are beginning to SEE the world differently. Each system, to one degree or another, has creative actors who share the values of social justice, inclusiveness, ecological sustainability, and deeper, democratic forms of participation. They are seeking and developing dynamic ways to manifest these values in practical terms. We call them co-producers in the task of building a "high road" economy.

International examples of this high-road economy are profiled in succeeding chapters. One among many is the Seikatsu Consumer Co-operative in Japan, which has shaped relationships between food consumers and private food producers cemented by ecological farming methods and fair prices. Further, the cooperative has transformed the supply chain in between: processing, packaging, recycling, and distribution involve private and democratically controlled firms in what can authentically be termed a "values"-added chain.

The central tenets of social and ecological economics compel us to seek balance, to respect and learn to live within the ecological limits of our planetary home. The solidarity economy compels us to craft the strategies and alliances that bring about that transformation. Social purpose, mutual aid, and reciprocity — the hallmarks of the social economy — need to flourish in all three systems. The social economy has an important, though not exclusive, role in making this happen. If we believe we must shift the paradigm from profit-driven economic growth to a steady-state economy, it will not do to continue working in system silos. We need to create a new ecology of innovation, alliances, and partnerships from which to build and secure the SEE Change.

Viewed this way, solidarity is much more than a concept. First, it is a framework for designing and implementing strategies that strengthen the resilience of communities, regions, and societies. Second, it elevates the idea of advancing the common good collaboratively rather than remaining preoccupied with the pursuit of individual interests. Lastly, solidarity is a vital resource, and a renewable one. It is a resource that we need from each other in order to sustain the efforts transition will require.

Pricing As If People and the Planet Mattered

> The "cowboy economy"...is symbolic of the illimitable plains and also associated with reckless, exploitative, romantic, and violent behaviour. The closed economy of the future might similarly be called the "spaceman" economy, in which the earth has become a single spaceship, without unlimited reservoirs of anything, either for extraction or for pollution, and in which, therefore, man must find his place in a cyclical ecological system which is capable of continuous reproduction of material form even though it cannot escape having inputs of energy.
>
> — Kenneth Boulding, "The Economics of the Coming Spaceship Earth"

The fact that high-road values are already shaping our discourse and our actions can be traced, at least in part, to the evolution of what is known as "ecological economics," which starts with a set of assumptions very different from those that mainstream economists have promoted so successfully over the last 40 years. According to ecological economist Malte Faber, this field is defined "by its focus on nature, justice, and time. Issues of intergenerational equity, irreversibility of environmental change, uncertainty of long term outcomes and sustainable development guide ecological economic analysis and valuation."

Pioneered in the 1960s by Kenneth Boulding, Fritz Schumacher, and Nicholas Georgescu-Roegen, ecological economics takes sustainability as the focus of its inquiry. It postulates that sustainability rests on three types of systems: the social, the environmental, and the economic (as shown in Figure 1.9). The field's most popular image is that of "spaceship earth" (a phrase and concept coined by Kenneth Boulding), which captures its basic tenet: we are absolutely dependent on the health of natural systems to sustain human life.

Ecological economists explore a broad terrain, everything from the carrying capacity of the earth or the threat that environmental degradation poses to our food and water, to the relationship of energy, the environment, and climate change, and the critical interdependence of systems. Among its most important contributions is the idea, popularized by Paul Hawken in *The Ecology of Commerce*, that we have evolved a system of commerce that thinks of itself and behaves as if natural systems were but a source of raw

Fig. 1.9: *Conventional economists and politicians often argue that the economy must be the first priority — "It's the economy, stupid" — and without it social justice and environmental cleanup will not be achieved. This is backwards. "It's the planet, stupid." A sustainable economy must live within the ecological limits of the planet. Our challenge is to organize economies with equity and ecological realities and goals at the forefront of our attention.*
Source: Sherman Morrison, "Sustainable U, 001: Sustainability Basics," accessed 26 January 2012, from shermanmorrison.hubpages.com/hub/Sustainable-U-Sustainability-Basics

materials for human benefit and a sinkhole for human waste. As a result, the systems are out of sync with each other because the market only responds to prices, and these prices fail to incorporate either the value of the services nature provides to our species or the costs of using nature as our collective refuse heap. As a result of this imbalance, we unwittingly have created a way of life that is by definition unsustainable.

Ecological economists argue that if we specified the dollar value of these damages and services, and if we integrated that cost into the price of goods and services, our economic behavior would change: we would become more cautious and deliberative about how we use the bounty of nature. Not to do so would radically increase what we have to pay because we would have to account for what economists call externalities. Ecological economists are developing tools to bring balance to this calculation.

Raj Patel chronicles a few of the countless examples of our failure to account for these externalities in *The Value of Nothing*. From Big Macs to the mining of water in China, from the erosion of soil fertility due to chemical fertilization to our failure to price carbon, the problem is far from fixed. Anaesthetized by a Walmart culture of cheap consumables produced by supply chains in which the lowest price is the only criterion, we are accessories to theft of two kinds — robbing ourselves and robbing each other. As Patel puts it: "When negative externalities are not paid for, the beneficiaries are in effect engaging in theft from those who bear the cost of their behaviour...If humanity had to pay for the consequences of a degraded eco-system the bill could, according to one recent study, run to about $47 trillion."

A recent study by the National Academy of Sciences looked at six areas of global environmental degradation in an attempt to determine who is generating the impacts and who is paying for them. It considered ozone-layer depletion, overfishing, deforestation, climate change, mangrove destruction, and intensified agriculture. Middle- and high-income countries are the big polluters, not only fouling their own lands and waters but also exporting pollution to poor countries. The estimated damage is $5 trillion. Poor countries, in contrast, were estimated to inflict $0.68 trillion in damages on richer countries. Ironically, the entire foreign debt that poor countries owe to rich countries is $1.8 trillion. Who owes who what? The math is pretty clear!

Establishing prices that take into account these externalities is of central importance if we are to successfully navigate the Great Transition. Without a clear, adequate, and firm price on carbon, even high-road investors, whether public, private, or social, will have trouble mobilizing the investment necessary to deploy existing technologies and innovate more. Carbon taxes must increase, emission quotas must be firmly set, and heavy penalties must be defined for those who exceed them.

Thomas Friedman, prize-winning journalist from the *New York Times*, pleads for recognition of the central role of proper pricing in his book *Hot, Flat and Crowded*:

> Repeat after me: when it comes to energy innovation, "price matters, price matters, price matters." If you want to bring about a mass movement toward more energy-efficient cars, windows, buildings, power generation systems, lighting and heating, the simplest way is to make sure that the true costs of using any and all hydrocarbon-based fuels is reflected in their price to consumers — the true climate costs, the true environmental costs...Consumers will adjust and demand more energy-efficient homes, more energy-efficient offices and schools, and more energy-efficient transportation. And, as a result, the level of carbon emissions will go down. It is simple economics. It is not rocket science. The cheap plastic junk you buy at big-box stores is cheap only because the externalities have not been priced in — the effects on air quality, the effects on water, the effects on climate. Price those into every product and the market will do the rest.
>
> Well, why doesn't the market reflect the true cost of the things being sold? When it comes to energy, the reason, at least in America, is that government has failed to shape the market with honest prices. It is not a market failure. Markets don't price externalities when they don't have to. It is a leadership failure.

Our persistent resistance, denial, and confusion about this basic tenet of ecological economics is akin to a toddler, who believes you can't see her when she covers her eyes. If you cannot see, touch, or count something, it is as if that thing does not exist. The reality is that it does exist, but we continue to think, and act as if, the planet we inhabit is the limitless domain of the cowboy.

Navigating the Transition to a Steady-State Economy

A major dilemma as we work to reduce economic growth and carbon emissions is determining how we can achieve this while maintaining economic stability. This is known as "the growth dilemma" or "the productivity trap."

Politicians are obsessed with maintaining economic growth — understandably, because jobs depend on it. Most corporations outside the financial sector concentrate much of their investment in research and development on technological innovation that will protect or increase profit margins.

Historically, this has translated into making more with less labor. The result is measured, at the level of the firm or of the national economy, by calculating if labor productivity is increasing or declining. The conundrum is that if labor productivity increases, employment levels in the sector concerned most often decline, and the way we currently deal with this is to do whatever is necessary to fan the flames of economic growth. Costs related to the environment or communities take a distant second or third place in the political and economic calculus.

As an alternative to this growth imperative, John Stuart Mill and John Maynard Keynes both argued that a steady decline in the workweek must accompany the increase in labor productivity arising from technological innovations that replace labor. To compensate for a loss in wages and salaries that results from such a scheme, Mill argued that reduced income from labor should be compensated for by increasing worker ownership of the capital. In this way, workers access income from two sources: from their labor and from their ownership of productive assets. According to Mill, various forms of cooperative ownership would make this possible — and when coupled with restructured property rights, they could reduce the cost of living, an objective we will demonstrate as achievable in later chapters.

The idea of workers earning their income from both labor and ownership is a core argument for economic democracy. Louis Kelso described it in the 1950s as binary economics. He envisaged a future economy where all citizens would have access to these two sources of income. The shift to more local and regional ownership structures are a key component of such a strategy, as we shall see. This shift is important in and of itself, but in combination with the need to radically reduce our carbon use, dependence on fossil fuels, and entanglement with unaccountable global capital, the argument for strategically recalibrating our efforts takes on a whole new level of significance. Increased local and regional self-reliance is a key component as we move off the growth treadmill and toward the resilience imperative.

Working with the new economics foundation (nef) in the United Kingdom, economists Tim Jackson and Peter Victor are part of a team designing macro-economic models to explore how a steady-state economy might be achieved. In their paper "Productivity: Rethinking Productivity for a Steady-State Economy," which they presented at nef's Great Transition summit meeting in October 2010, they showed their initial efforts to solve the conundrum presented by the priority conventional economists give to improving labor productivity.

Jackson and Victor found that between 1980 and 1995, labor productivity in 12 European Union countries increased by 2.7 percent a year. A 3 percent decline in working hours accompanied this increase. This seems like good news. However, from 1995 to 2005, labor productivity increased less than 1.4 percent a year. An 8 percent increase in working hours accompanied this decrease. Economists call this decline in labor productivity Baumol's disease, and it is characterized in Organisation for Economic Co-operation and Development (OECD) countries by a decline in the manufacturing sector and a growth in the service sector, where employment is more labor intensive.

All these factors inform the economic models Jackson and Victor are working on. As of 2010, they have confined their exploratory modelling to three scenarios aimed at cutting carbon use to 80 percent of 1990 levels by 2050 while maintaining economic stability.

In the first scenario, green infrastructure is expanded by 5 percent a year. This is achieved by investing in renewable energy technologies, instituting a range of low-carbon policies, and developing smart grid systems designed to both transmit electricity more efficiently and allow energy to be conserved more effectively. The projected outcome from the model indicates that economic growth would increase but that the 80 percent carbon reduction target would be missed by a wide mark.

The second scenario involves the same 5 percent yearly expansion of green infrastructure with an additional 1.5 percent annual reduction in working hours. This leads to a decline in economic growth and a fall in GDP, which may disrupt economic stability. As well, carbon reduction targets are not quite achieved in this scenario.

The third scenario includes the 5 percent yearly expansion of green infrastructure, a 1 percent reduction in annual working hours, and a 6 percent expansion in the local green services sector. This sector is described as producing and selling "dematerialized services" rather than "material products": for example, "selling energy services rather than energy supplies. Selling mobility rather than cars. Recycling, re-using, leasing..." Jackson and Victor envision building on already existing and "thriving local or community based social enterprises; community energy projects, local farmers markets, slow food cooperatives" and so on. In the model, growth declines slowly, not sharply; employment is maintained; and the 80 percent reduction in carbon emissions is realized.

This third scenario yields a more balanced outcome. In some ways it is reminiscent of Schumacher's "Small is Beautiful" argument, which called for a decentralized economy using a diverse mix of intermediate technologies, calibrated to make efficient use of local resources and regional markets, in order to transition to a more sustainable economy. In this vision, paid and unpaid "good work" would be equitably recognized.

Although their work is at a very early stage, Jackson and Victor's preliminary results are indicative of the importance of local and regionalized economic reconstruction. In the chapters that follow, we will share more robust (and scalable) examples that are meeting basic needs at the local and regional levels. By connecting the dots between shelter, food, energy, and different forms of structuring property rights, ownership and finance, people are blazing pathways that can help us transition to a steady-state economy where we live. In this sense, our contribution in this book is more on the micro-economic side of transition. This does not lessen the importance of the macro-economic research, which we touch on throughout, and periodically suggesting possible solutions to some of the key themes introduced in this opening chapter. Both macro- and micro-economics are crucial if we are to succeed in navigating the Great Transition from the growth imperative to the resilience imperative.

Moving on to Chapter 2, we examine the ascendency of the "free market," a fascinating story that is a central theme of the last 500 years of human history. The market's rough-and-tumble evolution has been fraught with opposition to the notion that the economy should trump social relations and nature. Within this story are propositions and experiments that reflect alternative ways of organizing our economic life, almost all of which foreshadow many of the innovations we deal with throughout this book. We discover that we are part of a long history, one that is inspiring, sobering, and instructive.

CHAPTER 2

Wealth versus Commonwealth

*It is a well-provisioned ship, this on which we sail through space. If the
bread and beef above decks seem to grow scarce, we but open a hatch
and there is a new supply, of which before we never dreamed. And very
great command over the services of others comes to those who as the
hatches are opened, are permitted to say, "This is mine!"*
— Henry George, *Progress and Poverty*

*The social problem for the future we consider to be how to
unite the greatest liberty of action with a common ownership in
the raw material of the globe, and an equal participation of all
in the benefits of combined labor.*
— John Stuart Mill, *Autobiography*

*I believe that the future will learn more from the spirit of Gesell
than from that of Marx.*
— John Maynard Keynes,
The General Theory of Employment, Interest and Money

FOR THE LAST 200 YEARS, the ideology of unregulated markets, free-flow-
ing capital, and minimalist government has waxed and waned. The
unbridled markets of the 1920s gave way to state investment and regulation
through the course of the Depression and World War II, right up to the
1970s. But over the last 40 years decked out in the language of "freedom"
and "individual rights," these libertarian ideas have surged back. We have
the influence of economic theorists like Milton Friedman and Friedrich
Hayek, and their respective political acolytes Ronald Reagan and Margaret
Thatcher, to thank for this, as well as the powerful corporate forces that
have lobbied incessantly for the unrestricted movement of capital across the

globe. Voices that challenge the priority of capital over social, cultural, and ecological values have been barely audible.

At issue is not whether markets have a place but whether so-called free markets should dominate our choices. Historically, the notion of free markets has existed for but a blink in time. Much of the human story reflects a different reality. Markets in most civilizations have been shaped and regulated by social and cultural goals. Economies have by and large been local and regional, not global. Rights to share "God-given" resources (the commons) were much more prevalent than the "sacred" rights of private property. Under the prohibitions against usury shared by Judaism, Christianity, and Islam, production and trade in Europe and the Middle East was strictly governed for centuries. These prohibitions were linked to a vernacular sense of justice. In *Customs in Common*, social historian E.P. Thompson described this as "moral economy" — customs and practices associated with a pre-capitalist cultural understanding of the "commons" and "common rights." Thus for much of human history it was considered avaricious to charge interest; laws existed to limit it or ban it outright. Today, by contrast, compound interest and indebtedness are pervasive.

Given the global predicaments of our times, one might be tempted to ask where the greater wisdom lies. Is the paradigm of economic growth and free-market capitalism constructive in a world where fossil fuels will inevitably become less accessible and where carbon emissions must be cut radically? Are we trapped between an unstoppable force and an immovable object? Or is human well-being possible without global economic growth? What can we learn from past societies? Can science help us SEE more vividly the possibilities for change?

We believe there is much we can learn. The perspectives we glean from our own history and from more recent scientific inquiry are sources of inspiration and guidance as we try to navigate the troubled waters of the 21st century.

The Demise of Moral Economy: The Great Transformation

Any economic system involves allocation of resources. The dominant assumption today is that the free market should rule how they are allocated, but views on this issue have varied dramatically over time. The 20th century witnessed a spectrum that ranged from free markets at one extreme to a fully planned economy that ignored markets as a means to allocate resources. The demise of the Soviet Union revealed the folly of this latter view. But in *The Great Transformation*, Karl Polanyi, a seminal theorist of social economics, suggested that the exclusive reliance on free markets is equally misguided. According to Polanyi and other pre-capitalist historians, allocation took place in three ways in many earlier urban civilizations:

1. **Reciprocity:** the ancient cultural system of gifting and mutual aid that is predominant in pre-capitalist societies, including traditional agricultural and hunter-gatherer societies
2. **Redistribution:** the social insurance mechanisms, developed over centuries, in which grain and other scarce resources are stored to enable survival when society faces such risks as disease, famine, and warfare
3. **Regulated markets:** guild practices, found in urban areas across the ancient and medieval world (i.e., guilds in Europe, koinon in Egypt, shreni in India, hangui in China, egbe in West Africa), that created social economic rules for production, exchange, and trade, ensuring cultural and social norms were respected and maintained

While they have played a role in all civilizations, markets have usually been closely regulated. Seldom have they been based on the unhindered operation of supply and demand. During the Middle Ages in Europe, for example, prices were set by producer organizations known as craft guilds. Ensuring an equitable return to skilled workers was a priority for local production. Guilds regulated the early urban economies.

The importance of reciprocity was affirmed by Polanyi's studies of rural African societies, in the early 1950s. Many local African economies made no sense to economists of that time. Most of the people did not own land (although they did have ancient use and access rights), nor did they own conventional economic assets. Yet they survived, even when, without buying, selling, and trading, they should have died from hunger. Polanyi and his fellow social economists uncovered rich and diverse cultures where social and ecological realities shaped and mediated "markets."

While many modern economists may reject such findings as passé, the very origin of the word "economics" reveals how close Polanyi was to the mark. The roots of the discipline's title are in two Greek words, *oikos* and *nomos.* Together they refer to "the management of household resources for the benefit of the whole household." Aristotle, one of the earliest and keenest observers of ancient economics, coined the broader term *oikonomia* — "the wise management of resources for the good of society." *Oikonomia* requires, first and foremost, that one satisfy the basic needs of the "household" in a self-reliant way. This could include the trade of surplus goods, which Aristotle viewed as a legitimate though secondary "social activity." However, he was concerned that the production, hoarding, or manipulation of goods to amass wealth could be socially destructive if it were not strictly controlled.

From his historical research, Polanyi concluded that Aristotle's analysis was indicative of the pre-capitalist world as a whole: economic interests were governed by social and political relations. Prior to the rise of mercantilism and nation states in 16th-century Europe, he found little evidence to substantiate the assumed individualistic and self-seeking propensities on which the contemporary free market arguments are founded. Indeed, in Polanyi's view and that of the American economic historian, Robert Heilbroner, Adam Smith's assertion of the inherent "human propensity to barter, truck and exchange" took insufficient account of the non-economic value system of earlier societies. They both argued that market behavior "with a view to private gain" was either strictly regulated to limit antisocial effects in pre-capitalist societies, or was confined to the sphere of international trade. Moreover, it appears earlier societies placed far greater value on religion, politics, and culture than on commerce.

Counter to the assertions of classical and neoclassical economists, Polanyi showed that the first markets were neither local nor competitive but, rather, long distance and complementary. Consistent with the guiding principle of reciprocity, their pattern of exchange was balanced and symmetrical: one region bartered or sold useful goods ("use values") they produced for other useful goods they did not have access to that were produced in another region. In distant meeting places, merchants, towns, and cities slowly developed. For hundreds of years the commercial activity of these towns was strictly controlled by an alliance of local rulers and guilds to guarantee high quality, achieve a "just price," and ban usury. Polanyi referred to these socially controlled places of exchange as "markets" with a small "m."

Small "m" Markets at Work

Before the existence of elected governments, rulers used charters to delegate authority and confer rights. For instance, William the Conqueror granted the City of London charter in 1067 to define the scope of its self-governance powers. Other royal charters were granted to monasteries and universities. Even guilds could be subject to charters issued by the king, though normally the local lord was their source. Usually the rights delegated were long term and came with a set of obligations to secure public benefits.

Guilds, the vernacular and oldest form of business association, came into existence by negotiating deals that set out clearly their rights to trade in exchange for tribute to their feudal lords. In some cases, the terms of the charters they agreed to enabled guilds to exercise a high degree of self-management. In other circumstances, local artisanal groups had to struggle for decades and sometimes centuries to gain a similar level of autonomy. Whatever the terms of their charter, all guilds had one common characteristic — their trade and their powers were locally rooted. Members of a guild were *con pagus* meaning "one of the same town." *Con pagus* coupled with *con panis* (meaning "to take bread together") denoted the master's obligation by custom, in many towns, to provide lunch for his apprentices and journeymen. Together the terms meant "good company." It is interesting that the convergence of local and reciprocal obligation is the root of the words we know today as "company" and "companion."

Indeed, reciprocity was at the heart of guild operations. Guild members pledged an oath to provide each other with social, economic, and military aid. Masters of each group of journeymen and apprentices normally had a seat at the guild table, where matters related to the management of their craft were discussed and decided. Agendas ranged from securing a fair price to procuring raw materials and supporting members who were ill. In turn, each guild appointed one of its masters to the local federation of guilds, where matters related to the regulation of trade between towns was discussed along with the procurement of food and provisions to meet the needs of households in the town.

Central to their deliberations was the setting of "fair prices," securing a "just income" for members, and setting and maintaining standards of quality. In other words, guild officials managed the market. They fixed the price of goods and used trademarks to maintain a uniform high standard. All goods in the town had to be sold in the marketplace. Preemptive purchases and sales outside the defined market were illegal. Food purchased for the townspeople was regulated to ensure that every household had enough flour and salt for bread making. The guilds also took care of a range of social functions. Working hours and holy days were regulated. Night work was illegal. Work on Saturday was restricted to half the day. The guilds organized mutual aid among members, which covered everything from provision of meals for sick guild members to funerals for the dead. In larger towns they built almshouses, hospitals, wells, churches, and chapels and sometimes provided forms of sanitation. In other words, the masters, as owners, were bound by obligations to their members, their customers, and their town. Social relations governed economic life. Reciprocity, mediated by local town charters and diverse accommodations with the local aristocracy, created complex and varied webs of group governance, where autonomy and mutual responsibility were intertwined.

From "markets" to "the Market"

This local approach to governing and managing economic affairs began to lose ground in the 15th century in Europe. Sovereigns began to delegate less and centralize more. Polanyi's many small "m" markets were slowly transformed into a growing big "M" Market. The Crown, looking for new sources of taxation, became the national market regulator, focused on encouraging commerce, fostering international trade, and capturing the benefits from exploiting resources in the "new world." Competition with other states for colonial spoils, control of trade, and national wealth became dominant. "Mercantilism" (or, in plain language, money grabbing for the benefit of the sovereign and mercantile corporations) gained ascendency. The craft guilds in England and France were displaced, increasingly repressed, and restricted by the sovereign.

In England, the death knell for the autonomy of the craft guilds took the form of the Statute of Artificers (1558–63), laws that expunged the power of artisanal guilds. No longer could the local guilds set terms for apprentice-ships or wages. Gone was their influence over local trade. Economic affairs were determined by the sovereign and the aristocracy prior to the industrial revolution.

Certain classes of guild workers managed to win exclusion from the sweep of this repressive legislation. Merchants, goldsmiths, and the profes-sional guilds — those who did not work with their hands — continued to set their own wages and govern their affairs at arm's length from the state, as most lawyers, accountants, and doctors do today.

While the professionals prospered, it was not until the 18th century that working-class people regained the right to form mutual aid societies that could raise money for people who were sick or who needed to be buried. Known in England as the Friendly Societies, these groups eventually became the base from which skilled workers organized into trade unions in the 19th century.

As nation states developed in Europe, the repression of the craft guilds was only one path, albeit a strategic one, that led to the ascendency of the big "M" Market. By removing the guilds' control of local trade, wages, and pricing, thus destroying their autonomy, the mercantilist instincts of emerg-ing trading nations were free to expand, unfettered by social or cultural obligations or constraints. However, reciprocity, the central economic prin-ciple of guilds, was a deeply embedded instinct, and it resurfaced regularly over the next 400 years in countless struggles that resisted the takeover of the commons by the Market. The mutualist thinking that shaped this ongo-ing opposition, and the innovations that have arisen from its transformative propositions, has produced a rich vernacular culture, as we will see.

Evolution of the Big "M" Market I: The Struggle for Land Reform

A key component in the ascendancy of the Market was the elites' capture of the common resources the majority of the population depended on. The land enclosure movement — an early example of privatization at work — was perhaps the most brutal. Separating rural people from their access to the land transformed their labor and their land into marketable commodities. Polanyi depicted it well in *The Great Transformation*:

> What we call land is an element of nature inextricably interwoven with man's institutions...The economic function is but one of many vital functions of land. It invests man's life with stability; it is the site of his habitation; it is a condition of his physical safety; it is the landscape and the seasons. We might as well imagine his being born without hands and feet as carrying on his life without land. And yet to separate land from man and organise society in such a way as to satisfy the requirements of a real-estate market was a vital part of the utopian concept of a market economy.

In *Discourse on Inequality*, Jean-Jacques Rousseau pointed to the enclosure of land as the root cause of rising social inequality and dire poverty. In the opening section he posed the questions: Is there any limit to what people can call "property"? How can one own what one does not create? He imagined what might have happened if the first man who "fenced in a piece of land, [and] said 'This is mine,'" had a neighbor with sense enough to pull up the stakes and denounce the imposter, warning others of this fundamental theft of a birthright: "You are undone if you once forget that the fruits of the earth belong to us all, and the earth itself to nobody." Or as the American Benjamin Tucker wrote a century later in *Instead of a Book*, "Things that are 'God given' such as land should not be 'owned,'" only used.

Rousseau might sound strange to the modern ear, but private ownership of land was a foreign concept to most cultures and civilizations of the past. True, it existed under the Roman Empire, but this was the exception rather than the rule. The custom was that rights to use the land were in the hands of the tribal group, clan, or other social grouping that depended on that land for a living.

In England, the enclosure of lands meant open fields and commons lands were fenced off, people evicted, and sheep moved in to expand production of fine English wool, a key commodity feeding the rise of the Market. The more demand grew, the more serfs were turfed.

Resistance sprang up in 1648 after Cromwell's Puritan New Model Army overthrew the monarchy, abolished the House of Lords, outlawed the Church of England, and proclaimed a Commonwealth republic governed by the House of Commons. To instigate land reform, a nonviolent protest movement known as the "Diggers" occupied former common lands in several areas near London in 1649, setting up shacks, growing food, and handing it out for free. Within a year, many of the Diggers were evicted, arrested, fined, and imprisoned, but their voices were not silenced. In 1652, Gerard Winstanley, a key leader, published the pamphlet "Law of Freedom in a Platform" to advance the Digger vision of a "cooperative commonwealth" in which land reform and economic democracy would figure prominently. Winstanley went on to help establish the Quakers in the 1650s, and his pamphlet inspired many other land-reform thinkers over the next 300 years.

Among them was Thomas Spence, who published a pamphlet, *The Poor Man's Advocate* (1779), which set out a compelling and practical case for cooperative land reform and economic democracy. Spence saw that democratic rights without an economic foundation were of little consequence. Why should landlords pocket the economic benefits of the land they had seized, while those it was taken from received nothing? Why should commoners not have a share of the benefits from the land to meet their basic needs? Why should all the benefits be captured by the aristocracy? To put an end to enclosure, he proposed the establishment of Parish Land Trusts, which would steward the land democratically as a common resource. Under the Spence plan, local residents would lease the land from the local parish council and could either rent or own the houses and workspace they constructed. Lease payments gathered by the community from residents and businesses would help pay for services defined by the people collectively as a public good.

Spence moved to London and promoted his land reform plan for decades through a small bookshop, the production of pamphlets, and the building up of a following, the Society of Spencean Philanthropists, which continued promoting his plan after he died in 1814. In 1817, amidst growing levels of unemployment and poverty, Robert Owen took up the cause of land reform, advocating for the establishment of Villages of Co-operation and Unity on mutually owned and governed land. A successful industrialist from Welsh working-class origins, Owen used his own capital to finance ambitious cooperative experiments in Britain, Ireland, and the US state of Indiana. Most of these failed, but lessons were learned, and Owen's practical vision inspired the development of the international cooperative movement.

The political goals of Spence and his followers, and the economic democracy goals of Owen were points of departure for British trade unionists and cooperatives that founded the Chartist movement in the 1830s. The Chartists' main aim was to win the vote for common people. No land meant no vote in 19th-century England, so one element of Chartist strategy was to raise capital from trade unionists in order to buy land to get the vote. The Irish Chartist leader Feargus O'Connor helped set up the Chartist Land Company, which established several cooperative villages where families could lease two to four acres to grow food and build a cottage. Under the Chartist land plan, each village was to have its own community center, doctor, and school. By 1847, 60,000 working-class members and supporters were investors, 600 local branches were established, and the first £90,000 had been used to build a number of villages on cooperatively owned land. However, in 1851 the government forced the company to cease operations because of allegations that it had been improperly incorporated and was keeping poor accounting records. This ended their land reform campaign, but other practical ways forward were inspired and seeded.

In the mid-19th century, John Stuart Mill, became a champion of worker cooperatives and other aspects of economic democracy, including fundamental land reform. In book four of his *Principles of Political Economy*, he advocated a progressive "stationary state" — a stable future economy facilitated by practical land reform and an economy that secured a greater level of participative democracy through the steady expansion of worker-owned and -governed firms. Mill was much more than an armchair political economist. He worked with the cooperative movement to develop legislation for mutuals and cooperatives, and he helped steer the legislation through Parliament — a major contribution to advancing economic democracy. He also helped found a campaign to nationalize the land, which, among other things, led to the establishment of city parks and allotments for urban food growing on common land in London and elsewhere. His writings and support for practical reform inspired the earliest development of public land for civic benefit.

Mill was the first mainstream economist to argue that while markets were useful producers of wealth, they were inequitable distributors of economic value. He was the first to argue that the distribution of wealth is a social economic issue that governments are absolutely free to decide upon. Measures to tax unearned wealth, to take land out of the market economy and set it aside for the people, to democratize ownership, and to ensure workers shared equitably in income from industry were common sense to Mill. He argued that if the conflicts between capital and labor and between property and liberty were ever to be resolved, reforming property rights was fundamental.

While Mill was advancing these arguments, John Ruskin and Octavia Hill set up the first nonprofit housing association in the slums of London, rehousing 3,000 low-income families. Equally concerned with rural depopulation, Ruskin appealed for donations of land and capital to repair village housing, halls, barns, and mills. In line with Spence's vision, local land trusts were set up under Ruskin's Guild of St. George; tenants secured long-term affordable leases at a fixed rent along with the option to buy the buildings. Sufficiency and self-reliance were core Ruskinian principles. As the tenant improved the land and increased soil fertility, Ruskin argued that rents should be decreased as just reward for "sweat equity" and local cooperative action.

Both Ruskin's and Mill's land reform visions set their sights on unscrupulous landlords, and Mill's work inspired Joseph Chamberlain to clear inner-city slums and set up the first municipal gas and water companies in Birmingham in the 1870s. Chamberlain's public ownership action galvanized other cities like Leeds, Glasgow, and London to forge a municipal socialism that was profoundly successful and inspired urban politicians in other countries.

These late-19th-century municipal and cooperative land experiments also inspired Leon Walras, the leading French economist, to support a more substantive reform: nationalization of the land to support the development of a social economy. Both Walras and Mill regarded unearned or "rentier" income as a vestige of feudalism. Progressively taking land into public ownership, they argued, would be socially beneficial; it would also enhance productivity and achieve a more equitable distribution of the market economy. Once land had become a significant public good, the cost of production for goods and services (especially food and housing) could drop dramatically, and land speculation could be phased out. Mill proposed the introduction of a land tax to secure for the government the "unearned increment" that landlords gain as a windfall from property development. Mill

"EVERYBODY WORKS BUT THE VACANT LOT"
I paid $3600 for this lot and will hold 'till I get $6000. The profit is unearned increment made possible by the presence of this community and enterprise of its people. I take the profit without earning it. For the remedy read "HENRY GEORGE."

argued that this high tax would encourage landlords to sell their land to the state at reasonable prices.

An American journalist, Henry George, was inspired by Mill's argument, corresponded with him, and developed an action plan six years after Mill died, which he described in *Progress and Poverty*. George concluded that a nationalization argument would not be acceptable in the United States. To more gradually achieve this goal, he argued for a "single tax on the land," which would mean the landowner was taxed rather than the tenant, a measure that would incentivize land redistribution in a steadfast way. George's ideas inspired the American populist movement in the 1890s and secured governmental support for a single tax in the UK under the "People's Budget" of the Liberal Party in November 1909. (The single tax was proposed by Lloyd George and Winston Churchill, but the House of Lords vetoed the idea, which led to a hung Parliament until the proposal was dropped in April 1910.) Beginning in Henry George's home state of Pennsylvania, 20 cities have introduced a "Land Value Tax." In Hong Kong, where the idea was taken up a century ago, the Land Value Tax today accounts for about a third of public revenue.

The struggle to implement practical land reform continues globally and is especially strong as a movement in Brazil. It is remarkable how the torch lit by the Diggers' spark continues to burn some 460 years later. But land enclosure is only one strand in the story of how the Market rose to its 21st-century dominance. It is a complicated web.

Evolution of the Big "M" Market II: The Ascendency of the Corporation

For tax reasons, local feudal lords frequently agreed to locally defined charters that delegated economic rights to the craft guilds, but only the sovereign could grant charters to merchants for long-distance trade. The first such mercantilist charter was issued by King Henry IV to the Merchant Adventurers in 1407 in exchange for exclusive national trading rights to cross the channel to Amsterdam with fine English wool as their cargo. Seven Royal Charters were granted in the next century. Terms were kept short, usually three years, which gave the Crown tight control over who got what and the flexibility to change the rate of taxation at will.

It was not until the 17th century that a longer-term lease was issued; the Dutch East India Company secured a 21-year charter for its activities in Asia. Investors were happy. The long term meant they could recover their original investment, just as they did with successful short-term charters, but then continue receiving profits well after their risk capital was recovered. Soon time limits of any kind disappeared. The English East India Company was the first to win the right to sell unrestricted investment shares that could be held in perpetuity.

No one foresaw the forces this decision would unleash less than a century later. Extortionate pricing by the East India Company, coupled with high taxation in Britain, raised the ire of the American colonies. The tipping point came in Boston, where the infamous Tea Party riots in December 1773 galvanized Americans to revolt against British rule and gain their independence. The cost of a cup of tea was but a symbol for what really irked the colonists: the ruthless powers of mercantile corporations that controlled trade at the expense of the colonies. Never again would this be allowed was the view. The right to incorporate a company, and the definition of terms under which it could operate, became the purview of citizen councils.

As Richard Grossman and Frank Adams put it in *Taking Care of Business,* "Having thrown off the English rule, the revolutionaries did not give governors, judges or generals the authority to charter companies." Each American state crafted recommendations to define the purpose of a company, the conditions it must meet to stay in business, and the period for which these arrangements would last. The conditions in each state were very different but commonly stringent, for example:

- Corporate charters were only granted for a limited period of time and could be revoked promptly for violating laws.
- Corporations could engage only in activities necessary to fulfill their chartered purpose.
- Corporations could not own stock or shares in other corporations nor own any property that was not essential to fulfilling the chartered purpose.
- To control the size of corporations and their power, limits on levels of landholding, capitalization, and debt were often included in charters.
- Owners of shares had only one vote, no matter the number of shares they owned.
- Corporations were to be terminated if they exceeded their authority or caused public harm.
- Owners and managers were responsible for any criminal act committed on the job. Directors could be imprisoned for failing to keep company actions in line with the charter.
- Corporations could not make any political or charitable contributions nor spend money to influence legislation.

"Citizen charters" were issued by early US states to for-profit and not-for-profit companies. Time limits varied from 3 to 50 years. The source of the charter depended on the size and scope of the company. State governments chartered companies operating across many communities, while local governments chartered companies that were locally owned and traded. Banks were commonly given the shortest charters — usually about three years and seldom more than ten. Two states, Indiana and Illinois, banned private banks altogether.

In the 19th century, most people living in the United States, apart from those in the slave states, were artisans, farmers, and people otherwise self-employed. They had won their freedom and their right to self-rule. Concentration of power was an anathema. From 1830 to 1850, citizens commonly revoked corporate charters. In Pennsylvania, ten bank charters were revoked in 1832 alone. If people suspected that charters were not being respected, citizen jury trials could be instigated to appraise allegations of corporate malfeasance and, if the company was found guilty, invoke criminal and civil penalties.

But the pressure to deregulate did not take long to build. Already in the 1830s a few states had passed general incorporation laws aimed at simplifying administrative procedures and eliminating "red tape." Over the next 50 years, time-limited charters, social responsibility clauses, and jury trials for corporate crimes were gradually phased out or became difficult to enforce through US courts.

The evolution in the United Kingdom was different, but the result was the same. In the midst of the severe depression of 1844, company law was amended to allow corporations to be formed without an act of Parliament. All that was required was to keep books of account, publish a balance sheet, and appoint an auditor. A few years later even these minimal requirements were abolished as "oppressive provisions" and "officious interference of the State." The biggest move in Britain occurred in 1862, when investors were freed from any constraints except one, to maximize shareholder profit.

The final relic of US citizen control over the rights and obligations of corporations was cast aside when corporate lawyers in the case of *Santa Clara County v. Southern Pacific Railroad* argued to the US Supreme Court that just as the slaves had been freed by the 14th Amendment to the Constitution, so should corporations. They won. Corporations, now imbued with the rights of any citizen and freed from the fetters of citizen charters, were set to become a powerful global force for advancing the priority of the Market over society. However, unlike a citizen, who could be prosecuted for his or her crimes, the people at the top of the corporate ladder enjoyed an enormous legal loophole. Their liability for committing crimes was limited.

The cumulative impact of this historical caving in to corporate enclosure has been, and continues to be, enormous. By 1955 the sales turnover of the largest US Fortune 500 corporations accounted for one-third of gross

Fig. 2.2: *In 1844, the same year the British Parliament freed the corporation from any vestiges of social responsibility, a cooperative of weavers in Rochdale, England, drafted the seven cooperative principles. They stand as a hallmark of the practice of corporate democracy and practicality against a rising tide of ever-more-powerful elites expanding their control over trade and capital.*

(i) *Democratic governance on a one-member, one-vote basis*
(ii) *Open and inclusive membership*
(i) *Distribution of surplus in proportion to trade*
(ii) *Payment of limited interest on capital*
(iii) *Political and religious neutrality*
(iv) *Cash trading (no goods on credit) and provision of pure and unadulterated goods*
(vii) *Education of members and households (paid for from a levy on surpluses)*

These principles were linked to practices that ensured full transparency. Quarterly meetings for all members, quarterly audited accounts, and a quarterly distribution of dividend surpluses were common practice. How different to the corporate world where, in the United Kingdom, companies were not required to show even a modicum of transparency until after the crash of 1929. Thereafter they had to assume the burden of publishing annual accounts.

domestic product (GDP); by 2004, it was two-thirds. Today, 51 of the 100 largest economies in the world are corporations, and the top 500 account for nearly 70 percent of world trade. In 2002, the top 200 had combined sales equivalent to 28 percent of world GDP, yet they only employed 0.82 percent of the global work force. Meanwhile, the United Nations estimates that poor countries lose about US $2 billion per day because of unjust trade rules — 14 times the amount they receive in aid.

The modern global corporation has become the most powerful instrument for enclosure the world has ever witnessed. And while there is a lot

Fig. 2.3: *Many people agree with the sentiment on these Occupy Movement banners in Los Angeles, including Senator Bernie Sanders. A movement to secure a constitutional amendment that would strip corporations of their legal status as "persons" is underway in the United States, one piece in a larger corporate reform struggle.* Source: © Gerry Boughan | Dreamstime.com

of talk about the growing movement for corporate social responsibility — some of it sincere — there is also plenty of evidence that low-road capitalism is still powerful and intent on continuing oligopolistic practices to advance private control over planetary resources.

Consider just one law. In 2005 the US Energy Act emasculated the Clean Water Act and the Environmental Protection Agency's right to regulate shale gas drilling. Dubbed the Halliburton loophole, it was inserted at the request of Vice President Dick Cheney, a former chief executive of Halliburton, a corporation that provides services to oil companies. Shale drilling, a process invented by Halliburton in the 1940s, involves injecting a mixture of water, sand, and chemicals, some of them toxic, into underground rock formations to blast them open and release natural gas. The practice is spreading rapidly across the United States and into many parts of Canada, and more recently the UK, as oil companies seek new supplies. Shale drilling, also known as fracking, has left an increasing incidence of poisoned water supplies in its wake, most dramatically reported in documentaries where households demonstrate the effects by setting their tap water on fire with a lighted match. Efforts to stop the use of this practice have been stymied. The oil companies involved have refused to reveal what makes up the chemical soup injected into the shale. Their defence is that to do so would reveal trade secrets, thus compromising their competitive position. Besides, the Clean Water Act now exempts them from acquiescing to such demands — the Halliburton loophole at work.

Evolution of the Big "M" Market III:
Banking Masters and Debtor Slaves

> *The modern banking system manufactures money out of nothing. The process is perhaps the most astounding piece of sleight-of-hand that was ever invented. Banking was conceived in inequity and born in sin. Bankers own the earth; take it away from them, but leave them the power to create credit, and with the stroke of a pen they will create enough money to buy it back again...If you want to be slaves of the bankers and pay the cost of your own slavery, then let bankers continue to create money and control credit.*
>
> — Josiah Stamp, Director of the Bank of England

As the financial industry has been deregulated over the last 40 years, the volatility of the global economy has significantly increased. In America, where banks were once regularly closed by citizens when they failed to meet the obligations of their charter, they are now so big they cannot be allowed to fail. Our seeming captivity to this argument is explained, in part, by the high level of our individual and collective indebtedness to the banks. We owe them, and they feel they own us. We can only begin to understand how we got ourselves in this modern debtors' prison by unraveling the mysteries of money.

Banking and accounting are much older than coins and dollar bills. In ancient times, what might be considered money came in many shapes and sizes — cattle, grain, salt, special stones, mystical totems, land, and slaves among them. People exchanged what they produced with others who had what they needed or as a way to pay tribute to the local lord or tithes to the church, to make amends for wrongdoing, or to amass a dowry that might attract a marriage partner.

Trading such miscellaneous items can be a difficult or unwieldy way to get business done. Not so with coins; they are compact, durable, and portable, perfect for trading and, as the Greeks and Romans figured out, a powerful tool in the business of building empires. Rulers and conquerors like Alexander the Great sent their merchants in ahead of the armies. Their job was to issue free money, knowing full well that once the country was vanquished, the paltry cost of issuing free money would be recovered by taxing the conquered.

Money is still issued freely by government and is still recovered through taxation. However, what most of us do not consider is that the state is now a minor player; its printing presses produce only a small fraction of modern currency. Instead, the banks control how much money is manufactured and, in contrast to the government mint, which would enter the money into the economy for free, the banks charge for this service. And we pay, dearly.

The first step toward the system of privately issued money in Europe was taken by goldsmiths and their customers in the Middle Ages. The goldsmiths provided a safe storage service for valuables, giving out IOUs for the gold customers stored in their vaults. Backed by the gold, the IOUs circulated as currency. When it became obvious that not all their customers were going to return at once for their gold, the goldsmiths began handing out more IOUs, in the process creating money not backed by gold deposits. They did very nicely and, voila, created for themselves a free secondary income as the first bankers.

We have traveled a long journey from the goldsmiths to the present displacement of government's free money by the banks' costly money. The result, as Josiah Stamp noted in the 1920s, is that modern banking has become a conjuring trick; it manufactures money out of nothing. About 3 to 5 percent of the money currently circulating in developed economies takes the form of coins and banknotes. The other 95 to 97 percent is electronic information that has little in the way of deposits to back it up — only the promise of others to pay their debts. For the privilege of receiving this electronic money, we pay the banks compound interest, and indebtedness grows exponentially.

Here is how it works. You go into the bank and ask for a loan. If approved, the bank credits your account. This creates a new deposit in your account and a credit to the bank at the same time. As these deposits grow, the law allows the banks to lend still more. As they are repaid, the money that has been created gets destroyed. Nevertheless, this is not a problem; the process of leveraging debts creates new money continuously. If the central bank requires banks to maintain 5 percent of real deposits as a reserve and hedge against bad debts, the banks are free to create 20 times that amount of money, always in the form of debt.

This is the fractional reserve system and theory of money creation. It is not widely understood. The conventional view of economists and the general public is that banks use savings to lend to households and to business. This is not the case. The Chicago Federal Reserve Bank described accurately how money is created in a guide called *Modern Money Mechanics,* quoted by Ellen Brown in *The Web of Debt:*

> [Banks] do not really pay out loans from the money they receive as deposits. If they did this, no additional money would

be created. What they do when they make loans is to accept promissory notes in exchange for credits to the borrower's transaction accounts. Loans (assets) and deposits (liabilities) both rise [by the same amount].

This is the goldsmith's IOU at work in today's world. Another form of IOU came in the late 1950s when bank credit cards were invented. This allowed the banks to manufacture additional volumes of money. The bank gives each card customer a credit limit, which it guarantees as long as the customer agrees to repay it. Typically, those who repay the balance each month pay no charges. Those who do not repay each month become the source of profits, paying typically close to two percent in monthly interest charges on unpaid balances. Unlike in the past, one need not save to show creditworthiness. Paul Mason reports that just prior to the 2007 credit crunch there were nine credit cards in circulation for every American citizen, with an average balance outstanding of $5,000 on each card.

Compound interest charged against the unregulated manufacture of money by the banks is a key part of their increasing share of corporate profits. Unlike simple interest, which charges a flat percentage annually, compound interest is charged at least monthly and in some cases daily.

For 4,000 years, religious laws proclaimed usury — the charging of interest — to be evil (in Hebrew, the word for usury is *neshek*, which means "to bite"). Usury was rife in the Roman empire, leading St. Paul to preach that the love of money was the root of all evil. The Catholic Church prohibited usury at the 1311 Council of Vienna. A fixed rate of interest was considered illegal because, as Aristotle pointed out, money itself is not productive in and of itself (he called it barren) and therefore warrants no return so long as loans are secured. A charge was considered legitimate by Aristotle only so long as it was appropriate to the level of risk — in short, if the price was just.

As land enclosures advanced and charters for mercantile trading corporations became more common, the ban on usury was lifted. After launching the English Reformation and dissolving the English monasteries, King Henry VIII legalized an interest rate of 10 percent. This benchmark was maintained in British law until reduced by Cromwell in 1651 to 6 percent. In 1776, Adam Smith argued in *The Wealth of Nations* that anything above 5 percent undermined small businesses and that the law should be changed to reduce the interest cap to this level.

In 1789, British utilitarian philosopher Jeremy Bentham disagreed with Smith, arguing in his *Discourse on Usury* that interest rates should be deregulated and have no cap at all. In 1854 the British usury laws were repealed and interest charges were allowed to rise. Over the past century the gloves came off completely. The 1927 Moneylenders Act increased the ceiling to 48 percent in the United Kingdom, and after World War II the United States raised the ceiling to 36 percent. In 1974 the UK ceiling was abolished, and similar deregulation took place in the United States in 1980.

To put this in perspective, in ordinary circumstances, when you borrow money at 3 percent compound interest, the amount you must pay back will double in 24 years. At 6 percent compound interest it will double in 12 years; at 12 percent, in six years; at 24 percent, three years; and at 36 percent, 18 months. Credit cards commonly charge compound rates between 20 and 40 percent. Even when homeowners use lower-cost credit to buy a house, with variable rates on a 25-year mortgage, they typically repay in capital and interest 2.5 times the sum they originally borrowed. And if they do not pay on time, they will begin incurring interest on the interest. Little wonder that the origin of the word "mortgage" combines two Latin words, *morte* (death) and *gage* (grip) — the "grip of death." Historically, a mortgage was the last resort of landowners or farmers, who would only mortgage their land in extreme circumstances, precisely because they risked losing a secure means of subsistence, to their own detriment and that of their community.

Since 1990, the interest rates on legal loans in North America and the UK have become extortionate. Payday loan rates of 2,000 percent or more are common, and the BBC recently reported that banks in the UK were charging their customers massive penalties for being overdrawn on their checking accounts, in some cases "eye-watering" rates between 300,000 and 800,000 percent.

Alternatives to the Modern Banking System 1: Public Banks

The situation in which we find ourselves, where the banking industry manufactures debt with no restriction on what it charges, is the result of corporate power inexorably influencing political choices. The alternatives are there, hidden away from the awareness of citizens who might otherwise press for an end to usury gone wild.

If interest is to be charged, why not allow more public ownership of banks? It is not such a strange question. In the heart of free-enterprise America, as citizens suffer the consequences of unrestricted bank-manufactured debt, one state is showing the efficacy of this political choice. To prevent farmers from losing their homesteads, the Bank of North Dakota was set up in 1919 as a public bank for the state. Faced at the time with rising levels of foreclosures, the farmers organized and secured a state law to establish the bank. It is now the only publicly owned bank in the United States and is highly successful. It is profitable and reinvests its earnings for public purposes. North Dakota in 2009 had the largest public sector surplus and lowest unemployment rate (3.3 percent) while other US states were floundering and continue to struggle with unwieldy fiscal deficits and soaring unemployment rates.

Other countries have established successful public banks. Municipal and regional savings banks are common in Europe. To achieve radical levels of carbon reduction, the German state bank, KfW is providing capital to Germany's mutual banks for upgrading all old housing nationally to high levels of energy efficiency at loans of under 2.5% for homeowners. The 300,000 new construction jobs annually repays the subsidy on the capital in new tax income generated. Central banks were recommended by Keynes to ensure that low-cost capital and low-interest-rate policies are pursued to fund public services. In his *General Theory* of 1936, Keynes set out his monetary reform theory. He called, in effect, for a cheap money policy that would be implemented by nationalized central banks that would intervene to ensure interest rates for investment by businesses and public sector organizations were kept low. As Geoff Tily has shown in *Keynes Betrayed*, what Keynes recommended to achieve this was a strategic long-term, low-interest policy, implemented through short-term and long-term bond rates set by government that would range from under one percent in real terms for three-month Treasury bills and under three percent for long-term bonds.

The Labour government elected in 1945 implemented this strategic Keynesian policy and these "cheap money" policies underpinned and operated well to maintain the so-called golden years of low-inflation and high employment policies enjoyed internationally from 1945 to 1970 by the main industrial countries of the world that followed this guidance. For example, as Tily shows, five-year government bonds in the UK operated for decades during the golden years after World War II at an average real rate of return of 1.4 percent. During the period of deregulation from 1977 to 2003, the average real rate of return on five-year UK government bonds was 7 percent.

The Bank of Canada was nationalized by the Mackenzie King government in 1938. King took the Keynesian message to heart and created interest-free money to help the country overcome the Depression, and the Bank of Canada still retains in its constitutional right to do so. By contrast, in the UK and the United States, the Bank of England and the US Federal Reserve can only create interest-free money under very restricted circumstances, and they are specifically forbidden from creating it for social purposes.

In 2010, Canadians paid $165 million daily in interest charges on governmental debt of $519 billion — this is equivalent to $136 a week from a family of four. According to Richard Priestman and Connie Fogal, between 1939 and 1945 the Bank of Canada produced 62 percent or more of the national money supply interest-free. From 1945 to 1975 the Bank of Canada provided a significant proportion of capital for public needs — at a nominal rate of about one percent. A major source of low-cost capital to lend was the private Canadian banks that were obliged under Keynesian policies to hold statutory reserves interest-free in the Bank of Canada, which the public bank could then lend out for public works and benefits. Over many years this put over $120 billion in interest-free money at the disposal of the Canadian government. Inflation and speculative lending could be reined in by the Bank of Canada requiring the private banks to increase their statutory reserves to slow down credit expansion where necessary.

Total federal debt in Canada was only $37 billion in 1975, and 22 percent was owed to the Bank of Canada. However, following the lead of Thatcher and Reagan, the Brian Mulroney government, which came to power in 1984, moved away from the statutory reserve system to free markets and the deregulation of the banking sector. Real long-term interest rates on Canadian government debt, which were 0.7 percent in 1980, escalated to 8.4 percent in 1984. After the policy shift, interest payable to the private banks on borrowing rose to levels from $5 billion to $8 billion a year on loans that had previously been virtually interest free. The use of the Bank of Canada to fund public projects has declined radically since. Interest rates on government debt rose to ranges of 6 to 18 percent in the 1980s, and the public debt soared to $408 billion in 1991 and then a peak level of $585 billion in 2000.

Alternatives to the Modern Banking System 2:
Cooperative Finance and Alternative Currencies

Interestingly, the practice of issuing low-cost or interest-free money is not restricted to government. Whether prompted by economic disaster or a strong moral stance against usury, the range of historic innovations in cooperative finance and alternative currencies is truly astonishing. Indeed, the early cooperative finance organizations sought interest-free solutions.

One of the earliest experiments (1775) was hatched in England by Richard Ketley, a Birmingham pub owner, and a group of his customers, who pooled savings interest-free in a "building society" that would help members buy land and build homes together cheaply. Under the mutual plan, each member, in solidarity with all the others, would save until the pool was sufficient to issue a loan to one of their number to build a house. The deal was that all members would continue the mutual savings process until the last member secured a loan, at which point the time-limited company formally terminated itself, and there was no more business in the pub except darts and the regulars imbibing their favorite suds. Almost 1,000 "terminating" building societies had spread across England, Wales, Scotland and Ireland by 1870, becoming one of the largest funders of housing construction.

Other experiments evolved throughout the 19th century, mutating, inspiring, and learning from each other. The idea of paying a fee for a loan, rather than paying compound interest, gained widespread support, especially in the United States. There was also strong support for the government to issue free currency, and the revival of Greenbacks (currency issued by Lincoln interest-free) was taken up by the Greenback Labour Party in 1874.

The struggle to end the practice of usury was diverse and continuous in the early cooperative movement. Dr. Thomas Bowkett set up cooperative savings and lending societies in England in 1843. Loans were allocated by lottery until everyone had received an interest-free loan. Richard Starr improved the cooperative system rules in 1862. Though made illegal in the UK in the late 19th century because of the lottery aspect, Starr-Bowkett societies were popular as a way to secure a loan for housing and other needs and operated in Australia until the 1960s. However, all such mutual ventures have had trouble figuring out how to make the idea work sustainably without charging interest.

In the depression of the 1890s, the German entrepreneur, Silvio Gesell began working on a new cooperative money system based on a widespread guild practice from the Middle Ages. In his essay "Economic Thought in the Middle Ages," David Boyle of the new economics foundation described the precedent that caught Gesell's creative imagination. Two forms of money became common in 12th-century Italy: silver coins were used for long-distance trade, and so-called black money for local exchange. Because they were minted from duller metals in local mints, the local coins quickly turned black. Similar coins circulated in German-speaking areas of Europe and in France. The black money was recalled every five or six years for reminting by the local ruler. On these occasions, the bearer would receive three new coins for every four handed in. The withheld coin was a tax charged by the local ruler. These coins were said to be the first "demurrage" (i.e., depreciating) form of money. This medieval money system became widespread under the Holy Roman Empire and lasted well into the 15th century.

Gesell revived and adapted this long-forgotten system, designing a unique way to overcome the challenge of financial sustainability. As a successful businessman oriented to cooperative thinking, he was keenly aware of the social injustice of the interest-rate system. However, his inspiration was not simply moral but also economic. He believed interest rates had a negative impact on the economic efficiency of markets. His rationale is intriguing. He questioned why, when everything in life wears out and dies, money is expected to grow and persist in "God-like" ways forever. Clearly money based on debt and the charging of interest was out of kilter with the reality of everything else on the planet. Fixing this design flaw, which

Fig. 2.4: *"Money as a medium of exchange increasingly vanishes out of working people's hands. It seeps away into channels where interest flows and accumulates in the hands of a few, who do not return it back to the market for the purchasing of goods and services but withhold it for speculation. As money is an indispensable wheel in the machine of production, an accumulation of great sums in a few hands means a gigantic danger for peaceful production. Every time the flow of money is interrupted, so is the exchange of goods and services, with a consequent fall in employment... Such a situation denies incentives to the population, threatening peace and wealth with destruction. Whole nations and states are under the threat of ruin. Our small place cannot liberate the world, but we want at least to give a sign. In the Wörgl area the sluggish, slow-circulating National Bank currency shall be replaced with a medium of exchange with a better circulating performance than ordinary money." (Excerpt from the statement of the mayor of Wörgl, 1932).* Source: Public Domain. Accessed 14 July 2011 from de.wikipedia.org/w/index.php?title=Datei:Freigeld1.jpg&filetimesta mp=20100501091650.

he considered a drag on the efficiency of markets, could only be accomplished with money that mimicked nature. The first step was to get rid of the idea that money was equivalent to a precious metal. The second step was to separate the unit of money, say a dollar, from the paper or scrip that represented it. He then logically proposed that money should "decay" over time rather than increase, just like everything else does. His proposed device for mimicking the natural order economically was a negative interest charge; in brief, Gesellian money would lose its value over time.

To put this idea into practice, he recommended a negative interest charge of 5.2 percent per year. If money lost this much value annually, Gesell forecast that it would become a pure medium of exchange. Why hoard it when it no longer stores value over time? Gesell called his idea *Freigeld* (free money), describing it as free of interest, stable, and democratically accountable if effectively managed locally. He also suggested such a currency would be much less risky in terms of either deflation or inflation, could possibly end the boom-and-bust cycles of market economies, and — something Aristotle, St. Paul, and Thomas Aquinas would love — would constrain hoarding and greed.

It sounds wild, but it only began to succeed just before Gesell died in 1930. In 1929, two of his supporters had established the WÄRA Exchange Society to promote *Freigeld*. Shortly thereafter they supplied a distressed business owner with a *Freigeld* loan of 50,000 "WÄRA" to revive a flooded coal mine in the small town of Schwanenkirchen, in Bavaria. The owner used the currency to pay 90 percent of his miners' wages. Importantly, he also persuaded the shopkeepers and local service providers to accept the currency; after all, it was backed by the value of coal from the mine.

The effect was dramatic. While the Great Depression was throwing people out of work across Europe and North America, the coal mine was revived, the workers bought and exchanged goods, and the town began a rapid revitalization, all fed by the rapid circulation of a currency that would lose 5.2 percent of its value within a year. Over 2,000 corporations across Germany began to use similar methods to revive their operations. But to no avail; the central bank felt threatened, and in 1931 it declared all such "emergency currencies" illegal.

However the idea of *Freigeld* had already jumped borders to Denmark, Austria, America, and Britain. Wörgl, Austria, introduced a Gesellian currency in 1932. Desperate to rein in an unemployment rate of over 30 percent, the mayor issued 40,000 "free schillings," using them to pay the salaries of municipal staff. Fully backed by the Austrian currency, the free schilling was free of interest but not free of charge. Every month the holder of free schillings had to go to the town hall and get a stamp affixed to the front of each note to revalidate it. The stamp reduced its value by 1 percent every month and 12 percent each year, more than double the 5.2 percent Gesell had recommended. People scrambled to spend their scrip even more quickly.

In the first year this scrip currency changed hands 13 times more than the Austrian schilling had done the year before. Debts declined. Demand for credit fell. To avoid the monthly devaluation, holders of free schillings opted to pay for work in advance, order goods and supplies, repay debts, settle accounts, and pay off taxes. It was a benefit to householders, businesses, and the municipality (only national businesses, like the post office and the railway, refused to accept the free schilling). Within the first year, new homes were built and old ones repaired; municipal buildings were improved; streets were repaved; a reservoir, bridge, and ski jump were built; and forests were replanted. Unemployment ended. A year later, 200 Austrian .towns were gearing up to adopt the reform. Guess what happened? Yes, as in Germany, the central bank declared the free schilling illegal. In 1934, the unemployment rate of Wörgl soared back up to over 30 percent.

Irving Fisher, the renowned American economist and developer of the quantity theory of money, thought Gesell's ideas a brilliant remedy for the ravages of the Great Depression. In 1932, a number of American towns were circulating local money, with some using Gesell's system. Fisher proposed that "Free-Money" be distributed to each state in proportion to its population. Half would be used for unemployment and welfare payments; half would finance infrastructure. Each Free-Money note would be good for one year. For a $1.00 note to remain valid, the holder had to affix a two-cent postage stamp to it every week. After 52 weeks the sale of stamps for each one-dollar note would have generated $1.04 for the post office, which would then redeem the "stamp scrip" for ordinary money and retain four cents to cover its costs. Such time-limited currency, Fisher argued, would not cause inflation.

Fisher produced a book to help local communities across the USA set up stamp scrip, and by early 1933, cities like St. Paul, Minnesota, the sparsely populated state of Iowa, and hundreds of small towns had issued their own money. President Roosevelt, so willing to try new things in so many ways, unfortunately decided not to include Fisher's reform in his New Deal. Advised by Harvard professor Russell Sprague that the American monetary system was rapidly being democratized and the government might lose control, Roosevelt banned stamp scrip in March 1933.

Why this constant closing down of innovation? What was the problem with a democratic, decentralized, and time-limited currency system that was creating such incredible social and economic results? Could it have anything to do with such systems being seen as a threat to the private profit priority of the Market?

Fortunately, one story of currency innovation in the 1930s comes with a happier ending. Danish farmers started the JAK "interest-free" cooperative in 1931 to stop farm foreclosures (JAK is short for *Jord Arbete Kapital*, or "Land Labour Capital" — the economic forces of production). Its first project, a local currency backed by farmers property, flourished in rural areas.

Within two years the new currency had expanded to 1.5 percent of the total money in circulation within Denmark. And, sure enough, it was declared illegal. In response to this setback, JAK launched two new experiments. One was an interest-free checking account system that allowed businesses and other members to trade goods and services without cash. It was shut down in 1935 (although this interest-free working capital system lives on in Zurich, Switzerland, where the WIR bartering system, adapted from JAK ideas in the 1930s, provides low-cost inter-trading and mutual credit of $2 billion annually for over 75,000 small businesses). The second experiment proved to be more enduring: an interest-free savings-and-loan system aimed at helping its members refinance expensive bank loans. Despite serious difficulties over the years, JAK has survived and continues to evolve and expand as a successful system of interest-free banking in Sweden and Denmark, with the generative results reflected in Chapter 3.

More recently, in 2003, an attempt to revive Gesell's stamp scrip money was begun in southern Germany, to assist the local economy in the towns of Rosenheim and Traunstein — both only 30 miles across the border from Wörgl in Austria. This project has secured support from the GLS Bank, a social bank in Europe. The currency, called Chiemgauer (named after the local region of 500,000 people), has a two-year lifespan and is renewable four times a year for a 2 percent charge. Like the euro it is denominated in 1 to 50 units of value. Four cooperative banks are promoting this currency, and there are 40 issuing offices. The Chiemgauer slowly gained support and is now accepted by 600 businesses (including eight supermarkets), used regularly by 3,000 people, and has become the world's most successful local currency, with an annual turnover 2.5 times faster than the euro. Christian Gelleri, who developed the Chiemgauer, has followed closely the Wörgl design features and the guidance from Irving Fisher. A key difference is that the currency is available both as stamp scrip notes and as electronic debit card money. The preloaded debit card facility has been provided by local cooperative banks. An additional recent feature is interest-free microcredit loans to local businesses from the GLS Bank. The success of the Chiemgauer is now spreading to other areas of Germany, and there are 36 similar projects under development through the national Regiogeld network. It remains to be seen whether the central bank will once again shut down such innovation.

Alternatives to the Modern Banking System 3: 100 Percent Money (Debt-Free)

The most obvious alternative is for the government to issue more debt-free money. It is hardly a radical idea. Henry Ford fully understood its efficacy: he railed against the dead weight that compound interest placed on businesses, on taxpayers, and on society as a whole. Why pay the banks interest, he asked, when the government could create debt-free money? In December 1921 he recommended to Congress an easy way to finance a hydroelectric dam to power one of his factories in Alabama: "Whenever the Government needs money for a great public improvement, instead of thinking of bonds with heavy interest charges, think of redeemable non-interest-bearing currency...Do you appreciate that 80 cents of every dollar raised by taxation is spent in the payment of interest?...Here is the way to get the improvements without increasing the debt."

It makes perfect sense. If the government can issue three percent of the money "interest-free" and "debt-free" as coins and notes, why can it not create the entire money supply the same way? The Romans did it; why not Brits, Americans, or modern-day Greeks and Italians? Indeed, it is only in the last few centuries, and in particular in the last five decades before the introduction of the credit card, that government has created such a small fraction of the money supply. For example, during the 1960s the UK government issued one-third of the money supply, interest-free and debt-free.

Governments historically have stepped in to increase the circulation of debt-free money in times of warfare or severe economic crisis. Britain freely issued £1 and £2 notes that were not redeemable in gold during the Napoleonic Wars, beginning in 1798, and continued this practice until 1821. (Some of these notes are on display at the British Museum, along with Bradbury notes that were issued in a similar way in August 1914, at the outset of World War I.) To pay the costs of the American Civil War, Abraham Lincoln issued the interest-free "Greenbacks." Most recently, governments in Japan, the United States, the UK, and elsewhere have been printing money debt-free (quantitative easing) to reflate economies damaged by the collapse of the global finance industry. Quantitative easing, carried out in the United States and the UK since 2008, is a modern method by which governments print money without borrowing. It has been used when interbank lending rates of interest are at or close to zero. The central bank increases the money supply by purchasing financial assets (mostly short-term), including both government bonds and corporate bonds, from financial institutions (such as banks), using money the central bank has created *ex nihilo* (out of nothing).

To limit inflation, any money issued as debt, whether interest-bearing or interest-free, needs to be repaid or redeemed so as to cancel it. In that case, as Henry Ford argued, why borrow expensive money from the banks when governments can issue redeemable non-interest-bearing currency? Would it not be in the public interest to do so? Who gains when banks charge compound interest on money they conjure up from nothing? Taxpayers can repay the debt for an affordable housing project at a fraction of the cost if the debt is interest-free money issued by the government. Taxation alone is a sufficient recovery mechanism. Alexander the Great seemed to have worked that one out over 2,000 years ago. Is this not a political choice we can make today?

Frustrated with his failure to get stamp scrip introduced, Irving Fisher produced a plan in 1936 for the US government to move to 100-percent debt-free money. He showed that debt-based money causes inflation in good times and leads to deflation in periods of depression. Therefore to stabilize economies, a critical reform is to take away the banks' power to create money and return this power fully to government. He summarized the plan this way:

> The essence of the 100% plan is to make money independent of loans: that is, to divorce the process of creating and destroying money from the business of banking. A purely incidental result would be to make banking safer and more profitable; but by far the most important result would be the prevention of great booms and depressions by ending the chronic inflations and deflations which have ever been the curse of mankind and which have sprung largely from banking.

Fisher developed strong support among other economists for his 100-percent plan during the late 1930s. By 1939 he had secured approval from 235 economists from 157 universities and colleges in the United States, though nothing came of the idea at the time.

However, several decades later, in 2011, the Positive Money campaign was launched in the UK to revive Fisher's plan. James Robertson, founder of the new economics foundation, has estimated that this reform would make an annual savings for UK citizens of £75 billion plus a one-off benefit to the public purse of £1,500 billion over a three-year period of transition from debt-based money to debt-free money.

The Economics of Sufficiency: Living within the Planetary Commons

Climate change, important as it is, is nevertheless a symptom of a deeper malady, namely our fixation on unlimited growth of the economy as the solution to nearly all our problems.

— Herman Daly

The notion of a future economy without growth is now the subject of a wide-ranging debate. Herman Daly, former senior economist in the Environment Department of the World Bank, has been raising his voice for decades in support of what was once called "green heresy." Polanyi is one of his key inspirations.

Daly has shown that steady-state economies were the norm for more than 99 percent of human history prior to the Great Transformation. He argues that since the end of the Roman Empire, the dominant economic paradigm has shifted in three ways: from the regulated just-price system of the Middle Ages to the free market system launched by the Industrial Revolution and then to the global casino banks that have developed since deregulation began in the early 1970s.

But with more than two centuries of growth now behind us, can humankind survive without it? Conventional economists think not; they say "progress without growth" is an oxymoron. Yet the real contradiction lies elsewhere. How can growth be sustained when it depends on oil and gas, which are becoming increasingly scarce, and on a money system out of control? Both have driven us as human beings to become isolated from the consequences of our behavior; we waste energy and incur debt beyond our means.

Part of the problem is that conventional economists ignore the interdependency of social, environmental, and economic systems. They treat the economy as if it were a closed system, a kind of perpetual motion machine. Nothing flows in and nothing flows out. Daly insists this is absurd because self-evidently the economy is a subsystem embedded within other social and biological systems. His scientific explanation becomes more interesting when you contemplate having a mouth to consume but no body parts to excrete. As Daly wrote in *Beyond Growth*:

> The first thing to change would be the circular flow diagram that conveys the pre-analytic vision of the economic process as an isolated circular flow from firms to households and back again, with no inlets or outlets...Maintenance and replacement in this picture would seem to be accomplished internally, requiring no dependence on an environment. It is exactly as if a biology textbook proposed to study an animal only in terms of its circulatory system, without ever mentioning its digestive tract! An animal with an isolated circulatory system and no digestive tract would be a perpetual motion machine. Unlike this imaginary circular-flow animal, real animals have digestive tracts that connect them to their environment at both ends. They continuously take in low-entropy matter/energy and give back high-entropy matter/energy. An organism cannot recycle its own waste products...But in economics there is only the

circulatory system. This is as true of Marxist economics as it is of neoclassical economics.

Economic assumptions that ignore the cumulative fouling of our own nests are just plain stupid. Calibrating our existence to fit within the constraints of ecological reality is nonnegotiable if the aim is the survival of our species. To make such a seismic shift, economic growth must decline. We are already overshooting the planet's capacity to absorb our excesses. This huge challenge is made exceedingly more difficult if we are to reverse the ever-increasing disparity in income, wealth, and resource use across the globe. The implication is radical: growth needed to meet basic needs must occur in some countries, and a strategic retreat must be navigated in others.

Daly identifies Frederick Soddy, who won the Nobel prize for chemistry in 1921, as the earliest scientist to advocate the redesign of the economy on ecological principles. Soddy abhorred the unwillingness of conventional economists to consider the underlying fact of global economics: that oil and gas were going to run out some day and that, as sources of energy, they were irreplaceable on any time scale relevant to human beings as a species. Scientists' acknowledgement of these facts might have induced a more conservative and intelligent stewardship of such resources, making them an asset to human life in perpetuity. Instead, unaffected by reality, the demand and supply models of economists assumed fossil fuels were going to be around forever. Soddy showed compellingly that the use of coal, oil, and gas was the source extending both human power and economic growth exponentially. How else could the world's human population grow sixfold in 150 years?

Soddy's thinking about the profligate waste of fossil fuels led him to consider the role money was playing in driving the treadmill of economic growth. Drawing on the innovative work of Gesell, he came to the same conclusion; charging compound interest on growing levels of debt had become a serious contributor to social and ecological problems, as exemplified by the crash of 1929. Ever the scientist, Soddy came to see the money problem stemming from entropy, a complete disregard for reality as expressed by the second law of thermodynamics.

From Ruskin and Gesell we have already heard the same story. Plants, animals, and humans arise from seed; they grow, some faster, others more slowly; they come in many sizes and use different sources of energy, which they expend at different rates. This is natural. We are born, we use and expend energy, and then we die. Although it is true that energy cannot be destroyed (the first law of thermodynamics), it does not stay the same once it has been used. Energy used for heat, light, and power, or energy used for eating, digesting, or defecating — any life-sustaining use — is irretrievably lost to a dissipated form of energy that is not useable. This is the second law of thermodynamics.

No wonder Soddy asked the profound and perplexing question: If the sun, the fundamental source of all energy, is dissipated once used, as the second law states, how is it that money can defy decay, as if it were some kind of perpetual motion machine? In his book *Wealth, Virtual Wealth, and Debt*, Soddy concluded it cannot, at least not without life-damaging consequences.

> Debts are subject to the laws of mathematics rather than physics. Unlike wealth, which is subject to the laws of thermodynamics, debts do not rot with age and are not consumed in the process of living. On the contrary, they grow at so much percent per annum, by the well known mathematical laws of simple and compound interest...For sufficient reason, the process of compound interest is physically impossible, though the process of compound decrement is physically common enough.

Like Ruskin before him, Soddy argued, in *Money Versus Man*, that "economic sufficiency is the essential foundation upon which national greatness and progress can be constructed." But sufficiency means enough. Growth beyond enough is akin to playing Russian roulette. Sooner or later, one of the chambers is going to fire.

The 21st Century: A Chapter the Living Must Write

Modern-day clearances are manifest and growing across the globe. The expansion of enclosure now has the entire planet in its grip, and the consequences keep rolling in like larger and larger tidal waves. Elites worldwide continue to angle for more from a finite base of natural and social capital to exploit. Citizens at the sharp end of the subprime mortgage travesty, countries gripped by the Euro-crisis, those losing jobs, the evicted and the homeless, those whose pensions are being curtailed, small businesses unable to secure working capital, the climate refugees, are all among the dislocated and the prematurely dying.

In *Progress and Poverty*, Henry George examined the absurd contradiction of rapid technological progress coexisting with rising levels of poverty. Obviously, the problem was not one of productive capacity. More and more was being produced faster and faster. The bottleneck was distribution of the means for people to live sufficiently, to meet their basic needs. Mill argued that to change this travesty we could not rely on the market; a political choice must be made. Over a century later we still refuse to make the hard choices our circumstances warrant. We need to recognize that this is our democratic prerogative and that the power is in our hands. Perplexed and without clarity on what could be done, the lack of a Plan B leaves so many concerned citizens meandering around in ever-smaller circles, unfocused, confused, and drifting toward apathy because they are unable to disperse the cultural fog created by the hegemonic myth that more is always better.

The visionaries and movement builders, the innovators and the diggers we have briefly introduced, suggest possible pathways forward. We are inheritors of their successes, their setbacks, and their learning. In the chapters ahead, modern pioneers demonstrate that the forces of enclosure can be rolled back, even if the scale is still not adequate. We can learn from what has been and scale up what is showing promise. When we look at the world through the eyes of the seers of the past and pioneers of the present, it does seem that we do indeed have the capacity to navigate our way through and to forge the Great Transition. It is a chapter of the human story we in this century must write, whether we like it or not.

We begin in Chapter 3 with a story that turns contemporary finance on its head. The JAK Cooperative Bank challenges the notion that we cannot loan resources to each other without charging compound interest. The Occupy Movement needs to hear this story and take its message to heart in the years ahead: it is possible to transform the usurious system that concentrates wealth. All it takes are shrewd approaches to financing based on solidarity and sufficiency.

CHAPTER 3

A Path beyond Debt:
Interest-Free Lending at Work

The trade of the petty usurer is hated with most reason:
it makes a profit from currency itself, instead of making it from
the process which currency was meant to serve. Their common
characteristic is obviously their sordid avarice.

— Aristotle

To take interest for money lent is unjust in itself, because this is to sell
what does not exist, and this evidently leads to inequality, which is
contrary to justice. Now, money was invented chiefly for the purpose of
exchange. Hence, it is by its very nature unlawful to take payment for
the use of money lent, which payment is known as interest.

— Thomas Aquinas

UNLOCKING THE DEBT TRAP is hugely difficult. Ironically, the primary solution advanced by banks and the International Monetary Fund is to issue more debt and charge compound interest for the privilege of borrowing. President Franklin Roosevelt commented on the intelligence of this refrain in his 1933 inaugural address to Americans: "Faced by a failure of credit, they [the banks] propose only lending more money."

Fast forward to 2012 — same story, different century. The list of European countries in danger of default on their debt grew longer month by month through 2011. And as the perceived risks increased, the charges imposed by the banks and bondholders became higher. Rates of compound interest climbed radically upward just when countries were falling to their knees under the crush of exploding debt levels. The worse off they were, the more they must pay.

If the consequences were not so tragic, we might think we were watching a farce. Just think about it. A deregulated and bloated industry designs opaque, predatory, and ultimately toxic financial products, wraps them up to sell in packaging that oozes security, and then spends six or seven years picking the pockets of millions of trusting consumers. Once the buyers start to understand the ruse, it blows up. The house of cards falls, small and large investors lose billions, and citizens and governments pony up to bail out the free-market banks that are "too big to fail." Government costs skyrocket, millions are thrown out of work, home foreclosures mount, government revenues plunge — and two years later the whole debate turns back to governments needing to tighten their belts and be responsible. Talk of financial reregulation is barely audible. Unearned bonuses return. Bank reserves are growing again, yet the credit crunch for the average citizen and small business remains.

Recall the stability of the financial system from 1933 to 1970 — not one financial crisis. Why? The central factor is simple: governments strictly controlled the cost of capital. They kept interest rates low and stable. In this setting, compound interest could not compound so fast nor drive citizens and governments so quickly into the debt trap. Not so now; the combined debt of US households, businesses, and governments rose from 1.6 times GDP in 1973 to over 3.5 times GDP in 2007. Under the Bush administration (2001–8), government debt almost doubled, from $5.7 trillion to over $10 trillion. Thanks to the bank-manufactured subprime-mortgage fiasco, US debt is now even higher. Indeed, the cross-the-board escalation in public debt since 1970 has catapulted compound interest into the "dominant revenue" of our times. The concept of dominant revenue, developed by French economist François Perroux, describes the type of income that by its rate and mass is decisive in the way the economy functions. Likewise, the social group that enjoys that income exercises decisive political influence. No wonder the finance industry commands 39 percent of corporate profits when only a few decades ago it was 14 percent, as noted in Chapter 1. And no wonder it is able to evade any threat of government regulation.

Drawing on the research of Helmut Creutz, Margrit Kennedy highlighted what percentage of the costs of providing various public services in Germany stemmed from compound interest. Like most enterprises, public services need equipment, buildings, and operating capital to do their job. It is tough to pick up garbage without a specially equipped truck, for example. Each service has its own chain of suppliers, and if one followed exchange transactions up the chain, the journey would reveal a complex web of interrelated businesses, each of which is paying compound interest for the working and fixed capital it needs from banks.

Kennedy's general conclusion was startling. Close to 35 percent of the costs of essential goods and services may be traced to the charging of compound interest; public provision of rubbish collection, 12 percent; provision of drinking water, 38 percent; provision of sewage disposal; 47 percent; and provision of public rental housing, a whopping 70 percent. These are astounding figures. Think of the impact on the costs of government, households, and every business along the myriad supply chains that provision human beings.

Helmut Creutz also conducted research to determine the impact of compound interest at the household level. His conclusion was equally astounding — 33 percent of all household expenditures can be traced to compound interest, triple the cost of the value-added tax paid to the German government. The difference is that the additional proportion of household costs represented by compound interest flows to the richest 10 percent of Germans, who own sufficient capital to lend it. As a result of compound interest, Helmut Creutz estimated that 600 million euros were transferred each day in 2010 from the bottom 80 percent to the top 10 percent of households (see Figure 3.1). By mortgaging future income this way, the excess cash created in the debt-based money process fuels the speculative and unsustainable casino economy, a conclusion that is reinforced when one considers data from the period 1950–2010. During this 60-year period, the gross domestic product in Germany grew eightfold.

The steadily rising ceiling on permissible lending rates in many countries, and the complete lack of a ceiling in Britain, accelerates this process. Licensed moneylenders in the UK can legally charge fees ranging from 80 percent for secured pawnbroker loans to 2,000 percent or more for payday loans. Subprime-mortgage lenders in the UK and the United States charge fees that for centuries would have been regarded as extortionate. The social costs continue to mount. In the United States, more than one in four low-income households spends over 40 percent of its income to service debts. In the UK, bankruptcies and personal insolvencies reached an all-time high in 2009.

Compound Interest: the secret tax

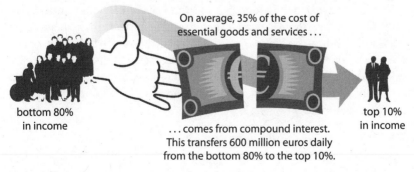

On average, 35% of the cost of essential goods and services . . .

bottom 80%
in income

. . . comes from compound interest.
This transfers 600 million euros daily
from the bottom 80% to the top 10%.

top 10%
in income

Fig. 3.1: *Compound Interest*

The economic logic of the growth imperative is fed by compound interest. If we do not grow the economy, how do we pay off those with the capital we need to borrow in order to live, work, raise children, run businesses, or function governmentally. The challenge is to figure out how to step off this treadmill in ways that enable households and communities to restore a measure of sanity to the process of financing our basic needs and the imperative of bringing our economies into balance with the ecosystems we depend on. Fostering self-reliance at the level of the household and community, while increasing local capacity to finance the Great Transition, depends, in part, on whether there are practical means to do so.

Interest-Free Lending at Work: The JAK Cooperative Bank

In the 1930s, a group of Danish farmers facing repossession of their land by the commercial banks set up a system that continues to operate successfully today. Building upon earlier practices of interest-free systems in Germany, Christian Christiansen championed the founding of a number of rural savings-and-loan cooperatives that went by the acronym JAK, short for *Jord Arbete Kapital* ("Land Labour Capital"). The personal savings and community benefits that have accrued to members of this democratic cooperative finance system are testimony to the dramatic impacts that can be realized when we replace compound interest with a fee-based approach to lending.

Sweden is now home to the largest number of JAK branches and members. Started in 1965, the co-op expanded rapidly in the late 1980s and secured a banking license in 1998. Today JAK has 35,000 members in Sweden, US$163 million in assets, and $147 million out on loan. It operates on the basis of mutual aid and financial reciprocity amongst its membership. JAK members agree to pool their savings and then lend them to one another, interest-free, for mortgages, home improvement, student loans, etc.

JAK Bank is based in Skövde but has 30 local branches and a large number of JAK member groups across the country. To keep overheads low, the local branches rely heavily on the assistance of the 650 community-based volunteers trained by JAK staff in interest-free lending principles and practices. These volunteers recruit new members through the JAK newspaper and educational events in local areas. Volunteers can tap into a number of JAK systems, including internet services and online forums, to get assistance with community engagement. A JAK school conducts courses for volunteers and members.

Key Points in the JAK Philosophy and Analysis

The high level of volunteer commitment cannot be explained simply by the cost savings that JAK members enjoy. It derives from a broader analysis that is consistent with the ideas of Margrit Kennedy, John Ruskin, and many of the visionaries referenced in Chapter 2.

First, JAK members agree that the cost of compound interest embedded in the cost of goods amounts to an indirect taxation of ordinary citizens by the wealthy. They see this as antithetical to the good of the household, the community, the environment, and the nation.

Second, they believe that compound interest fuels the notion that only projects yielding a higher profit than prevailing interest rates are worthy of investment. This leads to an overemphasis on large-scale projects (such as shopping centers, office buildings, etc.) or high-yielding short-term projects, (e.g., extracting finite natural resources) at the expense of long-term projects yielding a lower financial return (e.g., renewable energy, organic farming, energy conservation measures etc.).

Third, unsustainable economic growth is fueled by the pressure to service the costs of compound interest. This means compound interest is a key factor in the exponential growth of debt in the economy and an important contributor to unemployment, inflation, and the degradation of the natural environment.

Fourth, interest charges represent a depletion of life's energy. JAK members would agree with Ruskin that "wealth is life." Households, communities, and governments freed of the burden of interest costs can reinvest time and money in enlarging the round of life nurturing well-being and fulfilling livelihoods. They are also freed, in the view of Mark Anielski, "to re-establish a healthy relationship with money so that it is no longer a store of value (something to be hoarded) but a genuine medium of exchange amongst households and businesses to build real wealth and sustainable, flourishing communities." These core beliefs and values are reflected in all the aspects of the JAK's governance and management activities.

How the System Works

Operationally, the Swedish JAK is very similar to a credit union, except that members do not earn any interest on their savings or dividends on their shares. There is also a compulsory savings element. By foregoing interest and dividend income, members are entitled to fee-based loans at no interest. (The explanation below illustrates the operation of JAK in dollars rather than Swedish kroner.)

The following elements make up the total cost of becoming a JAK member and the cost of a loan:

- Loan appraisal and setup cost at a fee that is currently about 3.2 percent of the approved loan value (This makes up the loan cost.)

- An annual member fee of $37 to support the JAK educational system, volunteers, and the JAK magazine
- An equity deposit equal to 6 percent of loan value to cover risk on any loan in the portfolio (This is not a part of the loan costs; equity deposits serve as the bank's reserves and legally belong to the bank until the loan is fully repaid. If there has been no default, the deposit is then repaid in full to the member.)

The JAK maintains 20 percent of equity deposits in government treasury bills as a hedge against any unexpected withdrawal of savings by members. Bad debt has been kept below 0.5 percent, which also helps to keep loan costs low.

To develop and maintain liquidity, members are strongly encouraged to pre-save in order to qualify for a loan. This used to be a requirement in the Swedish JAK, but in 2003 the requirement was rescinded to allow lower income members to qualify for loans. Members can also contract to continue saving while they are repaying their loans. This is called post-saving, and it is structured as a separate savings contract that runs alongside the loan contract. By committing to continued savings while the loan is paid down, the member can negotiate a larger loan right from the outset.

New members receive an account immediately. Savings flow into a common pool, but instead of receiving interest, each member earns savings points — one point per dollar saved each month. Savings points give a member the right to borrow without interest. The amount that a member can borrow is based on the number of savings points accumulated (pre-savings) or contracted (post-savings). Savings points are essential to JAK's ability to maintain liquidity in the system, which in turn is essential to making interest-free loans available for a growing membership.

Figure 3.2 depicts how post-savings are calculated and combined with pre-savings to match the overall sum that is to be borrowed. In this example, if a member pre-saved $2,000 during a 12-month period prior to applying for a loan, he or she would be entitled to borrow a maximum of $2,000 over a similar term. However, the member could borrow an additional $3,000 if he or she agreed to continue saving (the post-saving contract referred to above) while repaying the loan over a 48-month term. Many readers may question such a system, in particular the revenue members forego by receiving no interest on their savings or dividends on their credit union shares. However, this is precisely where accessing credit based on payment of a fee shows its superiority to credit based on compound interest. When you consider the implications of a $20,000 loan over 10 years, the cumulative financial benefits to JAK members become very clear (see Table 3.1). The

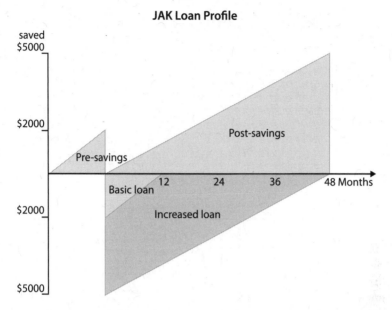

Fig. 3.2: *"Sweden's JAK Bank: Liberating Community Finance from the Ball and Chain of Compound Interest,"* Source: Pat Conaty and Michael Lewis. *Making Waves* 20, 3 (Autumn/Winter 2009).

JAK borrower enjoys net savings of $6,542 over someone who gets a loan from a conventional bank. However, while the JAK borrower saves a large amount of money in interest costs, his/her monthly payments are higher than those of a conventional bank customer (see Table 3.2). This is because the monthly loan payment must be matched by a post-savings payment: in this example, the member pays $166.79 in the monthly loan payment, an amount that is matched by an additional $166.79 in compulsory savings. The higher monthly payments total $336.62, compared to $241.18 for the loan from a conventional bank. As a result, the annual servicing of a JAK loan is about $2,000 more, about $20,000 over the 10-year term of the loan. However, this is the member's money, and all of it comes back to him or her. Thus a 10-year loan of $20,000 saves $6,542 in interest and creates for the member $20,000 in savings. In addition, the 6 percent equity deposit required at the front end of the loan is also returned, another $1,200. Together they represent a nice little nest egg for the borrower.

The average size of a loan in the JAK system is US$15,000. The smallest loans are about $3,000, the largest about $1 million. The aim of the JAK management is to run a stable operation on a nonprofit basis, though they do target making $140,000 each year to continuously add to the bank's

Table 3.1 Comparative Loan Costs for a 10-Year Loan of $20,000			
Charges	Bank loan with compound interest rate of 8.05% over 10 years	JAK loan over 10 years	Remarks
Loan appraisal and set up (3.2% of loan value)	0	$3,167	$49 per month over 10 years and compulsory savings of $167 over 10 years paid back at end of loan (not part of loan cost)
Loan equity deposit (6% of loan value)	0	$1,200	Paid upfront but repaid within 7 to 19 months of loan retirement (not included in loan cost)
Annual member fee		$370	$37 per year — not included in cost of loan as it covers other services
Annual service fees	$400		$40 per year
Interest cost on loan	$9,309		
Total cost of loan	$9,709	$3167	JAK borrower pays $6,542 less for the loan than the conventional borrower. Monthly payments are higher but half are savings ($20,000). This plus deposit of $1,200 means member gets $21,200 after loan repayment.

Note: This example illustrates fees and costs in dollars rather than Swedish kroner.

Table 3.2 Comparative Loan Payments for a 10-Year Loan of $20,000			
Payments on 10-year loan	Conventional bank loan at 8.05%	JAK Bank (assuming no pre-savings)	
Monthly loan payment	$241.18	$166.79	No interest This would be less if a pre-savings balance had been accrued. If $20,000 were saved, it would be recoverable three months after the loan was paid off.
Post-savings payment		$166.79 ($2,001 per year)	
Annual member fee		$3.08	$37 per year
Total monthly payment	$241.18	$336.62	

Note: This example illustrates fees and costs in dollars rather than Swedish kroner.

equity on the balance sheet and to comply with Swedish reserve-level requirements.

In order to keep credit transaction costs and default rates low, JAK loans above $16,000 are secured against assets. About 80 percent of JAK loans are for home improvements or to refinance high-interest loans originally obtained from commercial banks, including student and consumer loans. The other 20 percent is invested in ecological and social enterprises of various kinds.

The Local Enterprise Bank Innovation

JAK experimentation with enterprise financing began in 2000. The organization has developed this system in a way entirely consistent with JAK core principles, and it exemplifies their creativity and innovation. A Local Enterprise Bank (LEB) can be created by any group of JAK members that wishes to invest savings to advance a local enterprise that will generate community benefits.

The first LEB was for a small ecological slaughterhouse called Ekokött that applies ethical standards to the transport and treatment of animals. It serves the small farmers of the coastal region and islands of Bohus Province. Savings deposits to capitalize the business were made by local environmental groups, the Swedish Society for the Prevention of Cruelty to Animals, and JAK members, amongst others. A number of small farmers in the region have also switched their savings to the Ekokött LEB because the slaughterhouse has made it possible to sustain their traditional, ecological approaches to managing common grazing grounds.

The second LEB was started by the village of Hornbore to support the building of a replica of a 1,000-year-old Viking village. This combined cultural, youth, and eco-tourism project is important for local community building. When the local savings bank refused to lend the money needed for the project, JAK stepped in and set up an interest-free loan, which is being financed through savings that have been switched from other banks to the Hornbore LEB account. Another LEB was established to support Fjällbete, a cooperative whose mandate encompasses the rural industrial and educational aspects of Ekokött and Hornbore.

This simple system enables people to autonomously mobilize their collective savings for projects they consider worthwhile. It fosters community benefit enterprises, many of which advance the transition to a more sustainable economy, and most of which have been refused conventional, interest-based financing. The system comes with a clear advantage: when the public is asked for money, savings are less costly to a household than ordinary donations. JAK makes it easy for people to set up savings accounts targeted to finance a social or ecological enterprise. In addition to administering these

Fig. 3.3: *In alpine Jämtland, a Swedish province bordering Norway, Fjällbete is a means by which people link an array of local business, educational, planning, and consulting activities to the small-scale production and marketing of organic lamb. In form a cooperative, Fjällbete is in fact an entrepreneurial community that preserves and promotes a way of life that is sustainable socially as well as environmentally. JAK Bank has supplemented Fjällbete member deposits and loans with a loan of US$138,000 (in collaboration with Ekobank) as well as $40,000 in patient equity that interested parties have deposited in a JAK Local Enterprise Bank.* Source: Fjällbete

accounts, the JAK Bank vet the projects themselves, adding to the security of the savings. The system channels social solidarity efficiently and effectively.

Recently JAK extended the LEB approach through a program partnership involving three Swedish local authorities. It has been designed mainly for small ventures and community associations that can afford to pay the JAK loan fee and the capital installments but little else. Like all other JAK lending operations, these loans have to be balanced by savings. Fifty social enterprises have been financed to date. The largest is a $10-million community-based wind-power cooperative.

Impacts on the Household Economy: The Hartwick Family

In Chapters 3 to 6 we explore several innovations that represent transition pathways. Harking back to Aristotle's definition of economics as "the wise management of the household resources," we try to estimate how these innovations might affect householders in financial terms and in terms of life energy. Life energy, or imputed income, refers to the amount of time freed up from the necessity for income earning as a result of savings that lower net household costs.

Our hypothetical household, the Hartwicks, is a nuclear family of five. It is middle class in North American or European terms. Both parents work full time. Together they make the net equivalent after taxes of about $30 per hour, or $225 per day. Their three children are in their late teens and early 20s. The oldest has just finished college. The parents are both in their early 50s.

Assume the household has been paying off a $200,000 mortgage. This is lower than the average mortgage in the UK of $270,000, and much lower than average prices in Canada. The average interest rate on their mortgage loan is 8.05 percent (higher than the current 5 percent rate for 30-year mortgages, but far below the rates of 16 percent that were common between 1980 and 1991). They have another 10 years to pay off their 25-year mortgage. Their payments are $1,550 per month. By the time the Hartwicks can redeem their mortgage in full, they will have paid $465,078.84 for their house, a cool $265,079 of which is in interest charges — 32 percent more than the original purchase price. Such is the magic of compound interest.

If the Hartwick family lived in Sweden and became aware of the JAK Bank's fixed financing charge, they might well decide to switch the balance of their mortgage to a JAK fee-based loan. Many JAK members joined for this very reason. As shown in Table 3.3, the difference between conventional mortgage interest charges and the fee-based loan from JAK represents a saving of $67,090 in interest payments. This would be a tidy addition to their retirement savings — no small matter, since by the time the mortgage is paid they will be close to the end of their working lives.

Now let's translate these savings into the time spent working. With each parent netting about $15 per hour, together they will in the next 10 years

Table 3.3 The Impact of Fee-Based Lending on the Hartwick Household				
Comparison of JAK Bank and conventional bank mortgage costs	Bank mortgage (8.05%)	JAK fee-based system for loan	Savings $	Savings in hours
Last 10 years of 25-year mortgage	$91,821	$24,731	$67,090*	2,236

* For the sake of simplicity, we have not included the additional savings the Hartwicks would receive when their 6 percent equity payment was returned to them.

Note: With compound interest, the amount paid in interest declines over time. At first it makes up the largest proportion of the monthly payment. Later, the interest portion declines and more of the payment goes against the principal. For the sake of illustration, we have pro-rated the principal and interest as if they were being paid down at the same level as in the early years.

spend 2,236 hours less work time paying off their mortgage (that is $67,090 divided by $30 per hour).

In each of the next three chapters we will build on Table 3.3 to track the cumulative impacts and life-energy benefits of innovations related to land tenure, energy conservation, and food.

Transition Factors

The JAK cooperative bank operates inversely to virtually all conventional financial institutions.

- Like credit unions, it is member-controlled and democratically governed.
- It eschews compound interest in favor of simple and low-cost fees.
- It targets a modest annual profit, the purpose of which is to strengthen the co-op balance sheet and thus its stability.
- It has over 650 volunteers who actively promote, and educate people in, the basics of fee-based finance.
- It combines a highly professional, centralized, technically competent office with a small paid staff that facilitates dispersed lending activity through electronic means. The cost of management per member is very low: $144 in 2002.
- In the Local Enterprise Bank it has created an enterprise financing vehicle that is member-driven, decentralized, flexible, and capable of inspiring and channeling savings to community-wide benefit.
- Every loan is backed by real assets — other members' savings — and 20 percent is maintained in Swedish treasury bills for safety and to supplement earnings. This is diametrically contrary to conventional banks that loan $20 or more for every dollar on deposit.

Transition to such a system is not a simple matter. Redefining the purpose of banking is countercultural. Attitudes grounded in a view of money as a "store of value," coupled with the temptation to maximize profit by making money out of money, are not going to magically disappear. Indeed, current indications are that returning to "business as usual" in the financial world is a major preoccupation of most conventional financiers.

Nevertheless, more and more people have come to understand that they are vulnerable to an unaccountable, non-transparent financial system whose primary interest is shaped by shareholders expecting high returns and managers seeking large annual bonuses. Consumers who become aware of the impacts of usury represent the basis for replicating and scaling up a JAK model in many different settings.

Credit unions represent the most obvious starting point. They are democratic and can be influenced. Their roots still lie in social justice, cooperation, community outreach, education, and members helping members meet basic needs — however obscure that connection may seem at times. A wholesale change to interest-free financing will not be possible overnight. However, if credit unions established an account facility and staff capacity to provide this service, it would be a huge step in the right direction.

And a timely step, too. As the price of fossil fuel escalates, it will become more and more important to enhance our capacity to finance food production and processing, energy conservation investments, and renewable energy development in the localities and regions where we live. The JAK model offers a unique capacity to facilitate and mobilize solidarity savings. The idea of giving people local opportunities to invest in local capacity to meet basic needs is an innovation that needs to be adapted and scaled up. If communities are to become active agents in planning and adapting to the age of energy descent and climate change, the JAK model is one small but strategic pathway to a steady-state economy.

Resilience Reflections

The JAK Bank contributes directly to resilience at the level of the household (e.g., lower costs, more life energy, higher savings) and the community (increased local purchasing and potential for reinvestment). Arguably, the JAK model contributes to resilience at the societal level, and could contribute much more if replicated and scaled up. In any event, JAK clearly represents a net increase in *diversity* within the financial system. What is perhaps most significant: JAK is a modest but strategic demonstration that the chains of compound interest can be broken. This in itself is a major contribution to the possibility of creating a stable, low-cost source of finance capable of enabling the Great Transition.

In its values, goals, structure, governance, and practices the JAK Bank also exemplifies several other resilience principles. *Modularity* is well served by the local and regional nature of solidarity savings as well as by the enabling, flexible, and self-organizing attributes designed into Local Enterprise Banks. The LEB itself is evidence of JAK *innovation* at work, a capacity to think outside the box, invent new rules, and creatively adapt to evolving challenges. Equally important is the model's attention to federation. JAK's democratic structure and its engagement of volunteers in education and outreach create powerful linkages between branches and between individual members that strengthen the whole. *Social capital* is embedded in the culture of the organization.

Pulsating throughout this multi-nodal and multifunctional network are *feedback loops* that continuously transmit and receive information about the bank's performance. The fact that it is a member-owned institution with significant engagement of members, the solidarity savings requirements, the constant focus on education of the membership, the ability to autonomously mobilize savings for local or regional enterprises — all these provisions create a dense web of linkages that empower action and facilitate communication. It may seem a bit messy to the uninitiated, but from a resilience perspective these *overlapping functions and governance features* strengthen the local adaptive capacity of members. Thanks to these various features, JAK members themselves SEE and understand how financing can strengthen households, enterprises, and their communities. Their knowledge and skills, and those of the staff, are an invaluable repository upon which JAK can draw in the future. In the turbulent times ahead, such applied knowledge of how to mobilize local finance to meet local needs will be vital.

In a modest way, JAK is a creative demonstration that the market can be recalibrated to serve human beings, that the enclosure of our capital by "Wall Street" can be reversed. Chapter 4 extends the story to land, describing innovations that have a dramatic impact on the affordability of housing by removing land from the market and owning housing differently. It is a good-news story for householders, communities, and taxpayers, one that is consistent with the cooperative seers of the last three centuries.

CHAPTER 4

Uniting the "I" and the "We": Affordable Housing in Perpetuity

As soon as the land of any country has all become private property, the landlords, like all other men, love to reap where they never sowed, and demand a rent even for its natural produce.

— Adam Smith, *The Wealth of Nations*

Communism forgets that life is individual. Capitalism forgets that life is social, and the Kingdom of brotherhood is found neither in the thesis of Communism nor the antithesis of Capitalism, but in a higher synthesis. It is found in a higher synthesis that combines the truth of both.

— Martin Luther King, Jr., *Where Do We Go from Here?*

THE UNPRECEDENTED FINANCIAL, ECONOMIC, AND SOCIAL FALLOUT from the credit crunch presents governments with a structural set of problems when it comes to housing. A steep decline in prices in many countries since 2008 has led to widespread levels of negative equity, which means people owe more on their mortgage than their house is worth. Repossessions and evictions lead to depressed markets and abandoned properties in many countries. The situation is exacerbated by real estate investment companies' speculative purchases for "rack-renting," leading to what is being called in the UK "Generation Rent" — younger households with no realistic chance to buy a home, but whose rent levels are exorbitant and often extortionate.

For example, British real estate speculators buy foreclosed properties at knock-down prices, then turn around and rent them out at high monthly rates. In combination, people who have lost their homes and young people forming new households are increasing the demand for rental properties, thus pushing up rental levels in most big cities and many towns in the UK.

At the same time, the rising levels of mortgage arrears and upward pressure on repossessions leads to ongoing lender losses and underpins a severe contraction in the mortgage market. The decline in home purchasing since 2009 has been reinforced in the UK by the 15 to 25 percent deposit levels required of first-time buyers during 2010 and 2011. In the UK, the average age of a first-time homebuyer has increased now to 35 years. Younger "Generation Rent" households faced a national average monthly rent in late 2011 of £722 against a national average monthly mortgage payment, plus insurance and other costs of £600. But with a 15 percent or more deposit level, lower-cost buying has been impeded.

To make matters even more difficult, those in high-cost rental units are finding that they have no disposable income to save. These circumstances have led to a collapse of market demand and the withdrawal of housing developers from new construction.

Thus the problem of finding affordable shelter — a problem that existed before the collapse of the market — persists. The precise circumstances vary between countries, as do policies for addressing affordability. With deep deficits in the public sector as a result of the unprecedented costs of funding the bank bailouts and the subsequent recession, the solution for the persistent problem of affordability in the short and long term remains elusive. It can clearly not be solved through supply-and-demand management alone, although in some settings this is a factor. For example, British government research reveals a long-term requirement for the construction of 200,000 new home units a year to bring housing supply into line with housing needs. Certainly the structural problems outlined above, and the economic downturn, exacerbate this supply problem in the UK. But whether adequate supply leads to increased affordability is questionable when one sees how costs have continued to rise even in markets where supply and demand have been more in balance.

We have already seen in Chapter 3 how dramatically affordability increases when compound interest is taken out of the mortgage equation. The other major cost factor (other than construction costs, which are not so easily influenced unless one takes the self-build option) is the price of land. Indeed, land makes up 50 percent of the purchase price in some urban areas. Revival of the 19th-century innovations of Thomas Spence, John Ruskin, and Octavia Hill (see Chapter 2), which aimed to restore land to the commons (the "We"), could show the path forward in the 21st century. With land owned by a "trust" and buildings owned by local residents (the "I"), the land can be stewarded to the benefit of the household and the community. George Benello and his co-authors of *Building Sustainable Communities* describe this as a "duplex ownership tenure."

Herein lies the challenge: how do we remove the land from the market-place in order to increase the affordability and accessibility of shelter? The same challenge is relevant to a number of other areas of human activity — for example, land for growing food (see Chapter 6), for renewable energy generation (see Chapter 5), and for providing workspace. Can it be done? In a culture where private ownership is venerated as the cornerstone upon which wealth is generated, is there still room for Rousseau's assertion that one cannot own what "one did not create"; one can only use it?

In this chapter we examine two main issues. First we look at the idea of community land trusts, which are among the most promising ways to remove land from the market in order to create a permanent stock of afford-able housing. Then, given that public subsidies are a vital but stretched resource, we look at how land trusts stack up financially as a model for preserving the value of taxpayer investment.

The Community Land Trust Model in the United States

Community land trusts (CLT) develop affordable housing by separating the two cost elements: the market price of the land and the price of the house itself. By removing the land from the market and placing it in a CLT, the unearned equity resulting from escalating land values is taken out of the equation, to the benefit of low- and moderate-income households and the broader community. This is hugely important in preserving the affordability of housing over time. By allowing for individuals to own equity in the hous-ing itself (but not in the land), the incentive to maintain and enhance the quality of the housing is retained. This duplex ownership tenure, part private and part collective, is a challenging yet generative pathway to solving the long-term affordability problem for people with low and moderate incomes. Indeed, with land taken out of the equation, it is possible to halve the cost of homeownership or, in the case of rental housing, to lower the level of subsidy.

The CLT concept drew on the successful Gramdan (village land trust) movement in India, which was inspired by Gandhi. Activists in the US civil rights movement learned about Gramdan and contemplated how this model, developed on the other side of the globe, might be applied to the plight of the rural poor in the American South. Bob Swann and Slater King (a cousin of Martin Luther King, Jr.) examined Gramdan along with the *ejido* system in Mexico and even the land reform proposals Tolstoy argued for in his last novel, *Resurrection*. Tolstoy was influenced by Henry George, and what he calls for is reminiscent of Spence's and Ruskin's efforts in England. For example, Tolstoy argued for land to be gifted to villages, with any surplus rent from the land used to support schools, health clinics, road improvements, and the welfare of villagers.

Community Control of Land Preserves Affordability

Fig. 4.1: *Removing land from the market and placing it in a CLT dramatically increases affordability.*
Source: Champlain Housing Trust, "Community Land Trust: Model for the Big Society?" Presentation to the 2011 Southeast Conference of the Chartered Institute of Housing.

Another key influence on Swann and King was Ralph Borsodi, who had devised a land trust system for the American "back to the land" movement in the 1930s. In the mid-1960s, Borsodi was working in India with J.P. Narayan on a social financing system for the Gramdan movement. When he returned to New England in 1967, Swann persuaded Borsodi to help develop a US model. Together, Swann, Borsodi, and King designed the innovative legal structure of the CLT.

They set up their first CLT in Georgia in 1967, supported by Governor Jimmy Carter and Stewart Perry, then a War on Poverty officer. The project mission was to secure access to land in such a way that that African American sharecroppers and tenant farmers on 5,000 acres could become owners of their livelihoods. The goal was to lease the land to dozens of families who would own homes on the land, farm individual plots, and participate in cooperative farming. The plan was for the land to provide housing and income. The combination of land, decent homes, and a means of making a living would help those who had long suffered the injustices of a segregated South gain freedom. Financing costs were high for this first CLT, and due to a combination of high interest rates and the economic risks of farming, debt problems forced the sale of 1,300 acres in the early 1980s. This project ultimately failed, and in the late 1980s the remainder of the land had to be sold. However, much was learned in the process, and that shaped further efforts.

Since this first project 45 years ago, work on CLTs in the United States has had its ups and downs. Early development, land acquisition, and housing construction was slow, but Bob Swann and the Institute for Community Economics (ICE) persevered. Steadfast work and many experiments over the first 20 years yielded the current robust legal structure. To address the issue of access to capital, Swann and Chuck Mattei at ICE developed the first community development loan fund in America, which provided the risk finance for housing and other property developments on CLT-controlled land. For many years, securing financing for CLTs continued to be a formidable barrier to developing the model. Without the evolution of community revolving loan funds, CLTs would not have achieved their current scope in the United States.

In the last two decades, the dramatic impact on affordability of CLTs has begun to be more widely understood, and there is growing interest in most US states and a number of major cities confronted with an exploding affordability problem and a rapidly declining level of taxpayer funds.

Key Features of the CLT Model

A number of key features make CLTs a unique approach to securing affordable housing in perpetuity.

- **CLTs are nonprofit, tax-exempt corporations.** It is the mission of CLTs to preserve affordability, promote sound maintenance, and prevent foreclosures on buildings located on the CLT's land.
- **CLTs are very flexible.** They can provide housing for rent or for purchase. They can be used for such "place-shaping" facilities as workspace, gardens, renewable energy, and amenities. They can acquire land through purchase, tax abatements, and public or private donation.
- **CLTs allow dual ownership and dynamic property rights.** CLTs separate the ownership of the land from the ownership of the buildings on it. The land is retained in perpetuity in trust by the CLT for the benefit of the defined community by effectively removing it from the market. By contrast, buildings on the CLT's land are sold to and owned by families, cooperative housing corporations, small businesses, or nonprofit organizations.
- **CLTs make leased land and housing affordable.** The trust's land is never sold to the inhabitants; it is leased. Each CLT develops a resale formula to keep the housing affordable over the long term. The aim is to differentiate the land, which the CLT retains for community use in perpetuity, from the stipulated equity share an owner-occupant can receive on the sale of the housing units. The CLT exercises this power through a pre-emptive right to buy

housing units when they are resold. Each CLT maintains a waiting list for housing, and those leaving a CLT have a contractual obligation to sell their housing back to the CLT at a price set by the resale formula in the lease.

- **CLTs allow open and place-based membership.** CLTs operate within a specific geographical area. In the United States, this may be a rural town or rural county, an urban district, or an entire city.
- **CLTs have tripartite governance.** The board of a CLT is composed of three types of stakeholder. Normally a third of board members are elected representatives of the CLT's lessees. Another third are elected by residents of the wider community who are neither leaseholders nor tenants of CLT property. The final third are appointed to represent the local public interest and may include public-sector officials, nonprofit service providers, and local funders.

CLTs are a strategy that removes land from the housing market without disconnecting residents from their interest in owning, maintaining, and improving their homes. Let us see how one of the most successful CLTs in the US has achieved this.

The Champlain Housing Trust: Restoring the Commons — An Affordable Solution

Vermont is a rural, mountainous state with very few large employers and the lowest wages in New England. Many residents commute two to three hours to work each day. The gap between average incomes and housing costs in Vermont is one of the highest in the United States: 47 percent of renters and 38 percent of homeowners pay more than 30 percent of their gross income on housing.

Burlington is a small university town in the state and the home base of the Champlain Housing Trust (CHT), the largest CLT in the United States and the first to expand its landholdings through partnership with a municipality. The trust's origins lie in the mid-1980s, after the first Reagan administration ended federal government programs to fund affordable housing. An expanding downtown and rising enrollment at Burlington's three colleges pushed housing prices through the roof, and attempts by Burlington mayor Bernie Sanders and his Progressive Coalition to implement rent control failed. They turned to the Institute for Community Economics, which had been developing and promoting the CLT concept since the early 1970s. Sanders and the Coalition established a Community and Economic Development Office at City Hall and in 1984 drew up a strategy to create two nonprofit organizations, the Burlington Community Land

Trust and Lake Champlain Housing Development Corporation. The land trust was started with a $200,000 grant from the city and, later, a $1-million line of credit from the city employees' pension fund. Over time, the geographic territory, services, and funding sources of the two organizations overlapped, and in 2006 they merged to form the Champlain Housing Trust.

At present, CHT has in its portfolio over 2,000 units of permanently affordable housing located inside Burlington city limits and scattered across three adjacent counties. Approximately 60 percent of the units are resale-restricted, owner-occupied houses and condominiums; the other 40 percent are rental apartments. Since 2001 the organization's staff has grown from four to over 70, according to the CHT website. CHT offers several components that in combination can serve to improve the quality and affordability of housing dramatically:

- Two Homeownership Centers, one in Burlington and one in the rural town of St. Albans, integrate homebuyer education with debt and budgeting advice and home maintenance courses for first-time homebuyers. Over 300 people a year learn how to meet the criteria of conventional mortgage lenders and steer clear of predatory lenders and mortgage brokers. The advisory service helps households bring consumer credit and other debt problems under control.
- Financing packages offer down-payment grants funded by local, state, and federal government sources in addition to mortgages at interest rates almost two percent lower than the average. CHT has worked with local banks to develop financing packages with payment structures affordable to low-income households.
- CHT mobilizes its membership to contribute to a pool of funds that is used to cover operating costs. Currently, there are 4,000 members in a region with a population of 100,000. Members include local businesses as well as individual citizens. Some join with a payment of $50 or less (the "carpenter" rate); others make a larger investment (the "community developer" rate is $250 to $500, and the "visionary" rate is $1,000 and over). Many members regularly donate to further the trust's work. These grassroots funds are used to leverage additional capital grants from the Vermont Housing and Conservation Board, the City of Burlington Housing Department, and the federal government. Support from the city and the state has been crucial in expanding the trust's operations since 1999.
- To complement its housing work, CHT has developed a day center for the elderly, a nursery facility, social enterprise and nonprofit

offices, a storefront for the local credit union, an office for the community legal advice center, and a multi-unit business incubator.

Unlike the Gramdan land reform movement in India, American CLTs rarely receive land through gifts and donations. Instead, they use a variety of methods to purchase real estate at a reduced cost. The process involves considerable time and effort, but CLTs have been able to steadily acquire land for affordable housing and/or acquire existing housing and make it more affordable over time. The combination of private donations of money and public subsidies enables CLTs to leverage and maintain subsidies at a cost to the public purse that is far lower than conventional approaches to the subsidization of low-income housing.

For example, let's look at the CHT Homeland Grant program, which enables low-income households to buy properties on the open market. A grant of $22,000 (raised mainly from federal, state, and municipal sources), a low-interest-rate mortgage, and a resale stipulation accomplish two things. First, the quality of the housing accessible to low-income households increases significantly in the here and now. Second, the same housing remains affordable to low-income households in perpetuity. Table 4.1 shows how the program works for a family of four with an annual income of US$39,350, compared to a similar household with a conventional mortgage. The monthly mortgage entitlements of the two households are similar, but the household that qualifies for the CHT option benefits from both a grant of $22,000 and the lower interest rate of 4.25 percent. This combination of grant and low-interest mortgage enables the household to afford a property that is $48,926 (42 percent) more expensive for virtually the same monthly payment. This analysis shows how the CLT can stretch the impact of a public subsidy.

Table 4.1 The CHT Homeland Grant Program		
	Conventional mortgage	**CHT option**
Household income	$39,350	$39,350
Mortgage entitlement per month @ 30% less CLT ground rent for lease	$714	$709
Mortgage interest rate	6.15%	4.25%
Maximum mortgage	$117,197	$144,123
BCLT Homeland Grant	0	$22,000
Maximum house price that the household can afford	$117,197	$166,123

In 2003, a full-scale cost-benefit study examined the impact on the long-term affordability of 97 homes resold by the CLT in Burlington between 1984 and 2002. This research by Burlington Associates, the first such study ever undertaken, reached the following conclusions:

- In 1984 the homes sold were affordable to households earning 62 percent of the area median income (AMI). By 2002 they were affordable to households earning 56.6 percent of AMI.
- The value of the initial public subsidies increased over the 18 years by 33 percent.
- Only 2 percent of public subsidies were lost due to unavoidable mortgage foreclosure.
- Homeowners averaged a 17 percent annualized return on resale on the value of the house.
- After selling, 60 percent of CLT homeowners moved on to open-market properties.

A more recent study carried out in 2009, with a larger sample of 205 house resales, revealed how CHT has increased the net affordability of its homes since 2003 to the lower level of 53.4% of AMI.

The land trust model can also achieve dramatic savings for taxpayers. In another research appraisal, the costs of a CLT-funded unit of housing were compared with the costs of housing through a traditional government-subsidy program. Table 4.2 shows how conventional and CLT subsidy performances compare when the same property is resold five times over 30 years.

In the example, a $50,000 public subsidy, when protected by the land trust and the CLT resale formula, preserves a CLT home's affordability over 30 years, even if the home is resold every seven years to a new family. In contrast, under the conventional affordable-housing subsidy program, the public subsidy is repaid each time the home resells, and the seller is allowed to claim all the capital gains. As a result, a greater public subsidy is required after every sale to keep the housing affordable. With an annual inflation rate of 6 percent, raising the house's sale price to $375,000 for the second low-income owner, the government would have to invest 60 percent more, for a total of $80,000, to keep the house affordable. The public subsidy keeps going up after every sale: $132,000 in Year 14, $216,000 in Year 21, and $342,000 in Year 28.

It does not take a rocket scientist to figure out which system is more beneficial and efficient. The CLT model costs taxpayers $50,000. To achieve the same affordability objective, the conventional subsidy approach costs the taxpayer $820,000. The results demonstrate how important it is to take the land permanently off the market and to impose permanent controls on the

Table 4.2 Subsidy Performance Over Time: Conventional Homebuyer Loan v. CLT		
Initial sale	**Homebuyer loan***	**CLT model***
Initial market value	$250,000**	$250,000**
Grant (public subsidy)	50,000	50,000
Initial sale price	250,000	200,000
Resale in Year 7		
Sale price	375,000***	245,000***
Repay first mortgage	(174,051)	(174,051)
Repay public subsidy	(50,000)	0
Sales cost (6%)	(22,500)	(14,700)
Proceeds from sale	**128,449**	**56,249**
Affordable price to next buyer	245,000	245,000
Recaptured subsidy	50,000	0
Additional subsidy required	**80,000**	**0**
Total subsidy for next buyer	130,000	0
Resale in Year 14		
Sale price	565,000	303,000
Additional subsidy required	**132,000**	**0**
Resale in Year 21		
Sale price	850,000	372,000
Additional subsidy required	**216,000**	**0**
Resale in Year 28		
Sale price	1,278,000	458,000
Additional subsidy required	**342,000**	**0**
Total subsidy invested over 30 years for 5 families	**$820,000**	**$50,000**

* The homebuyer loan is repaid without interest upon resale of the house. It enables the buyer to afford the home but does not reduce the actual price of the home. The CLT subsidy stipulates that the resale price may not exceed the initial price, plus an adjustment based on the annual change in the area median income (AMI).

** The home is assumed to have a value of $250,000 in an area where the family in the target income range can afford $200,000.

*** Assumes 6 percent annual inflation in home price, 3 percent annual income inflation, and stable interest rates.

Source: John Emmeus Davis and Rick Jacobus, The City-CLT Partnership: Municipal Support for Community Land Trusts (Lincoln Institute of Land Policy, June 2008), pp. 8-9, accessed 25 October 2011 from www.ihtmv.org/PDF/City-CLTPolicyReport.pdf.

resale price of the housing in order to assure long-term affordability. It also shows what CLTs alone can accomplish: namely, the capture of any public subsidy or land gift within the land trust balance sheet, thus preserving for perpetual community benefit a public or social investment in land.

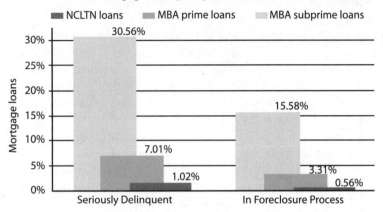

Comparison of National Community Land Trust Network (NCLTN) and Mortgage Bankers Association (MBA) Data for Mortgage Delinquency and Foreclosure, 4th quarter 2009

Fig. 4.2: *Mortgage delinquency.* Source: Champlain Housing Trust, "Community Land Trust: Model for the Big Society?" Presentation to the 2011 Southeast Conference of the Chartered Institute of Housing.

The success of CHT has spread. Through its Homeownership Initiative, the Vermont Housing and Conservation Board has provided support to develop five more CLTs in the state, each operating in a population area of about 100,000. There are now approximately 250 community land trusts in the United States, and fledgling movements in Great Britain, Australia, and Belgium. They are increasing in number whenever and wherever real estate markets are very hot, and have also demonstrated their effectiveness in preventing foreclosures in cold real estate markets.

These examples show the CLT model is a dynamic solution for the local stewardship of land for the benefit of low- and moderate-income citizens and their community in perpetuity. It has also proved itself to be very resilient in the face of the subprime mortgage crisis in America. Figure 4.2, which compares CLT data with that from the Mortgage Bankers Association (MBA), shows just how much more resilient they are in the face of crisis.

What this graph does not depict is the significant cost savings CLTs are creating for municipalities in the United States. Foreclosures cost money. The demolition and clearance of vacant housing, rising public administrative costs, and loss or decline of property tax revenue are all features of what home repossession costs the public. Studies in Chicago and Minneapolis between 1995 and 2005 indicate that each foreclosure costs the taxpayer between $27,000 and $34,199. In short, the stability of the CLT duplex tenure model saves taxpayers millions and could save billions if scaled up.

Scaling up CLTs in the Cities: Irvine, California

City governments faced with ballooning housing prices from 2000 to 2007, massive foreclosures since 2008, and dwindling budgets for affordable housing are turning to CLTs as a possible solution. In Irvine, California, the high cost of housing (average price of $700,000 in 2005) and the imminent closure of a military base triggered the city government to set a strategic target of making 10 percent of the entire urban housing stock permanently affordable by 2025. Passed as its development plan in 2006, the Irvine affordable housing strategy requires that 9,700 units be added to its existing base of affordable housing by 2025. The key plank in the Irvine plan is that all new low-cost housing must be designed for permanent affordability.

Over the years Irvine has tried many strategies to improve affordability. Deed restrictions have proved to be costly and difficult to enforce. The city's down-payment assistance program became irrelevant to people with low and moderate incomes as housing prices skyrocketed. Subsidy programs also lost any residual value as the benefiting families sold off their homes at market rates. True, these subsidies were paid back to the city, but as Table 4.2 shows, it took even more public funds to make the house affordable for the next low-income family.

It was this challenging context that drove city leaders to make CLTs the core of Irvine's new strategy. To implement the plan, they established the Irvine Community Land Trust and aligned their affordable housing policies to support the CLT's core role. For example, the city has a zoning law that requires all new development to have an affordable component. Developers can produce the low-cost housing units or they can pay a capital sum in

Fig. 4.3: *Doria Apartment Homes were developed as a joint venture between Irvine Community Land Trust and Jamboree Housing Corporation. Doria's first 60 units were made available to households earning 30 to 60 percent of the area median income. Ten units were reserved for recipients of mental health services.* Source: Juan Tallo. Courtesy of Jamboree Housing Corporation, Irvine, California.

lieu of choosing not to do so. The other option for private developers is to donate land of equivalent value, and this is the option the city encourages.

Contrary to the classic tripartite governance of CLTs, the first board members on the Irvine trust were appointed by the city and supported by city staff. Eventually, lessees of the CLT will get three seats, two seats will remain for city appointees, and two more will be available for appointed at-large representatives.

Irvine also maintains significant control through its design of contractual agreements. When the city transfers land and financial resources to the Irvine CLT it is under an agreement that includes performance standards. The city will monitor the performance, and if problems do occur the city can take back control and fix the problem before handing the land back to the CLT.

Community Land Trusts in Britain: Rekindling Land Reform in the 21st Century

The most ambitious land trust system in Britain was designed by Ebenezer Howard. Like his forbears who struggled to restore the commons, Howard wanted a system to capture the unearned increment of property development for community benefit.

In 1899, Howard established a "cooperative land society," First Garden City Ltd., and raised initial share capital of £20,000. His vision was to use the money to build new cities where the land was owned collectively. Letchworth, Hertfordshire, north of London, was launched in 1903. Over the next 50 years its population grew to 33,000 and it thrived for a short period after that. By holding the land (5,600 acres), First Garden City was able to capture lease income from the land, from commercial buildings, and from a variety of social enterprises it owned, and continuously reinvest that money in community improvements. Residents were engaged in a mutual benefit system of unprecedented scale. Living was affordable and convivial, and people had what they needed close by.

In 1961 a group of corporate raiders and financiers attempted to take over the land, demutualize the organization, and break the back of the cooperative land society. The national government successfully fought off the onslaught, but victory came at a cost. The cooperative ownership of the land was transformed into public ownership. In 1995 it was changed back to a tax-exempt mutual structure, and the land assets were transferred to the new Letchworth Garden City Heritage Corporation, with a legal structure like that which Ebenezer Howard established in 1903. Essentially a CLT, this new cooperative land society has regained a number of land assets with 999-year leases. Many of the homes were established with 99-year leases, however, and the 1967 Leasehold Reform Act gave owner-occupiers in the

UK the right to buy their lease at an affordable price. As a result, as the 99-year leases come up for renewal at Letchworth, residents are purchasing the properties and, following the logic of the real estate market, reselling them at a significant profit.

Aside from Letchworth, the CLT idea didn't really take hold in the UK until the late 1980s. Inspired by projects in the United States, new developments in Britain have required considerable effort and a lot of learning by trial and error, with groups in rural Scotland pioneering the new approach.

Land ownership in rural Scotland is concentrated in the hands of a few hundred very large landlords. In one leading grassroots struggle in the 1990s, the local community on the Isle of Eigg, blocked by an absentee landlord from having any control over decisions concerning economic development of the island, started organizing to change this. Led by tenant farmers, known as crofters, the community succeeded, against all odds, in raising sufficient funds from social investors to buy the entire island in 1997 and establish the Isle of Eigg Heritage Trust — a pathbreaking CLT.

This success inspired other rural and island communities to follow suit, and they attracted growing support from the Highland and Islands Development Agency. In fulfillment of Tony Blair's pledge to devolve authority if he was elected prime minister in the 1997 UK election, the new Labour government established the Scottish Parliament. Community land trusts had become a popular cause, and in 2003 the Scottish Parliament passed the Land Reform Scotland Act, which created an enabling framework for advancing the CLT tenure. Work has focused on supporting economic regeneration, affordable housing and renewable energy generation in isolated and depopulating rural areas, where about 25 CLTs have been established.

Since 2004 a CLT movement has been emerging in England and Wales. The UK Parliament has approved a legal definition for CLTS (for England, see Section 79 of the Housing and Regeneration Act 2008). Progress on the ground has been steady, and about 20 rural CLTs are actively building housing — from 2 to 39 homes per site. Financing has become difficult since 2009 as a result of the collapse of the housing market and the withdrawal of lenders. Innovative financing methods have been put in place to provide development and construction loans, but there is a need for a loan guarantee facility to secure easier access to longer-term finance. Nevertheless, progress has been steady since 2010. Fifty new rural and urban CLTs have been registered, strategic support from the Welsh government is developing, and construction activity continues to expand.

A key factor facilitating the expansion over the last five years is the development of an efficient and effective method under the CLT national demonstration project to transfer knowledge of the democratic ways to

The Commonwealth Wheel

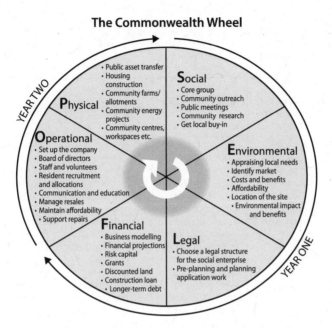

Fig. 4.4: *SELF-OP six step methodology provides a foundational tool that, properly supported, helps community stakeholders get organized, knowledgeable, and effective in putting in place a CLT and affordable housing projects.* Source: Community Finance Solutions

develop community-owned assets. The basic six-step process is summarized in the Commonwealth Wheel, depicted in Figure 4.4. Referred to as the SELF-OP method (Social, Environmental, Legal, Financial, Operational, Physical), it has been central to helping local stakeholders get the basics right much more quickly than they did in the early days of experimenting.

SELF-OP provides a logical route map and strategic tool to enable a local group to come together and link up a partnership between local activists; local residents in village, town, or urban neighborhood; an architect; sympathetic local planners; and social finance providers. The tool is used in training courses to help CLT formation groups carry out local demand research and to give guidance on how to develop affordable cost systems for the housing against localized affordability data. The tool, and this systematic approach, helps a group plan and organize the work in the right order and helps engage professional help from planners and technical specialists.

Significantly augmenting this SELF-OP tool is a national CLT Fund that facilitates the risk financing in ways that enable local groups to draw down social financing as their readiness advances on completion of each stage of the six step SELF-OP methodology (Table 4.3).

Table 4.3 The Funding Available for Community Land Trusts in England and Wales				
	Feasibility Study	Technical Assistance	Pre-development	Development Finance
Summary	One day of consultancy to help you scope a project	A small grant to fund initial costs	Funding your project prior to planning permission	Funding the costs of construction
Who is it for?	Community groups keen to tackle affordable housing needs in their community	Organizations that meet the legal definition of a CLT and have definite ideas about an affordable housing project but require both additional expertise and small amounts of cash to advance the project further	Organizations that have an outline plan for a housing project but lack funds for pre-development work such as paying for the planning process, appointing architects, and conducting site surveys.	Organizations that have a business plan, designated land with planning permission, and fully costed plans for an afford-able housing project but that lack commercial funds to finance the building work.
What funding is available?	One day of support from an expert who, if appropriate, will work with you to apply for technical assistance support.	Up to £2,500 of support to be used on further professional and expert support, setup, and initial costs.	Up to £4,500 per unit of housing. To fund the costs of working up a develop-ment proposal for submission of a planning application, procuring construction, and raising further finance for the project.	About £30,000 per unit of housing loaned to you, and secured by at least a second charge over the land and buildings.

"What Funding Is Available," Community Land Trust Fund, accessed 29 January 2012 from www.cltfund.org.uk/how-to-apply.

The methodology of the SELF-OP six step methodology is now being adapted as a tool for developing other decentralized local economy services such as workspace, community renewable energy, community gardens, and local food growing. The latent and active democratic potential inherent in this process needs to be noted and underscored. If it is effectively facilitated among multilateral local stakeholders, the Commonwealth Wheel can mobilize an active process of economic democracy in ways that Ivan Illich described as "tools for conviviality." This place-shaping approach, which is already actively involving citizens in rural CLT projects in England, offers a system that makes democracy an active, experiential verb rather than the remote, every-four-to-five-year limited noun called "national elections." Implementing the SELF-OP methodology in partnership groups is equivalent to experimenting, practicing, and evolving a system of daily democracy to advance the commonwealth of diverse communities.

Any village, town, or city neighborhood can take up the tools to address a range of issues in this cyclical way. With more practice, mutual and locally democratic action among diverse stakeholders will improve, and this participative and horizontal process among engaged stakeholders can build up local confidence and enable countless local areas to commence the journey to a low-carbon, steady-state economy.

The Mutual Homeownership Model: Scaling up Urban Affordability

The CLT model has recently been joined up with other approaches to create a new model known as the Mutual Home Ownership Housing Society model (MHOS). This new model is the result of the co-op sector working together to innovate affordable housing solutions in high-cost urban areas. CDS Cooperatives, England's largest cooperative housing service agency, worked with the new economics foundation, to redesign the early-20th-century Letchworth cooperative land society model for the 21st century. Described in the nef publication *Common Ground For Mutual Home Ownership*, the MHOS model developed by CDS Cooperatives has been inspired and informed by three models: Letchworth, the original Garden City designed by Ebenezer Howard; the CLTs that have evolved in the United States; and a tenant-owned co-op model from Sweden.

The Swedish model is a multi–tiered approach of mutual aid in which two national "mother" co-ops develop new housing co-ops and mobilize low-cost financing, respectively. These "mothers" bring 50 to 70 percent of the development and lending resources together for a new housing project. Their "daughters" are tenant-owned local housing cooperatives that manage themselves and get help from the "mothers" needed for further development. The tenant-owners also bring money to the table through a mix of down payments, tenant savings schemes, and bank financing, which they apply to the purchase of an existing equity share from a departing tenant-owner or, alternatively, to the purchase of a home in a new co-op. Each tenant owner is able to earn equity. The two "mothers" have produced 5,500 "daughters," a generative partnership to say the least.

The challenge for the team of researchers led by CDS Co-operatives and its CEO, David Rodgers, was to figure out how to combine the best features of each of these models while avoiding their respective weaknesses.

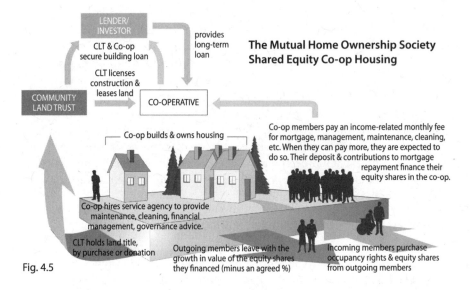

The Mutual Home Ownership Society
Shared Equity Co-op Housing

LENDER/INVESTOR

CLT & Co-op secure building loan

provides long-term loan

CLT licenses construction & leases land

COMMUNITY LAND TRUST

CO-OPERATIVE

Co-op builds & owns housing

Co-op members pay an income-related monthly fee for mortgage, management, maintenance, cleaning, etc. When they can pay more, they are expected to do so. Their deposit & contributions to mortgage repayment finance their equity shares in the co-op.

Co-op hires service agency to provide maintenance, cleaning, financial management, governance advice.

CLT holds land title, by purchase or donation

Outgoing members leave with the growth in value of the equity shares they financed (minus an agreed %)

Incoming members purchase occupancy rights & equity shares from outgoing members

Fig. 4.5

As Figure 4.5 shows, the CLT is central to the MHOS model. The trust owns the land and holds it for the purpose of preserving affordability in perpetuity. The trust issues a head lease to a tenant ownership cooperative, which enables both the land trust and the co-op to organize the financing, with help from CDS. The tenant ownership co-op is then responsible for getting the actual construction completed, with support from an expert development agent, a service which CDS also provides.

The mortgage that pays for the cost of building is held corporately by the co-op. As in the Swedish model, member-owners lease their units from the co-op. One prerequisite is a deposit of 5 to 10 percent, which is converted into equity shares in the co-op. Thereafter, equity shares are also funded through members' rental payments. These payments, the asset and land security provided by the trust, and the co-op's projected lease income form the basis for financing each project. The pooling of resources into a single mortgage package helps reduce the cost of financing, which is an important contribution to affordability — especially in the UK's risk-averse market since 2009 where individual mortgages have been especially hard for first-time homeowners to come by. Another cost saving flows from the assignment of equity shares and occupancy rights by members. This eliminates the legal and other closing costs that are part of buying and selling houses.

Once construction is complete, the co-op issues 20-year renewable leases to members. They can stay as long as they want, so long as they meet their obligations. One of the most important obligations is to make lease payments, which are calculated at 35 percent of monthly household income, after taxes and deductions. If, for example, my household's take-home income were $1,500 per month, we would pay $525. Were we earning $5,000 per month, we would pay $1,750 per month for the same unit.

This seems fair and equitable (it's a formula widely used by co-ops in Canada). However, the designers wisely found a way to recognize the higher contributors. This is where the shares come in. Everybody pays the deposit up front, and this payment becomes shares, with a face value at their issue date of £1,000 each. As the corporate debt goes down, and as (or if) average earnings rise over time, the value of the shares goes up. Since the lease payments are what pay down the debt, those who pay higher lease charges finance more equity shares. The designers also learned from the Swedish experience and built a resale formula into the lease to ensure long-term affordability. That is why equity share value is linked to average earnings.

Finally, co-op members democratically control the management and maintenance of their homes. They jointly organize housing repairs and control management and services. They could also introduce low- or zero-carbon heating and energy solutions, such as combined heat and power systems or photovoltaics, as is being done in the LILAC Ecovillage in Leeds — the first 20-home MHOS now under construction.

A Closer Look at Mutuality and Equity

Those are the basics of the model. Now let's look more closely at the equitable mutuality it features. Table 4.4 illustrates how Mutual Home Ownership provides for equitable lease rates based on income level, and how lower and middle income members can earn limited equity returns as well. To keep things simple, the table shows how the model works for a household occupied by two working adults living either on their own or with one or two children. The income figures are aggregated for both earners and are net of UK tax, pension, and other wage and salary deductions.

The key is the monthly payment (line 4) and the equity shares funded and "owned" by the member (line 8). The corporate debt that a leaseholder services through his/her lease payments or deposit is progressively converted into equity shares. As members service the debt of the cooperative at different levels (because their payments are income-related), it is fair that they "own" units of equity, represented as their household's shares in the mutually owned housing assets. The net value of the member's equity shares increases as the collective corporate loan is repaid and in line with the increase in average earnings over time. (This assumes that average earnings

Table 4.4 Mutual Home Ownership: Monthly Costs (£) and Equity Shares for Two-Income Household						
1. Total net household income.	14,406	16,688	18,845	23,108	26,318	32,738
2. 35% of net household income for housing costs	5,077	5,841	6,596	8,088	9,211	11,548
3. Less revenue costs payable for all members						
(i) Management	33	33	33	33	33	33
(ii) Maintenance	53	53	53	53	53	53
(iii) Service costs	18	18	18	18	18	18
4. Net monthly payment for corporate mortgage loan repayment	319	382	445	570	663	850
5. Capital value of corporate loan serviced	64,336	77,190	89,892	114,997	133,900	171,707
6. Number of equity shares funded by monthly payment	64	77	90	115	134	172
7. Add equity shares paid as 5% deposit	7	9	10	13	15	19
8. Total equity shares owned	71	86	100	128	149	191
Monthly cost of each additional equity share	4.95	4.95	4.95	4.95	4.95	4.95

Data in this table is drawn from information provided by David Rodgers of CDS Co-operatives.

increase. If they do not, equity share values could fall.) Line 5 shows the smaller and larger portions of debt to be repaid by members with different levels of income.

A resale formula permits a modest return on the sale of equity shares. The following example of a resale formula assumes an annual increase of 4.5 percent in household income (i.e., an annual rise of 3.5 percent in the retail price index, plus a growth of 1 percent in real earnings). In ten years this example would yield members the following net equity values (net of the outstanding corporate loan balance):

- 71 shares = £13,314
- 86 shares = £16,271
- 100 shares = £18,919
- 128 shares = £24,217
- 149 shares = £28,190
- 191 shares = £36,136

Scaling Up Mutuality

Financing is key — for land acquisition and for mortgages. With the growing interest among social investors and pension funds in longer-term, safe, and performing assets, there is much to recommend this model. For one thing, if MHOS developers can purchase land at below-market value with support from national governments or local authorities, they can offer investors a good level of security on a loan-to-value basis (the ratio of the asset value to the corporate loan). Purchasing the land at less than market value provides the asset cover required by the lender/investor. This is welcome news to municipalities where housing is becoming unaffordable to large numbers of residents — not least those in key public sector jobs, including teachers and fire department employees. The municipality that owns land or has leasehold land coming up for renewal would do well to use these as opportunities to jump-start and expand on the MHOS model.

Another advantage in the UK is that the Co-operative Housing Finance Society Ltd., established by CDS, can provide a one-year interest guarantee, an additional level of security. In addition, the national Community Land Trust Fund can assist with initial risk-financing costs and secure additional financing for the construction financing phase. Broadening the current scope of loan guarantees would be helpful, and CDS Co-operatives is working with financial advisors and lenders, including the Co-operative Bank and the Co-operative Group, to determine the feasibility of establishing a £200-million lending facility to support new MHOS projects. The Welsh government has just announced a project to work with CDS to develop MHOSs across Wales in the next few years.

Finally, MHOSs can be funded corporately either by bank lenders or through mutual housing investment bonds. The latter offer a secure rate of return for ethical, municipal, trade union, or other types of social investors. Currently CDS is using this means to try to secure 40- to 60-year mortgage finance from pension funds. This strategy was employed successfully by Letchworth, where a mix of long-term mortgage finance below 4 percent was used to build the Garden City a century ago.

In summary, mutual home ownership is affordable for the following reasons:

- Lease payments are a set ratio (35 percent) of net household income.
- Lower-income members can acquire equity shares. (In ten years, the equity available to low-income members is almost equal to their annual income.)
- Members can buy more shares as their incomes rise.

- Transaction costs are reduced. Properties are not bought and sold; instead, equity shares and occupancy rights are exchanged by assignment.
- Over the longer term, borrowing costs should be cheaper as longer-term financing is secured from pension funds.
- The linkage to average earnings helps reduce risk and maintains the affordability of the home.

Mutual home ownership societies combine the best of three models: community land trusts, tenant cooperatives, and cooperative land societies (the tenure system developed for Letchworth Garden City). The MHOS model keeps housing permanently affordable while giving current member-tenants incentives to maintain their dwelling and to contribute as much as they can to paying down the collective debt. The LILAC Ecovillage in Leeds is under construction as the first application of the MHOS model (see Figure 4.6). In its low-carbon housing design, it shows precisely how the model encourages environmentally sustainable housing, which is proving easier to finance. Its combined heat and power heating system, and its solar photovoltaics for renewable electricity, have attracted development finance from the European social bank, Triodos (see Chapter 8).

Fig. 4.6: *LILAC (Low Impact Living Affordable Community) hopes to build 20 homes and a common house by mid-2012, integrating cooperative community with ecological design and long-term affordability. LILAC sits on 0.7 hectares, site of a demolished primary school, which offers plenty of heat and light for homes that minimize carbon emissions by means of Modcell, a prefabricated strawbale building system.* Source: Artist's sketch courtesy of White Design

Collective mortgages can secure interest rate discounts, which give tenant-owners the money to invest in renewable energy measures and higher levels of thermal insulation. Active citizenship and community engagement are invited in two arenas: the tenant ownership cooperative and the community land trust. Quite simply, MHOS is a model that manages to recycle its benefits from one generation of occupants to the next.

The Household Economy: Land Trust Impacts on Transition

The Hartwick family accrued a 10-year saving of $67,090 by switching to a JAK Bank fee-based-lending model (Chapter 3). Let's presume now that their house was held by a CLT. In urban areas, CLT ownership could reduce the cost of a house by 50 percent.

We presume for the Hartwicks a much more modest reduction of 35 percent. The mortgage would then become $130,000. This reduction in purchase price, combined with the fee-based JAK mortgage, is good news for the Hartwicks, as shown in Table 4.5.

Table 4.5 The Hartwick Family: Cumulative 10-Year Savings by Adding in Land Trust				
Comparison of JAK Bank and Convention Bank Mortgage Costs	Bank interest charges (8.05%)	JAK fee charges	Savings $	Savings in hours
Last 10 years of 25-year mortgage of $200,000	$91,821	$24,731	$67,090	2,236
Impact of land trust on financing costs (130,000) in last 10 years	$67,530	$17,780	*$49,750*	*1658*
Actual capital cost saving of land to the householder	$70,000	$70,000	*$ 70,000*	*2333*
Total Reduction in Costs and Increase in Life Energy			119,750	3991 hrs

Transition Factors

The idea of restoring land to the commons is countercultural. Private property — indeed, the whole idea of owning a piece of land — is deeply embedded in our contemporary psyches. Questioning the right of individuals or companies to capture equity on the land by removing it from the ownership equation would, in many circles, be considered a betrayal of the free market and the rights of capital. This is true, to an extent, but the land trust formulation affirms Rousseau's assertion that one cannot own what "one did not create"; one can only use it. However, when we unite the "We" with the "I" by enabling ownership of assets created by human effort — a house or apartment, for example — individuals can own property and earn equity that provides a fair return on their investment.

The public benefit created by this dynamic approach to property rights is a crucial underpinning of transition. The Burlington Associates study dramatically shows the benefit to taxpayers of removing land from the market. The cumulative savings projected are an impressive 1,640 percent over 30 years. The additional quality-of-life benefits for low-income householders is obvious. However, the community benefits are not captured very effectively in these calculations. How do the reduced financial pressures in the lives of low- and moderate-income people actually accrue to the community? Might there not be a reduction in crime, better educational and health outcomes, and more stability and security for the workforce as a result? Might the significant savings that accrue at the household level lead to stronger families and better prospects for community members? If so, is it not common sense to argue that bringing the "I" and the "We" into closer proximity will likely lead to better societal outcomes? We think it does. Moreover, the evidence supports our contention.

In the health care field, the Population Health movement has captured this shift from a focus on just the "I" to a balance with the "We." Rather than focusing only on individuals, this movement analyzes the distribution of health outcomes throughout an entire population. The large body of evidence which shows that beyond biological and genetic factors, the physical, social, and economic environment are important contributors to good health.

- The Canadian Senate's subcommittee on population health found that social and economic factors — things like housing, education, and income — are the "social determinants of health." Over 50 percent of health outcomes are attributed to these factors.
- According to the BC Healthy Living Alliance, stable and affordable housing frees up income to purchase essentials like healthy food. It also reduces stress levels due to financial insecurity.
- And Maya Brennan, a researcher with the Center for Housing Policy, found that affordable housing enables families to participate more in community life and fosters a stronger sense of belonging. Good housing has also been proven to contribute to better educational outcomes for children.

Another argument related to community benefit goes well beyond the interests of people with low and moderate incomes and highlights the broader public benefits of improved housing affordability. Increasingly, for a wide variety of communities, people working in key employment sectors — such as teachers, police officers, and nurses — cannot afford to live near where they work. In high-amenity communities internationally, where wealthy people congregate for vacations or retirement, those who are serving them in the restaurants, the car repair services, the grocery store, the local hospital, etc., cannot afford housing in the district. Forced to live at a distance and commute to their jobs, these workers absorb the personal costs of time and energy. They have less time for their families. In carbon terms, their increased transportation requirements add to their unavoidable carbon emissions. In many large cities the turnover of teachers has become an obstacle to sustaining and paying for the educational system, and similar problems are affecting a growing range of public services and adding a new term to the lexicon: labor market housing. The result is a growing recognition that the housing affordability problem has extended well beyond the sphere of low- and moderate-income people.

As a broader constituency comes to understand these realities, more people may come to accept the land reform agenda embedded in duplex land tenures. It is hard to see how the increasing problems of housing affordability are going to be resolved without restoring the commons and uniting the "I" and the "We."

Resilience Reflections

Nothing could more dramatically illustrate the lack of resilience at the intersection of shelter and finance than the collapse into recession triggered by the bursting of the housing bubble. Few understood, when they were buying triple-A-backed mortgage securities, that the secure financial return they sought was feeding a frenzy in the market, with predatory mortgage brokers and companies making money based on nonexistent lending criteria. Where were the *feedback loops* that would have signaled the disaster in the making? The answer seems obvious. The lack of transparency or regulation in the international market place ensured obscurity. There was no lighthouse warning of the reef the housing bubble was heading us towards. And few understood that they were in the midst of a hurricane.

This lack of *feedback loops* is linked to the lack of *modularity* in a financial system that is "too big to fail." The credit union movement, the JAK Cooperative Bank, and a number of European social banks bring the relationship of finance and people closer to home. This local aspect is virtually absent in the international banking and investment system that fed and benefited from the growth of the housing bubble.

In cities like Vancouver, where in early 2012 the price of an average three-bedroom house hit $1 million, the speculative impacts of the private property system are excluding everyone but the very well heeled. *Diversity* is declining; the poor are becoming more and more marginalized, and the mid-income professionals and services workers must commute longer distances to their jobs. If the long-expected earthquake hits and a bridge goes down, most of the police, firefighters, nurses, and other health workers will be cut off from the city. In short, the price of housing is eroding resilience.

Uniting the "I" and the "We" through land trusts and cooperative approaches to improving affordability preserves the income *diversity* of the population, which in turn increases the distribution of income groups across the city or rural region. One can understand this impact in resilience terms as enhancing *modularity* — for example, all the community safety personnel do not have to live 40 miles away in order to afford shelter. This in turn potentially reduces the *ecological* impacts of a community, at least insofar as people are able to live closer to where they work.

Of course it is possible to imagine that if the pioneers of CLTs had not existed — that is, if the societal culture accepted the status quo — there would have been none of the *experimentation and innovation*. However, those pioneers did not accept the status quo and persisted in leveraging their learning and growing *social capital* to overcome many obstacles. The result is a blended model of *overlapping property rights and governance* that is much more dynamic, equitable (for more people), and flexible than conventional renting and buying.

Multi-stakeholder, democratic structures (a form of *social capital*) that steward land for public benefit in definable territories are, by definition, diverse, autonomous, and capable of being understood and tracked. And the process continues. The MHOS model is the result of a new round of *innovation* that leverages what has been learned in the last 40 years from very different national contexts. Creative and adaptive solutions emerge that are counter to the dominant cultural pattern. This is no more so than in the case of land and finance reforms that appear heavily impeded by both prevailing assumptions and a deep cultural attachment to traditional private property and private profit. Where land reform succeeds in uniting the "I" with the "We," the potential for navigating the challenges of transition successfully is, in our view, substantially improved.

CHAPTER 5

Seeking Strategic Pathways to Energy Sufficiency

The so-called energy crisis is, then, a politically ambiguous issue. Public interest in the quantity of power and in the distribution of controls over the use of energy can lead in two opposite directions. On the one hand, questions can be posed that would open the way to political reconstruction by unblocking the search for a postindustrial, labor-intensive, low-energy and high-equity economy. On the other hand, hysterical concern with machine fodder can reinforce the present escalation of capital-intensive institutional growth, and carry us past the last turnoff from a hyperindustrial Armageddon.

— Ivan Illich, "Energy and Equity," *Le Monde*, 1973

This curious faith is predicated on the notion that we will soon develop unlimited new sources of energy: domestic oil fields, shale oil, gasified coal, nuclear power, solar energy, and so on. This is fantastical because the basic cause of the energy crisis is not scarcity: it is moral ignorance and weakness of character. We don't know how to use energy or what to use it for. And we cannot restrain ourselves. Our time is characterized as much by the abuse and waste of human energy as it is by the abuse and waste of fossil fuel energy.

— Wendell Berry, *The Unsettling of America*

I'd put my money on the sun and solar energy. What a source of power! I hope we don't have to wait 'til oil and coal run out before we tackle that.

— Thomas Edison

OUR ENERGY DIET HAS PUT US BETWEEN A ROCK AND A HOT PLACE. On one hand, we are hooked on oil and demand is increasing. On the other hand, if we do not radically reduce our fossil-fuel use, we radically increase the likelihood of catastrophic, irreversible climate change.

It is this stark dilemma that drives James Lovelock, among others, to advocate massive investments in nuclear power, solar thermal installations, and smart grids. Some of these options are highly controversial. A massive shift to nuclear power may not be politically possible, even if, as Lovelock argues in *The Vanishing Face of Gaia*, possibly correctly, nuclear waste poses less risk to humanity and ecology than greenhouse gas (GHG) emissions do. Moreover, reports on the availability and price of uranium suggest that conventional nuclear power may not be economically feasible.

Even if such measures were implemented, it is doubtful they would be enough. Centralized strategies such as massive solar-thermal installations and nuclear power hooked up to smart grids may bridge the yawning gap in electricity supply, but they are not enough, in and of themselves, to replace fossil fuels. They are also highly vulnerable to disruption, as we saw in the wake of the Japanese earthquake and tsunami of 2011. Distributed energy strategies, diverse in type and scale, that increase local and regional self-reliance, may well be more prudent and resilient options for the transition to a low-carbon, powered-down, conservation-oriented future.

A 2009 briefing paper by the new economics foundation reports that, starting in the 1970s, "Denmark pursued an extensive energy efficiency programme, including the capture of waste energy (combined heat and power), that has improved its energy security by 150 per cent. It is now a net exporter of energy, due to its hundreds of small-scale 'distributed' generators making use of wind, biomass and a range of bio-fuels manufactured from waste."

Energy efficiency is a near-term priority. According to Canada's National Round Table on the Environment and the Economy, "significant reductions in greenhouse gasses [GHGs] can be achieved only if energy is used more efficiently and if energy is produced while emitting less carbon. Energy and climate change policy in the 21st century means addressing both energy use and energy production. The question is not which technologies to deploy, but how to deploy effectively all of the potential GHG reduction technologies." The Round Table has suggested that Canada could achieve 40 percent of the 60 percent reduction in GHGs targeted for 2050 by deploying a comprehensive suite of available conservation and energy-efficiency technologies.*

---

* It should be noted that several jurisdictions are now aiming to reduce carbon levels by 80 percent by 2050. The Canadian estimate dated 2006 may thus be too low as new information has outstripped the rate of GHG emissions actually being measured.

The potential of this strategic path for reduction of carbon emissions is huge. For example, approximately 27 percent of all carbon emissions in the UK come from the residential housing sector (see Figure 5.1), so comprehensive action on carbon reduction could also help take some of the edge off another knotty problem. The new economics foundation paper mentioned earlier noted that, in the UK, "fuel poverty" is defined as having to spend more than 10 percent of household income to keep your home adequately warm. The combination of low incomes, poor access to energy services, poor insulation, and inefficient heating systems renders more than five million British households fuel poor. It is estimated that for every 1 percent increase in the price of energy, 40,000 UK households join the ranks of the fuel poor.

How can communities be empowered to mobilize public and local resources to achieve radical reductions in household energy consumption, carbon emissions, *and* fuel poverty? This is the first theme we explore in the chapter. The path taken by the city of Kirklees in the UK provides a

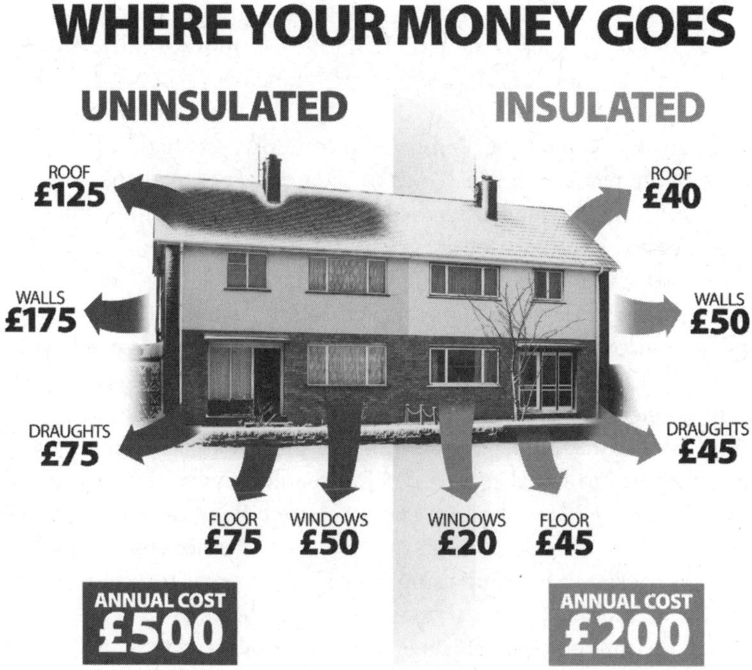

WHERE YOUR MONEY GOES

UNINSULATED   INSULATED

ROOF
£125

ROOF
£40

WALLS
£175

WALLS
£50

DRAUGHTS
£75

DRAUGHTS
£45

FLOOR   WINDOWS
£75   **£50**

WINDOWS   FLOOR
£20   **£45**

ANNUAL COST
£500

ANNUAL COST
£200

Fig. 5.1: *For every 1 percent fuel prices go up, 40,000 UK citizens enter fuel poverty. Residential energy efficiency keeps people warmer, healthier, and cleaner in relation to the atmosphere on which we all depend.* Source: Smye Holland Associates

fascinating and instructive glimpse into what is possible and what it takes to generate energy-conservation solutions. The second theme we explore is how renewable energy developed, owned, and operated at the community and/or regional level can create clean energy and economic vitality. The commitment of the leadership and citizens of Kristianstad, Sweden, to become fossil-fuel free shows the dramatic results that can be achieved.

YES to Conserving Energy: Yorkshire Energy Services at Work

Kirklees in the 1980s and 1990s was typical of many medium-sized cities in the UK and elsewhere. A large stock of poorly insulated housing drained cash from fuel-poor households while emitting vast amounts of carbon. True, a complex of assistance programs was available, created over the years by a plethora of national government departments. Good intentions, however, were not enough. Designed and implemented in silos, and without reliance on any local capacity to mobilize and coordinate resources, these programs had little impact.

In 2000, the Kirklees metropolitan council made a decision to transform the community's relationship to energy. An energy-efficiency program launched by the European Union (EU) in 1998 became the vehicle of change. The Specific Actions for Vigorous Energy Efficiency (SAVE) II Program could supply up to 50 percent of the budget for innovative pilot projects. (A local authority and other public or private partners had to provide the balance.) One plank in SAVE II was to pilot energy-management agencies at the local level. In light of its carbon-reduction targets under the Kyoto Accord, the EU considers local capacity for action to be vital. Indeed, the decisions of private citizens are directly responsible for over half of all final energy consumption in the EU, so it is critical to have local energy agencies that disseminate to consumers good practices in demand-side management.

Kirklees Energy Services (KES) was established in 2000 by the metropolitan council as a separate legal entity, a not-for-profit social enterprise. Within three years, KES programming enabled a total of 2,080 energy-saving measures to be taken in 1,455 households. Some of these measures included energy-efficient heating and insulation; floor, cavity wall, and loft insulation; draft-proofing of doors and windows; gas-heating controls; hot-water tank jackets; and condensing boilers. Permanent carbon reductions across Kirklees, even at this early stage, were significant: 34,304 tons.

The targeting of households living in fuel poverty added social value to these early efforts. For example, KES was able to organize partnerships that offered free insulation and heat-recovery ventilation units to householders whose respiratory illnesses would be mitigated by a warmer home. In another example, where poor households were still relying mainly on coal for heat, KES worked with Scottish Power to help them convert to full gas central heating.

Apart from some initial setbacks due to unprofessional installers, KES maintained a steady record of success. Advice, prequalified and registered installers, fixed-discount pricing, preferred credit, and up to 25 percent rebates enabled householders to realize significant energy savings conveniently and affordably. In addition, by 2007, KES had informed 3,000 householders about the effect that their new-found energy efficiency was having on local carbon emissions. Diverse promotion and advertising schemes have increased interest in KES programs still further.

The key to the KES success has been its capacity to join together and coordinate partners from the public and private sectors and from civil society to provide services and programs tailored to the needs of a wide range of households (see Figure 5.2). Three local credit unions offered preferential loans to householders. A combination of local authorities and the power utilities funded the rebates. KES charged its slate of approved private contractors a 10 percent referral fee for insulation installations and a 5 percent referral fee for heating measures. These fees covered the administration costs of the scheme.

By 2004, KES and Kirklees had learned several lessons. A big one was that designing the service as a one-stop shop for promoting and managing household energy efficiency eliminated time, cost, and hassle for householders. It

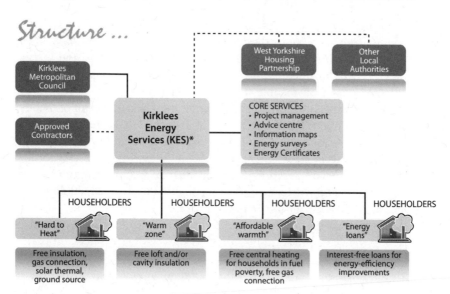

Fig. 5.2: *KES-YES structure.* Source: Yorkshire Energy Services, www.yorkshireenergyservices.co.uk

also reduced the risks involved in finding a quality installer. The following are some other early lessons:

- Build a team of registered and reputable installers who offer superior customer service and have an interest in energy efficiency. This is crucial for customer satisfaction and thus to the ongoing success of the scheme.
- Specify stringent standards of "customer care" in the tender to installers. This is essential to building the trust of community members who will use the service.
- Set up a loan scheme that offers flexible criteria. This makes financing directly accessible for householders, and as a result generates more implementation of measures.
- Create substantial rebates to get householders engaged. This involves convincing organizations or companies that they should fund the rebates. In KES's case, rebates were an important way for local authorities to meet their commitments under the Home Energy Conservation Act and for utilities to achieve their prescribed energy-efficiency targets.
- Charge contractors referral fees in order to create a meaningful income stream. When the 5 percent referral fee for heating measures proved insufficient, KES raised it to 10 percent.

With seven years of experience and capacity-building under its belt, KES became a provider under the UK Warm Zones program in 2008. Warm Zones coordinates the delivery of information, advice, grants, and installation services to low-income and vulnerable households in designated urban and rural areas. Low-income households qualify for C$2,850 (£1,800) in fuel-efficiency measures.* Those with senior members in receipt of income-related benefits are eligible for a grant of up to $5,550 — and up to $9,510, if oil central heating is recommended because the home is not on the gas network. Grants available under this scheme enlarge the range of measures still further. In 2009 the insulation work that KES coordinated in its early stages expanded to include support for micro-renewables, including solar thermal heating and air-source heat pumps.

KES shot to the forefront in piloting Warm Zones and expanded its reach to the western Yorkshire subregion surrounding Kirklees, ultimately

---

* All currencies in this chapter are converted to Canadian dollars at the rate current on 1 December 2010 (C$1.5851 to the Pound Sterling, C$1.3359 to the euro). Totals less than $10,000 are rounded to the nearest ten dollars.

servicing a population of 500,000. Local authorities within this region committed $20.3 million over the next three years, matched by funds from the Warm Zone program. KES's established track record in 2009 was leveraging $4 for every $1 of public investment. In short, KES was positioned to help channel and deliver an integrated system of energy-efficiency services worth over $160 million (4 x $40.6 million) into targeted energy conservation and carbon reduction measures.

As the program was about to launch, the funding available was cut back to $31.4 million — $14.1 million from local governments and $17.3 million from Scottish Power. However, despite this 20 percent drop, the evaluation of the KES program revealed that the leverage ratio had been expanded to 5:1. Even with a major program cut, KES was projected to stimulate a total investment of about $157 million over the four years.

Under the new program, every household across the district was scheduled to be visited, ward by ward, street by street. Households initially learned by direct mail that representatives would soon be in their area. At the same time, district-wide marketing reinforced the program's brand recognition and affirmed its backing by the local council. Community and volunteer groups helped spread the message, and local events raised awareness. Trained assessors carried out door-to-door visits to check insulation status. If required, a contractor installed mineral-fibre insulation in lofts and cavity walls, at no cost to the homeowner. This area-based approach saved

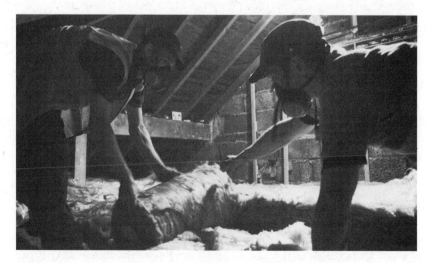

Fig. 5.3: *Private contractors lay rolls of loft insulation. Loft insulation and cavity wall insulation were two of the simplest, most cost-effective ways to reduce energy use and carbon emissions from homes in Kirklees.* Source: Andy Aitchison/Ashden Awards

significantly on the surveyors' and installers' travel time, and contractor productivity went up 50 percent.

By July 2010, all 171,000 households had been visited and 127,007 energy assessments carried out. As a result, 40,238 properties had loft insulation and 20,324 had cavity wall insulation installed (over 51,000 separate residences in total). Savings to each household from insulation measures alone have averaged $317 per year. By its third year, the program was reducing carbon emissions by almost 55,000 tons per annum. Household savings are calculated to achieve around $16 million per year — money that is now available to spend in the region or on other things. There were 100 direct jobs created and another 60 indirect jobs for insulation specialists, furnace installers, energy auditors...the list goes on. At least 1,000 households have climbed out of fuel poverty. As oil prices rise, however, some of them are likely to slide back under the wire.

As a social enterprise with a regional market, KES is now known as Yorkshire Energy Services (YES). It runs the Energy Saving Trust advice center for south and west Yorkshire that is part of a national network of advisory organizations. YES also manages a range of award-winning projects for public sector organizations across northern England. In 2010, YES established a subsidiary to install such renewable technologies as solar PV and solar thermal. It is now diversifying both into the development of low-carbon transport, especially electric vehicles, and modal shift redesign measures to make it easier for people to move from car use to public transport.

While Yorkshire Energy Services has demonstrated dramatic results on the energy-conservation and carbon-reduction fronts, it is just starting to facilitate the production of renewable energy. As indicated earlier, Denmark has made remarkable progress in this regard, with the government taking action to create an effective, decentralized, renewable-energy production system, a story we return to in Chapter 10. Not all national governments are quite so forward thinking, unfortunately, but we turn now to a story of prescient local politicians at the cusp of a new century helping to build effective renewable energy supplies at the community level in Sweden.

Fossil-Fuel-Free Kristianstad

In the council chambers of Kristianstad, Sweden, in 1999, the representatives of a unique amalgamation of a small city (population 33,000) and 25 nearby towns and villages gathered to make a momentous decision: they wanted to make Kristianstad the first fossil-fuel-free municipality in the Western world.

Spread out over an area of about 1,300 square kilometers in southeastern Sweden, this rural district is home to some of the best agricultural land in

Europe, a food-processing industry, and the production center for Absolut Vodka. Committing the scattered population of 77,000 to becoming fossil-fuel free was not something to be taken lightly. Nevertheless, council members were unanimous, and their "Yes We Can" attitude, the strong commitment and vision of the local government staff, and a systematic planning and citizen-engagement process is making it happen. By 2008, Kristianstad had cut its use of fossil fuels in half.

To be sure, the region had shown signs of a strong progressive streak since the mid-1980s, when Kristianstad Energy Ltd., a municipally owned energy company, began working to replace oil with biofuel (wood chips). Biofuels have also been key to the development of a combined power and heating plant in Kristianstad. Major parts of the city are served by a district heating network, and new areas are continually added to the system. The biofuel-powered heat and power unit Allöverket, established in 1994, is estimated to have reduced the municipality's emissions of carbon dioxide by 120,000 tons in the last 15 years. The wood chips come from mills within a radius of 100 kilometers and from the waste of the local hardwood flooring industry. Additionally, to improve sustainability and energy production, the municipal waste company, Renhållningen Kristianstad, established a biogas production plant just outside town in 1997.

Since setting out the fossil-fuel-free vision in 1999, Kristianstad has stepped up its investment. By 2008, 55 million euros (about C$69 million)

Fig. 5.4: *Allöverket co-generation plant.* Source: Stephen Salter PEng, Farallon Consultants Limited

Table 5.1 Financial resources and partners: Kristianstad Renewable Energy Vision at Work

Financial source		Budget		% of total budget
Grants from the Swedish government (7 million €)		6 992 163 €		13%
Financed by investors (47,7 million €)		47 765 732 €		87%
Sum		**54 757 895 €**		
Achieved	**Year**			
Biogas for Transports, new upgrading plant	2006	17 000 000 SEK	1 789 474 €	473 700 €
In progress				
New boiler at the CHP plant in Kristianstad	2007	150 000 000 SEK	15 789 474 €	0 €
Extension of district heating system	2005-2008	41 000 000 SEK	4 315 789 €	647 400 €
Cycling, building infrastructure, and campaigning	2005-2008	4 000 000 SEK	421 053 €	0 €
Biogas for Transports (cars, buses, and heavy vehicles)	1999 – 2008 (2010)	8 350 000 SEK	878 947 €	357 000 €
Conversion of private houses to renewable energy sources	1999-2008	38 000 000 SEK	4 000 000 €	757 900 €
Climate information and mobility management	2005-2008	5 000 000 SEK	526 316 €	55 400 €
Insulation of private houses	2005-2008	10 800 000 SEK	1 136 842 €	352 600 €
Solar heating for private houses	2005-2008	5 200 000 SEK	547 368 €	168 400 €
Conversion of municipal buildings from electric heating to biofuels	2005-2008	9 000 000 SEK	947 368 €	0 €
Planned				
Biogas for Transports (more filling stations)	2007-2008	10 500 000 SEK	1 105 263 €	331 579 €
New boiler at the district heating plant in Åhus and new network in Tollarp	2007-2008	40 000 000 SEK	4 210 526 €	221 000 €
Extension of the biogas plant, Karpalund	2007-2008	14 650 000 SEK	1 542 105 €	230 500 €
New biogas plant, Nöbbelöv	2006- 2008	35 900 000 SEK	3 778 947 €	1 133 000 €
Biogas for Transports (production on farms)	2005-2008	15 000 000 SEK	1 578 947 €	473 684 €
School buses running on biogas	2007-2008	4 800 000 SEK	505 263 €	0 €
Bioboiler in Nöbbelöv replaces 2000-ton gasol	2006-2008	85 000 000 SEK	8 947 368 €	1 790 000 €
Energy performance contracting for municipal buildings saves 30% energy	2007-2008	26 000 000 SEK	2 736 842 €	0 €
Sum		**520 200 000 SEK**	**54 757 895 €**	**6 992 163 €**

Source: "Fossil Fuel Free Kristianstad, Municipality of Kristianstad, Sweden," Case Study 254 (European Commission Directorate-General for Energy and Transport, January 2011),www.managenergy.net/download/nr254.pdf.

had been invested or committed; 13 percent came from Swedish government grants, and the balance from municipally owned companies and private investors. Table 5.1 shows the range of investments brought forward in the first nine years, and it illustrates the range of strategies Kristianstad is employing to realize its vision of fossil-fuel freedom.

As a complement to the combined heat and power plant in Kristianstad, the village of Fjälkinge operates a district heating plant using wood chips. The target customers are households. Biomass-fueled district heating is cheap and clean, but it is an energy system suitable only to densely populated areas. Where sparser populations make district heating inefficient, wood pellets are the best alternative, economically and environmentally. Therefore, the municipality has converted 44 oil-fed boilers in schools and other public buildings to burn pellets. This saves 3,000 tons of carbon yearly. In 1998, municipal buildings relied on fossil fuels for 48 percent and on biofuels for 27 percent of their heat. By 2002 those proportions had shifted to 9 percent and 78 percent, respectively. A grant program gives households an incentive to convert from oil to pellets.

Biogas is another key sector, and two anaerobic digester facilities are operating in the Kristianstad region. One is a municipal wastewater treatment plant. The other is the Karpalund plant, built in 1997 by Renhållningen Kristianstad, the local municipal waste management company, to serve primarily as a treatment plant for waste from the local food industry. This was the first to co-digest municipal solid waste from households (sorted into paper bags) and food industry waste together with farm manure for coproduction of energy and fertilizer. Average annual input to the Karpalund digester is 70,000 metric tons. That yields 40 gigawatt hours (GWh) of energy. According to Renhållningen Kristianstad, feedstock from the food

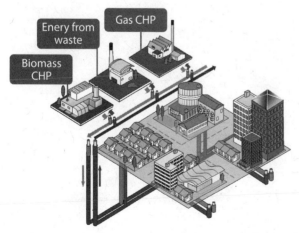

Fig. 5.5:
District heating More energy efficient, less polluting, and ultimately more cost effective, district heating and cooling is rapidly gaining more attention.
Source: Aberdeen Heat & Power Company, Scotland. CO2Sense Ltd. Leeds, UK.

industry accounts for 34 GWh, household waste contributes 4 GWh, and farm manure yields 2 GWh. Roughly 63,000 metric tons of digestate is produced each year, the equivalent of about 1,000 metric tons of artificial fertilizer. (Note that the average US home uses 10,000 kilowatt hours of electricity per year. One gigawatt of power — 1 million KWh — can support 100 homes. The 40 GWh produced by biogas, if used just for electricity, would be sufficient to supply over 4,000 average US homes.)

The municipality is also working to increase the use of biogas as a vehicle fuel, with households, companies, and municipal units as the target market. In addition to coordinating promotion and education, the municipality has offered a grant for up to 50 percent of the extra cost to purchase biogas-fueled buses. As a result, 35 buses and 250 other municipal vehicles operate on biogas. Additional capacity for producing biogas vehicle fuel was installed in 2006. This has raised local production to 10,000 liters a day, annual production to 4 million liters, and has reduced carbon emissions by an additional 11,000 tons. A recent assessment report projects that by 2018, 800 buses will be fueled by biogas in the region.

This carbon benefit is even bigger when one considers where the feedstock for the biogas refinery comes from. Waste from the agricultural industry, including abattoirs and vegetable waste, comprises 60 percent of the feedstock. Household waste (6 percent) and farm manure (34 percent) make up the balance. Much of this waste stream, along with the waste water and the landfill mentioned earlier, would otherwise be naturally emitting methane, a greenhouse gas 21 times more powerful than carbon (see Figure 5.6).

Combined district heating, small-scale heating, and biogas for transport yield an annual direct carbon reduction of about 140,000 tons.

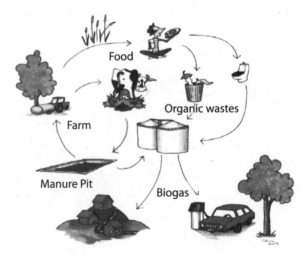

Fig. 5.6: *Biogas cycle.*
Source: Municipality of Kristianstad

Renewable Electricity (GWh/yr)

☐ Hydro power ■ Combined heat and power ☐ Wind power

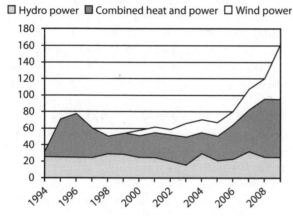

Fig. 5.7:
Renewable electricity
Source: Lennart
Erfors, "Kristianstad
Mitigating Climate
Change! Strategies
and Achievements,"
Municipality of
Kristianstad, 6 May
2010, p. 12.

Apart from introducing biogas as a fuel, the municipality is vigorously working to change transportation behaviour. Since there will not be enough renewable fuel to fill today's need, the number of journeys made by car must decrease. The municipality therefore runs several mobility management projects. For example, European Mobility Week distributes information about car pooling and car sharing, and encourages people to take a bus or bicycle to work.

Beyond these initiatives, wind power is playing an increasing role. Generating capacity currently produces about 65 GWh of electricity per year. The growth in local electricity production, illustrated in Figure 5.7, represents sufficient electricity for 6,500 average American homes. This wind provision was put in place in 2008.

Kristianstad's commitment to renewable energy is just getting started. The current objective is to cover the entire annual electrical demand of the district municipality using local sources. Another 500 GWh/year of onshore wind power is currently in process, and 500 GWh more is on the books to be developed from future offshore wind power. And the sun has not been forgotten. Although solar is not yet a major strategy, a pilot installation is currently producing 11 MWh per year. Adding up the numbers yields an impressive 1,160 GWh from renewable sources, enough to supply energy for 116,000 typical three-bedroom homes — an amazing result when one considers the total population of the district is only 77,000.

To date there has been no evaluation of the impact of these multiple initiatives on the municipal economy. However, Lennart Erfors, the manager of Fossil-Fuel-Free Kristianstad, notes that a lot of money has been saved at the household and municipal levels by converting from oil to bioenergy.

Moreover, the conversion from oil to district heating or to woodchip heating has a very short payback period. In contrast, wind and solar will likely be more expensive in the short term — unless Friedman's plea for a much higher price on carbon (described in Chapter 1) is taken seriously. If and when his warning is heeded, Kristianstad will be well ahead on the transition curve and making money. Indeed, given the municipality's current plans, it will soon be exporting clean energy to adjacent regions.

The Impact on the Household and Community Economy

Our little family of five would make some modest financial savings if their community had a program similar to Kirklees Energy Services. As noted earlier, by 2010, Kirklees had helped 55,000 households achieve an average annual saving of $317. If we assume that domestic energy prices will increase 3 percent annually, this represents a 10-year savings of about $3,642 for the Hartwicks (see Table 5.2).

The broader community impacts are important to note. If Kirklees stopped doing any further work, the 55,000 households already served will, over the next 10 years, be saving an average of about $18.6 million per year. If 60 percent of this amount is spent locally, Kirklees and the region will gain a direct benefit from $11,200,000 flowing through the local economy. This money of course creates a multiplier effect. Using a modest multiplier of 2.5, this amounts to a $28 million reinvestment impact on the local economy. Both the energy savings and the leverage effect will contribute to new jobs and enhance the stability of existing jobs and businesses.

Then there are the societal benefits of carbon reduction to consider. Carbon is being reduced. Assuming reduction is worth $23 per metric ton,

Table 5.2 The Hartwick Family: Cumulative 10-Year Savings by Adding in Energy Savings				
Comparison of JAK Bank and Convention Bank Mortgage Costs	Bank interest charges (8.05%)	JAK fee charges	Savings $	Savings in hours
Last 10 years of 25-year mortgage of $200,000	$91,821	$24,731	$67,090	2,236
Impact of land trust on financing costs (130,000) in last 10 years	$67,530	$17,780	$49,750	1658
Actual capital cost saving of land to the householder	$70,000	$70,000	$ 70,000	2333
Kirklees conservation savings over 10 years			$ 3,642	121
Net savings due to CLT, JAK, and Kirklees model			$123,392	4113

the annual carbon reduction of 55,000 tons from the Kirklees Warm Zone initiative is worth $1.265 million by Year 3 (this was the price in June 2011). This would be available for reinvestment in ongoing transition initiatives. However, if one accepts the European carbon brokerage market estimate of what is needed to meet the third phase of the Kyoto protocol (i.e., 80 percent emissions reduction by 2050), a carbon price of $84 dollars from 2013 onward will be required. Pricing at this level would yield a carbon offset on the Kirklees Warm Zone project of $4.62 million.

Transition Factors

In the case of both Kirklees and Kristianstad, the municipal government was the key agent.

- They each jump-started and sustained the investment of time, talent, and resources.
- They both played key planning, coordinating, oversight, and financing roles.
- Kirklees incorporated and then delegated certain planning and all delivery functions to a social enterprise, a provision wisely required by the European Union.
- Key in the case of Kristianstad is the municipality's ownership of two low-carbon energy corporations: one focused on waste, the other working to develop renewable energy production. This enabled Kristianstad both to direct investment and to capture cash flow for continuous reinvestment in the renewable energy strategy.
- Each municipality leveraged national and local programs and investment resources to create a blend of different kinds of money tailored to their specific objectives.
- Each municipality has built its strategies based on a comprehensive, long-term perspective.
- Each organization measures and reports on outcomes for carbon reduction, energy efficiency, energy production, and cost savings. Kirklees extends its reports to action on fuel poverty and jobs.
- In both cases, a wide range of partnerships has been created and wielded to extend capacity and broaden participation. Government, local business, social enterprise, affordable housing organizations, citizens, and (where necessary) outside businesses have been engaged to create a diverse and expanding circle of committed actors.

Resilience Reflections

Both Kirklees and Kristianstad are significantly contributing to increasing the resilience of their respective communities. The *diversity and modularity* of their energy systems are radically enhanced at the household, community, and subregional levels. Their investment outcomes, in terms of carbon emissions, energy savings, energy production, and economic effects, are direct and ample evidence of *shorter feedback loops* at work. There is a distinct sense that citizens, organizations, and institutions are embarked on a learning process that is steadily enhancing their capacity to both act and adapt; in short, *social capital* is being strengthened. The *innovation and experimentation* undertaken in each setting have fed the engagement, learning, and capacity-building of the multi-stakeholder and cross-sector partnerships that have been vital to the success realized thus far. One gets a strong sense of the social solidarity economy at work.

An outstanding feature of the positive strengthening of resilience in Kristianstad flows from its capture of economic and financial benefits. It is interesting to ponder whether, without being an owner, this farflung district municipality could have realized such rapid progress towards becoming fossil-fuel free. How could this have been accomplished if reinvestment was not framed as a public good goal? The simple truth is that the private business sector could not and would not undertake such a long-term process unless provided with guarantees. Nor is it likely that the private sector would have reinvested continuously.

Herein lies the dilemma introduced in Chapter 1 and so eloquently put by Thomas Friedman: it is all about price, price, price. Friedman strenuously argues for governments to shape the market by setting clear prices for carbon and establishing a regulatory framework that will give nervous investors, focused on financial return, the right incentives to invest.

There is no question that shaping the market to meet public good goals is fundamentally important. But we can see how low the price of carbon is in Europe, where it is generally higher than in other markets. Change is just not happening, at least not broadly enough or fast enough. True, the growing use of feed-in tariffs (see Chapter 10) is having a big impact on renewable development in jurisdictions like Denmark and Germany, and it appears their approach is facilitating a wide range of ownership models.

In the absence of a much higher and consistent price, private investment will remain muted. In the meantime, in the case of Kristianstad, it is the municipality's ownership of the means of production that has been central to implementing systematic and profitable business strategies and to enabling continuous reinvestment for the benefit of citizens. The municipality is making money, reducing carbon, and radically increasing the resilience, the *ecological* health, and the energy self-reliance of the region.

CHAPTER 6

Seeking Pathways to Sustainable Food

You look at the labels and you see farmer this, farmer that. It's really just three or four companies that are controlling the meat. We've never had food companies this big and this powerful in our history.

— Eric Schlosser, *Fast Food Nation*

Only farming that nourishes Nature and supports biological activities, efficient use of water, climate, seeds, breeds and naturally developed soils — rather than industrial agricultural that creates deserted monotonous landscapes and relies on external energy — can guarantee food for all: now and in the future"

— Laureates of the Right Livelihood Award,
"Declaration for Living Change"

IF ONE CLIMBED TO THE CHURCH BELL TOWER in most European villages in 1789, one could approximate a bird's eye view of a local landscape that produced 95 percent of the food necessary to sustain local villagers. Even 150 years later, the change was not that dramatic. In *The Right to Useful Employment*, Ivan Illich pointed out that, as the Second World War was breaking out, 96 percent of food consumed was a mix of local and regional production. So where are we now, only 70 years later? In 2009, only 5 percent of the food consumed by the 750,000 inhabitants on Vancouver Island (a 300-mile-long island that sits off the southwest coast of British Columbia) was produced on the island. The balance was transported by truck across North America and across the globe by ship and air.

In less than a lifetime, food production has been transformed from a local affair into a complex web of supply chains crisscrossing the planet that miraculously deliver a multitude of foodstuffs right to our doorstep. Today, farming, including crop and pasture land, covers 40 percent of the globe, accounts for 70 percent of consumptive water use, and employs approximately 40 percent of the population worldwide. By contrast, less than 2 percent of the US population lives on productive farms today.

Cheap Food and Its Price

The army of humans who used to work on farms has been replaced by cheap oil, wondrous in its flexibility and possessing uniquely high energy values. Imagine: a single barrel of oil has been estimated to be equivalent to approximately 25,000 hours of human labor, or one person working 12.5 years at 40 hours per week. It is little wonder we struggle to sober up from our oil addiction. Oil is so integral to our economy, society, and culture that disentangling ourselves from our dependence on it is a hugely complex challenge. This is particularly so when it comes to the food system. From the plowing of the fields to the weekly big-box grocery run, we rely on an oil-dependent global supply chain, controlled by multinational corporations, for our food. Fertilizers, pesticides, manufacturing, and machinery of all kinds — pumps for water-hungry irrigation schemes, processing equipment, plastic packaging, right through to the energy-sucking open freezers of big box supermarkets — are all links in a chain feeding the global cafeteria.

Fig. 6.1: *Cheap oil delivers cheap food. The commodity-based food system depends on it so much that when the price of oil soars, so too does the price we pay for our groceries.*

Source: © Julien Tromeur | Dreamstime.com

Agricultural Emissions — Greenhouse Gases and Nitrogen

In the United States, 10 to 15 calories of fossil-fuel energy is used to create 1 calorie of food. This adds up to the equivalent of 1,500 litres of oil (20.3 barrels) to feed each American per year. Natural gas is a key component in this mix. As the main feedstock for nitrogen fertilizer, it has been responsible for raising global crop yields approximately 35 to 50 percent over the last half century. For cereal crops it accounts for 80 percent of the increase in productivity.

Unfortunately, nitrogen used on the land seeps into rivers and is carried to river deltas and oceans. Nitrogen destroys oxygen, creating an effect known as hypoxia. As a result of the extensive use of nitrogen, and the resulting runoff, rivers and oceans are suffering from the accumulated deposits to the point of death. In an August 2008 article for *Scientific American*, David Biello reported that over 212,000 metric tons of human food was lost to hypoxia each year in the northern Gulf of Mexico, much of which has become a dead zone. Nitrogen and other oil-based agricultural inputs were originally heralded as innovations supporting the "green revolution" that would feed the world. They have now become part of the problem.

Agriculture is also a major contributor to greenhouse gas (GHG) emissions. A 2006 report from the UN's Food and Agriculture Organization, *Livestock's Long Shadow: Environmental Issues and Options,* estimated the meat and livestock industry alone contributed 9 percent of total carbon dioxide emissions, 37 percent of methane, and 65 percent of nitrous oxide. In New Zealand, 50 percent of daily GHG emissions came from the farting, burping, and breathing of 40 million sheep, 9 million cattle, and 2 million roe deer. (The emissions of methane and nitrous oxide are particularly disturbing. Nitrous oxide has 296 times the global warming potential of carbon. Methane is 23 times more potent than carbon, though it lasts a shorter time — four years to carbon's 100. However, given the worry about a tipping point at which GHGs will reach concentrations that create self-reinforcing feedback loops, these more powerful gases are a big problem.)

The UN predicts that the number of livestock will double by 2050. Food expert Felicity Lawrence, in a 2011 article in the *Guardian* newspaper, counters that this is impossible because the meat industry in Europe already requires an area of vegetation seven times the size of the European continent to feed the animals. If everyone in the world ate meat at a North American rate of intake, we would need to raise cattle on the moon.

Corporate Concentration and the Price of Food

Oil use in food production has also delivered something many of us in our everyday lives take for granted — cheap food. In the United States today, an average of 9.9 percent of disposable income is spent on food; 80 years ago it was 25 percent. German consumers on average spend 10.9 percent of their disposable income on food at home, followed, among high-income countries by Japan (13.4 percent), South Korea (13.4 percent), and France (13.6 percent), and in middle-income countries by South Africa (17.5 percent) and Mexico (21.7 percent). China (28.3 percent) and Russia (36.7 percent) are seeing rapid decreases, but the percentage of income spent on food is still relatively high. India (39.4 percent) and Indonesia (49.9 percent) are among the highest when it comes to the amount of disposable income spent on food.

The linkage between oil and food and narrowly defined commercial efficiencies appears to be one key factor in the low price of food. According to the US Department of Agriculture, labor accounted for almost 40 percent of the value of resources used in farming in 1950; by 1993 it had declined to 9.5 percent. In contrast, machinery and chemical use in agriculture increased from 25 to 43 percent during the same period. Fertilizer use increased fivefold since 1950. It seems logical that as the price of fossil fuels escalates in the years ahead, agriculture is going to become more labor intensive again. The need for an increased supply of labor at a wage that can sustain workers may push up the cost of food, which will squeeze consumers, especially those with lower and moderate incomes.

Ironically, while the low percentage of disposable income currently spent on food is good news for consumers, it has not necessarily translated well for the producer. On average, US farmers get back less than 20 cents of every dollar spent on food. Sixty years ago they received almost 40 cents, and as recently as 1981 the figure was still 31 cents on the dollar. The striking implication cannot be ignored by any citizen concerned with basic notions of fair trade, sustainable livelihoods for farmers, or long-term food security. If 10 percent of consumers' disposable income goes for food purchases, and 20 percent of that amount gets to farmers, only 2 percent of a consumer dollar actually ends up with the farmer.

Meanwhile, many farmers cannot make a living, require off-farm income, and suffer from debt levels and cost increases that drive them off the land. Recent Statistics Canada data makes the point: net farm income, net of government support payments and adjusted for inflation, reveals 2010 as the third-worst year of losses since 1926, and the years 2003 to 2010 stand out as the worst period yet.

The profits are being captured by the colossal corporate concentration of production right through the value chain. For example, three companies retail and distribute the bulk of Canadian oil, gasoline, and diesel; a few corporations control Canada's nitrogen fertilizer capacity; and a small handful control the chemical and seed sectors. Three dominate the farm machinery sector. Farmers face similar concentration among processors and retailers. Cargill, for example, now controls about 50 percent of Canadian beef-packing capacity, and when one adds Tyson, these two companies alone control 80 percent. Four companies mill most of the flour; three make Canadian soft drinks; and six control the food retail sector.

Corporate concentration and energy-intensive agriculture fit hand in glove. Some argue the result is a highly efficient process. But they do not weigh the ecological and health costs. For example, consider the impact of housing a million pigs in a multi-story production center where each pig produces as much manure per day as eight people — the total is equivalent to the amount of sewage generated by the entire population of London.

The lopsided energy equation of these types of production is equally disturbing. Traditional farming yields 10 units of energy output in food compared to every one unit of energy input. According to C. Tudge in *Feeding People Is Easy*, industrial farming turns this thermodynamically

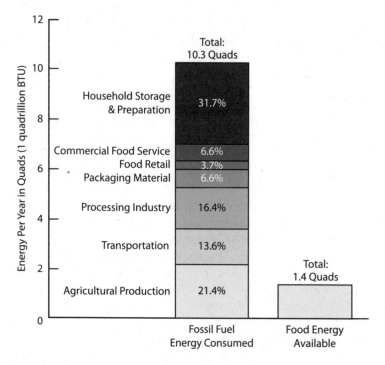

Fig. 6.2: *We are spending more and more fossil fuel to produce less food on more land. Thus we emit more and more carbon, which is becoming more and more of a threat to a food system that grows less and less resilient.* Source: Center for Sustainable Systems, University of Michigan, "U.S. Food System Factsheet," Pub. No. CSS01-06, 2011.

efficient energy equation on its head, squandering 10 to 15 units of energy inputs to achieve just one unit of energy output in food (see Figure 6.2).

It makes one think about what one eats. Perhaps returning to a traditional mixed-farming practice that combines grains, vegetables, and a bit of meat production might make more common sense. As Tudge argues, the diverse cuisines of the world have evolved in sync with such practices — plenty of vegetables, nót much meat, and a mix of grains. Certainly such a diet would significantly reduce carbon emissions and water shortages, especially if meat consumption was sharply cut. Beef, for example, requires an estimated 100,000 liters of water to produce one kilogram of meat (about 26,500 gallons for two pounds).

So it seems there are a lot of downsides to the so-called productivity of the industrial food system that delivers our cheap food supply. Any thoughtful reflection on the conundrum must pay attention to the provocative question of ecological economist Hazel Henderson. Commenting on the oft-repeated appeal to increase economic efficiency and productivity, a common refrain of economists and politicians, she argues that the question that must be asked is: Productivity for whom and for what? One might additionally ask: And at what cost?

Climate Change

Climate change is the other major challenge to our long-term food security as fertile land dries up at an alarming rate. China, Australia, South America, and the United States, which together contribute two-thirds of the world's agricultural production, experienced unprecedented drought conditions through 2009. In some areas, the drought continues. For example, northern China in 2010 experienced its worst drought in 50 years, and conditions had become dire, threatening over half the wheat crops in eight provinces. From 2004 to 2010, Australia had an unrelenting drought — the worst on record in 117 years. La Nina–fed rains came in 2010 but pockets of drought remain, and 41 percent of the country's agriculture is threatened due to dried-up rivers, toxic lakes, and abandoned farms. In California, thousands of acres of row crops have been fallowed. Argentina, the world's fourth-largest wheat exporter, was in a state of emergency in 2009 as the worst drought in half a century turned fertile land into dust. The country halted all exports for the first time when yield for 2009 dropped 50 percent.

Decreasing yields due to drought are being exacerbated by two other factors — water shortages and the rise in temperatures. Agriculture is the largest consumer of fresh water, with approximately 70 percent of all freshwater withdrawals going to irrigated agriculture, which today covers 275 million hectares (about 20 percent of cultivated land) and accounts for 40 percent of global food production, according to the World Water Assessment Programme's *Water in a Changing World* report. Renewable sources of water for irrigation, such as glacier-fed rivers, are now at severe risk due to climate change. Gigantic aquifers such as the 450,000-square-kilometre Ogalla aquifer, which underlies eight midwestern US states, are being depleted more rapidly than they can be replenished, despite stringent conservation efforts.

When crops are exposed to high temperatures, crop development slows. In the United States, a study by W. Schlenker and M.J. Roberts suggests that a 1.2°C increase from the current mean (which is what the Intergovernmental Panel on Climate Change predicts will occur over the next three decades) would cause yield decreases of 4 percent in corn, 6.7 percent in wheat, 12 percent in rice and 5.7 percent in cotton.

Weed, disease, and pest pressures will likely also increase. Pests that thrive in warm weather will gain a foothold in regions previously too cool to support their growth, and increased carbon dioxide levels will likely benefit weeds more than food crops. Monoculture crop systems, which make up the bulk of US agriculture, will be particularly at risk from increases in weed and pest pressures, as well as changing microclimates. Unlike polyculture systems, where a diversity of crop types are planted in close proximity, thus ensuring some protection against devastation from pests or weather, monocultures are highly vulnerable systems that can be wiped out entirely from a single pest, blight, or weather event.

Navigating Transition to a Resilient Food System

So from whither will come our food? The short and rather oblique answer is that it depends on where you live; there is no global answer. However, no matter where we live, we have a common challenge: how can we radically shorten the food supply chain, decrease fossil-fuel dependency, conserve water, and reduce the carbon footprint of our current food system?

If we want to consciously create local and regional markets that pay fair prices for sustainably grown food, we must coordinate this with rebuilding the local and regional infrastructure — processing, warehousing, labor supply, investment, and local credit sources being prime examples (Figure 6.3). These elements existed in most localities 50 years ago but have been incrementally hollowed out by oil-greased production systems and long supply lines designed to compete for market share in the global marketplace.

Accomplishing such a transformation is anything but simple and has many parts. In the following sections we consider three pathways we could take to transform our food system. Each reclaims the commons in new and creative ways, and each forges effective partnerships and alliances that manifest the social-solidarity economy and economic democracy in action.

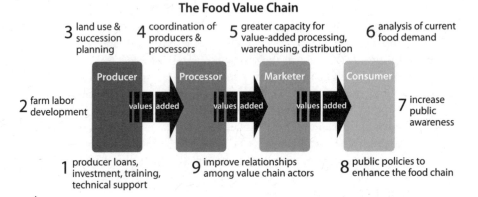

Fig. 6.3: *Hollowed out by globalization, local and regional infrastructure needs to be rebuilt if we are to secure a resilient food system. It is a puzzle with many pieces and an appetite for a ton of cooperation between diverse actors.*

Seikatsu: "Living People" Transforming their Relationship to Food and Each Other

"Seikatsu" means "living people." The significance of this for members of Japan's Seikatsu Consumer Co-operative is a down-to-earth story of transformation in process. The cooperative's humble beginnings involved women sitting together at kitchen tables talking about food. Some disturbing trends in their region bothered them — an increase in imported foods, the consistent loss of farmland to development, and the accelerating migration of farmers to the cities. They were also worried about the quality and safety of their food, a concern closer to their kitchens that was deeply rooted in the privation so many suffered in the post-war years. Hunger from the period marked the consciousness of a broad swath of the population. It was from this fertile ground that cooperatives grew, aided by the introduction of legislation in 1948 and the rapid formation of the Japanese Consumer Cooperative Union in 1951.

In 1965, a group of women approached a local farm family with an idea to address the issues of concern to them. The essence of their proposal was that the farmer would provide their families with fresh milk, fresh fruits, and vegetables, and the families would guarantee to pay a negotiated fair price. The farmer agreed so long as they organized a large enough number of people willing to commit to purchasing the farm's production. A contract was drawn and the *teikei* concept was born. Translated literally, *teikei* means "partnership," but philosophically it means "food with the farmer's face on it." Twenty years later, the *teikei* idea migrated to the United States, inspiring the first community-supported farm at Indian Line Farm (see the "Who Will Grow Our Food?" section in Massachusetts).

The heart and root of the Seikatsu movement is a collective purchasing model that seeks to make the co-op itself a "living instrument" for social and ecological change. The basic building block of Seikatsu is the *Han* ("small group"), which in local areas collectively plans and purchases food. The *Han* was not a new type of group. They were first used in 1956 as an organizing tool for member participation by the Tsuruoka Co-op in the northeast of Honshu, Japan's largest island. They became a key strategy for distributing products within the burgeoning co-op movement and strengthening relations between members, both of which were important to the creation of a federated system for coordination across larger geographic areas. What emerged as an ideal *Han* consisted of seven to ten members, each representing a household that would participate on a voluntary basis. Today there are about 11 million members of *Hans* throughout Japan, most of them belonging to co-ops associated with the Japanese Consumer Cooperative Union.

Underpinning the *Han* concept within Seikatsu is a countercultural perspective on human time and how it can be used creatively to strengthen human connection with each other and with the environment. *Han* members consider time in relation to three forms of work: employed work, work for others (care and social support), and work for the collective good. For example, Seikatsu Club members view the time and energy required to shop in corporate supermarkets as a waste of time, better invested in realizing their goals of safe food, healthy farmland and farmers, and living more sustainably. Thus, through Seikatsu practice, cooperation has become incarnated as a "living instrument."

Founded with the aim of acquiring safe food at a reasonable price, the Seikatsu *Hans* concretely express their values by specifying strict standards for materials, production processes, packing materials, and environmental practices, which are then negotiated with producers. The resulting agreements are the basis for the pre-order collective purchase system, which in turn enables a well-planned production and supply system. The purchase of safe food at reasonable prices, the minimization of waste of natural resources, and the reduction of environmental impacts are among the generative results. More than 350,000 members now operate through thousands of *Han* groups, aggregating their purchase plans within one or another of the 32 Seikatsu Consumer Cooperatives (SCC). These in turn are affiliated nationally into the Seikatsu Union Club (SUC).

The SUC has adopted the term "consumer materials" to describe the products they purchase. The language is indicative of the principles they operate under. Members see themselves as employing their collective purchasing power to secure goods for their "use value," not as "commercial goods." Every month the SUC's Consumption Committee meets to determine the items to be purchased collectively based on the demands and views of the members. Members participate in extensive testing of new consumer materials. Taste, packaging, and price preference are determined through member engagement, combined with market research to design draft specifications. These are then discussed with producers. A critical appraisal of the production process reviews what can be done; packaging, content, volumes, and price are among the key focus of such discussions.

Seikatsu gains efficiencies by limiting the number of regular items provided to 1,600 annually. (This is in contrast to the 9,000 items carried by the 600 other consumer co-ops in Japan, with 22 million members — and to the much larger number of products and brands in modern mega-supermarkets.) Keeping the system simple significantly reduces inventory costs, thus creating one source of savings that allows the co-op to increase the price to the farmer while keeping prices to the consumer reasonable. By concentrating on a narrower range of high-quality products, producers and processors also gain important efficiencies.

Further efficiencies are gained through adherence to some basic principles.

- Purchasing is viewed as an ethical responsibility. Seikatsu members regard mass production, consumption, and disposal as a negative, disconnecting consumption from ethics. By developing "consumer materials" for basic needs, they try at every stage to solve problems of health, environment, and safety.
- The well-planned production of a more limited selection of high-quality foods enables efficient shipment, thereby reducing unit costs for transportation.
- Goods are delivered directly to either the *Han* or the individual though member-run pickup depots. Delivery eliminates the financial risks of high retail overheads, huge inventories, and the waste they generate.
- The SUC has developed a standard of eight types of returnable bottles for a wide range of food products. This has helped reduce the price of this type of packaging and raises the efficiency of collection, sorting, and washing. Seikatsu has organized a Bottle Re-use Council, which in 2007 estimated its system was reducing carbon emissions by 2,121 tons a year.

To ensure its specifications are met, the SUC has established its own independent control and auditing system. Members and producers set the standards together through sector committees for agriculture, fishery, livestock, processed food, packaging materials, etc. Between 2007 and 2010, 6,500 people participated in 790 unannounced spot inspections. This participatory approach to certification is much less bureaucratic and much less costly than the third-party audits most certification systems require. Moreover, the learning and relationship-building between members and producers is much more profound, a benefit the annual audit by an outside consultant or accountancy firm cannot achieve.

The relationship between the purchasers and the producers of food extends to the planned participation of consumers as a source of labor supply. Because the average age of a Japanese farmer is 67, planting and harvesting demands can limit their capacity to assure the supply of healthy, nutritious food. Organizing labor in solidarity with farmers began in 1995; its initial success was to secure stable production of tomatoes for organic juice for Seikatsu members.

In another example of solidarity, Seikatsu organized member capital, which, along with farmer investment, enabled the start-up of three milk-processing plants to supply urban consumers. One hundred producers owning 5,000 cows are now co-producing a product with a high level of raw milk, an alternative to the ultra-high-temperature (UHT) sterilized milk dominant on the Japanese market.

By 2010 the annual turnover based on the purchasing *Hans* was US$1.1 billion. Accumulated equity was close to $1 billion due mainly to each member voluntarily paying $11 per month until he or she has contributed $3,500. There is also a $60 membership fee for the local SCC and another $60 for the SUC. This equity underpins the financial stability of the system. It is indicative of the importance placed on members being co-responsible for the health of the system, a fundamental cornerstone of the "Living People" model that Seikatsu represents. By investing time and money in various parts of a mutually supportive relationship with producers, they realize a key value of their movement: their democratic autonomy as members.

Today, the SUC is not only implementing a "values added" strategy aimed at transforming the food system but has also taken up recycling, green energy development, and social services.

- SCC members have been encouraged to lobby their municipally owned utility to allocate 5 percent of the monthly utility bill to the Hakkaido Green Fund. These funds have been used to capitalize five "citizens wind turbines" — and the SCC is seeking to expand this model.

- To address the challenge of being the oldest population in the western world, SCCs are establishing day service centers and special nursing homes. About 10,000 people are now involved in providing home or institutional care services for the aged through 448 organizations. Home care, another feature of the evolving system, provided over 1.4 million hours of volunteer service. Since the start of the nursing care insurance system in Japan, these services have expanded and are now generating $87.4 million per year. Parallel efforts targeting the needs of people with disabilities, infants, children, and mothers raising children are also evolving.
- Worker collectives are another Seiktasu manifestation of the innovation and drive for economic democracy. In 2006 there were 582 democratically owned and run businesses with 17,000 worker-owners operating across a wide range of sectors and generating $126,300,000.
- Another fundamental principle of Seikatsu is the concept of citizens advancing their values by shaping the political discourse. Beyond ensuring high ethical and environmental standards in their own purchasing, they have actively campaigned to outlaw synthetic detergents and to foster a "genetically modified free" food movement in Japan. This civic participation has evolved further through the establishment of independent local political parties to press Seikatsu goals. By 2006 there were 120 network parties with about 10,000 members, who had succeeded in electing 141 local councillors.

It is little wonder that the Seikatsu movment received the honorary Right Livelihood Award in 1989. Considered to be the "alternative Nobel Prize," the award was given to the "housewives' movement" for its success in generating a form of "alternative economic activity against industrial society's prioritization of efficiency." The prize commended the movement for its continuing interest in human health and the environment through its production of essential materials for living.

"Living People" indeed.

Transition Factors: Transforming the Value Chain

Rooted in local communities, the Seikatsu movement builds from a base of intentional small groups with concrete objectives and mobilizes around a clear function (collective purchasing), thus embedding its values in actions grounded in meeting everyday needs. The evolution of the Seikatsu Club has secured a federated, multifunctional, democratic, profoundly local, but strategically linked, national movement for transformative change that operates through horizontal networks and vertical production chains as appropriate. Every stage of the food value chain is subject to member reviews, principled evaluation, constant scrutiny, and regular adjustment. In this way members leverage their purchasing power to transform the food system and the production and distribution of other essential goods and services, supported by multi–tiered capacity to aggregate functions where effective.

The financial health of the movement is impressive. It is fed by the efficiencies gained through a strategic approach to product specification, principled negotiation with producers, guaranteed fair prices (which stabilize supply chains), and rationalized distribution directly to end-users. Producers and consumers share in the benefits of reduced costs through procedures that require constant dialogue to understand each other's position.

The relationship between ethical consumption and production is profound, standing in stark contrast to the mass merchandizing and mindless consumption perhaps most vividly exemplified by the just-in-time global supply chain of Walmart. Founded on getting the lowest price possible to the individual consumer, Walmart largely succeeds, but with no heed to the consequences for those who live along the chain. In contrast, SCC members view consumption as a social rather than an individual activity, hence their reliance on the *Han*, neighborhood-level organizing, and the investment of both financial and sweat equity.

Seikatsu is also a profound expression of the solidarity economy at work, particularly the cooperation and complementary exchange mechanisms forged between civil society and the private sector. The SUC is a comprehensive counterpoint to the so-called free market, where atomization, isolation, and competition among people predominate.

An outstanding feature of the Seikatsu movement is its democratic autonomy. Its grassroots democratic base, along with its financial self-sufficiency, protects it from being co-opted or manipulated by the state, and also enhances its capacity to advocate credibly its views and advance its goals. Seikatsu incarnates what Francis Moore Lappe argued, in *Democracy's Edge*, is central to transforming the food system: the practice of "living democracy." The voting booth is insufficient; we must live democracy through our daily choices of what we buy and how we live.

Forging such a path is profoundly countercultural. Consumers who depend on others, who buy services they have had no part in shaping, who slavishly choose between high-cost brands or cheap no-name brands, who mindlessly chatter about material desires, achieved or not, stand in contrast to people who cooperatively shape their own choices, ethically meet their needs, honor the dignity of all life, manage their exchanges with consciousness and an eye to their transformative potential, and reclaim their deep cultural inheritance as gifted human beings capable of living actively, expressively, meaningfully — these are the characteristics of a living democracy. Katsumi Yokota, a founder of Seikatsu, has argued that this cooperative yet personally mediated change in lifestyle is what democratic transition entails.

Seikatsu — Living People. Seikatsu Club — a living instrument to shape social and ecological change. Living Democracy — conscious citizens choosing to act in favour of transformation.

All are incarnated in the Seikatsu experiment, an inspiring illustration of the possibilities of local innovation that is strategically federated into a powerful agent for profound change. "Living people" consume in a manner that aggressively and consciously considers the existence of planetary life, integrates ethical considerations into every aspect of their decision making, and, in so doing, points us toward practical transitional pathways.

Resilience Reflections

The Seikatsu system walks the talk; it addresses the resilience imperative in profound ways. The entire system incarnates a strategy to enhance social, economic, and environmental *diversity*. The *Han* groups, whose democratic decisions are aggregated at strategic points to enhance economic, social, and environmental benefits are a sterling example of *social capital* and *modularity* in play. Tight but flexible *feedback loops* are intricately built into the overall system of *overlapping governance* and communication functions, from the small *Han* groups to the federated Seikatsu Club. The result is that members, producers, and partners are fed a constant stream of data on the results being achieved. This tracking of results feeds ongoing *learning and innovation*, leading to new ways of reducing the *ecological impact* of food systems.

There are, however, warning signs with respect to the intergenerational resilience of the Seikatsu model, as pointed out by John Restakis in *Humanizing the Economy*:

> The changing nature of Japanese society is having an impact on Han and the involvement of members in the work of the co-ops. Japan's consumer co-ops are contending with aging memberships and a base of volunteers that grew up in a very different age. The sense of communal purpose is waning in Japan. Young people are not joining the co-ops. The changing role of women means that the traditional housewives that stayed at home and were the backbone of Seikatsu Club are now entering the labour market and have less time for co-op activities in

the neighborhood and within the household. As with other consumer cultures, these factors have contributed to a growing individualization within the membership of Seikatsu Club as well as the other consumer co-ops. Communal distribution of food has declined sharply and has been replaced with home delivery.

Such trends are worrisome when one considers the intersection of aging demographics, changing cultural patterns, and the demands of time and energy on which the Seikatsu model was built, particularly the time and energy of women. Whether a new generation is positioned, economically and culturally, to rediscover the "values added" of collective action remains to be seen. Perhaps the depth of the challenges we face with respect to securing our food supply in the decades ahead will spark a consciousness among younger people of the wisdom of reclaiming the heritage of "Living People" invented by their forebears.

Community Supported Agriculture (CSA)

Community supported agriculture (CSA) migrated to North America via the concept of *teikei*, which arose from the Seikatsu movement.

A CSA in North America typically involves one or more farmers directly producing for local people, who become CSA members. The consumers advance the farmer cash well before the next growing season. This secures them fresh produce on a weekly basis during the following season. It can also involve meat products. The cash flow of the farmer is improved by this provision of non-interest-bearing working capital, and the members guarantee the farmer a market. Customers stipulate varying conditions related to the way food is grown, but they tend toward organic production. Fair price is usually an important consideration. More and more CSA members are connecting the dots between ethical consumption, fair price, local food, and long-term food security (see Figure 6.4).

One of the challenges for farmers establishing and running CSAs is that it appears they have to take on most of the responsibility for marketing, promotion, and servicing of CSA members. Experiments are underway to adapt this basic CSA model.

An urban pilot set up in 2009 in Edmonton, Alberta, illustrates an equitable means of co-production. A coalition of local groups contracted eight somewhat skeptical farmers, who were selected to secure a diverse but complementary line of fresh produce. Rather than having the farmers organize the membership, the local group marketed the pilot, and in 10 days 500 potential members came forward. Of these, 290 were selected for the service

Community Shared Agriculture (CSA)

Fig. 6.4: *CSA members pay a fee to the farmer at the end of a season. In return the farmer contracts to produce fresh food for them next season. This creates a local market that farmers can depend on, with a higher margin. The more food items and consumers the market includes, the greater is local/regional food security.*

based on geographic proximity — a matter of some importance given the household distribution system they were designing. Delivery routes needed to be efficient and to minimize costs. The pilot was a significant success. The farmers' evaluation was that this was a quality market which yielded fair prices and significant efficiencies over selling through farm gate or farmers market outlets. Consumer members receiving the produce evaluated the fresh food and the service highly.

Based on the pilot, a feasibility analysis indicated that this basic system could be self-sufficient at a membership level of 1,000 people. It also showed that having members work closely with producers to maximize complementarity and diverse products was an important next step. By optimizing efficiencies through a greater degree of product specialization and coordination among individual farmers, more effective production and marketing could be possible. As well, the successful pilot showed the potential for servicing this emerging market with a broader range of products, including meats and locally processed food products.

Who Will Grow Our Food? The Problem of Succession

Farmers in many OECD countries are getting old; in Canada the average age is 52. In Japan it is a startling 66. Many are asset rich but cash poor. Most have few options to secure their retirement except by selling their farms. Sometimes this can be arranged within a family, but often it cannot. Land is expensive, and producing food does not pay the bills. When a farm does sell, the land often is no longer farmed; gentrification of farmland into country estates or new subdivisions is common, at least in North America. Preventing this loss is crucial to any effort to increase long-term local and regional food security.

Two strategic questions frame our exploration.

- How can we transfer increasingly valuable land in a manner that is affordable for a new generation of farmers, while ensuring aging farmers are assured a fair and respectful retirement?
- How do we ensure that the economic, social, and ecological value of the land is transferred into a tenure that carries with it the responsibility to contribute to the public good and the food security of local and regional populations?

Fundamental to addressing this knotty issue is the problem of financing such a transaction. The question of how to structure ownership of the land to maximize producer and community interest in long-term food security is another tricky part of the equation, but finding a workable answer is vital if we are to strengthen the resilience of local and regional food systems.

Restoration: From Old Garbage to New Farmers

In 1983, the flood plain of the Winooski River, a mile and a half from the center of Vermont's largest city, Burlington, was a mess. Garbage four feet thick, junked cars strewn across the landscape, seepage problems from the adjacent sewage plant — not exactly a setting that triggers visions of organic farming. Nevertheless, the land was reclaimed to produce local food, and just two decades later, in 2007, a mere 120 acres were producing more than 1 million pounds of high-quality produce and generating over $1 million in annual sales. Stewarded and managed by the Intervale Center, a nonprofit organization that has been strengthening community food systems since 1988, a once-desolate 350-acre site has been transformed into a local ecological treasure and a vital agricultural resource.

Today the Intervale Center leases over 140 acres to farmers enrolled in its Farms Program to build a local supply of sustainably produced food and help new farmers get started in the business of farming. Founded in 1990, the Farms Program leases land, equipment, greenhouses, irrigation, and storage facilities to small independent farms. Each year, these farms — many of which are linked to community-supported agriculture (CSA) and other direct markets — create 60 seasonal jobs.

This system creates significant benefits for young farmers. First, not having to buy land is a huge capital savings. Creative design of leases lowers the financial risk considerably. Similarly, structuring cooperative arrangements

Fig. 6.5: *Sustaining farms: Since 1990, the Intervale Center's Farms Program has helped nearly 50 farms get their start in the Intervale. These independent, organic farms grow and sell healthy, delicious food to the greater Burlington community.* Photo courtesy of the Intervale Center.

to share buildings, equipment, and irrigation reduces capital costs and increases the cost efficiencies. Several other agricultural development programs, including Success on Farms and the Intervale Food Hub, support local market development, business planning, and technical support services for new farmers. Together, these factors create a reasonable and realistic gateway for younger people to grow food as a viable livelihood.

Providing a diverse food supply is a key objective of the Farms Program, which the Intervale Center achieves by carefully selecting lessees based on their individual interests and by studying local and regional niche markets, and the capacity of the land.

The Intervale Center has several revenue-generating enterprises that produce about 60 percent of its $1.3 million in annual revenue, the balance coming from grants and community fundraising. Other revenue generation streams include the various leasing arrangements with Intervale farmers, fees for technical services, contracted services related to education and training, and rentals of Intervale facilities.

Its revenues were higher by $800,000 in 2008, when it still operated its first and largest enterprise, one that was key to the Intervale transformation from garbage dump to productive farming land: Intervale Compost.

This break-even operation, the largest composting service in Vermont, sold its products, packaged and in bulk, to individuals for household use, landscapers, farmers, and the city. Quite apart from its contribution to the local economy and soil-fertility enhancement, this social enterprise diverted over 30,000 tons annually from landfill sites and employed a number of marginalized people. In 2010 it was sold to Chittenden Solid Waste District and has become integrated into a state-of-the-art facility in Williston, Vermont.

Solidarity and Succession: Securing Local Food

What the Intervale example does not answer is the question of how to transfer land in an equitable and financially viable way from a farmer nearing retirement to an Intervale-type community land trust.

When one does an internet search for land trusts dedicated to preserving land for agricultural purposes, scattered examples turn up. In North America, groups or individuals often use the legal device of conservation easement to prevent farmland being sold off to developers. However, while protection is an important first step, it does not mean the land will be productively farmed. British Columbia, Canada's westernmost province, passed a law to protect farmland in 1973, but in the 2000s more and more people with a lot of money are buying these farms and turning them into rural estates. The land may be preserved, but the farm is no longer producing food.

Most farmers have a deep attachment to the land and a deep desire to see their life's work of husbanding that land sustained into the future. Selling off their homestead for cash to a developer or to the wealthy may be tempting in the absence of other options, but maximizing profit is hardly the driver of people who have committed their lives to farming. Indeed, the increasingly prevalent pattern of farmers taking jobs off the land in order to support the farm suggests the opposite motivation. Farmers want to farm but cannot sustain themselves. Herein lies part of the transition challenge: we as consumers have come to expect cheap food, yet the farmers we need to feed us in the future cannot afford to put their full efforts into doing so. Having invested for years, aging farmers reaching the end of their worklife have assets, but remain cash poor. And if the problem of retirement is not solved, the likelihood is that they will sell their land and assets to someone with lots of money and no intention to farm. As many farmers lament, you have to be either rich or crazy to buy a farm these days.

Indian Line Farm in Great Barrington, Massachussets, provides an example of one method of solving this problem. A creative series of transactions reveal several important pieces of the puzzle necessary to address the challenge.

First, the Indian Line farm, a small 22-acre operation, was one of the first CSA farms in the United States. Thus there were already a number of conscious consumers from the local area, members of the CSA, who had a relationship with the farmer putting food on their tables. In short, there was existing social capital.

Second, the CSA members' relationship to the farm fed a desire to preserve it in perpetuity. They were willing to donate funds and tell other people about the opportunity to preserve the farm. CSA member donations to a regional conservation land trust kicked off a broader campaign that successfully raised enough cash to secure the means to pay out the farmer's heirs following his death and to buy a conservation easement, the function of which was to place a covenant on the land that permanently protected its use as farmland. In this case, the easement also required that particular ecological values on part of the property be maintained and, indeed, enhanced. (Typically, conservation trusts get their money from a combination of public fundraising, foundations, and, at times, state or federal government agencies.)

Third, the title of the land was placed under a separate community land trust. With technical assistance from the EF Schumacher Society, a long-term (99-year) lease document was devised that required any leaseholder to use ecologically sound farming methods and sell to local markets. All the core values of the various CSA partners were intertwined into a covenant that was designed to endure.

Fig. 6.6: *Indian Line Farm was the first CSA farm in the USA. Without an alternative land tenure system, local markets, and creative financing, this little girl's family would likely not have been able to farm; indeed, it is unlikely the farm would still exist.* Source: Jason Houston.

Fourth, the next-generation farmer secured financing to purchase the house, barn, outbuildings, and whatever equipment was deemed useful. This completed the payment to the farmer's heirs. The lease allowed the new farmer to earn equity on any improvements made to the farm during his or her tenure, thus providing a limited but important incentive for investment. The community land trust retained an option to purchase the buildings and improvements back, and to resell them at their replacement cost to another farmer. Thus, long-term affordability is firmly established.

Fifth, the community land trust recovered its transaction costs through the capitalization of the deal. Over the longer term, the lease was structured to deliver a modest but ongoing management fee as well.

Transition Factors Related to Succession

Addressing the critical connections between ecology, economy, and community, CSAs, conservation easements, and community land trust projects are restoring and protecting habitat, preserving agricultural land, and making intensive organic farming viable for local and regional markets. The Indian Line Farm example, with the participation of two land trusts, shows a way for local consumers to partner with a new-generation farmer to successfully finance the purchase of the land, the buildings, and the farm equipment. If the farmer had still been alive she would have had enough to retire with dignity. As it was, her heirs were able to be paid out fairly. The new farming family had access to land on a long-term lease that gave them the opportunity and obligation to grow food organically and practice wise stewardship. The CSA members secured an important part of their annual food supply.

Commodity-based producers and the agro-food industry often discount the contributions of small farmers, but their small-scale, more labor-intensive style of farming may be of critical importance to rebuilding local food systems. A 2001 study of 200 sustainable agriculture projects in 52 countries calculated that "nine million farmers were using sustainable practices on about 29 million hectares. More than 98 percent of these small farms emerged in the last decade." Jules Pretty, the British agronomist who directed the study, found that the increase in yield per hectare of production ranged between 46 and 150 percent.

However, this kind of transformation does not happen by itself — at least not in settings where industrialized agriculture is dominant. The transition is challenging, and four elements stand out in both the Intervale and Indian Line Farm cases as critical enabling factors:

- A capable, value-driven development agent
- An alternative land-tenure option

- Accessible low-cost finance
- A capacity to bring together producers, consumers, capable community organizations, alternative land tenures, and local businesses in a circle of mutual interest and solidarity

In both cases, community land trusts were the key development agents. They acquired sufficient capacity to identify the opportunity, raise the capital, put together a deal, structure the covenants, work out the business model, recruit the younger farmer(s), and provide the basic administrative supports required to sustain the effort to finalize the deal. Supplementing these factors was the availability of technical assistance and expert guidance from committed professionals able to frame the legal, organizational, and sector-specific advice necessary to make the local development system work. Without fitting these jigsaw pieces together creatively, it is hard to see how the new generation of farmers could have put the elements together in a way that secured a livelihood focused on feeding local people.

Resilience Reflections

In a modern farming context, where an oil-soaked monoculture feeding global supply chains is the norm, the signposts emanating from the cases presented here appear radical. The *diversifying* of production, the localizing of markets, the covenants built into the ownership models, the more direct relationship to consumers (*social capital*), and the *ecologically* based agricultural practices run directly counter to the industrialized model of agriculture.

What these pioneering experiments show is that the centralized and highly interdependent global food system could be steadily replaced by a much more *modularized* system of production serving local and regional markets. The consumers' direct link to the production of food and even the financing of food production provides a level of relationship that *tightens the feedback loops* between all the actors in what has been transformed into a much shorter supply chain.

Underlying the resilience gains in both Intervale and Indian Line Farm is the duplex ownership tenure, without which the transition from garbage to organics and from old to young would have been very difficult, if not impossible, to achieve. The mix of *common and private property rights*, combined with creative and collaborative financing methods, was central to making the transition.

Restoring Salmon: Restoring the Commons in Alaska

Before Alaska became a state, the US federal government managed the region's salmon and was making a mess of it. Harvest levels in 1938 were close to 120 million fish. Twenty years later the harvest had declined to 20 million. This precipitous erosion of a resource so important to the coastal communities of Alaska became a key issue in the movement for statehood. According to D.F. Amend, Alaskans felt that gaining control of the mismanaged fisheries would allow them a far greater degree of regional self-governance.

But the decline continued even after Alaska became a state. Different harvesting methods, habitat pressures, too many boats chasing fewer fish, conflicts, and inequities between different gear types made managing fisheries exceedingly complex. In 1972 the harvest fell even lower. The ongoing crisis finally led to five significant decisions to:

- Limit the entry of new fishing vessels to the fleet
- Invest in rebuilding the wild stock
- Initiate construction of salmon hatcheries
- Improve the stock enhancement program
- Design an approach for what was called "ocean ranching"

Ocean ranching involves the release and recapture of fish from hatcheries into ocean waters (see Figure 6.7). Eggs are stripped from the broodstock and reared for a time in a hatchery located near the mouth of a river. Once the offspring are large enough, they are put in net pens located somewhere offshore in an area that avoids the migration of wild stocks. Three or four weeks in the net pens is enough time for nature's magic to imprint the young salmon with a personal homing beacon that will guarantee the survivors return to the precise point they were released. Once they do they are easy pickings. No chasing fish around — just wait and scoop them up. The question is: who will benefit?

Private ocean ranching was already being piloted in Oregon. Weyerhaeuser, a major multinational forest company, bought out the first Oregon project in the early 1970s and other states were beginning to consider replicating the private model.

In Alaska, the fight about who should benefit was first focused not on ocean ranching, but on who should own the hatcheries. Private investors argued that private businesses should do the job, as they were more efficient than government. The fishers disagreed. Knowing the pivotal role hatcheries played in ocean ranching, they feared a takeover by large multinationals and fought back. As far as the fishers were concerned, the commons was not for sale. Privatization was not a solution. They argued that hatcheries should be owned by nonprofit corporations governed by all stakeholders in the resource. The state government listened, at least in part, and brought all of the key stakeholders together to design and agree on a strategic action plan. Ocean ranching was a main component.

Once this battle was won, however, it turned out that fishers had little input. The government decided it should run the hatchery program, and the results were a disaster; salmon runs declined to 4 million fish. Fishers blamed poor hatchery site selection and mistakes in the choice of salmon species to be reared at those sites. All the different groups practicing different fishing methods (known as "gear groups") shared this opinion and launched another lobby.

Typical Ocean Ranching Scenario

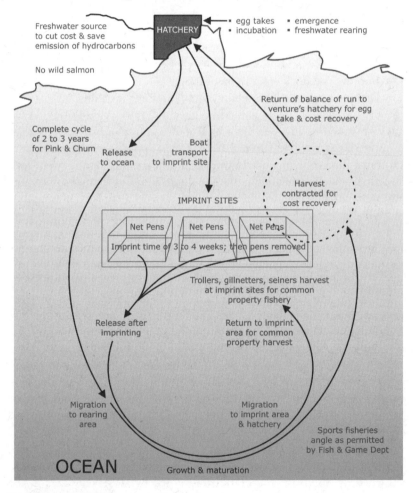

Fig. 6.7: *Ocean ranching.*

This time the fishers prevailed, and in 1976 the Regional Aquaculture Associations were established. Fishers in each of the five designated regions automatically became members of the relevant regional association. The associations are designed to provide direct economic and social benefits and management control to the fishers and other stakeholders of the local communities in each region. They were also designed to be financially self-sustaining. What has emerged is a collaborative and mutually beneficial multi-stakeholder partnership between the state and a carefully defined cross-section of community and local business stakeholders.

From a resilience perspective, the results have been transformative: 200 million salmon were being harvested by the late 1990s, 80 million more than in the 1930s. Through careful management of ecological risks (e.g., mixing wild stock and ranched stock), this number is made up of 65 percent wild salmon and a significant 35 percent of ocean-ranched stock. Moreover, over 70 percent of the harvest is designated common property.

Co-Managing the Commons

The Alaskans had one central goal: to increase the number of salmon available as a common property resource for fishers and common property users. The multi-stakeholder prescription for mutual and regional governance reflects this goal, though variation is possible between regions.

In the Northern Southeast Regional Aquaculture Association (NSRAA), for example, each of the gear types (troll, gill-net, and purse seine) elects five members. Ten other board members are appointed from this core body, representing aboriginal organizations, municipalities, sports fisheries, processors, conservationists, subsistence fishers, and the public at large (two members). This group of 25 elects an executive board of eight.

The NSRAA owns and operates the hatcheries in its region. But, as indicated earlier, ocean ranching involves a lot more than just the hatcheries. Associations were given significant planning responsibilities, including the design of a long-range management plan to enhance and manage salmon in a way that would create sustainable economic benefits for fishers and other users. The target of the NSRAA plan — to have 85 percent of the fish produced in their region available for harvesting as a common property resource — is being achieved. Traditional conflicts over how many fish are allocated to each group of users, especially the gear types, have been radically reduced by applying innovative management techniques designed and agreed to by the fishers themselves.

Making all of this work requires money. The cost to plan, construct, and operate hatcheries is high. The professional expertise and management to undertake the planning, site the release points, determine allocations, and manage nonprofit harvests is an ongoing operating expense. Within a very short time after the regional associations were established, it became apparent that financing was going to be a problem. Conventional banks were not interested in financing a new and untested business.

The first problem was collecting capital to build the hatchery and related infrastructure, not a simple matter in remote coastal sites. The initial solution was to set up a State Fisheries Enhancement Loan Fund to get low-interest credit to the associations. Six- to ten-year holidays for payment of interest and principal were designed into the loans. Given the long lead time before revenue could be expected, this was a crucial feature; without patient capital, nothing would have happened.

However, by 1980 it was apparent that low-cost debt financing was not going to be enough to cover development and operating costs. The enabling legislation had provided for voluntary self-taxation of fishers, but this was not proving to be a steady or sufficient source of revenue. Viability demanded a reliable long-term source of equity and operating capital.

The solution the fishers devised was unprecedented: they demanded the state government put a mandatory tax on all licensed fishers. The regulations that were adopted required fishers to place a mandatory tax upon themselves. They had the choice of 2 or 3 percent tax on the value of the salmon they landed, and the rate chosen had to be approved by a majority of the permit holders within the region. Fish buyers collect the tax and send the proceeds to the government, which in turn disperses it back to the association for the region in which the fish were caught.

The other key revenue flow comes from allocating a portion of salmon for the nonprofit body. The original legislation let associations harvest the early returns of salmon for broodstock and for sale, the proceeds of which go directly to the association to offset operating costs.

The state government's responsive legislative and financial role has been fundamental to launching the process. Also important, it retains control of issuing permits for the transportation of fish and is responsible for measures to protect the genetic integrity of the wild stock. Without question, these regulations have at times been a source of friction, but the consensus is that the overall effect is positive. Indeed, Pete Esquiro, manager of the Northern Southeast Regional Aquaculture Association since its inception, has suggested that there were times when having the state filling this regulatory role prevented people from damaging their own interests.

The results achieved by the NSRAA are among the most impressive of the five regional associations.

- By 1980, its $5 million in original capital was paid off.

- The target of 70 percent of the fish being harvested as a common property resource has been regularly exceeded, averaging between 80 percent and 85 percent.
- Annual operating costs and some capital improvements are being covered by association cost-recovery harvests (10 percent of the total annual return) and enhancement tax revenues. Five percent of the total return is used for broodstock.
- As of 2000 the association had a $1.5-million capital reserve set aside.
- NSRAA has 23 full-time employees and a further 20 to 30 seasonal and part-time employees. Positions include biologists, fish culturalists, maintenance engineers, hatchery managers, tagging supervisors, and general laborers. There are also administrative, accounting, and shipping positions.
- Of significant importance, the self-imposed tax of $22 million between 1980 and 2000 ensured the equity and working capital needed to produce an increased harvest yield of $122 million.
- The association has developed an organizational culture driven by the goal of meeting the needs of fishers and communities.

In an era when the public's image of Alaska is dominated by Sarah Palin's talk of rugged individualists and their wholesome families living close to the land and far from the reach of big government raiding their purse, the story of restoring salmon and defending the commons is a breath of fresh air. Without solidarity and cooperative cross-sector investment of time, effort, and money the Alaskan fishing commons would likely have continued to decline.

Transition Factors

The political influence of persistent, active citizens and fishers is a central underlying factor in this story. Even before Alaska became a state, citizens' frustration with distant, disconnected, and incompetent management of the resources they depended on for a livelihood was so profound that it became a key issue in the push for statehood. Their involvement continued long after that goal was achieved, leading to the creation of the first action plan, the push for decentralized multi-stakeholder associations in each region, and the self-taxation model that created the equity so necessary to securing the long-term viability of restoration efforts. Perhaps most strategic was the outright rejection, by fishers and many citizens groups, of the private ownership model being applied to ocean ranching. Cooperation and mutuality were fostered by the focus on achieving a public good—the restoration of a common property resource. It is hard to imagine a multinational like Weyerhaeuser arguing for the state to increase its tax load in order to ensure success. Yet private local fishers, rooted and connected to their place, with their livelihoods at stake and their cultural knowledge of the environment to leverage, did just that. Elinor Ostrom would not be surprised.

Equally important was the state's capacity to take leadership, listen, and address financing issues intelligently and flexibly. As well, state officials proved flexible when necessary, adapting rules and regulations to achieve the central goal of restoring the common property resource for community benefit. By delegating ownership and management responsibilities to regional associations, they unleashed the energy and commitment of stakeholders to restore the commons where they lived. By retaining key regulatory functions, they were able to create a framework that ensured the ecological integrity of the wild stocks was maintained and legislation respected.

Resilience Reflections

One of the remarkable achievements of the Alaska story is the level of *innovation, experimentation, and learning* embedded in the process of restoring the salmon within a common property framework. This was not without risks. Environmentalists and professionals of many kinds had real worries about the contamination of wild stocks by ranched salmon, fearing that genetic diversity would be eroded. Indeed, these concerns were shared by the fishers; they were the most stringent critics of state decisions on hatchery siting and species selection in the early days.

Nevertheless, once the centralized state-led approach was dropped in favor of the regional associations, the common interests and knowledge of the state, fishers, and other resource users were able to unite in a *modularized* system of *overlapping governance structures* that facilitated experimentation and shared learning. This collective wisdom and skill meant planning and management could be more effectively tailored to the *ecological and species variation* in each region. Most importantly, siting decisions for hatcheries and imprinting pens were improved, thus minimizing contact between wild stock and ocean-ranched fish. Genetic *diversity* has been protected; wild stocks have thrived, while the *diversity* and overall population of stocks has been radically expanded.

Feedback loops between regional and state actors, and between a *diversity* of stakeholders in each region, have been tightened. In the process, *social capital* has been significantly strengthened. As evidence, one need only note the reduction in conflict between resource users, the radical improvement in resource planning and management, and the exponential increase in self-reliance and socio-economic benefit.

Impacts on the Household Economy: The Hartwick Family

Thus far the pathways identified have saved the Hartwick family $123,392 over 10 years, about $12,400 per year. When it comes to food being produced on a sustainable basis, however, the direct costs to the family will go up, not down. Fair pricing to sustain livelihoods and the environmental criteria to sustain the planet require setting prices to cover these costs, something that is largely absent in the mainstream global food system.

How to calculate such a cost is complex and is not explored here. Nevertheless, given the purpose of exploring the impacts of alternative pathways on the Hartwick family household we offer a modest formulation to calculate an increase in the cost of food.

Consider two pieces of evidence cited in the introduction to this chapter. First, recall the declining percentage of the food dollar captured by farmers and the tiny percentage of our food dollar that gets to the farmer.

> On average, US farmers get back less than 20 cents of every dollar spent on food. Sixty years ago they received almost 40 cents, and as recently as 1981 the figure was still 31 cents on the dollar. The iniquitous implication cannot be ignored by any citizen concerned with basic notions of fair trade, sustainable livelihoods for farmers, or long-term food security. If 10 percent of consumers' disposable income goes for food purchases, and 20 percent of that amount gets to farmers, only 2 percent of a consumer dollar actually ends up with the farmer.

Second, consider how the average percentage of disposable income we spend on food has steadily declined. In the United States today, an average person spends 9.9 percent of disposable income on food; 80 years ago, 25 percent was the share.

Without determining the fair price needed to allow a full-time farmer to earn a reasonable income, and without making adjustments for the costs of transitioning to a low-carbon system of production, let's assume a 50 percent rise in the amount of household disposable income devoted to food. Assuming the Hartwick family is American, they would start spending 14.7 percent of their income on food, up from 9.9 percent. This is only 1.1 percent higher than the average household spends on food in France, and 2.8 percent lower than in South Africa.

Now let us recall the economic circumstances of the Hartwicks. Together they make the net equivalent after taxes of about $30 per hour, about $225 per day. The combined disposable income of the two parents is $62,400. Applying the 9.9 percent US average would suggest an expenditure of

$6,178. At the higher 14.7 percent, the expenditure would rise to $9,173, an increase of $2,995 dollars per year.

Table 6.1 connects the dots we have been plotting since Chapter 3. Even with more disposable income going to food, the cumulative impact of the reforms introduced is impressive. And assuming the Hartwicks had access to some land for growing food, they could choose to translate some of their time savings of 312 hours per year into home-grown production.

A person can grow an impressive amount of food on a small plot. A San Francisco–based urban farmer reclaimed a 4,360-square-foot (one-tenth of an acre) plot of concrete and relatively lifeless soil. Five years later this small urban farm yielded three tons of food, which does not include the crop from several fruit trees that are not yet producing. If the Hartwicks decided to try their hands at intensive urban farming, they would be making money and becoming healthier in the process.

In the last four chapters we have examined innovations in finance, shelter, energy and food. We now turn our attention to shaping the places we live, drawing from place-based strategies that build citizen engagement and multi-sector collaboration in order to address difficult challenges specific to one's own community and region.

Table 6.1 The Hartwick Family: Cumulative 10-Year Savings when Food Prices Increased				
Comparison of JAK Bank and Convention Bank Mortgage Costs	Bank interest charges (8.05%)	JAK fee charges	Savings $	Savings in hours
Last 10 years of 25-year mortgage of $200,000	$91,821	$24,731	$67,090	2,236
Impact of land trust on financing costs (130,000) in last 10 years	$67,530	$17,780	$49,750	1658
Actual capital cost saving of land to the householder	$70,000	$70,000	$ 70,000	2333
Kirklees conservation savings over 10 years			$ 3,642	121
Net savings due to CLT, JAK, and Kirklees model			$123,392	4113
Subtract Increased Food Costs over 10 Years			**-29,950**	
TEN YEAR NET SAVINGS			**$93,442**	**3,115 hrs**

CHAPTER 7

Reweaving Our Economies Close to Home

*People do not live globally. Measured in global scales, people
spend most of their life time at one place. There they work, live and
develop themselves as well as their environment. An economy that
pays attention to these facts, would organise itself more locally and
with the people in the centre of all its processes.*
— Norbert Rost

*The world seems to be looking for the big solution,
which is itself part of the problem, since the most effective
solutions are both local and systemic.*
— Paul Hawken, *Blessed Unrest*

*As soaring energy-induced increases in transport costs swing the
economic pendulum from the global economy back to the local
economy, we suddenly need to become generalists. We have to refocus on
smaller, more local markets that may not be large enough to support the
specialization that the broader global market previously provided.*

— Jeff Rubin,
Why Your World Is About to Become a Whole Lot Smaller

FEW LIVING A MERE 100 YEARS AGO would have imagined the rapidity of
global travel and communication so commonplace today. Patterns of
life unprecedented in human history are seen as the norm. Middle-class
Londoners can catch an Easy Jet flight to Berlin for the weekend for a return
price of less than US$60. Peasant farmers in Senegal keep track of prices in
distant markets on their cell phones. It is truly amazing.

Yet despite 60 years of global economic expansion, incomes over the last
30 years have stagnated. People who were once beneficiaries of spiralling

growth are no longer participants. The migration of manufacturing from North America to Asia's lower-cost, less-exacting regulatory environment is a prime example of why this is so. Hundreds of thousands of jobs have been lost. Entire neighborhoods and communities have been pushed down the path of economic decline. Most recently, the global financial meltdown has thrown millions more out of work across the globe.

Deregulation of the financial system, the proliferation of free trade agreements, and the increased influence of the World Trade Organization converged to release capital to roam the globe. Constant technological innovation in computers and communication has freed people to relate in new ways, some positive, others questionable. Certainly, instantaneous communications aided and abetted the efficiency of capital migration. Gone was talk of national industrial strategies, the need to keep balance of payments reasonable, and so on. Investment flowed from the productive economy into the casino economy. In the process, income disparity exploded across the globe, especially in America.

> The rising concentration of income can be seen in a special *New York Times* analysis by David Cay Johnston of an Internal Revenue Service report on income in 2004. Although overall income had grown by 27% since 1979, 33% of the gains went to the top 1%. Meanwhile, the bottom 60% were making less: about 95 cents for each dollar they made in 1979...Johnston concludes that only the top 5% made significant gains ($1.53 for each 1979 dollar).

This situation of increasing income and wealth disparity on one hand, and the increased vulnerability of communities to overnight capital flight on the other, has fed the efforts of a wide range of people, acting where they live, to try to recover more local control over local resources and productive assets. In Canada and the United States the struggle to revitalize and rebuild marginalized economies is called community economic development (CED). Similar movements have emerged elsewhere under the banner of local economic development. The thrust of these initiatives is the integration of social goals with the economic and broader community development needs of particular places (i.e. neighborhoods as well as entire communities and regions suffering decline). Typically this work is led by citizens and their organizations becoming active agents shaping their own development.

CED, at least as it is practiced in North America, is often linked to the social economy and various strands of economic democracy, although the nomenclature varies. The social economy, which we introduced in Chapter

Total Productive System of an Industrial Society
(represented as a layer cake with icing)

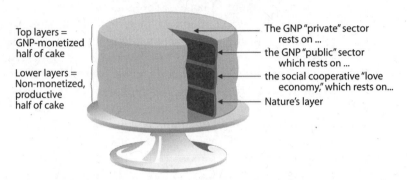

Top layers =
GNP-monetized
half of cake

Lower layers =
Non-monetized,
productive
half of cake

The GNP "private" sector
rests on ...

the GNP "public" sector
which rests on ...

the social cooperative "love
economy," which rests on...

Nature's layer

Fig. 7.1: *Hazel Henderson's cake reminds us of the multilayered interdependence of modern society. But make no mistake — the foundations on which we all depend have not changed in the history of our species.* Source: © Hazel Henderson 1982.

1, is characterized as the market-trading arm of the "third system" (the first system being the for-profit private sector and the second being the public sector). The third system includes the market-engaged social economy and a wide range of nonprofit associations, cooperatives, charities, trade unions, NGOs, and economic activities at the family level.

Like CED, the social economy focuses on gathering citizens and their organizations into a diverse array of community- and cooperatively-owned enterprises. A hallmark of the social economy is the specific aim to integrate social goals into business operations. The leading Quebec federation in this field, the Chantier de l'Economie Sociale, defines it as made up of any association-based economic initiatives focused on the values of solidarity, autonomy, and citizenship. A dynamic relationship exists between CED's "place-shaping" strategies, sector-focused initiatives, and the work of building local and social enterprises. Several cases presented thus far illustrate it well.

For example, Seikatsu members' desire for ecologically produced food from local farmers receiving fair prices was inherently place-based but concentrated on a sector strategy to ensure environmental and social values were applied to shortening the supply chain. In turn, several different kinds of enterprises capable of producing products that met the standards of a socially and ecologically determined market were required. Place, sector, and enterprise were woven into the diverse ecosystem of producers, consumers, and institutional linkages to begin transforming the food system.

Kristianstaad illustrates a different starting point. Here, a local authority with jurisdiction over a specific territory — 1,100 square kilometres and 26 communities — provided the leadership. Here too a sector-focused strategy was of central importance. Concentrating on renewable energy created the basis for a powerful and unified range of coordinated innovations and initiatives. Two municipally owned enterprises were vitally important players, providing the core tools and reinvestment necessary to implement the renewable energy in the region. Would it have been possible to make so much progress if the local authority had not owned its own waste management company and its own energy utility? We think not. With ownership came cash flow that in turn enabled direct reinvestment over time. Would investment in the momentous tasks of transition be sustained if there were no collective ownership as part of the mix? It is an interesting question.

Likewise, Kirklees points to the importance of YES, a community-based energy services company dedicated to an integrated approach, without which the results achieved would not have been possible. Without the linkage to place and a capacity to mobilize and coordinate a wide range of enterprises and financial tools, it would not have attained the buy-in of householders and such rapid success.

Overall, it is fair to say that without the interplay of a variety of tools and techniques relevant to territorial, sectoral, and subregional enterprise strategies, it is doubtful that transition to a low-carbon, more resilient, local economy can be practically implemented. Reviewing the elements of successful CED practice from the last 40 years can aid in thinking through elements of what is necessary in the next 40 as globalization gives way to a greater emphasis on local and regional economies.

In this chapter we set out a basic framework to guide thinking about the functions that must be attended to as we set out to reweave the economies of local communities and regions. The two case studies examined, one urban and one rural, demonstrate what can be done. Though both have emerged over the last 30 years and do not speak directly to navigating the challenges we face in the decades ahead, they do give us a view of the inclusive and democratic architecture of local and regional institutions we must expand and scale up.

The Core Economic and Social Functions

Before proceeding to the case studies, it is useful to introduce the basic economic and social functions that effective CED and social economy organizations address, either directly or indirectly. Whether you are urban or rural, the process of stemming the tide of economic decline and social decay begins with figuring out how these functions are being fulfilled, where the gaps are, and what strengths and weaknesses exist. These are very basic conceptual markers that will help you understand the economic and social

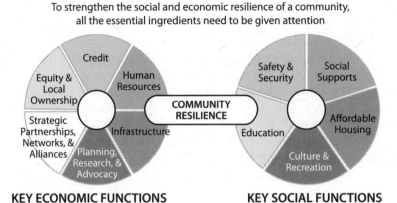

Fig. 7.2: *Essential ingredients*

landscape, a prerequisite whether the aim is to overcome impoverishment or navigate the stormy waters of transition.

Figure 7.2 depicts the essential ingredients that must be woven together to strengthen a local economy. Decline and dependency stem from interrelated factors. So too does the revitalization of a community. A more robust and self-determining citizenry and multi-stakeholder, collaborative organizations are central to advancing resilience, as we shall see in the next section.

The Economic Ingredients: Key Functions
EQUITY AND LOCAL OWNERSHIP

Equity is directly linked to ownership. If I own my house outright, I have equity equal to the value of the house if it were sold. If I own a business, I have equity to the extent that the value of the assets (e.g. buildings and equipment) is greater than that of the liabilities (e.g. outstanding loans). In a business context, equity is created from profits that remain in the business. This equity, or ownership interest, is available for reinvestment — for example, to buy new equipment or to invest in expansion.

Without local ownership of productive assets, reinvestment in the community is likely to be undermined, especially in difficult times. Equity is thus a precious resource that requires careful husbanding. Localizing and democratizing ownership is thus a critical function, and capturing equity for reinvestment in transition is vital. There are various ways to do this. The JAK cooperative bank, Kristianstaad, Seikatsu, and the Alaskan regional aquaculture associations are examples of the vitality that can be sustained if careful attention is paid to ensuring there is sufficient equity on the transition balance sheet.

CREDIT

Transition requires credit, not just equity. Seldom does a community or an individual have sufficient equity or investment capital to pay all the costs of starting or operating a business, acquiring real estate, or investing in transition.

There are many different types of credit. For example, credit to buy equipment and buildings is usually structured as term loans. The lender provides a mortgage in return for interest payments and a combination of loan guarantees and security on the assets being bought (collateral). Another type of loan is for working capital, which enables businesses to pay their staff, hold inventory, and pay suppliers on time.

Unfortunately, almost all banks are averse to risk financing, especially when confronted with projects in marginalized communities. As we saw in the case of JAK Bank, ecological and social enterprises denied loans by the banks were the opportunities that members mobilized around through the local enterprise bank system. Without such patient capital, many viable social and ecological enterprises would never get off the ground. For example, the huge social and economic returns achieved in Alaska would not have happened without the State of Alaska offering long-term, low-cost credit.

HUMAN RESOURCES

People displaced from participation in economic life for extended periods of time often feel daunted and discouraged when faced with the challenge of applying for a job or retraining. Strategies that help people become willing, ready, and able to participate in jobs, to become self-employed, or to band together with others to build a social enterprise have helped countless numbers of people make tough transitions. This is familiar territory for CED organizations committed to fostering social inclusion, reducing poverty, and strengthening community.

To succeed, we need to know what is going on in the local labor market. Where are the jobs? What kinds of skills are needed for available jobs? What bridges need to be built to get displaced people ready for productive employment? For those who aim to become self-employed, how can they be trained, advised, encouraged, and financed? Where are there opportunities for social enterprise that can leverage existing skills and, with appropriate technical and financial support, create livelihoods that are sustainable? What are the strengths and weaknesses of existing organizations with a mandate to serve the community? Can they do the job? If there is a gap, how do we fill it?

Ongoing training and leadership development are other important dimensions. The board members and staff of community organizations involved in CED and the social economy need orientation, training, and knowledge to perform their role effectively. Leadership is vital for sustaining the development process over the long haul. For regionally based initiatives, whose members come from geographically dispersed communities (as is often the case in rural and remote areas), this often means providing training and technical support to increase the capacity of individual communities to strengthen the local economy. In the context of transition, the quality and interconnection of community leadership is perhaps even more vital.

One last point is that organizations leading community revitalization always have to take on the responsibility of educating and engaging a range of other stakeholders. Helping people understand the ingredients of successful efforts elsewhere can inspire and motivate. CED organizations that successfully built local coalitions that made a real difference over time have usually developed methods to engage people in the task of assessing their own context and building a set of collective priorities and strategies.

INFRASTRUCTURE

Infrastructure is not normally the direct focus of CED and social economy initiatives. This level of investment and project implementation usually falls to larger public- and/or private-sector institutions. Nevertheless, there may be instances when infrastructure development becomes a strategic priority. For example, in the case of First Nations, when infrastructure is to be put in place for a major resource development or when the physical infrastructure of the local community is being improved, aboriginal development organizations may endeavor to maximize business and employment benefits by leveraging their aboriginal rights to secure new economic opportunities.

Where a lack of infrastructure constrains the development of the local or regional economy, advocating for investment in certain kinds of infrastructure may be taken up by a CED organization — perhaps improving electrical or water and sewage system capacity or securing internet access for communities in a remote region. The importance of infrastructure development is powerfully illustrated by the example of the regional aquaculture associations of Alaska. On a more modest scale, one could include recycling programs as an infrastructure-related undertaking. In Quebec, Canada, this sector has become an active focus for a number of social economy enterprises across the province.

PLANNING, RESEARCH, AND ADVOCACY

It is impossible to successfully weave together a strategy relevant to all of these functions without planning and research capacity. In order to establish priorities and advance action, it is critical to carry out active research and intelligence gathering to learn what is going on in the local and regional economies. Research is also a key function in the process of identifying and developing business opportunities. Equally important, knowing what is going on and who is doing what is a prerequisite for forming partnerships and alliances that can achieve more effective outcomes.

Lastly, poverty reduction requires advocacy beyond the local arena and usually involves senior government agencies and the private sector. Knowing what needs to be changed, who needs to be targeted, and, when necessary, how to mobilize the political pressure needed to foster changes in larger systems is an inevitable part of the territory covered by many CED and social economy organizations.

BUILDING STRATEGIC PARTNERSHIPS, NETWORKS, AND ALLIANCES

One could argue that building and maintaining partnerships, networks, and alliances should be included as a core function. Building partnerships of various kinds is of central importance if an organization is to gain the capacity to influence local or regional economic activity, or address the needs of a particular sector or segment of the population. With respect to equity, for example, a strategic partnership could take the form of a joint venture that secures for the development organization an important role in a vital economic sector. With respect to credit, it could create a partnership with a public institution, like a credit union or a bank, that makes credit more accessible to people and business initiatives too marginalized for conventional financing. With respect to human development, it could mean a partnership with a training or education institution that helps create programs that meet the priorities of a CED or social economy organization. An example is customized training aimed at preparing the unemployed for available employment opportunities or emerging social enterprises.

The Social Ingredients: Key Functions

There are several social functions that can become important domains for planning and action by CED and social economy organizations.

EDUCATION

Access to education, and the quality of that education, has a profound influence on the life trajectories of individual human beings, both children and adults. To the extent that either access or quality is compromised in particular localities, such as an inner-city neighborhood or a rural town with a declining tax base, the long-term prospects for community revitalization can be seriously compromised.

SAFETY AND SECURITY

In settings where there are risks (or even perceptions of risk) to the safety and security of citizens and businesses, there are often negative social and economic impacts. On the social side, people's sense of security and safety can have a significant impact on their willingness and ability to participate in the various facets of community life. On the economic side, chronic safety and security concerns can lead to businesses closing or moving, people with means moving out of declining neighborhoods, and a general decrease in overall investment and local economic activity.

Social Supports

A capacity to reach out and help citizens meet their basic needs and participate in the life of the community is fundamental to strengthening the social interconnectedness among citizens and between citizens and their institutions. Weak connections inhibit the building of trust, and without trust it is difficult to forge agreement around priorities for community action. Without conscious commitment to common priorities, it is next to impossible to mount an effective mobilization of resources and people in a common development effort.

Affordable Housing

It is a truism that affordable housing not only has a major influence on the quality of life of citizens but can also determine their ability to adequately meet other social and economic needs. Many researchers and commentators define adequate housing as a cornerstone for the physical, social, and economic health of people and communities.

Culture and Recreation

The physical and emotional health of citizens and communities is reinforced by active physical and cultural engagement. Programming and support that makes such involvement possible can be an important platform from which to extend the opportunities for participation in other aspects of community life.

Weaving the Strands Together: Constructing Local Development Systems

It should be apparent that each of these ingredients has an impact on the quality of life within any particular community or population. The extent to which there are organizational, financial, and institutional resources for each shape the social and economic landscape of the community.

In disadvantaged or distressed settings, there is typically a deficit in some or all of the identified economic and social functions. This means some community's needs are unmet, which can in turn feed the cycle of decline. One practical benefit of examining a particular community or region through the lens of these social and economic functions is that by analysing what is going on in each area, who the actors are, and what strengths and weaknesses exist, we can see community assets, deficits, and needs. A rudimentary map emerges that enables activists and researchers to better understand the terrain. As we will see in the case of RESO in Montreal, this is an early step in the process of revitalizing a community. It helps the community SEE its context more clearly and lets citizens and a range of community organizations SHARE a dialogue, which is a prerequisite to effective planning, priority setting, and SEEKING effective change strategies. Done well, the analysis and dialogue build the basis for action, which in turn advances learning and social capital, all of which creates community capacity to both defend and advance its interests.

Unsurprisingly, the portrait of community reality that emerges from this process is complex and multidimensional. Yet government responses tend to be anything but. Communities in crisis are offered short-term projects focused on a single function — for example, business finance, housing, or small-business development. The result is services and funding formulas that mobilize particular tools — entrepreneurial development, microcredit, resume and job-search skills, etc. — which are not thought of or deployed within any broader change strategy. The old adage "To a hammer, the whole world looks like a nail" is a good way to characterize the problem. What we learn from the history of revitalizing communities is that longer-term, more integrated, multifunctional strategies and action are required (as implied in Figure 7.2). In short, the local or regional *development system* needs to be strengthened, and the community must increase its capacity to marshal resources and apply them in a more integrated way. The aim is to address priority functions and needs in a way that can create a more synergistic and durable development process.

US research on how certain devastated inner cities were transformed into thriving, liveable spaces affirms the basic idea of a community-based development-system approach to addressing the multiple difficulties of distressed communities. Some of the findings are outlined below.

- **Successful initiatives combine action in the economic, service, educational, physical development, and community-building domains.** Successful initiatives share one common principle: a "comprehensive mindset." The community change practitioners use this mindset as a lens through which they survey problems, opportunities, and solutions. They understand the necessity and the effectiveness of working at the same time on economic and physical development, service and educational reform, as well as in community building. But they are strategic in choosing where to begin, in sequencing their activities, and in working out how much they can take on at once.

- **Successful initiatives rely on a community's own resources and strengths as the foundation for designing change initiatives.** Successful community-based change initiatives reflect the specific assets, needs, institutional relationships, and power structures of individual communities. Community building, a central characteristic of successful initiatives, is more an orientation than a technique, more a mission than a program, and more an outlook that an activity. It catalyzes a process of change grounded in local life and priorities, and changes the nature of the relationship between the specific community and the systems outside its boundaries. This strong orientation to community building is based on the belief that inner-city residents and institutions can and must be primary actors in efforts to solve the problems of their neighborhoods.

- **Successful initiatives draw extensively on outside resources, including public- and private-sector funds, professional expertise, and new partnerships that bring clout and influence.** While this finding may seem a contradiction to the second one, it is not. Many of the problems faced by inner-city residents arise from powerful economic forces and from deficiencies in public and private systems that originate far beyond the borders of distressed communities. Effective interventions aimed at transforming neighborhoods require a new relationship between insiders and outsiders — a strong relationship that allows for a flow of information and the leveraging of the wisdom and skills of all stakeholders. Outsiders perform the following functions in support of successful community-based initiatives:

  ✓ **Provide funding.** They make their money available in amounts and under conditions that are related to the objectives to be achieved. Funding is structured to be predictable over sufficiently long periods to get results.

  ✓ **Provide clout.** Outsiders can help remove or reduce political, bureaucratic, and regulatory obstacles that interfere with a coherent approach to interventions.

  ✓ **Provide technical assistance.** They can mobilize and broker expertise that may not be readily available otherwise but is crucial to securing ongoing development and to realizing community-based initiatives.

- **Focusing on Long-Term Outcomes Is Critical.** Another critical theme of the American research is that successful initiatives are oriented toward achieving concrete outcomes. In doing so, they remain focused on long-term, durable outcomes even while recognizing that, from a community mobilization point of view, short-term results are also important.

These characteristics of success derived from American research parallel the results of research carried out in Canada in the early 1990s. Successful place-based revitalization efforts share the following common patterns, among others:

- They are the result of a multifunctional, comprehensive strategy or development system of ongoing functions and activities, rather than the result of any individual economic development project or other isolated or unrelated attempts at community betterment.
- They integrate or merge economic and social goals and functions to make a more significant impact on community revitalization.
- They provide a base of operating principles that empower the broad range of community residents to take over the governance of both their development organizations and their community as a whole.
- They display a businesslike financial management approach that builds both ownership of assets and a diverse range of financial and other partners and supporters.
- They use an organizational format that is nonprofit, independent, and nongovernmental, even when for-profit and governmental entities are linked to their work.

These lessons are well illustrated in two very different settings: urban Montreal and rural Maine.

RESO: Transforming Montreal's Poorest Neighborhoods

Propelled by the 1850 construction of the Lachine Canal, the southwest Montreal neighborhood of Point Ste Charles rapidly became a thriving industrial district, exporting goods south into the United States and west through the Great Lakes. More than a century later it was the complete opposite, a district caught in a spiral of decline, seemingly beyond hope. By the 1950s the narrow streets and infrastructure of yesteryear were proving unsuited for the efficient application of new technologies, and the economic vitality of the neighborhood was becoming depleted. The final blow came when the Lachine Canal was closed. The 1965 opening of the St. Lawrence Seaway flushed out many of the remaining businesses. Almost 60 percent of the population left the neighborhood. Of the remaining 13,000 people in 1986, 43 percent were living below the poverty line, 17 percent were unemployed, and 25 percent were living on government welfare.

Though prospects seemed bleak, residents did not take the changes passively. Community groups organized throughout the 1960s and 1970s. A consumer co-op and a housing information service were established. Within a decade, 23 housing co-ops were formed and 300 homes built. But after 30 years of decline, these grassroots efforts failed to stem the tide. Businesses and jobs continued to leak out (Figure 7.3).

Cheap real estate and proximity to downtown Montreal made the neighborhood a target for real-estate developers who planned to stem the decay by building upscale condos. Again residents organized, this time to resist the threat of gentrification and the accompanying displacement. By the early 1980s they had formed a permanent coalition ready to defend "the Point" from encroachment.

There were some attempts to create jobs during this period. Government money was used to create businesses that would hire young people. All such public programs failed. Financing and management services were wholly inadequate.

Turning Point: PEP

A turning point came when the YMCA agreed to fund two community organizers to help the local groups and residents come up with a plan for revitalizing *the Point*. The two helped locals establish what was working elsewhere, educate themselves on the emerging lessons, commence dialogue on how it applied to their neighborhoods, and begin the process of assessing the social, economic, and business dynamics of the neighborhood. These

Fig. 7.3: *To stem decline, plugging the leaks in a community economy is one step that advances self-reliance and strengthens resilience.*

were the elements that led to the formation of Programme Économique de Point Ste Charles (PEP).

Modeled after community development corporations (CDCs) in the United States, PEP was incorporated by nine community organizations in 1984 and launched several months later with a neighborhood-wide meeting to elect a board of directors that would guide work to achieve four major goals:

• Local renewal guided by neighborhood priorities
• Business development to create good long-term jobs
• Training programs to prepare the unemployed for those or other jobs
• Secure funding for PEP

Armed with a small staff, a $100,000 investment fund, and some seasoned business professionals, PEP launched an entrepreneurial training and development program. Many business start-ups were supported, and many failed, including three cooperatives. Despite the failures, 50 long-term jobs emerged — a success that was dimmed by the failures and by disagreement among the founder members about business development strategies and working with the private sector. Three founders left. However, 140 individuals and 13 businesses and other organizations joined. Working with local business owners to retain and expand businesses became a core strategy. Even if PEP created 50 jobs per year, many more jobs were still being lost annually.

The work of PEP inspired other Montreal neighborhoods to begin organizing. New CDCs were set up across the city. PEP and two other CDCs teamed up to deal with the issue of securing developmental funding, so crucial to their long-term success; together they pressed a reluctant government for a three-year funding package and won. PEP immediately focused on drafting a new strategic plan to increase its impact. It also set new priorities: improving job access for the unemployed, creating and retaining businesses, strengthening its own network of supporting institutions, and diversifying its funding sources.

With new priorities in place and three years of funding secured, PEP took several more strategic steps. First, it reorganized its board: four places were maintained for the community organizations and four were created for local business, four for local residents, and one for PEP staff. Second, it instituted a program of assistance for local businesses aimed directly at stemming their departure or closure and protecting existing jobs and services. Among the services that PEP provided to business were local relocation planning, management consultation, search for expansion space, direct financial assistance, and referral to other sources of help, including on-the-job training.

By the end of 1988, 188 jobs were maintained and 76 jobs created. PEP was developing a reputation for being helpful to business. For example, it had successfully encouraged local retailers to set up a mutual self-help association and had financed a consultant study on local markets and the renewal of the commercial shopping district. While this was helpful to the retailers directly, it also met a need expressed by residents for good shopping facilities.

From its beginning, PEP had recognized that business development could not be pursued effectively unless friendly sources of capital were put in place for new and expanding ventures. Its experience with a small fund of its own had not been encouraging, but the need was still there. With the two other Montreal CDCs, PEP established Fonds de développement Emploi-Montréal, a business development fund that over the years has made many loan and equity investments for new and expanding local businesses.

Despite these clear indicators of progress, a new round of plant closures and the threat of more to come had growing numbers of people in Point Ste Charles and adjacent neighborhoods along the canal reeling. The extent of the crisis brought into play a new set of relationships that had hitherto eluded PEP. Labor unions, once cool to PEP and its community partners, but now faced with further decimation of their ranks, began to collaborate with community groups. PEP had a simple message that was key to the change in union policy: "Your current members may not need the services of a CED group, but your ex-members are in our offices looking for help." Now it appeared there would be a lot more ex-members, and the unions recognized the importance of developing a broad front.

Together they built a major cross-sector coalition that took in the five southwest Montreal neighborhoods and finally won recognition for what became known as CREESOM, the Committee for Economic and Employment Revitalization in Southwest Montreal. With $200,000 from the government, they got to work on reviewing the situation in depth and developing practical recommendations for concerted action.

The resulting report documented the disinvestment and job loss as well as the dollars lost to government. CREESOM also produced a series of recovery recommendations, which included improvements in infrastructure, housing, and employment services, as well as government investment of $140 million over five years in business and job expansion. Among the recommendations was a proposal that the revitalization of the five neighborhoods should be vested in a local organization, Regroupement économique et social du Sud-Ouest (RESO), which would be based on an expanded and reorganized PEP. What started as a CDC in Point Ste Charles now took on work in all five neighborhoods with an aggregate population in 1986 of about 68,000.

A struggle ensued immediately over control. Many in the business community insisted that they be in charge of the new organization. However, in the end, they lost the argument. The broad-based coalition that had made up PEP and achieved the results won the day. The business sector received four board places (one each for big industry, small industry, financial institutions, and the commercial/retail sector), community groups got four, labor unions two, and RESO staff one.

RESO Successes

An early project of RESO was the establishment of an "early warning system" that would signal when there was a risk of plant closure, relocation, succession issues, financial difficulties, etc., any of which could mean significant job loss. Information from the unions triggered a warning that jobs were at risk. Typically, this would be followed be a process of reaching out and listening to the business managers tell their stories and identify their challenges; then RESO would bring managers and workers together to solve the problem.

A striking example of the ripple effect of RESO's emphasis on strengthening the local business sector was an incident involving the largest local manufacturer, whose CEO was on RESO's board. His experience as a board member led him to put the firm's $80-million annual procurement budget under the microscope so he could identify opportunities for bringing jobs to the southwest area of the city. A Spanish supplier, faced with the possibility of losing a long-standing contract, decided to establish a Montreal office in order to maintain its business with the local manufacturer. The new facility created 35 to 40 new jobs, the majority of which were filled by residents that RESO was working with. The program developed for this local recruitment emerged as another feature of RESO's CED work — competency-based training.

Because RESO was involved so deeply with the businesses in its neighborhoods, it possessed more detailed information than any other group about what human resource challenges the businesses were facing. RESO systematically translated this labor market intelligence into a system for identifying and recruiting residents into training programs tailored to address the gaps specified. The results were effective. People were trained with the concrete needs of local business clearly in mind. At one point 1,500 residents were involved in training through RESO each year. Today, 1,000 people still use these services annually.

Another example of the early warning system at work was the heads-up RESO got from the shop steward of a manufacturing business that was going to lay off 60 workers who didn't have the numeracy and literacy skills to adapt to new technologies. RESO met with the union and management, brokered a program with a local nonprofit specializing in literacy, and helped design a curriculum, which they delivered in the factory during working hours. All workers remained on the job. From this success, the nonprofit went on to form a social enterprise specializing in this kind of service citywide.

RESO's first five-year mandate (the length of time it had core funding of $500,000 per year plus training-program funds) was dominated by the process of building its outreach and services to businesses and its training of local residents. Statistics Canada reported in 1994 that for the first time in over 30 years, the decline of manufacturing in southwest Montreal had stopped.

Among the next CED steps taken by RESO was the establishment of RESO Investments Inc., a $5-million venture capital fund, based on contributions from the federal and provincial governments, trade union-controlled investment funds, and capital from the private sector. It was time for a more proactive and strategic approach to creating new businesses and expanding on innovations of existing businesses. Since its inception, this fund has injected equity and subordinated debt into a range of businesses, taking equity positions worth between $50,000 and $450,000. The priority initially was manufacturing and advanced technology sectors. Business criteria were used in the final stage of decision making, but social criteria shaped investment strategy, particularly in achieving the objective to create long-term jobs for residents in the five targeted neighborhoods.

Into the Future

Fifteen years later the talk and work in southwest Montreal had turned from revitalization to how to ensure sustainable development. By 2005, signs of revival were everywhere: the Lachine Canal reopened and was being developed; employment growth was more than twice the Montreal average; Montreal's downtown and the new economy were spreading toward the southwest; locally owned businesses and social enterprises were established and expanding; the cultural sector was blossoming, as were building projects and commercial revitalization...and the list goes on.

The RESO board has expanded to include representatives of health, educational, and cultural institutions; social economy enterprises; participants in RESO employment services; and an elected municipal official who represents the borough. But unlike many boards of community organizations of one kind or another, the board members of RESO are not invited or recruited to sit on the board. They are elected for two-year terms by their peers in each of the constituencies. Unions gather and elect their two representatives; small business members do the same, and so on. Every year 250 to 300 people gather to take part in eight sector-based electoral colleges. This dynamic and democratic process indicates the importance placed on citizen engagement.

The esteem for democratic engagement shows up in many other ways. RESO has become the key convener of strategic public forums. For example, the reopening of the Lachine Canal was shaped by the hundreds of residents RESO convened across the neighborhoods. At the annual meeting, large numbers of residents and organizational members attend, not just to vote, but to debate priorities. By mid-2005, RESO had about 300 organizational members (from business, the community, unions, etc.) and 1,500 individual members. They regularly convene round tables and consultations that bring people in various sectors together to assess neighborhood issues and create joint strategies to address them.

Nevertheless, despite all this success, there are two long-standing challenges that persist and new ones emerging. Poverty remains a problem for a significant segment of the population. The success of the revitalization is drawing new people to this area of the city. Housing prices are rising. Early-stage gentrification is creating worries. Urban sustainability has emerged as a major theme for RESO, one that cuts across its citizen engagement, advocacy, and business development work. Advancing the diversification of the financial base, especially through earned revenue, remains a strategic and puzzling challenge, especially given the broad scope of work undertaken. And the task of integrating its diverse functions (business development, recreation and tourism, housing, culture, training, and community

RESO's DEVELOPMENT SYSTEM

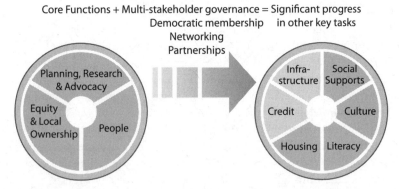

Fig. 7.4: *Local focus, citizen engagement, multi-stakeholder cooperation, and democratic governance are cornerstones of the community architecture necessary to navigate transition in tough times.*

representation and advocacy) is an ongoing challenge, driven by community-determined priorities and an ever-evolving context.

Coastal Enterprises Inc. — Community Development Finance in Rural Maine

On the way to his first posting in Maine, Ron Phillips, a new graduate from a New York City divinity school, had his life transformed. When he encountered poverty, poor housing, and insecure employment in rural Maine and saw no apparent means by which people could overcome the barriers of economic exclusion, Phillips committed his life to building an organization that could make a difference to structural injustice.

Since 1977, Coastal Enterprises Inc. (CEI) has pursued a mission to "help people and communities, especially those with low-incomes, reach an adequate and equitable standard of living, working and learning in harmony with the natural environment." With initial backing from the state and local faith-based groups, CEI is now considered one of the leaders among the 4,000 community development finance institutions (CDFIs) in the United States, many of which grew out of the civil rights movement and the war on poverty in the late 1960s and early 70s. Over this period, CEI has mobilized and leveraged over $1.8 billion in private and public capital from diverse sources: public entities, private foundations, insurance companies, financial institutions, and religious organizations (see Table 7.1). Its continuous and systematic approach to organizing and convening a wide range of stakeholders to carry out strategic projects and investments is remarkable.

CEI's founding priority was to improve the economic prospects of Maine's fishers and the coastal communities they lived in. Concentrating its first investments on fishers, the nascent mussel and oyster aquaculture industry, and then small-scale farming and value-added forestry ventures, CEI slowly situated itself as a partner that listened first, organized appropriate resources second, and then systematically delivered a combination of organizing, technical assistance, training, and financing to make projects happen.

Two years into the start-up period, its first major investment rescued a traditional fish-processing plant from closure when the land it was on was about to be sold for marina and hotel development. Without the plant, scores of fishers would have lost the base where they landed, processed, and marketed their catch. Today the plant still exists — under town ownership now, a pulsating working waterfront. Over the subsequent 30 years, CEI has stayed close to its roots, investing and brokering over $40 million in 160 marine enterprises dotting Maine's beautiful coastline.

CEI has also branched out to become a creative and effective player in diverse sectors, helping to organize, support, and expand affordable housing, a range of innovative social and health services, markets for organic local food, energy efficiency and conservation, preservation of forestry lands (linked to greening their management practices), and environmental industries at local, county, and state levels. More generally, CEI has played a central role in strengthening the community economic development field as a whole through its promotion and its efforts to help secure hundreds of millions of dollars in new resources to extend the work of CDFIs in poverty reduction and community development across the United States.

Table 7.1 CEI's Impact, 1977–2010	
Number of staff	78
Number of loans/investments outstanding	421
Capital under management/committed	$715.4 million
Businesses financed	2,040
Amount financed	$556 million
Amount leveraged	$1.5 billion
Businesses/people counseled	30,727
Full-time jobs at loan closing	24,496
Affordable housing units created/preserved	1,261
Child care slots created/preserved	4,664

Source: Coastal Enterprises Maine, Inc.

CEI's Sector Approach

CEI has used the sector-focused approach (fisheries, forestry, etc.) to guide and inform its work. Given its enterprise and job-creation priority, and the dispersed populations across rural and small-town Maine, CEI has found this more effective than targeting a particular community. The approach is in contrast to that of many CDFIs and CDCs, RESO being but one, that concentrate on a particular territory. This is not to say CEI ignores community development. Quite the contrary — it is constantly consulting and convening local leadership to discuss its work and specific projects. This includes a rich and generative maintenance of the relationship to faith communities in Maine — communities that CEI considers vital partners. They refer projects and potential enterprises to CEI and themselves generate social enterprises that CEI can assist and support through start-up and expansion.

A principal question in CEI's determination of a sector strategy is "Where can we add the most value?" It bases a decision to enter a sector largely on signs of economic opportunity, the sector's importance to rural communities, and the talent and institutional capacity in the sector relative to CEI's own strengths. Specifically it looks at the following factors:

- Potential for new products and markets
- Existing capacity, limits, and reproduction of the natural resource base
- Community infrastructure
- Skills and knowledge in the sector
- Potential partners
- Institutional capacity and vision

Obviously, the more informed and involved CEI is in a particular sector, the better able it is to design an intervention that advances social, environmental, and economic sustainability. CEI determines a sector's life cycle by systematically analyzing its "production continuum" — that is, what makes up the product, how and where it is processed, how and to where it is distributed, who it benefits, what waste the life cycle generates, and what happens to it. Such thorough assessment helps CEI foster viable businesses, stronger communities, and minimal environmental harm.

Fig. 7.5: A conveyor streamlines packaging at Whitney Wreath (www.whitneywreath. com) in Machias, Maine, the world's largest balsam-fir-wreath maker. The company's 600+ seasonal and 18 full-time jobs take a big bite out of the 11.2 percent average unemployment rate in the county. The owner, David Whitney, has devised numerous strategies for improving the company's performance, including providing housing for his migrant staff. With loans provided by Coastal Enterprises Inc. (CEI) and its partners, the company expanded operations in 2009 to fill orders for balsam products from L.L. Bean and the QVC shopping network, supporting an additional 250 jobs. Source: CEI Maine

Nonetheless, it does not select a point of entry solely on the basis of a comprehensive analysis of sustainability. Background research is done to understand economic forces, environmental and regulatory issues, as well as the community and social development context. Key leaders and organizations in the industry are interviewed, secondary industry data sources consulted, and CEI often organizes advisory groups made up of various stakeholders.

CEI has developed the following sustainability criteria for selecting, designing, and financing projects and enterprises. The first three (added value, equitable distribution, and local ownership) flow from its social justice roots and have traditionally formed the cornerstones of the screening criteria.

- **Added value.** The project creates potential for more income and economic value to accrue to local communities.
- **Equitable distribution.** The project generates increased economic activity that benefits Maine's people and communities, especially those with low incomes.
- **Local ownership.** Because of the project, economic activity is more likely to stay in local communities.
- **Available local products.** The project provides goods and services for local needs and basic necessities.
- **Low environmental impact.** The project reduces waste, energy costs, and pollution, and conserves natural resources.
- **Institutional capacity.** Existing businesses, trade organizations, or other support groups can help implement and sustain the project.
- **Economic risk.** The project has viable markets and entrepreneurs; the scale of the project itself is viable.
- **Environmental risk.** The project has little or no potential to create unintended environmental impacts.

Related to the environmental criteria, CEI prefers prevention to remediation, and substitution of new materials for toxic or scarce resources. CEI mobilizes and deploys a range of tools to implement its sector-strengthening strategies.

- **Gap financing** consists of subordinated debt for small and microenterprises, and small-scale equity investments through a for-profit venture capital subsidiary.
- **Technical assistance** is extended to businesses in the form of management training, marketing, credit, and strategic planning.

- **Market development** is undertaken, including market research, organizing, and education, as well as the testing of new products.
- **Targeted job development** links people with low incomes and public assistance recipients to jobs created by the businesses financed.
- CEI builds **new institutions** as needed to help develop markets and cooperative relationships among businesses, such as trade organizations and research collaboratives.
- **Policy development work** creates resources and a favorable regulatory environment to support CEI's work.

Although each of these is common in the work of CDFIs, it's rare that all are present under one roof. CEI's capacity to wield effectively this range of tools is one of several reasons it is so successful. CEI exemplifies the kind of capacity we must develop if we are going to transition to more self-reliant local and regional economies.

Deepening the Integration of Sustainability into the Financing Function

CEI's earliest effort to integrate sustainability into its work started in 1993. By 2001 it was ready to try to influence the larger CDFI movement in the United States. Convening CDFIs with environmental and policy groups at a national round table led CEI leadership to a more systematic dialogue on how to improve, extend, and scale up the integration of environmental goals into their financing and developmental work. A double bottom line that looked only at social and economic outcomes was clearly no longer sufficient.

In 2004, with support from the Ford Foundation, CEI cofounded the Triple Bottom Line Collaborative (TBLC) with ShoreBank Enterprise Cascadia, a CDFI based in rural Washington state. TBLC is a 10-member alliance of community development finance groups striving to integrate economic development and poverty alleviation with a third focus on environmental sustainability. The goal is to refine and grow triple-bottom-line lending and investment practices.

The TBLC developed a TBL Scorecard to document, demonstrate, and assess the impact of its members' TBL deals — that is, deals that meet each of three metric categories, the "Three Es":

- **Economy:** Measures how TBL loans/investments generate income or assets for individuals and enterprises and how this then improves community or regional economic health. Metrics include tracking jobs created or retained, payroll and benefits generated, capital leveraged into the region, housing units constructed, and goods or services locally sourced.

- **Environment:** Measures both the increase in positive and the reduction in negative effects on nature's macro systems through sustainable management of resources, protection of water quality and systems, reduction in the use of materials and toxic substances, and reduction in energy consumption and greenhouse gas emissions.
- **Equity:** Measures the investments' contribution to building social capital by providing capital, technical assistance, and asset development to historically disadvantaged individuals, sectors, and communities.

The TBL Scorecard focuses on the direct impacts of loan investment as reported by the borrower. The scorecard can be adapted to the local environment and conditions of any CDFI. The environmental bottom line is sometimes easy to see — such as when solar energy replaces an oil-fired water heater. In other cases, the environmental benefit may simply be to reduce or eliminate the environmental dangers that a project might pose.

TBLC continues to seek ways to develop the capacity of CDFIs to practice TBL lending and investing. New partnerships with the environmental and conservation movements will be required to further TBL lending and investment practice opportunities, to access new capital sources, and to promote supportive state and federal policies.

Transition Factors

There are several lessons embedded in this chapter that can help guide transition to more local and regional economies.

The first is captured well by the phrase "If you ain't organized you ain't gonna contend" — attributed to Saul Alinsky, one of America's most famous community organizers in the 20th century (see his book *Rules for Radicals*). Ongoing engagement of the community, citizens, and the sectors of economic activity is necessary to sustain effort over time. Without engagement, dialogue, and sometime fractious debate to determine what is most important, it is not possible to set strategy effectively or to learn from what works and what does not. Without securing this local level of buy-in from the main stakeholders, any kind of transition will be difficult to navigate. The story of RESO richly illustrates this point.

Second, while local roots are vital to building democratic organizations that can contend with the tough work of transition, not every function can be effectively fulfilled at the local level. CEI would not be succeeding if it was serving only a single rural community. Development finance, one of its key functions, requires a broader geographical reach if it is to become sustainable. Without access to a broader market, CEI's investment activity could not pay for the overheads needed to sustain the work. What is unique about these kinds of CDFIs is that they are not merely serving a market where demand for financial products is already organized; they are creating new markets, primarily among the most vulnerable citizens and communities. If it were not employing methods that authentically engage industry sectors and communities in problem-solving and opportunity creation, the market it has shaped for triple-bottom-line financing would not exist, nor would the benefits being generated at the local, regional, and state levels across Maine.

Both cases richly illustrate two of the themes introduced in Chapter 1: the nature of the solidarity economy and the compelling logic of the need to reenvision the scope and shape of democracy.

The history of RESO is one of agitating, educating, animating, and communicating across old divides in order to build bridges between the private, public, and civil society silos in its five urban neighborhoods. We can think of RESO as a developer of the "high road economy." Even when some of its founding members put pressure on the organization for getting too close to business, the RESO leadership resisted becoming framed and constrained by ideological assumptions. Rather, it focused on constructing a place-shaping coalition that could get things done in a principled, pragmatic, and democratic manner. This is the core of the solidarity economy.

Coastal Enterprises approached its development work from a similar base. Driven initially by the values of its founder, CEI cut across and engaged actors in all three systems (public, private for-profit, private nonprofit) in the fight against impoverishment, the empowerment of local producers, and the revitalization of their rural communities.

RESO compellingly illustrates the second point, the extension of democratic practice far beyond the limited influence gained by voting politicians in or out of office. Initially organizing in a single neighborhood, with a board representing only community organizations, the entity evolved into a multifunctional organization with a board elected from key stakeholders — community organizations, labor, small business, large business, finance, health, social enterprises, and even the municipality — in each neighborhood. The result today is a creative and durable CED organization with the capacity to mobilize effectively citizens, sectors, and enterprises. This is a dynamic form of economic democracy at work and exemplifies the untapped potential of associational democracy, a concept we introduced in Chapter 1.

What RESO has managed to accomplish through its inspired grinding over the last 25 years is no less than a redefinition of the domain of authority exercised by the community. It is an example of the Catholic social doctrine of subsidiarity at work: "that power should as far as possible be distributed to distinct domains of authority," in the words of Paul Hirst. The difference in the case of RESO is that the authority was not devolved to the community by government; rather, the community organized to enlarge the scope of its own authority by politically challenging the effectiveness and efficiency of the state — and of the private sector, for that matter. By becoming a broader form of local, participative democracy, a genuinely accountable network of actors has been mobilized and organized for long-term neighborhood revitalization and renewal.

The examples of RESO and CEI testify to the wisdom embedded in the theory of associational democracy, which sees self-governing associations becoming the primary means of democratic governance of economic and social affairs. As we pointed out in Chapter 1, associational democracy is based on the idea that

> ceding selected state functions to such associations, and creating public mechanisms to finance them, could remove from centralized bureaucracies those functions beyond their level of competence, while providing the potential for a much greater level of citizen engagement and accountability. Enabling democratic associations to expand the resources and tools available to address the challenges of transition is a key objective. As we will see, this can be achieved by mobilizing local and regional financial tools and shaping markets and production relevant to meeting basic needs.

Interestingly, both CEI and RESO have mobilized a wide range of resources from public, private, and civil society to finance their activities; this includes generating revenues from the citizens, communities, and the diverse sectors they serve. The diversity of resources, combined with the sustained engagement of people and organizations with a stake in communities and regions, is essential to achieving the impressive results evident.

These innovations, like others advanced earlier, are powerful provocations to conventional thinking. Again, as noted in Chapter 1:

> This is a far cry from the classic liberal democratic assumption that democratic government is based on accountability to the individual citizen. Indeed, the outlines of associative democracy might evoke derision from some, who charge that it is stripping representative democracy of its right to govern based on the consent of the governed. Such arguments are weak, especially when, as Hirst points out, the "bulk of economic affairs are controlled by large privately-owned corporations, and the great bulk of social affairs are controlled by

state bureaucracies." Increasing the space in which local and regional associations exert significant democratic influence over economic and social functions advances democratic participation and ownership of the responsibilities of citizenship.

As the crises of transition deepen, communities and regions that have the kind of capacities represented in CEI and RESO will be much better positioned to navigate the forthcoming array of challenges. Those that do not, and that continue to be held captive by the mantra of individualism, consumerism, and globalization, will be at much greater risk.

Smart governments will recognize their role as strategic enabler and partner. Playing out old narratives is not an option. Associational democracy is about "democracy as verb." Its aim is to empower communities to transcend current limits on democracy, which relegate citizens to being spectators in a public-/private-sector tennis match rather than active agents of democracy in the things that matter to their daily lives in the places they live.

Neither centralized big government nor minimalist, get-them-out-of-the-way ideologies are relevant to the challenges at hand. If communities and regions are going to maximize their capacity to adapt and to devise creative responses to energy depletion and climate change, they will need to extend and deepen democracy and solidarity.

Resilience Reflections

In Chapter 1, we defined reilience as "the amount of change a system can undergo (its capacity to absorb disturbance) and essentially retain the same functions, structure and feedbacks." Both RESO and Coastal Enterprises show why resilience is such a powerful lens for navigating transition. In southwest Montreal, the spiral of decline caused by technological, economic, and transportation changes left once-thriving neighborhoods reeling. The industrial heritage and the vibrant community that had grown up around these neighborhoods became overwhelmed. The level of disturbance was too great. Community functions weakened. A large segment of the population lost its self-reliance and became dependent. Resilience eroded. But it did not pass the tipping point.

The tipping point is where the cumulative impacts of stress on a system are so severe that it loses any capacity to maintain its original functions and structure. It thus "tips" over the upper boundary of the system and falls into new patterns that typically are very difficult to reverse. An example of an ecosystem reaching the tipping point is a lake stressed by a cumulative saturation of pollutants to the extent that the entire system becomes depleted of oxygen, killing off all life in the lake. In human terms, a region that has arguably gone over the tipping point is the Darfur region of Sudan. The stresses of war, drought, environmental degradation, and persistent hunger have virtually destroyed the social and economic fabric. Local populations, refugees, governments, and international aid organizations are all struggling against what seem insurmountable odds to restore some kind of decent basis for survival. Will they succeed? Or has the entire region passed the point of no return, incapable of restoring the basic functions and structure of the human communities it once supported?

Similarly, in the case of climate change, refugees and casualties are already appearing. Entire communities are being permanently displaced. Floods, droughts, extreme weather...if they multiply as predicted, the stress will amplify. Tipping points will be reached. Communities and regions that are not organized or that have insufficient energy, too many people, and too few resources will be unable to contend with the changes and stress. Moreover, as the crisis evolves, the capacity of the international community and national governments to respond will decline as they are overwhelmed by the immediacy of each crisis, the compelling nature of the demand for help, and the distress of too few resources.

When faced with this spectre, the imperative of resilience takes on added meaning. John Kunstler's description of the coming period as "The Long Emergency" compels us to think about resilience: Just how resilient is the community I live in? What are the signs? Is there anything that can be done?

The stories of RESO and CEI suggest that resilience can be strengthened in practical and strategic ways. We can see that both are also beginning to incorporate the principle of doing their work with the health of ecosystems in mind, especially CEI with its triple-bottom-line lending system. RESO and CEI show that with appropriate community organizing, governance, resources, strategy, and a persistent reaching out to engage citizens and their organizations, core economic and social functions can be strengthened, and sophisticated adaptations molded and shaped.

In Chapter 8 we continue our exploration of the cross-cutting theme of finance. The JAK Bank and CEI are innovations that evolved over a 30- to 40-year period. What is exciting today is that the pace of innovation is accelerating. At the same time, innovation is diversifying, creating a plethora of small and large applications targeted to meet a variety of needs. As the fallout from a dysfunctional global financial system continues to appear, the motivation for innovation increases. It needs to. Convivial and appropriate finance is centrally important to all aspects of transition.

CHAPTER 8

Convivial Banking Innovations:
Seeds for Transition

*During the "golden age" banks were originally focused on local clients,
and bank managers had a strong bond with their borrowers.*
— Simon Thompson, Chartered Institute of Bankers

*In future the question will not be, "Are people credit-worthy?"
but rather, "Are banks people-worthy?"*
— Muhammed Yunus, Grameen Bank

*Tools are intrinsic to social relationships. An individual relates
himself in action to his society through the use of tools that he actively
masters, or by which he is passively acted upon. To the degree that he
masters his tools, he can invest the world with his meaning; to the
degree that he is mastered by his tools, the shape of the tool determines
his self-image. Convivial tools are those which give each person
who uses them the greatest opportunity to enrich the environment
with the fruits of his or her vision.*
— Ivan Illich, *Tools for Conviviality*

IN THE NORTH DURING THE 1970S, mainstream banks moved away from relationship banking with their small-business and household customers. In the South, as rural land enclosure and poverty drove dispossessed people to the cities in search of work, microcredit was invented and relationship banking reinvented by Ela Bhatt, the founder of SEWA Bank in India, and by Muhammed Yunus, the founder of the Grameen ("village") Bank in Bangladesh.

The movement away from relationship banking in the North parallels the deregulation of the financial industry since the 1970s. Before the rapid globalization spurred by deregulation, community residents and local businesses in the commercial strips of towns and cities had a long-term relationship with the local bank's branch manager. These up-close relationships with the individual customer, and the bank manager's understanding of the local context, were vitally important to lending decisions.

This is no longer the case. Banking decisions are now driven by an automated credit score rather than an evaluation of the customer's character or an assessment of the local context within which the loan is being sought. In general, computers make the decisions. Only a few cases on appeal may require senior management — actual human beings — to review decisions on regular mortgage and commercial loans. Large loans are treated differently.

Simon Thompson of the Chartered Institute of Bankers believes that a rebirth of relationship banking was nevertheless taking place — until the credit crunch of 2007 left millions of householders and small and medium-size business owners with little attention from the bankers. According to Samira Khalil, executive director of Global Talent Intelligence Strategies, they continue to have huge difficulties accessing credit. Indeed, in the globalized market, most professional bank managers focus their attention on the top one percent of borrowers — the large multinational corporations and the high-net-worth individuals. These are the kinds of clients who continue to receive personalized relationship-banking service from the big banks. JP Morgan Chase, Citibank, HSBC, and Barclays have even set up special branches for the elites. Little wonder the credit needs of social and cooperative enterprises, and of local and regional small-business innovators, are not on the radar of conventional financial institutions. Time is money, and the big banks are looking for quick wins and big-ticket corporate deals to appraise.

Nevertheless, where needs exist, resilient and creative folks innovate new solutions, and the absence of credit and the challenge of mobilizing equity are definitely unfilled needs for many, which need solutions. This chapter introduces a range of tools and solutions invented to bridge this yawning chasm between need and access. They are, by and large, modest, but each has demonstrated success. Many are in early stages. Others reveal the emergence of scale. Together they constitute an evolving ecology of alternative financing tools and strategies. When joined with a range of nonfinancial tools described elsewhere in this book, the array of lending and equity strategies creates a rich and diverse mixture of ingredients that can be woven into tailored solutions for specific contexts.

For example, Coastal Enterprises Inc., described in Chapter 7, demonstrated the innovation, impact, and scale achieved by a mission-driven organization wielding an array of financial tools. One can imagine CEI being well-positioned to adopt and adapt many of the innovations we explore in this chapter. Each innovation has its own capacity to inspire ideas and effort that, with focused intention, persistence, human creativity, and cooperative relationships, can help create the resilient financial ecosystem we will need to navigate the challenging transitions ahead.

Before proceeding with our survey, it is useful to remember that money and capital are entwined in a variety of complex tools that take many different forms. Gifts, endowments, tax rebates and credits, grants, seed capital, participation finance, mezzanine capital, "withdrawal" share capital, micro-equity, traditional risk equity, and a variety of debt structures are financing tools that can be creatively wielded to design innovative and flexible financing strategies.

This is the craft of development banking: a creative process of blending different kinds of money and forms of capital to address unmet needs. Get it right and the blend will be generative. Get it wrong and toxic brews emerge, including mortgage foreclosures, over-indebted enterprises, and insolvent countries. What we need is development finance managed and guided by a triple bottom line that has both equitable and homeopathic qualities. This is the lost art of banking that so vitally needs to be understood and reclaimed.

Linking Money and Debt Advice to Finance: Community Banking Partnerships

Community banking partnerships (CBPs) are a new group of initiatives in the UK. Along with their Irish and American predecessors, they offer a glimpse of a radically reconceptualized and inclusive approach to community development banking. In *Community Banking Partnership Prospectus*, the National Association of Credit Union Workers, new economics foundation, and Rebuilding Society Network argued that cash in the UK is no longer king; plastic is, although, given current trends, mobile phone banking may displace plastic before too long. Payment systems today are configured to serve only those who qualify for plastic or electronic payments. Because the poor live outside the banking and electronic payment networks, three in ten British households pay much more for a long list of everyday goods and services most of us take for granted, for example:

- **Energy costs.** A majority of low-income UK households use pre-payment meters. Lacking a bank account, they do not qualify for term service contracts. But consumer watchdogs affirm that this "pay as you go" method costs such households an extra £255 per year for one fuel and £485 for two.

- **Food prices.** On tight budgets and without access to affordable credit, low-income households lack the means to buy in bulk and can't afford many supermarket discount deals ("buy two and get one free").
- **Phone charges.** Finding the connection fee for a landline unaffordable, low-income households rely on mobile/cell phones. But without a bank account, they are not eligible for phone contracts. The cost of a "pay as you go" service that the poor can access typically costs six times that of mobile phone contracts.
- **Clothing and household goods.** Using retailer credit to finance the purchase of a kitchen stove and oven will typically increase the cost of the appliance by 30 to 35 percent. An extended guarantee for repairs and replacement will increase the total cost by well over 50 percent.
- **Credit and cheque cashing.** The UK, unlike Europe and many US states, abandoned usury laws in 1976 with the passage of the Consumer Credit Act, which abolished ceilings on interest rates and credit charges completely for the first time since Henry VIII. As a result, there is no legal cap on the interest or fees that banks and subprime lenders can charge in the UK. Those without bank accounts can legally be charged anywhere from 85 percent by a pawnbroker to 2,000 percent or more by a payday lender. Cheque cashing incurs a commission charge of 7 percent or more. In its *Profiting from Poverty* report, the new economics foundation exposed predatory lending to a value of £16 billion in 2003, with legal charges to low-income households that amounted to 160 to 2,000 percent annually.

As a result of these charges, unbanked households with annual earnings of £10,000 a year pay 10 percent extra (about £1,000 a year) in surcharges for gas, electricity, telephone, cash machine withdrawals, and credit. In stark contrast, households with bank accounts enjoy free cash machine withdrawals and receive discounts from utility companies by paying through bank transfers monthly.

To seek solutions to this vexing problem, new economics foundation and the National Association of Credit Union Workers researched and piloted a model that seeks to develop multi-stakeholder partnerships. On the basis of this research, CBPs have been set up in urban and rural subregions of Great Britain. They were inspired by the Money Advice and Budgeting Service, an Irish network that over the past 20 years has successfully integrated the provision of advice on money and debt with credit union services nationally.

A CBP links up a range of institutions providing education, advice, and financial services — for example, a credit union or a community development loan fund and nonprofit debt and money advice agencies (see Figure 8.1). These institutions then develop a joint approach or partnership that targets low-income households and offers four main products and services, identified by the acronym ABCD.

- **Advice** on money matters and debt
- **Banking** services to pay bills and budget
- **Credit** that is affordable
- **Deposit** services to meet future needs

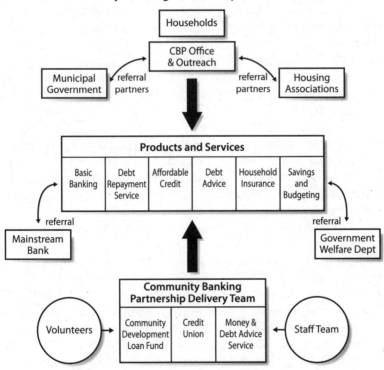

Fig. 8.1: The community banking partnership (CBP) brings autonomous organizations together in a group structure to create an integrated strategy and framework of accountability. Adapted from the work of the US National Federation of Community Development Credit Unions, the model is creating solid economic results for low-income citizens, for housing providers, for taxpayers, and for communities.

Fair Finance, a CBP in London, has pioneered a model for linking money management, financial advisory, and debt counselling services with the provision of microcredit. Its Fair Money Advice service is backed by a consortium of six nonprofit housing associations that pay to refer their tenants for help. In the past four years the CBP has helped over 5,000 people access affordable credit and banking services, set up more than 2,000 debt repayment plans, and saved over 1,000 people from eviction. The multilingual staff have provided one-to-one support that enabled tenants to manage over £12 million of debt; 75 percent of those tenants have maintained their rent repayment plans.

The nonprofit housing associations have also drawn on Fair Finance expertise to give their housing managers basic training in money management and budgeting advice for their tenants. This has increased the success in resolving debt cases and led to expanded money advice services. Low-cost credit that tenants can use as an alternative to loan sharks, energy advice that allows them to secure lower utility bills, and additional debt and money management services have become more widely accessible. Fair Money Advice workers communicate with their housing partners through monthly email updates and quarterly meetings to discuss and track case referrals. Fair Finance even provides legal representation to households facing debt-related court actions.

It is hard to imagine any other financial institution playing this role. Fair Finance has proven that the close interlinking of advice, support, and finance has contributed to reducing rent arrears and other debts. Success has come through building strong partnerships and closer relationships with service users who are attracted to the "fair trade" banking aspect. As its name says, Fair Finance makes equitable treatment for every participant in a market integral to its social banking services. In "walking the talk" with this simple yet novel idea, Fair Finance has inspired other British CBPs to follow its lead.

A rural example is South West Pound, a CBP supported by Devon County and 13 nonprofit landlords in Devon and Cornwall. Over 5,000 households were assisted by the service in the first three years. Credit union partners in the South West Pound alliance advanced over £630,000 in affordable credit to low-income households. Debt cases of over £7.8 million were handled.

South West Pound's core service provided three hours of free welfare and tax credit advice, general money-related information, plus access to low-cost banking, savings, and credit services. In addition, financial and money advice workshops were offered to staff in the public, private, and nonprofit sectors.

Fair-trade banking is not just wishful thinking. By collecting comparative data, Fair Finance and South West Pound demonstrated a convincing business case for CBPs. For example, each eviction in the UK costs £6,000 or more in legal costs, court fees, and bailiffs' charges. CBPs argue to creditors and landlords that the carrot is cheaper than the stick. Mediation through CBP debt advice, refinancing, and direct help can be much cheaper than litigation.

From 2005 to 2008, CBPs provided money and debt advice to over 9,000 households in England and Wales and £18.5 million in affordable loans. Table 8.1 shows the savings realized by the Southern Housing Group, a non-profit landlord in southeast England. Contrary to the narrow calculation of risk and benefits that conventional financial institutions rigidly adhere to, CBPs demonstrate the extent to which financial institutions practicing smart community development can create multiple benefits for several stakeholders.

A CBP is unique to its local area. To achieve significant social and economic benefits, crafting hands-on partnerships is fundamental to success. Landlords and creditors are hard to win over, and setting up contracts is a slow process. To keep overheads low, autonomous partners must be persuaded to cooperatively deliver services. This aspect of CBP development has been challenging, as third-sector organizations tend to compete for scarce resources rather than cooperate strategically to leverage limited capacity. Hence the importance of developing horizontal networks in which social economy organizations can learn the principles and practices of mutual aid and work together toward common social justice goals.

Table 8.1 Southern Housing Group: Cost Benefit of Financial Inclusion		
Annual costs of financial inclusion program (in pounds)		£92,582
Annual stats		
Tenants assisted	160	
Positive outcomes	96	
Cost benefit to social landlord		
Evictions prevented	14	97,248
Court hearings prevented	14	37,344
Other satisfactory outcomes	67	5,578
Total	95	**£140,170**
Net benefit to the social landlord		**£47,588**

Source: National Association of Credit Union Workers, new economics foundation, and Rebuilding Society Network, "Community Banking Partnership — The Joined-Up Solution for Financial Inclusion and Community Economic Development" (NACUW, April 2009, www.varotherham.org.uk/financial-inclusion-news/1177-community-banking-partnership-prospectus-published).

US Credit Union Innovations: Federating Solutions

There are 8.4 million American households with no banking service, almost 10 percent of whom live in New York City. Most have no savings and show negative net worth because of debt problems. Neighborhood Trust, a community development credit union (CDCU), teamed with Credit Where Credit is Due (CWCID), a nonprofit anti-poverty organization, to create a fair banking group structure to serve the 300,000 people, mainly Latinos, packed into the three square miles of Washington Heights, a New York neighborhood. Incomes are among the lowest anywhere in the United States — 20 percent of residents live on less than $10,000 a year, and 60 percent of households are single parent.

CWCID's financial education and money advice programs are joined with the credit union's financial services, and money and debt advice programs are offered in collaboration with over 30 community-based partner organizations. As with Fair Finance in London, the success is visible as the institutions directly help low-income clients refinance high-cost payday loans and reduce their debts significantly — there has been a net average savings of $12,000 per household. Each $1 invested in this CDCU strategy is yielding $2 in savings for its members, and the model is now being established at other CDCUs across New York and in other states.

For example, the Borrow and Save service recently launched by two other CDCUs in Harlem and the South Bronx offers a low-cost community development finance service as an alternative to payday lenders. A portion of each loan is used to set up a savings account for the borrower, with a small initial deposit. The idea is simple. By shifting away from payday lenders and pawnbrokers to a CDCU, households can save a lot. (It is important to note that payday lenders in the United States and the UK secure significant supplies of capital from casino banking providers such as private equity firms.)

Table 8.2 New York CDCU Borrow and Save Service v. New York Payday Lender	
CDCU $500 loan for 90 days	**Payday lender $500 loan for 90 days**
Average annual percentage rate of 18% and $25 application fee	Fees and interest equal to $15 per $100 borrowed every 14 days
Total cost for 90 days: $40.07	Total cost for 90 days: $450
Average amount in savings account for the Borrow and Save product: $30	Amount in savings: $0
Financial education provided	No financial education
Confidentiality	Personal information sold

Source: National Federation of Community Development Credit Unions, "NYC Community Development Credit Unions Launch Affordable Small-Dollar Loans with Savings Component" (press release, 19 September 2011).

Table 8.2 highlights the stark difference. This is what a huge difference convivial banking can make!

There are 235 CDCUs in the United States, with an aggregate membership of over 1.7 million and combined assets of $11 billion. CDCUs are owned by low-income Americans and specialize in providing services to this constituency across the United States. The CDCUs are hugely creative, a quality amply demonstrated by their invention of the group company structure, from which the UK community banking partnership model was adapted. A key strategic issue is determing how to scale up their capacity so their community development finance innovations can be extended to low- and moderate-income communities, both urban and rural, across America, which have their own complex and diverse financing needs. The National Federation of Community Development Credit Unions is developing a strategy by which it will federate in collaborative ways with the much larger US credit union movement, with its 7,400 credit unions, 91 million members, and $866 billion in assets.

To expand the reach of their innovations, CDCUs have been promoting a program to link the smaller CDCUs with larger credit unions. The benefits of this Community Development Partners program are two-way. The larger credit unions access CDCU training to improve their methods of reaching and serving lower-income households, leading to more inclusiveness in the markets they serve. CDCUs, in turn, access the technical and infrastructure systems of their larger counterparts, something they could not afford on their own. There are now 50 partners that have linked up to support the CDCU national network.

A dramatic early success has been the Latino Community Credit Union (LCCU) in North Carolina, a state that has the fastest-growing Latino immigrant population in the United States, with more than 500,000. Launched in 2000, LCCU has become the fastest-growing credit union in US history. In a mere seven years, 51,000 members joined, mainly immigrants and refugees from 18 Latin American countries. Today they have more than $100 million in collective assets. 95 percent of members are low-income, and 75 percent are first-time banking customers. A strong and dynamic partnership linking the LCCU to the Self Help Credit Union (one of the largest CDCUs in the United States), El Centro Hispano, the North Carolina Minority Support Center, and the State Employee's Credit Union has been a contributor to this success. Staff are bilingual, and the requirements for personal identification needed to open an account were streamlined to make it easier for people to become members. Marketing is done in partnership with church networks. Most importantly, access to the office services of larger credit union partners reduces LCCU overhead costs and improves efficiency.

LCCU fosters the empowerment and self-reliance of members by offering them money advice and financial education. Education sessions are run at credit union branches as well as in the workplaces of local employers, in community centers, and in churches. Topics are diverse and include how to save, budget, build credit, buy household goods, manage a credit union account, and purchase a home. Since 2000, LCCU has provided its members with $114 million in affordable credit and assisted almost 10,000 members with its financial education programs.

Beyond Microcredit: Integrated Approaches that Work

Over 3 billion people globally are self-employed — the largest sector of the international workforce. The proportion of self-employment varies widely from rates of 80 to 90 percent in India, Bangladesh, and many countries of Africa, to 20 to 60 percent in areas of southern Europe, the Middle East, and Latin America. Even in the UK, sole traders and microbusinesses with under five employees account for about one in four jobs, and rural areas frequently have 30 percent or more self-employment. Self-employment in all countries has been expanding since the widespread promotion of free markets and deregulated labor markets. As a result, this is a huge market for innovative forms of microfinancial and related support services.

The International Monetary Fund and the World Bank promote microcredit, but the real innovation is happening where services tailored to low-income and self-employed people are integrated into credit provision. World Bank policy has little to say about this appproach, and global banks increasingly seek to provide wholesale capital to microfinance institutions as they smell opportunities for profit. This usurious approach to credit leads to disastrous consequences; loan rates in Mexico and other countries are now between 80 and 100 percent. Widespread debt problems are resulting, and reports of borrowers committing suicide are chillingly frequent.

SEWA Bank and Working Women's Forum in India

It need not be so. Inspired by Gandhi, two leading Indian microfinance institutions are demonstrating the homeopathic power of the integrated strategies practiced in the social solidarity economy. Founded in the 1970s, the SEWA Bank (established by the Textile Labour Association, a trade union that Gandhi helped organize in the 1920s) and the Working Women's Forum (WWF) in India have developed a broad range of services that go well beyond stand-alone microcredit. Through an organizing strategy of "horizontal cooperation" they have forged links between trade unions advocating for just pay, market cooperatives for the self-employed, bulk-purchasing cooperatives for buying supplies, and community and social finance services to address a number of business and household financing needs. Over 1.6 million members in different urban and rural subregions of India have been inspired to collaborate and innovate solutions for a wide range of challenges. For example, WWF has created its own trade union for members, the National Union of Working Women (NUWW). WWF has also set up a social insurance cooperative with 120,000 members, many of them self-employed.

Organizing the Self-Employed

The Indian strategy of linking services to produce integrated solutions for the problems of the self-employed has inspired interesting experiments in Europe, where the protection afforded by trade unions is covering fewer and fewer people every year. Those who lose their union jobs often add to the growing number of self-employed people with little access to social protection insurance, legal advice, advocacy, or pension services — a condition European research reveals extends to nearly 40 percent of the workforce. This includes almost all of the self-employed as well as the staff of community organizations, casual workers, homeworkers, tenant farmers, agricultural laborers, and those working for family businesses. A growing number of trade unions are paying attention.

Indeed, in some countries, organizing the self-employed is one of the few sources of new trade union members. In the Netherlands, Germany, Italy, and the Scandinavian countries, significant progress is being made. For example, in the Netherlands, since its founding in 1999, FNV Zelfstandige Bondgenoten has become a broad-ranging and effective trade union for the self-employed. It uses direct mail and telemarketing to contact 15,000 microbusinesses every six months and has gained members from nontraditional sectors including professionals, IT specialists, interpreters, financial advisers, consultants, couriers, taxi drivers, ballet dancers, piano tuners, and those in the organic food sector.

London Rebuilding Society

A very different strategy is under development at the London Rebuilding Society (LRS), a community lender that focuses on financing for social enterprises and ethical businesses. As one of its several services, LRS developed in 2006 a mutual aid fund (MAF) targeting immigrants and refugees with no access to conventional sources of enterprise finance. Many of the attracted groups are immigrants from African countries. The MAF has two categories of members — investors and MAF borrowers. LRS helps each group establish a mutual aid fund from which it can distribute small loans to its members. Investments from MAF groups form a pool of share capital that LRS holds to guarantee loans. Up to $4 in loans are leveraged from every $1 provided as a guarantee. As the MAF groups are established, a share account is put in place so groups can add to the share capital in the guarantee fund. Typical groups are nonprofit, social enterprise, and self-help organizations representing a particular community. LRS encourages share investment of available unrestricted funds or community donations raised by the MAF group.

As its name indicates, the primary methodology of MAF is to foster mutual support of members who have similar ideas and interests. For example, a MAF group of self-employed people working in the same sector would collaborate to identify ways they might work together — a group of small-scale caterers might consider leasing space for a collective kitchen or organizing bulk purchasing.

In order to extend its capacity to support MAF groups, LRS reaches out to a range of community organizations willing to help, providing them with training and coaching on how to support enterprise development within MAF groups. An attraction of the MAF approach is that it is similar to the group-based savings-and-loan systems used in rural African communities.

In its first four years, the LRS program has seen the establishment of 21 MAF groups of between 50 and 100 members. A unique feature of this model is that it is the MAF members themselves who recommend loans to the people and enterprises in their group. LRS trains each MAF in lending methods. Once a decision is made, the loan is advanced by drawing down a multiple of the MAF group's share capital from LRS. Interest is charged at a rate of 6 percent up to a maximum sum of £10,000, and loans are repayable over three to five years, with no capital repayments required in the first year of the loan. By 2009, LRS had provided over £350,000 in loan guarantees. The loans secured through the guarantee are for diverse purposes, including social enterprise loans, working capital for women market traders, and finance for enterprise start-ups.

Each MAF group designs its own loan products and services to meet the needs of its members and the different MAF communities. In some MAF groups, personal loans are entertained — for example, to cover funeral costs. LRS works with each group to design its own products and services to support the borrowers, and also gives the groups access to software and loan-management systems. The LRS training program has expanded to provide MAF groups with a range of money-management courses that can then be offered by the groups to their enterprise, organizational, and household members.

Mutual for the Self-Employed

The new economics foundation's research into MAFs mapped out a broader range of services, similar to that offered by SEWA Bank, that the London

Rebuilding Society and other community development financial institutions (CDFIs) might support. The research revealed that the self-employed have two key worries: fear of failure and fear of debt. (For women, the fear of debt and failure is higher than it is for men.) The nef proposed and modeled a mutual for the self-employed as a possible solution. Drawing on lessons and existing services provided by SEWA, WWF, and the growing network of trade unions for self-employed people, the social solidarity economy services that the mutual could offer would include the following:

- **Marketing opportunities:** Inclusion in one or more supportive business networks
- **Tax advice:** Access to tax advice tailored to issues around specific business situations
- **Financial services expertise:** Access to personalized services from a specialist money adviser and/or an independent financial adviser to identify tax credit opportunities, offer generic pensions and insurance advice, and provide guidance for improving and managing cash flow more effectively
- **Peer support:** Networking sessions with other microbusinesses and a chance to develop closer links with others in the same trade
- **Bulk purchase scheme:** Opportunities to make major savings on business operating costs and other overheads
- **Microfinance:** Access to low-cost insurance services, affordable credit, and other cost-effective financial services from a trusted source
- **Legal and professional help:** Access to legal advice and other professional help from sources empathetic to the needs of the self-employed

This proposal was taken up in July 2011 by a specialized credit union and mutual guarantee fund for the self-employed, backed by a consortium of German microfinance organizations. The new organization, Kreditunion eG, is based in Berlin and plans to extend its services across Europe through a federation supported by the European microfinance networks.

Equity Angels Grounded in Community

Access to equity is a challenge for many types of enterprise and is a particularly severe impediment for social enterprises integrating social and ecological goals. However, in France, 400 groups of social investment "angels" grounded in their communities have been organized since 1983. Cigales, registered investment clubs that invest in and provide enterprise advice to locally owned businesses and cooperatives, focus on local enterprises that reduce poverty or contribute to sustainable development within the community. The clubs use the 3 Ms approach — monies, management, and marketing — to ensure that equity investment is integrated with business and social support services. The result is new or expanded businesses, strengthened social capital, and a cost-effective way of mobilizing and integrating know-how with equity. Social investors receive tax relief of 25 percent and can hold their investments for up to a maximum of five years. Thus the number of Cigales in operation varies from year to year as new ones form and old ones complete their legally restricted life.

Similarly, BCA Holdings Ltd., based on the island of Cape Breton, Nova Scotia, started its novel approach to the provision of patient capital with a lending pool. Founded in 1989 by a group of local activists and businesspeople fed up by the banks' lack of interest in financing the revitalization of their community, BCA Holdings decided to take a different tack. It negotiated a no-interest loan of $500,000 from the provincial government, with the promise that it would raise another $500,000 from fellow Cape Bretoners. It succeeded. The capital raised from community members, borrowed and packaged in diverse ways, provides a return of 5 percent interest annually, a much better return than the average stock market return in Canada.

As with Cigales, most of the work is done by members of a small volunteer board of directors, with only one part-time professional staff person and an assistant. Investments are made primarily by way of secured loans at affordable rates. Also as with Cigales, technical assistance is provided directly by board members and other businesspeople from the community. The results have been solid and ongoing.

When the province of Nova Scotia made a tax credit available to investors in local enterprises, a sister organization called BCA Investment Co-operative was formed to make only equity investments. To date, 400 local investors have put up $1.5 million, all of which is invested in local businesses that retain capital and jobs in the region. Investments cut across a wide range of sectors and include a number of successful worker buyouts and business start-ups owned by people committed to the island and the wellbeing of Cape Bretoners.

Cooperative Capital in the UK — Withdrawable and Transferable Shares

Few social enterprise development financing programs address the need for equity investment. One reason is that the conventional nonprofits and charity legal forms are all that is available, and these preclude investor participation; they have no share capital structure and thus are unable to attract equity, leaving the organizations reliant upon either grants or loans. This is a big problem. Loans require monthly payments right away, which slows cash flow and hamstrings promising start-ups and businesses with expansion potential. Patient capital is needed to give such businesses breathing room, capital that can be shown on the balance sheet as equity.

In the UK, legislation recently drafted was meant to address the problem of financing social enterprises. The Community Interest Companies (CIC) legislation created two options, one of which was for the express purpose of facilitating equity investment. However, the new system is not working as hoped. The legal costs of a CIC share issue are not much different than those for a public limited company. This is just too expensive, and given the reasonably modest equity needed by most social enterprises, the formation costs are completely disproportionate to the amount of equity sought from investors.

As it turns out, the revival of co-op legislation that John Stuart Mill helped steer through Parliament in 1852 has begun to resolve the equity problem. The Industrial and Provident Societies (IPS) governed by this legislation can legally issue what is called "withdrawable share capital," which gives investors the means to withdraw their capital under specified conditions. This, along with dividends, creates attractive flexibility. IPSs have enjoyed a resurgence in the UK because they allow people to invest in businesses that are starved for capital but perform vital functions, many of them relevant to transition. Since the mid-1990s, a broad range of social enterprises have received investment this way, ranging from community land trusts, self-build and co-housing, community wind farms, and micro-hydro projects to community-supported agriculture, community ownership of village shops and pubs, community ownership of football clubs, and the community buy-out of businesses facing closure.

Recent reforms of tax legislation have increased the attractiveness of IPS enterprises, as it allows them to secure tax relief for investor shareholders under the Enterprise Investment Scheme, a welcome new addition to the social enterprise finance tool kit.

A pioneer in the application of "withdrawable share capital" is Shared Interest, a UK cooperative lending society that has been involved with the fair-trade movement for 20 years. Known as the world's only 100 percent fair-trade lender, the Shared Interest ethical cooperative investment fund has 8,700 social investors. This support enables lending of over £33 million a year in 36 countries around the globe. Investment levels from £100 to £20,000 provide trade finance for both sellers and buyers of fair-trade products. Producers in Africa, Latin America, and Asia typically receive working capital against orders or loans for equipment. Buyers in Europe and North America are helped to finance inventory. Even though security is not required for most loans, Shared Interest has never suffered a loss that

Fig. 8.2: *Customers of the Natural Food Store in Headingley, Leeds, were dismayed to learn that the owners were retiring. After public discussion, the Headingley Development Trust, a membership-based community enterprise, concluded that a community buy-out was feasible. With support from a cooperative development body, Co-operative and Mutual Solutions, the trust completed a business plan and launched a share issue in 2007. In five months, the necessary £103,000 was raised and the business opened as a cooperative with 230 investing members.* Source: The Community Shares Programme and Co-operatives UK

affected its members' investment capital. Dividends to its investor members are modest and always kept below the market rate of interest.

Two other examples of enterprises benefiting from IPS investors are the Phone Co-op and Energy4All.

- The Phone Co-op, an award-winning UK social enterprise, set up in 1998 and has been expanding steadily ever since. Financed by IPS investors, its telecom service for the social economy sector yields dividends of between 2.5 percent and 4 percent (in 2010, Phone Co-op members received 2.25 percent interest on share capital held and an additional dividend of 1.5 percent; this was payable on withdrawable shares held from £1 to the current maximum amount of £20,000), a rate of return that is continuously attracting more subscribers.

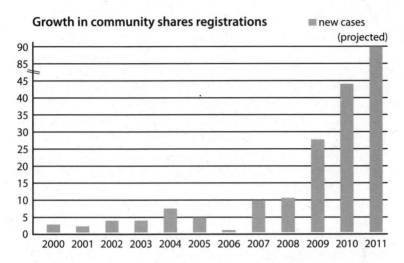

Fig. 8.3: *Community shares program.* Source: Petra Morris, "The Community Shares Programme: One Year On" (National Trust Association and Co-operatives UK, March 2010), p. 1. Revised with permission. Courtesy of Jim Brown, Baker Brown Associates.

- Energy4All, a network of seven community-owned wind cooperatives in Britain, has raised over £13 million in what is known as "transferable share" capital. Because it takes long-term capital investment to amortize the costs of expensive wind turbines, withdrawing capital in the middle of the paydown period does not work. Investors locking up their capital in this way can thus only transfer their shares to another buyer in the pool of energy co-op members or to other social investors who can benefit from Enterprise Investment Scheme tax relief incentives. The dividend levels are significant — between 7 and 8 percent — and unlike conventional equity investment in the market, transaction costs are very low.

The revitalized use of the IPS legal structure shows how linking membership, a low-cost investment tool, and a valued service or product facilitates an "up close" and localized form of mutual ownership that is flexible and effective. The number of IPS share issue launches in England and Wales over the past three years is greater than it has been since the 1920s.

Relationship Banking from a Distance

A range of web-based enterprises springing up internationally serve to demystify banking and mobilize credit through an innovative, relationship type of banking that is facilitated by electronic "peer to peer" lending and borrowing, at a distance.

Zopa

Zopa, founded in the UK in 2005 by Giles Andrews, has led the way. The service allows those with funds to lend to make direct contact with borrowers, offer a loan at a rate of interest they choose, and, if the borrower agrees, make a deal. Zopa has facilitated over £150 million of loans in this way. It runs credit checks for its lenders and spreads the risk for lenders by pooling loan offers across borrowing communities. Thus, if one borrower defaults, the risk and possible loss is spread across the lending group. Out of its first 10,000 loans, Zopa had only 59 defaults. The service also chases borrowers in arrears.

Lenders pay a fixed annual fee of 1 percent of the loan. Zopa charges borrowers for credit appraisal checks and other set-up costs. Fees are currently £118.50 per loan, and there are two loan terms — 36 months or 60 months. Zopa has achieved low overheads, low lending transaction costs, and low default rates, in part because it screens out those with low credit scores. For microcredit, this methodology has major attractions and is making headway in tough markets.

Kiva

Based in San Francisco, Kiva uses a different method for brokering long-distance loans. It is also growing faster than Zopa, in part because Kiva partners with an increasing number of the over 7,000 microfinance institutions operating around the globe. By bringing the huge credit delivery capacity and loan portfolio management of microlenders into the equation, Kiva has assisted more than 700,000 microenterprise borrowers, 80 percent of which are low-income women.

Microentrepreneurs post their photo and trade profiles on the Kiva system, indicating their credit needs, the loan purpose, and the identity of the microfinance institution they are working with. An average loan is $385 and can be made to either self-employed people or groups of traders. The repayment rate to date on Kiva has been well within international microfinance standards of 98.92 percent.

By March 2012, counting both investors and borrowers, Kiva had over 1.1 million participants located in 218 countries. Total loans advanced had reached US $296 million. Investors are in the North and borrowers in the South. The success of Kiva is inspiring others — for example, Lending4Change in Los Angeles and Lendwithcare, developed by Care International. A Kiva partnership to lend in the USA is getting underway.

Fig. 8.4: *In San Jose, Antique province, the Philippines, Ronabee Nomat sells fish, shrimp, and crab from her own stall in the town's largest public market. Kiva lenders enabled Ahon sa Hirap, Inc. (ASHI), a microfinance institution modeled after the Grameen Bank, to extend a loan that she used to purchase more inventory. ASHI (from the Tagalog, meaning "to rise up from poverty") lends exclusively to women living on very low incomes.* Source: John Briggs, Kiva

Low-Interest, High-Impact Lending for Vulnerable Homeowners

Low-income homeowners in Britain have difficulty securing affordable finance for home repairs and energy savings. This void has led to many scandals over the years involving usurious second-mortgage lenders who strip the value from pensioner assets with expensive equity release products that offer home finance solutions but can end up in evictions and dispossession. Like usurious operators in the microfinance field, this kind of sharp dealing drives some borrowers to suicide.

Over the past ten years, eight community development loan funds in England and Wales have developed home improvement partnerships with a small but growing number of local municipalities in seven regions. To improve housing that is in a serious state of disrepair and poses health risks to low-income homeowners, these partnerships have experimented with varied lending models to replace scarce local government grant funds with low-cost, flexible loans. All models have been based on the following design features (used by many community lenders):

- Repayable grant funds (essentially interest-free loan stock) and a social investor membership fee is provided annually by the municipalities to the community development loan funds.
- Interest payable on home repair loans is shared equitably; low-income borrowers pay half and the local government partner pays the other half of the loan charge to the community development loan fund.
- Loans are secured by a restrictive second-mortgage charge with no legal right of repossession or eviction.
- For the poorest older homeowners, no repayments are required and the loan is structured as an equity loan, with repayment due on death or when the house is sold. The balance due at loan maturity is based on a low-cost percentage of the rise in the house price over this period. There is normally a cap on the uplift value of the loan.

After a decade of development, this low-cost, fair-lending system is performing well. Interest rates charged range from 2 to 5 percent, and loan performance has been excellent, with slow payers and bad debt below 1 percent.

A leading pioneer of this model of fair-trade finance is Wessex Home Improvement Loans (WHIL). It was the first to develop a "shared interest" system to tackle home repair problems for those unable to attain a bank loan. WHIL's innovative system has attracted investment from 19 municipal authorities in the southwest of England. Its dynamic approach has converted previously provided grants for low-income homeowners into a zero-interest loan pool. Local governments provide interest-free loan capital for WHIL's regional revolving loan fund, which has allowed WHIL to offer affordable secured loans ranging from £1,000 to £20,000 at a fixed rate between 3 and 4 percent. WHIL has achieved rapid expansion over the last five years with few delinquencies and no bad debt.

The WHIL approach is similar in many ways to a simple JAK lending system (described in Chapter 3). The difference is that the pre-saving at no interest is provided by the local government rather than the low-income borrowers, who are asset rich but cash poor. This two-way deal enables the low-income borrowers to simply service the administrative costs of operating the regional loan fund that WHIL manages. Unlike JAK, WHIL does not use a savings point system, but a small adaptation could move this British community development finance innovation toward a JAK model. Indeed, the WHIL approach is close to that of the JAK Local Enterprise Bank service for funding community wind projects.

Capital invested to date by the community development lenders is £111 million. A shared interest system or a JAK model has prospects for rapid growth across the country if supported by a national policy framework that mandated retrofitting all housing stock on a long term basis and that provided the repayable capital for low-interest lending. A number of the community development lenders are well positioned to lead the expansion of these models as they have already piloted lending for energy-saving retrofits for low-income homeowners.

Revolving Loan Funds for Affordable Housing: Risk Pooling

Millard Fuller and Clarence Jordan worked with Bob Swann and Slater King in the Civil Rights movement during the late 1960s in Georgia. While Swann and King were experimenting with the first community land trusts (CLTs — discussed in Chapter 4), Fuller was establishing another housing solution related to finance. He shared with Swann and King the view that the poor needed capital, not charity. In 1968 he and Jordan had the idea to convert charitable donations into a simple revolving fund to support people building their own rural housing projects.

With this epiphany, the Fund for Humanity was born, set up by Fuller as a permanent, revolving loan fund to provide interest-free capital. With the social finance system in place, an innovative self-build housing methodology emerged in 1976 and expanded internationally into the well-known Habitat for Humanity. This organization is active in over 100 countries; it has built over 500,000 homes and provided housing solutions for over 1.75 million people in more than 3,000 communities spread across five continents.

The fund continues to grow and develop. Borrowers are organized into groups to construct self-build housing and are charged a small administration cost but no interest. In return for this low-cost finance, group members must invest at least 500 hours of volunteer "sweat equity." Habitat for Humanity has recently forged a co-development partnership with the US Community Land Trust network to integrate some of these methods with CLT innovations.

Like many other affordable housing developers, CLTs in the UK face the problem of securing risky up-front development financing. It is not a simple process. One of the major challenges is the lack of housing development experience among community groups, which is exacerbated by the lack of access to the seed funds necessary to get a track record. In the UK, this problem is being overcome through the use of a CLT facilitation fund (see again Table 4.3). If practical land reform through CLTs can deliver solutions for meeting local housing needs affordably, then it makes sense for local government and foundations to facilitate the process. The CLT facilitation fund provides the following four layers of support:

1. An initial feasibility grant that provides one day of technical assistance to a CLT formation group to scope their project
2. A technical assistance grant to provide specialist expertise to the group so it can develop a business plan for the CLT
3. A pre-development finance fund to help pay for the requisite architect fees, survey costs, and legal fees involved in gaining planning permission
4. A development finance fund to help leverage finance from CDFIs and other bank lenders to pay for the construction period before housing units can be sold or rented

These features help clear away key pre-development obstacles. Even a small project to develop six units of housing in the UK may require £20,000 of capital at risk. Architect design fees and planning permission costs are expensive and risky. If a group succeeds in gaining planning approval, repayment is simple; up-front costs can be included as an expense that is recoverable when the housing units are sold or rented. However, if planning consent is not given, the up-front professional fees still have to be paid, and the impact on a community-based housing-development venture can be tough.

The CLT facilitation fund covers these inherent risks by charging each group that accesses the fund a risk premium charge. The fund managers assume 20 to 25 percent of CLT projects will not succeed and builds this into a surcharge on each project. To share the risks equitably, the CLT projects that secure planning permission and build homes have to repay an interest rate of about 25 percent for this high-risk, pre-development finance. This covers the liabilities of CLT projects that do not secure planning consent. The latter do not have to repay their loans, as the risk of not gaining planning permission for construction is largely outside their control. By pooling the risk transparently and fairly in this solidarity way across all the projects, the CLT facilitation fund can recover its lost capital for the projects that are unsuccessful.

Social and Ecological Banks: Investing in the Unconventional

Since the 1970s an interesting form of social and ecological banking has developed in Europe — first in Germany, with the establishment of GLS Bank in 1974, and then spreading to other Western European countries. The earliest social banks arose out of the ideas of Rudolf Steiner, a pioneer of biodynamic farming in the 1920s. Steiner's philosophy of social economy was rooted in a profound form of cooperative theory inspired by Goethe, who sought to prevent the separation of artistic and scientific thinking. It was framed by a perspective of what Steiner regarded as the three key interconnected structures of modern societies. He described this as the threefold order of the social economy, which includes:

- the cultural milieu (communities, civil society, and the arts)
- political and legal structures (institutions and government)
- economic activity (markets and informal economic exchange)

Steiner argued that social and environmental problems are symptoms of unbalanced and unclear relationships between these three spheres. Overemphasis on one sphere at the expense of others leads to imbalances, distortions, and ultimately, if pushed too far, social, ecological, cultural, and economic dysfunction. This dysfunction will grow worse and become volatile if the imbalances are not corrected. In other words, as Hyman Minsky pointed out in the 1980s, if the market economy is allowed to grow like a cancer as a result of unrestricted predatory lending, the cumulative impact will destroy the cultural milieu and could lead to the breakdown and breakup of the legal and political order.

European social banks focus their financing on the development of a healthy social and ecological economic system. Inspired by thinkers like Steiner and Fritz Schumacher, they seek to reframe the use of money to achieve a balance between the three fundamental parts of the social economy. As Rudolf Mees, an early leader of the European social banking movement, described the philosophy in *Money for a Better World*, the fundamental belief is that "money, used consciously, can be a powerful tool for social good."

Triodos

Triodos was inspired by Steiner's ideas. It was founded in the Netherlands and over the past 15 years has grown through mergers with other social banks and social finance organizations in Britain, Ireland, Belgium, Germany, and Spain to become a European social bank. The mission of Triodos is to help expand the social economy; it accomplishes this by developing in-depth knowledge and financing methodologies for various niches — for example, the cultural and environmental sectors. With this market intelligence and sector knowledge in hand, it works collaboratively with social economy organizations to design financing products that take into account the nuances of sector needs and their growth potential. Triodos additionally works closely with social investor members and borrowers to experiment, solve problems, advance solutions, and limit risks to all participating stakeholders.

In the UK alone, the growing list of social and ecological investments made across the diversity of sectors financed by Triodos is impressive and includes organic food, renewable energy, environmental technology, affordable housing, social care projects, nonprofit social services, a diverse range of social enterprises, fair-trade businesses, community nurseries, healthcare projects, the arts and culture, and a range of projects sponsored by faith communities. Social enterprises and affordable housing projects in the UK have received investment from Triodos of more than £225 million. Renewable energy projects have secured more than £150 million. Triodos has also developed a low-cost share-selling service that allows investors in IPS shares to exchange their transferable shares in, say, community wind projects with funds from other social investors.

Caisse d'economie solidaire Desjardins

In Quebec, Canada, a similar and dynamic approach to European social banking has grown steadily over the past 40 years. This system for investing in civil society has evolved through a credit union that has become an important source of development finance in the social economy of the province. The Caisse d'economie solidaire Desjardins (CESD), founded in 1971 by the leadership of the CSN (one of the two trade union confederations in Quebec), is unique in the way it links the trade union, credit union, and social enterprise sectors.

The CESD operates across Quebec with an annual turnover of $913 million. It has 2,694 organizational members, including 619 cooperatives; 647 trade union bodies; and 856 NGO, community, and cultural organizations. There are also over 9,000 individual members, mainly employees of its organizational members. CESD has an annual loan program of $112 million aimed at the enterprises that make up its membership. Further, it invests $1.2 million of its annual profits in community development services.

Transition Factors

The creative innovations introduced in this chapter are impressive in their range, scope, and the scale some are achieving. They are also hopeful. In a context where financing has become dominated by speculation, they represent an organic tide of creative resistance to the maxim that shareholder profit needs to be the core driver of the financial calculus. Gandhi would have been pleased that, in the face of pervasive exploitation, so many are willing to heed the ancient Chinese proverb that advises it is "better to light a small candle than curse the darkness"— and to follow the advice he included in his autobiography for civil resisters: "experiment socially to find the truth." Social solidarity financing organizations are on the rise, from SEWA in India to CDCUs in the United States and Triodos in Europe.

Think again about Ivan Illich's analysis in *Tools for Conviviality*:

> Tools are intrinsic to social relationships. An individual relates himself in action to his society through the use of tools that he actively masters, or by which he is passively acted upon. To the degree that he masters his tools, he can invest the world with his meaning; to the degree that he is mastered by his tools, the shape of the tool determines his self-image. Convivial tools are those which give each person who uses them the greatest opportunity to enrich the environment with the fruits of his or her vision.

If he were still alive, Illich would be pleased with the range, scope, and texture of the many tools being invented, applied, and shaped by reintegrating relationship and vision into the financing equation.

Kenneth Boulding would also be pleased. He argued in the 1960s that the process and substance of innovation was increasingly dependent on "knowledge capital."

> Economic development manifests itself largely in the production of commodities, that is, goods and services. It originates, however, in ideas, plans, and attitudes in the human mind... This whole process indeed can be described as a process of the growth of knowledge. What the economists call "capital" is nothing more than knowledge imposed on the material world. Knowledge and the growth of knowledge, therefore, is the essential key to economic development. Investment, financial systems and economic organizations and institutions are in a sense only the machinery by which a knowledge process is created and expressed.

It is the addition of knowledge to the long list of different types of capital — financial, natural, built, human, cultural, social — that led Boulding to exclaim before he died that knowledge is "the hope of humanity." It is knowledge capital that is fundamental to the transformation of the other forms to ends that can sustain life on spaceship earth.

The mass of diverse experiments depicted in this chapter are each building on existing knowledge and creating new knowledge. In some cases they are resurrecting lessons of yesteryear, that ethical relationships are central to building and sustaining success in tough times. Their tailoring and integrating of services to meet the needs of their members, their transparency, their emphasis on education and the transfer of knowledge for empowerment of diverse stakeholders, their focus on building trust and social solidarity — all bear testimony to the power of knowledge being applied and created.

These characteristics are the hallmark of what is emerging as an alternative ecology of finance, rising like a phoenix from the wasteland and ashes of a financial system that breeds ignorance and invents overly complex financial instruments to cover up usurious and predatory practices. As Bob Hope once commented, "A bank is a place that will lend you money if you can prove that you don't need it." While this may not have been true among the relationship bankers of yesteryear, the casino bankers thrive on debt and dependency. Usury was outlawed in the past and it needs to be outlawed again.

Unfortunately this will not be easy. Nor will it happen overnight. There is a long hard road to travel to secure fair-trade banking and economic systems internationally. While this ecosystem of social and community finance innovation is growing, it remains off the radar and marginalized for most people and most politicians. Even under the Obama administration, with a president whose roots are in community organizing and who is very familiar with the remarkable results being achieved by CDFIs such as Coastal Enterprises Inc. in Maine, public investment is infinitesimal when compared with the bailout of the big banks.

Regardless, this chapter illustrates the seeds from which we will grow and expand our collective capacity to finance transition. Add the JAK Bank, CEI in Maine, RESO in Montreal, several others in the chapters that follow, and the many we have not even hinted at, and one gets a sense of what is possible. This is encouraging and hopeful. Many commercial bankers trained in the big banks have jumped ship for the social banking world, and they love it. They love the transparency and the honesty of the approach that seeks to empower borrowers and businesses and repudiates any cunning deception that takes advantage of widespread financial illiteracy. The formidable challenge is the task of combining the community and social banking parts into more visible and powerful consortiums that can be federated to shape public discourse, social investment policy, and priorities. This is not easy in a context where the ideological and cultural predisposition remains weighted to individual gain rather than the common good.

What is missing is leadership to bring diverse networks together, forge intensive cooperative links, mobilize a social/ecological justice vision, and develop creative ways to deliver knowledge capital through dynamic services that make money our servant and no longer our master. Knowledge and patient forms of cooperative finance strategically address the broad-based needs of citizens globally. This is the way to transcend unjust, usurious banking practices that are anathema to the social and ecological economic goals so urgently needed in the 21st century.

Resilience Reflections

An unjust, opaque, unaccountable, and highly centralized financial system is a source of stress across many sectors of society. The fact that there is such a wide and *diverse* array of *experimentation and innovation* emerging with ever greater rapidity is a testimony to human resilience.

Many of the examples in this and other chapters are inherently *modular*; that is they are decentralized and linked to specific territories. They both create and leverage *social capital*, sometimes by creating new partnerships and *collective governance structures*; at other times by reorganizing existing relationships. The community banking partnership model increased resilience by creating partnerships between local groups that had not previously been linked, creating a common strategy and *collaborative governance structure* to create impacts none could achieve on their own. The community development partners program brings together individual credit unions within the American credit union movement to reap reciprocal benefits through common goals that in turn required *tightening up feedback loops* and *increasing social capital*. Examine almost any of the *innovations* in this chapter and it is not difficult to discern the resilience principles in play.

Yet there remains a problem. These convivial banking innovations need to be joined together more broadly. *Social capital and tightened feedback loops* between innovators need to be woven together into federated forces for change. Given the power and hegemony of the global financial system, and given the urgency of mobilizing and focusing huge amounts of capital on the tasks of transition, there is a need for more powerful and organized means to contend, both in the discourse and in changing the rules of the game to favor the survival of planet and people. Otherwise, it is difficult to see how we will secure and expand those innovations that are working and how we will continue the process of experimentation and innovation in the field of finance. Federating for change is a central task, one we turn to in the next chapter.

CHAPTER 9

Federating the Change Agents: Securing the Gains

*The Roman arena was technically a level playing field.
But on one side were the lions with all the weapons and on the other
side the Christians with all the blood. That's not a level playing field.
That's a slaughter. And so is putting people into the economy
without equipping them with capital, while equipping a tiny
handful of people with hundreds and thousands of times
more than they can use.*

— Louis Kelso

THE FIRST STEP in the SEE Change pedagogy we have advanced in this book is to SEE the world differently. We must redefine our field of vision, broaden our understanding of the context and challenges we face, and open our eyes to new ways of meeting our basic needs.

Second, we must SEEK strategic pathways through which to bring into balance our relationships with each other and with the earth. We have seen ample evidence that when people, organizations, and institutions become engaged and organized around a shared vision and values, and a shared analysis of what is most important, options for acting emerge and strategic transition projects are advanced.

Third, we must SHARE what we are learning. Inspiring others with the possibilities and responsibilities for navigating the transitions we are called to make is an ongoing task.

Fourth, we must SECURE the innovations that are getting results by scaling up and broadening their applications. This is the final pedagogical element in the SEE Change framework. Many of the cases we have set out show how particular innovations have been scaled up and their successes replicated elsewhere. Often, political action that changes the rules of the game in order to support expansion or strike down policies that thwart success has been part of the story. For example:

- A cross-section of Alaskan citizens lobbied hard for regional aquaculture associations; without that victory they could not have achieved their amazing results.
- Southwest Montreal's RESO emerged from a broad-based coalition aimed at leveraging innovations in order to win adequate resources and political space so it could drive a community-controlled strategy of social and economic revitalization.
- Kristianstad would not be nearing its vision of freedom from fossil fuels if its political leadership had not been willing, ready, and able to defend such an ambitious and contentious agenda.
- The social solidarity cooperatives of Italy (described in Chapter 10) also required a broad-based lobby to win appropriate legislation, which allowed them to create the framework for their rapid growth.

The strength of the strategic pathways we have charted thus far lies in their local and regional roots, though, as we have seen, some have grown beyond their regions through various kinds of federated structures. Where political action was taken up, it was focused on a specific target and sought a particular gain.

Important as such action is, is it realistic to think it can be effective against the global powerhouses of wealth and control, who believe economic growth is an unalloyed public good most expediently advanced by keeping government out of the way? The proposition of moving to a steady-state economy is laughable to many in this camp. After all, they will argue, millions have been lifted out of poverty. Wealth is the basis for investment, and without the freedom to pursue profit, investment will dry up. Besides, is it not by virtue of successful corporations that the jobs and taxes needed to support social and environmental programs are created and sustained? These are powerful arguments. Indeed, they are difficult to counter if you are limited to basing your argument on the last 40 years of supply-side economics, deregulation of capital markets, and huge expansion in fossil-fuel-dependent economic growth.

Nevertheless, the rejection of these arguments is being fed by what businessman, author, and environmentalist Paul Hawken calls "blessed unrest." Deepening disparity, human dislocation, and ecological threats are feeding a different kind of growth — a virtually invisible but global movement that cuts across outdated ideologies, different classes, and varied cultures.

Autonomous and diverse, often local or issue-specific in their focus, outgrowths of this movement are multiplying across the globe. Some grow out of propositions to solve local problems; others out of opposition to forces compromising the health of the local environment. Others cut their swath more widely, advancing propositions or mobilizing opposition, linked together, often unwittingly, by a broad concern for the protection, healing, and health of people and planet. Few have substantial monetary resources at their disposal, though among their numbers are a surprising number of billionaires alleged to have had an epiphany on their way to the 21st century. Their breadth and diversity, arguably one of their strengths and a key contributor to their successes, "also leaves the movement singularly vulnerable," suggests Hawken in his book *Blessed Unrest*:

> However adaptive, diversity can also prevent connection, cooperation and effectiveness. Inevitably there is jockeying for position and territory, and lack of collaboration, especially when organizations are forced to compete for scarce resources. There is narcissism, when small groups begin to stare into the waters of just causes and imagine themselves to be saviours... Strongly held beliefs can breed fanaticism as easily as genuine breakthroughs...While issues grow in importance, a balkanized movement does not match the scale of the problems. This is particularly obvious with respect to climate change. On one hand, the practical implementation of hands-on energy reduction needs to be implemented on a local scale. But the major policy changes and initiatives that must be taken on the national and international levels with respect to public transportation, oil company subsidies, and renewable energy are stymied by the corruption of politicians and special interests; as yet there has been no coming together of organizations in a united front that can counter the massive scale and power of the global corporations and lobbyists that protect the status quo.

Fewer in number but strategically important are those that have managed to create a united front. This evolving capacity to weave proposition and opposition into broadly based, multilayered federations succeeds in shifting the discourse about what ends the economy should serve and, in modest ways, makes some inroads into changing the rules by which the economy is governed.

Prime Minister Margaret Thatcher's most famous and oft-repeated utterance was "There is no alternative!" The acronym, TINA, was shorthand for her audacious claim that any deviation from free markets, free trade, and capitalist globalization was certain to lead to disaster. This is the voice of the "Lions" set loose in the "Roman arena" of the last 40 years.

Meanwhile, a growing numbers of "Christians" are finding their voices. Though their means of defense may seem laughable from the perspective of a lion, with all its ferocity, teeth, claws, and strength, it may yet surprise. Sufficient numbers of inspired, determined, cooperative, and smartly organized folks occupying every square meter of the arena, armed with a fist-sized rock in one hand, blinding dust in the other, and a good measure of solidarity, may yet prevail. They know there is no alternative.

Reinventing the Guilds: A Way Forward?

Before sharing two contemporary examples of the power of federating for change, we will take a brief detour to examine why some of the greatest minds of the early 20th century believed that reinventing the guilds was a promising pathway for progressive change.

Arthur Penty, a British Christian socialist, triggered a major debate in 1906 when he advocated reinventing the guilds as a possible method to organize a wide range of workers, artisans, tradesmen, and small-business people into an effective federation that would reconnect productive property and social purpose. Some of the most brilliant minds of the generation vigorously debated his ideas in *New Age* magazine. A central and ongoing focus in this rich debate was practical ideas and policies for closing the gap between social purpose and property rights.

Background

Penty's ideas were no doubt fed by the ideas of economic democracy, including worker ownership and self-management, that were bubbling across Europe a century ago, fed by the Long Depression that began in the 1870s and by growing levels of inequality in this age of the Robber Barons. Many workers felt threatened by emerging assembly-line techniques of mass production. They worried that the technological shift in industry would both deskill them and deprive them of what little independence remained. This may have been why the possibility of a modern incarnation of the guilds was appealing.

The worker self-management movement became especially strong in France, where, after the legalization of trade unions in 1884, worker organizations established the Bourses du Travail. Viewed as centers to strengthen working-class culture, the Bourses provided training and educational services, community facilities, job placement, libraries, meeting halls, theaters, political education, and support for cooperatives and mutual aid associations.

Controlled and managed by the trade unions and local workers' associations, the first Bourse in Paris (1887) expanded to 158 local branches by 1913, inspiring similar worker self-management movements across Europe.

In North America, the self-managed and federated nature of medieval guilds inspired nine Philadelphia tailors to found the Knights of Labor in 1869. They sought membership from the broadest range of workers possible: homeworkers, craftsmen, industrial workers, miners, farmers, and shopkeepers. Unique for the time, women and ethnic minorities were actively recruited as members. Excluded were bankers, stockbrokers, gamblers, and other rentiers who lived off their capital rather than their effort. Beyond advancing worker ownership and producer cooperatives — their initial focus — the Knights campaigned for women's suffrage and a range of tax, land, banking, and monetary reforms.

Less than 20 years later there were more than 700,000 members of the Knights across the United States and Canada. While they made progress in advancing worker ownership, a combination of strikes in the 1880s and a further depression in the early 1890s seriously depleted their funds and their membership. Insufficient equity and difficulties in accessing credit left the Knights weakened and poorly positioned to compete with the expansion of assembly-line methods of production and the increasing size of industrial plants in urban manufacturing centers. However, they continued to organize farmer–trade union alliances in rural areas, which led to the later growth of agricultural cooperatives in places like Saskatchewan, Canada (described by Seymour Lipset in his book *Agrarian Socialism*).

The vision and efforts of the Knights inspired others, including Cardinal Manning in London and Cardinal Gibbons in Baltimore. Together they drafted a statement of Catholic social philosophy that influenced Pope Leo XIII. His encyclical letter of 1891, *Rerum Novarum*, argued that ownership of the means of production should be spread as widely as possible among the general populace.

Rise of Guild Socialism

It was in this context that Penty's advocacy of a 20th-century adaptation of the medieval guilds kicked off a creative dialogue between leading intellectuals, which took the form of a substantive and extended debate in the pages of the *New Age*. If ownership of the means of production should be "spread widely," as advocated by Pope Leo XIII, whose responsibility was it to do the spreading? Should it be the task of a centralized welfare state that efficiently captured taxes and then deployed them for health and social services, as advocated by H.G. Wells and Sidney Webb? Or should the state's role be to facilitate as much as possible the ownership of property and production by

Fig. 9.1: *The Guildhall, Fordwich, England. The guild houses persist, and the ideas behind them continue to be reinvented and reinterpreted right into the modern day.*
Source: © Photodynamx | Dreamstime.com

a broad cross section of the population as a way of increasing self-reliance, as advocated by G.K. Chesterton and Hilaire Belloc?

Two other key players in the debate, R.H. Tawney and G.D.H. Cole, saw the merits in both approaches, and ultimately their work, along with that of others, became focused on Penty's advocacy of reinventing the guilds. They envisioned a vast and diverse network of worker cooperatives, trade guilds, and social investment funds becoming dominant players across the industrial spectrum. By designing decentralized and complementary systems of coproduction and co-delivery, producers, consumers, and capital providers could be organized to come together to reunite work with social purpose. The transfer of ownership implied by this ambitious model of economic democracy, combined with the decentralized but federated organization of production and governance, was called Guild Socialism. It reflected what two of the earliest contributors to the *New Age*, Tawney and John Hobson, had argued: that injustice could not be solved if the grossly unequal distribution of property rights was not addressed. Without reconnecting workers and other stakeholders in production to new forms of social ownership, inequality would prevail.

This was not a monolithic strategy. Rather, guild socialism was premised on a pluralistic and democratic approach that was locally focused but also federated into national guilds. To achieve the vision, Cole and Tawney called on trade unions and cooperatives to work together to advance the cause of a broad diversity of consumer and producer cooperatives. They advocated allotments for food growing, and agricultural guilds to oversee food production in the green belts they envisioned for garden cities; affordable housing and social services (similar to what is provided by Champlain Housing Trust, described in Chapter 4); utility ownership by local authorities, who could partner with cooperatives to provide energy and water service (as has happened in Kirklees and Kristianstaad — see Chapter 5); and public ownership for larger industries, such as, for example, railways, shipping, mining, and steel production. The overall idea of guild socialism was to democratize and functionally decentralize economic management within a federated model of collaboration and coordination between various forms of public, private, and cooperative ownership. The guild motto was "Not for profit, not for charity, but for service." Profit was fine as long as it was a means to an end, not an end in itself.

Guild socialism was also seen as a means to transcend the limitations of representative democracy. It reconceptualized democracy as an active verb rather than just a hollow noun. Proponents believed diverse local economic action was necessary to foster the spirit and the practice of democracy in everyday life. The theory was that, as capacity and influence grew, an increasingly active and self-confident citizenry could take back powers from the nation-state. This would reduce bureaucratic inefficiency and vest decision making, more appropriately, in decentralized and participative forms of ownership and governance.

In *Guild Socialism: A Plan for Economic Democracy*, published in 1920, Cole advanced a vision of civic co-sovereignty. He proposed a Guild Congress that would decentralize power and coordinate strategic initiatives taken at the local and regional level. The Congress would comprise four types of guild: producers, including small business and farmers; consumer councils and cooperatives; civic services and citizens associations; and other voluntary organizations. The Guild Congress would complement local authorities, and together they would shape a "functional economic democracy" to serve as a national and regional counterweight to Parliamentary democracy. In other words, the guild socialists were calling for a more diverse, pluralistic system of checks and balances.

Over the course of World War I, growing support for guild socialism came from intellectuals, trade unionists, Christian socialists, and some politicians in Britain. Bertrand Russell declared himself a strong advocate of guild socialism and wrote two books explaining his reasons: *Principles for Social Reconstruction* and *Roads to Freedom*. A National Guilds League was formed in 1915. Trade union interest was strong in the railway, construction, and mining industries and among postal workers. Starting in 1918, guilds were established in the arts, clothing, furnishing, construction, and farming sectors. Trade unions also advanced ideas to show how the public sector could be involved and ambitiously designed a national plan for organizing the mining industry under a guild system.

The largest project in guild socialism took place in the building industry (described by Geoffrey Ostergaard in *The Tradition of Workers' Control*). By 1921 a hundred local building guilds were established and federated into the National Building Guild. Each involved a procurement partnership between local authorities and cooperatives to build council housing. Finance for construction was arranged with the banking division of the Co-operative Wholesale Society, a federation of consumer cooperatives. The system worked well for 18 months. Then, in 1923, an economic slump and a reduction in government subsidies created a cost-price squeeze. Inadequately capitalized (that is, without the necessary equity) and with insufficient access to credit, the largest guild of the time went broke.

Interest in guild socialism waned. The inspiration of the Bourse and the Knights of Labor, and guidance from some of the leading intellectuals of the time, was not enough to break out of the box. Guild socialism, with its aim of reuniting ownership with social purpose and extending the reach of democracy, had failed to solve the capitalization dilemma.

All was not lost, however. In 1921 the prospects seemed good that the cooperative movement would play a key role in rebuilding cities, tackling the slums, and redistributing wealth. Consumer and agricultural cooperatives were winning more of the market in several European countries. Worker-owned firms, still relatively small but expanding, were finding a voice in the international co-op movement that was evolving. Trade union interest in cooperatives for mining and auto manufacturing industries was taking hold.

And Fall — the Repression of the Cooperative Economy

Then the assaults began.

Johnston Birchall, in *Co-Op: The People's Business*, described how, starting in 1921, Italian fascists, led by Benito Mussolini, arrested and killed the leadership of Italy's 8,000 cooperative societies, dissolved the Co-operative League, burned and plundered cooperative shops, and forced the remaining co-ops to be incorporated under the Fascist Union.

In the early 1930s, Germany had 1,100 consumer co-ops; 21,000 credit unions; 4,000 cooperative savings banks; and 7,000 agricultural co-ops —

with a total of 4.5 million members. They suffered a fate similar to that of the movement in Italy.

In Austria, consumer co-ops were rapidly expanding, and one in every three households were members. In Vienna alone, membership was over 170,000; the sector provided goods and services for more than half the city's population. When Hitler marched in, co-op movement leaders were arrested, dismissed, and replaced by fascist supporters; assets were seized and transferred to private business owners.

In Spain, General Francisco Franco's victory in the civil war led to the seizure of consumer and worker co-op assets, the arrest and killing of leaders, and the exile of many to Latin America.

Russia, in 1918, had 26,000 cooperative societies handling and distributing 65 percent of food supplies in central Russia. The mutual movement had its own central bank and a Co-operative University in Moscow. After the Bolshevik Revolution, all who had been cooperative members were forced to join the Communist Party. Without the cooperative food distribution network, famine and starvation spread across the country. Three years later, Lenin did an about-face: markets were allowed to reopen, cooperatives were given autonomy again, and the agricultural cooperatives expanded rapidly until 1928, when central planning again became the order of the day. Under Stalin agricultural co-operatives were forced into a collectivization model under authoritarian control.

Yet out of the ashes of guild socialism's failure to solve the capitalization conundrum and the savage assault on the cooperative movement in much of Europe, the phoenix arose in a poor, remote region of Spain. A rural Catholic priest committed to putting Catholic social teaching into practice started a school, helped its six first graduates form a co-op, and figured out how to solve the puzzle of the equity gap (a story we pick up in the next chapter).

Constructing the Social Solidarity Economy in Quebec

What kind of organizations might individuals seek to join if their ultimate goal was to transition to an economy based on the core values of care, sustainability, democracy, and inclusiveness?

- **Consider the kinds of businesses that might be included at the table.** Think of a community-owned radio station that is committed to relaying progressive news and positive innovation in a small region. Think of an enterprise, owned by a nonprofit, that is recycling waste and employing a workforce that is 80 percent people with disabilities who would otherwise not be working.

Think about cooperative and nonprofit day-care centers that look after thousands of children whose parents are earning a living. Think of a group of artisans and craft workers who have organized a social enterprise to advance their art. Think of a cooperative that is organized to provide reasonably priced, high-quality home care to ailing elders. Think of a federation of cooperatives, large and small, that represent democratic businesses across many sectors of the economy.

- **Consider the type of community-based infrastructure that could help build more of these kinds of businesses.** Think about community development corporations committed to mobilizing citizens and organizations to revitalize disadvantaged neighborhoods (as RESO did in southwest Montreal) or marginalized rural areas that the mainstream economy has left behind. Consider the idea of a network of community-controlled development organizations providing loans and technical assistance to small businesses and social enterprises that otherwise would not gain access to credit.

- **Consider the kinds of organizations that could add the clout and resources which might help convince governments that business as usual has to change — that a fairer, more democratic economy is both necessary and possible.** Think of a federation of labor unions with a deep history of defending the rights of workers to a "living wage" and decent working conditions. Think of the potential of active social movements — women's, anti-poverty, aboriginal, environmental, and others — joining together to press for change. Think of a federation of housing cooperatives from across an entire province that aim to continue their efforts to expand affordable housing. Think about the key networks evolving around local food, sustainable production, and low-carbon consumption of energy.

- **Consider what financing institutions and mechanisms would be important to have exposed to the social entrepreneurial energy and innovative products/services that require financing so as to expand the numbers of those producing, consuming, and acting within a framework of solidarity and transition.** Think of a federation of credit unions owned by a membership that includes 80 percent of the citizens in an entire province. Think of labor-sponsored investment funds with a mandate to invest in small and medium-sized businesses. Think of community and social enterprise loan funds operating in a range of local communities.

- **Finally, consider what role academics and university researchers might play in a movement for significant change in the economy.** Think of the economists, political scientists, business professors, sociologists, geographers, finance specialists, environmental design specialists, and resource management specialists who inhabit the academy. What might they contribute if they focused their research on questions leaders and practitioners from all these other groups felt were really important to build an economy based on the core values of care, sustainability, democracy, and inclusiveness?

Just imagine what all of these groups sitting at a common table with a common purpose might accomplish. If you do, you have begun to envision what the Chantier de l'économie sociale has become in a little over 15 years. A network of networks, the Chantier (which in French means "construction site") emerged out of a crisis in Quebec in the mid-1990s.

Facing major budget deficits, the provincial premier of the time, Lucien Bouchard, announced plans to convene an economic summit of government and business leaders, a well-established tradition in the Quebec context. However, this time there was a new player demanding to be at the table. In 1996 the women's movement and its allies flooded the streets to fight against poverty and exclusion. Potential budget cuts that would disproportionately hit the poor, workers, and the community sector galvanized strong resistance and a growing opposition. Among their numbers were dynamic, self-confident organizations that had emerged in Quebec over the previous 10 to 15 years. Community economic development (CED) corporations had been making significant impacts, revitalizing some of the poorest urban neighborhoods. Rural community development corporations (CDCs) had taken shape in many parts of the province. A new generation of cooperatives and social enterprise was beginning to blossom.

These groups contended that opposition, while necessary, was not enough. They began formulating propositions for democratic, decentralized, proactive approaches to economic and social development. The community and its citizens were viewing themselves as actors in their own development rather than passive recipients of development fomented by others. Multi-stakeholder CED corporations, such as RESO, working in five of the poorest neighborhoods in Montreal, had brought together business, trade unions, and the community movement in neighborhood economic and social action. And they were achieving concrete results.

In response to the growing pressure from social movements and the emerging CED movement, Premier Bouchard invited them to take a seat at

the table for the 1996 economic summit. It was the first time these movements had taken part in such an event, and they took full advantage of it.
By the end of the summit they had forged agreements with government,
the private sector, and the labor movement that recognized their contribution and their legitimacy as actors in the economy. Following this

The Chantier de l'économie sociale

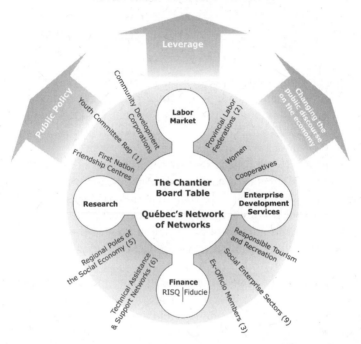

Technical Assistance & Support Networks
- Local Development Corporations
- Community Economic Development Corporations
- Community Loan Funds
- Cooperative Development Organizations
- Housing Development

Ex-Officio members
- Fiducie
- RISQ
- Labor Market Committee on the Social Economy

Social Enterprise Sectors
- Housing
- Training Enterprises
- Child care
- Perinatal
- Home Care
- Sheltered Workshops
- Community radio
- Community Television
- Recycling

Fig. 9.2: *Chantier is French for "construction site." Through a federated network structure
that cuts across key sectors and constituencies, this construction site for the social solidarity
economy in Quebec is changing the public discourse on what the economy is for, securing
positive policy change, and leveraging benefits for communities and regions across the
province.*

political recognition, a task group was created to put in place the Chantier de l'économie sociale, the construction site for the social economy (see Figure 9.2 which is elaborated in the text which follows).

Federating a Development System to Build the Social (Solidarity) Economy

People in Quebec see the social economy as made up of association-based economic initiatives focused on the values of solidarity, autonomy, and citizenship. Consider just a sampling of sectors included within the social economy in the province: recycling, cultural businesses, alternative media, forestry, child care, manufacturing of various sorts, agriculture, transport, health, funeral services, training businesses, technology businesses, ecological and cultural tourism, etc. By 2005 there were 7,150 social economy enterprises in Quebec. These enterprises hired 124,000 people and generated $17.2 billion in turnover.

These firms bring the core values of solidarity, autonomy, and citizenship into practice through democratic forms of participation and ownership. And while there have been examples of these kinds of initiatives in Quebec for a long time, their expansion has accelerated since the formation of the Chantier. Several factors contribute to this growth, but the main ones, listed and described below, are the strategic support services put in place to facilitate the start-up and growth of these enterprises.

Planning, Research, Promotion, and Advocacy

The Chantier member networks represent hundreds of organizations, which in turn represent hundreds of thousands of members committed to promoting the social economy. Within the broad-based membership, there are very particular resources that shape its promotion and support role.

The Chantier umbrella houses partnerships with territorially based local development centers (LDCs), community futures development corporations (CFDCs), rural community development corporations (CDCs), and cooperative technical assistance organizations. This density of community-based actors across the entire province plays an important role in supporting the planning and development of new social enterprises and cooperatives, as well as providing backing for other local entrepreneurs. The capacity for outreach and technical assistance is a key factor fostering start-up and expansions; it improves the quality of financing proposals significantly, thus reducing the transaction costs of lenders.

Another important factor at work is the Chantier's formal partnerships with university researchers, who for ten years have been documenting what is working and what is not, codifying best practice, building the rationale for and details of innovative financing tools, mapping the field to document its scope (including the characteristics and results being achieved), and undertaking policy research and development. All of this is tremendously important when it comes to elaborating the context and rationale for expansion of the social economy. Researchers also work strategically with practitioners to co-create new knowledge and tools that will advance the social economy.

CREDIT

Réseau d'investissement social du Québec (RISQ), a province-wide organization dedicated entirely to making capital accessible for the social economy sector, was founded by the Chantier in 1997. Seed money came from a $10-million loan fund made up of investments from the private sector, labor-sponsored investment funds, and the Quebec government. This was one of the results facilitated by agreements made at the 1996 summit. RISQ has consistently leveraged other sources of financing , including loan funds held by local development organizations (LDCs and CFDCs) as well as by credit unions.

Ten years on, the Chantier created a second financial instrument, the FIDUCIE (*fiducie* means "trust" in English). For several years, social economy entrepreneurs had been identifying the need for a more diverse set of financial products. Traditional grants and loans were not enough; they wanted financing to take their social mission into account. They also wanted to find a way to retain long-term capital in their businesses. The FIDUCIE was the result.

Capitalized to the tune of $52.8 million by the federal government and two trade union-owned investment groups, this social venture fund is a big step forward. Bridging the gap between financial markets and social economy enterprises, it pools the risk and reduces the costs of financing for both investors and enterprises. The FIDUCIE also leverages a network of competent stakeholders to evaluate projects. Those social enterprises that qualify are offered a "patient capital product" — loans with a 15-year capital repayment moratorium that can be used for two things: working capital, which is critical for purchasing equipment and for marketing new products; and loans to finance the acquisition, construction, or renovation of real estate assets.

Having successfully launched the FIDUCIE, the Chantier and researchers are now working on creating a secondary market for the much larger loans they are making. The objective is to sell off performing loans to other lenders in order to accelerate the redeployment of the FIDUCIE's patient capital for the ongoing expansion of the social economy.

EQUITY

While the local development centers have been an important source of equity for start-up grants to social economy enterprises, there remains a strategic equity gap in the Quebec development system. Clearly, the social financing scheme of the Fiducie is an important new resource, and its patient financing products help social enterprises build equity in their balance sheets. However, even this it is not sufficient. It was estimated in 2004 that $100 million in equity could be productively utilized over a ten-year period. A federal tax credit is one possible method for raising this kind of finance. It has been used successfully in Nova Scotia to leverage citizen investment to start and expand social enterprises in a variety of sectors.

HUMAN RESOURCE DEVELOPMENT

Businesses within the social economy can call on RISQ and the other technical assistance organizations, already noted, for support to improve management capacity or worker skills. These organizations, along with stakeholders associated with the FIDUCIE, are important resources for developing a cadre of competent social entrepreneurs who can develop new enterprises and put the financial packages to good use. There are also several university-based diploma and degree programs in Quebec that offer training for the leadership that will expand the social economy well into the future.

Transition Factors

In 12 years the Chantier has woven together a dynamic, federated development system. It aligns and coordinates action around key economic functions and imbues them with social purpose. Born out of opposition, the Chantier has been adept at advancing propositions during its short history. It is constantly leveraging resources, and its capacity to coherently advance a concrete agenda is getting results. And, importantly, it has demonstrated its capacity for opposition when necessary. When a new government tried to increase the cost to parents of Quebec's high-quality, nonprofit and cooperatively run child-care system, the Chantier played a major role in mobilizing protests that within one week saw 25,000 people hit the streets. The government backed down. This ability to propose first and oppose when necessary has allowed the organization to protect its gains while continuing to enlarge the economic and political space occupied by the social economy in Quebec.

In contrast to the Seikatsu movement presented in Chapter 6, which has never had any notable financial support from the state for its activities, the Chantier has maintained funding for its core functions and has successfully promoted a large increase in state funding to the social economy in Quebec.

These funds support a range of programs that directly finance some key parts of the social economy, the largest of which is child care. The state also systematically supports a wide variety of funds for capacity building and technical assistance and, as noted above, key investments in the financial instruments managed by RISQ and the FIDUCIE.

This relationship with the state is evolving into a partnership in which mutual accountability is becoming apparent. Active discussions, research, and collaboration around what is called the co-production and co-construction of public policy are emerging as a tense but nevertheless operational norm.

On a conceptual note, it is interesting to contemplate how the language that dominates the discourse in Quebec is changing. Early debates after the 1996 economic summit pitted some of the social movements, notably the women's and labor movements, against the new-found recognition of the social economy. The former felt this recognition was a betrayal of a political project of transformation, siphoning off energy to play an accommodating role at the margins and putting Band-Aids on the endemic wounds created by capitalism. Labor fretted about whether well-paid public service jobs were going to be offloaded into a government contracting-out strategy to cut costs. On the other hand, leading practitioners and researchers in Quebec positioned the social economy within a pluralistic vision of Quebec society, focusing on building the social economy sector within the third system referred to in Chapter 1.

More recently, however, the term "social solidarity economy" has come into use, and it has become clear that the intent of the solidarity economy is to change the whole economy. It is not content with confining its activity to collective enterprise trading with a social or ecological purpose, or operating at the margins. As Michael Lewis and Dan Swinney explained the concept in 2007:

> The solidarity economy as a conceptual framework in progress may have significant theoretical and strategic implications for actors in the social economy. The distinct boundaries most social economy actors draw to set themselves apart from the private and public sectors shape their perception of the terrain upon which action is viewed as either desirable or possible; the "third" sector is the primary locus of strategy and action. In contrast, the solidarity economy thrusts social economy actors into the spaces among and between the three economic sectors and inserts reciprocity as the dominant animating driver, creating a space for expanding solidarity.

At the Social and Solidarity Economy Summit, held in Montreal in November 2006 to celebrate the 10th anniversary of the social economy initiative, over 600 participants clearly linked the concept of *solidarity economy* with that of the *social economy*. Two excerpts from the Declaration show well this more global vision.

> Collective enterprises are not alone in their contributions to economic democratization. We are pleased to see the constant rise of responsible investment, the commitment of labour to economic development, public policy that favours sustainable development, responsible consumption practices, and companies that are acting in a socially responsible fashion. Clearly, the social economy is part of broader movement that is constructing alternatives to pervasive neoliberalism, and a more democratic solidarity-based economy.
>
> Today, we invite women and men in Quebec to join this movement to establish a solidarity-based economy that seeks a more just response to social, economic and environmental imperatives. We encourage Quebeckers to innovate and adopt more responsible consumption practices. We, the actors and partners of the social and solidarity economy, are determined to reinforce the social economy's contribution to the sustainable development of Quebec, and, through our partnerships, to sustainable development in others parts of the world.

An interesting evolution indeed.

Resilience Reflections

Organizing *diversity* is a hallmark of the Chantier. Its success in mobilizing a broad cross-section of networks around a common table and agenda is a powerful foundation. Each of the network partners maintains its autonomy while concurrently acknowledging that its ability to affect the public discourse, shape public policy, educate the market, and mobilize intellectual and financial resources is significantly enhanced through joint cooperation and action. Mobilizing diverse networks has expanded the societal space for the diversity of enterprise forms and values to be substantially enhanced. There is little doubt that in this aspect, the Chantier is strengthening resilience at the level of the firm, the sector, the community, and the province as a whole.

Modularity and *a layered approach to governance* are evident in several ways. The autonomy of network members is preserved. Financial instruments

(RISQ and FIDUCIE) linked to the Chantier are key to expanding the governance structures to include investors. Their support for developing enterprises that are committed to inclusiveness, democratic governance, and the priority of people over capital enhances autonomy at the firm and community level and enhances the space and supports for citizens to take responsibility for their own development.

The inter-linkages between the several layers of action and co-responsibility embedded in structures of the Chantier represent a viable system of *feedback loops* that enable ongoing *social learning and innovation*, feeding *social capital formation* as well as benefiting from the trust built among the leadership and constituencies of member networks.

One last comment is in order. When one compares and contrasts the Seitaksu (Chapter 6) and Chantier cases, one major feature that stands out as distinct between the two is the relationship with government. Seikatsu's history with respect to government has been its advocacy of a change in policy — for example, a request that genetically modified foods be labeled. Other than that, it has had little discernible financial support from government. The Chantier, on the other hand, has a more complex and interdependent relationship with governments, one that includes major financial support from the state. It is interesting to ask if this fundamental difference renders one more resilient than the other. Arguably, the Chantier's support from the state is a major advantage as well as a potential vulnerability. It is possible that a change in the provincial government to one akin to the current federal regime in Canada, which canceled all funding for the social economy when it came to power, could lead to major funding cuts for the Chantier. Seikatsu appears more resilient when viewed from this vantage point. Government has no direct way of undercutting its financial viability — it is entirely self-supporting.

However, it is interesting to note the high degree of interest the Seikatsu movement has in the Quebec experience. Several delegations have come to study what is being achieved by the Chantier. One of the reasons may be the Chantier's relationship with the state, and the extended influence and positive impacts that have thus far evolved from this partnership. Could such a model, built on the highly resilient Seikatsu foundation, be a significant means of accelerating the scaling up of the highly innovative Japanese model?

La Via Campesina: Building a Global Movement for Food Sovereignty

The farmer is one of the most important professions in society, at least as important as doctors and far more important than lawyers.

— La Via Campesina

La Via Campesina (LVC) grew out of the radical erosion of rural life experienced by the peasant organizations of Latin America in the second half of the 20th century. Policies of the World Bank and the International Monetary Fund (IMF), as well as the fossil-fuel-intensive "green revolution" of the 1970s and 1980s, represented an assault on peasant and small farmer agriculture across the continent. Social and economic relations between rural people and the state deteriorated as the state carried out a flurry of moves to transform food into an export commodity that would earn foreign currency, at the same time as heavily indebted governments were forced by the IMF to cut services — including education and social supports — in order to borrow from Northern capital markets. As markets opened up, as commodity-based agriculture became more dominant, and as cheap, subsidized food from the North was dumped in the South, prices paid to farmers serving local and regional markets declined.

The relationship between associations and networks of farmers collapsed as governments withdrew their support. The destruction of old patterns created a political space within which new questions were posed and a fresh analysis carried out. As capital became more global and concentrated, and as free-trade agreements emerged, the livelihoods of farmers were threatened. Simultaneously, the rapid growth of an energy- and water-intensive monoculture of cash crops was destroying the natural health of the land upon which sustainable food production depended.

This analysis is reflected in the Declaration of Quito, a statement that emerged from a major conference of mainly indigenous people from across the Americas in 1990. The declaration articulated a strengthening resistance to the extensive plans of governments to celebrate the arrival of Columbus 500 years earlier. It also depicted the moral foundation of the movements out of which La Via Campesina emerged.

> We do not own nature...it is not a commodity...it is an integral part of our life: it is our past, our present and our future. We believe that this meaning of humanity and of the environment is not only valid for our communities of Indoamerican people. We believe that this form of life is an option and a light for the people of the world oppressed by a system which dominates people and nature.

Continental organizing of peasants and farmers coalesced in 1992 with the formation of a Latin America-wide network that aimed to resist destruction and build a new model that brought food production home from the grips of the global market. In Europe, India, and even North America, more and more farmers were coming to the same conclusion. The brutal impacts of free trade, declining prices, and industrial agriculture were hollowing out rural life in communities across the globe. A new round of enclosure was underway. Global capital and the big "M" Market were well into privatizing for profit the control of everything from seeds to water. As peasants and small to medium-size farmers began to understand the forces at work, the organizing across borders, cultures, and languages accelerated. In May 1993, 70 leaders of peasant and farmer organizations met in Mons, Belgium, and formally committed to work together to defend their rights and resist neo-liberal assaults on their role as the world's food producers.

From the outset, LVC strategically set its terms of membership to ensure that the voices of grassroots peasant and small-farmer organizations would not be compromised or muted:

- NGOs, foundations, and aid agencies cannot be members.
- Financial support with conditions is rejected, as are attempts of outside agencies to influence LVC decisions.
- LVC maintains a deep suspicion of constant attempts by international agencies to involve it in consultations, multi-stakeholder dialogues, and conflict resolution.
- It speaks in its own name. No one else can represent member interests at any international forum or negotiating table.
- It is militant, makes clear demands, and views conflict — aggressive debate and protest — as an important tool for building a critical mass for positive change.

However, LVC's oppositional strategies and tactics are balanced by a wide range of positive propositions for change. These are hammered out through extensive democratic discussion and debate. This core commitment to deliberative process has shaped the political and developmental character of what today is the largest global social movement in human history, involving some 500 million families who are members of one of 148 organizations in 69 countries. Members come from the ranks of organizations representing peasants, the landless, rural workers, family farmers, artisans, fisher folk, indigenous people, rural women, and youth.

The central proposition of LVC is food sovereignty, a formulation it inserted into the debate of the World Food Summit of 1996 (Table 9.1 illustrates the stark contrast between the food sovereignty model and the dominant neoliberal system). La Via Campesina rejects the view that food is just another exchangeable commodity, to be traded to the highest bidder in a world market. It sees local and national markets as the priority and states

Table 9.1 Dominant Model versus Food Sovereignty Model		
Issue	**Dominant Model**	**Food Sovereignty**
Trade	Free trade in everything	Food and agriculture exempt from trade agreements
Production Priority	Agro-exports	Food for local markets
Crop Prices	What the market decides (leave mechanisms that create low crop prices and speculative food price hikes intact)	Fair prices that cover costs of production and allow farmers and farm workers a life with dignity
Market Access	Access to foreign markets	Access to local markets; an end to the displacement of farmers from their own markets by agri-business
Subsidies	While prohibited in the Third World, many subsidies are allowed in the US and Europe, but are paid only to the largest farmers	Subsidies are okay if they do not damage other countries via dumping. Subsidies should only be to family farmers for direct marketing, price-income support, soil conservation, conversion to sustainable farming, research, etc.
Food	Chiefly a commodity; in practice this means processed food full of fat, sugar, high-fructose corn syrup, and toxic residues	A human right: specifically, food should be healthy, nutritious, affordable, culturally appropriate, and locally produced.
Ability to Produce	An option for the economically efficient	A right of rural peoples
Hunger	Due to low productivity	Problem of access and distribution due to poverty and inequality
Control over Productive Resources (land, water, forests)	Privatized	Local, community controlled
Access to Land	Via the market	Via genuine agrarian reform
Seeds	Patentable commodity	Common heritage of humanity, held in trust by rural communities and cultures, "no patents on life".
Rural Credit and Investment	From private banks and corporations	From public sector; designed to support family agriculture
Dumping	Not an issue	Must be prohibited
Monopoly	Not an issue	The root of most problems
Overproduction	No such thing, by definition	Drives prices down and farmers into poverty; we need supply management policies in the US and Europe
Farming Technology	Industrial, monoculture, green revolution, chemical intensive, uses GMOs	Agro-ecology, sustainable farming methods, no GMOs

Table 9.1 Dominant Model versus Food Sovereignty Model cont.		
Issue	Dominant Model	Food Sovereignty
Farmers	Anachronism, the inefficient will disappear	Guardians of culture and crop germplasm; stewards, repositories of knowledge, internal market, and building block of broad-based, inclusive economic development.
Urban Consumers	Workers to be paid as little as possible	Need a living wage
Genetically Modified Organisms	The wave of the future	Bad for health and environment, an unnecessary technology
Alternatives Possible	Not possible, nor of interest	

that countries have the right to define their own food, farming, and agricultural policies, no matter what the World Trade Organization (WTO) rules say. It argues that food has a central role to play in addressing goals related to poverty reduction; preservation of rural life, economies, and environments; and sustainable management of natural resources. Prices must be fair to the producer and consumers, and the practices that undercut fairness must be changed. Accordingly, LVC seeks a ban on food dumping, the enforcement of anti-monopoly rules nationally and globally, the effective regulation of overproduction in the large agro-export countries, and the elimination of direct and indirect, open and hidden subsidies that enforce low prices and overproduction. It proposes maximum limits on farm size; equitable local control over seeds, land, water, and forests; and the abolition of seed patenting by private interests. The broad strategic range of LVC's propositional measures and oppositional aims is impressive.

On the World Scene

The building phase of La Via Campesina, which ran through to 2000, was characterized by militant insertion of the LVC point of view in protests — at the Seattle WTO meetings, for example — and honing its capacity to articulate clearly the moral dimension of human rights over the dominant free-market ideology that treated food as a profit-generating commodity. In the process, LVC catapulted food sovereignty into the public discourse. In the 1990s it also consolidated its regional structure and identified gender equality as a central goal to be achieved in order to realize its vision of change. LVC's self-definition as a movement of peasants and farmers, rather than as an NGO helping peasants, marked it as a new kind of force on the international scene.

After seven years of organizing, protesting, and advancing an alternative path to decide how food is produced and for what purposes, the LVC took advantage of its 2000 conference in Bangalore, India, to launch a new strategy of building alliances to broaden and deepen the pressure on certain policies of the WTO, the World Bank, the IMF, and United Nations agencies, especially the Food and Agriculture Organization (FAO). LVC's ranks and alliances expanded rapidly. Recognition by other movements, NGOs, some governments, international financial institutions, and some UN agencies grew, and LVC became a key voice in debates about rural revitalization and sustainability. Its ascendant leadership showed up in 2003 at the ministerial meetings of the WTO in Cancun, Mexico, where in civil society forums, lobbying, and protests, LVC played a key role in the collapse of the WTO meeting.

Attempts by the World Bank and WTO to co-opt the movement by engaging in expensive, jet-setting dialogues were rejected. Indeed, LVC defined these agencies as "clear enemies," worthy only of direct opposition. In contrast, the FAO was seen as a potential alternative space where agricultural policies that might counter those of the World Bank and WTO could be developed.

In 2002, the United States and Europe began dumping food in South American countries. Dumping is the export and sale of products at prices below the cost of production in the exporting country. For example, the price of wheat dumped into South American markets was 43 percent below the US cost of production; the price of soybeans was 25 percent below cost; maize, 13 percent below; cotton, 61 percent; and rice, 35 percent. Thousands of peasant farmers were economically devastated, and many committed suicide. As Peter Rosset pointed out in *Food Is Different*, "This hurt farmers worldwide. Nor do US or European family farmers benefit from their nation's low price export practices. Chronically low crop and livestock prices, coupled with subsidies that go to larger, corporate farms, leave family farmers in the North without either a price or a subsidy that can cover their living expenses and farm loans, leading to massive farmer bankruptcies."

The clear analysis, moral stance, and militancy of LVC in the midst of the turmoil created by US and European policy inspired a rapid expansion of alliances around the food sovereignty agenda. Throughout the balance of the decade, the LVC governance system and leadership continued to be strengthened.

Structure

The international conferences of LVC, held every three or four years, are the organization's highest decision-making authority. It is here that the structure and governance of the movement are refined. The process of building a shared analysis, developing policy, and negotiating political direction and strategies takes place, in tandem with critical examination of the movement's internal functioning.

The International Coordinating Committee (ICC), made up of two representatives, one male and one female, from each of the nine LVC regions, meets twice a year. The committee reviews compliance of members with agreements made at the international conference, evaluates international conference decisions, undertakes a situational analysis of each region, and considers the global political and policy context in relation to strategic adaptations that may be needed. Out of these discussions, the plans for advocacy are framed.

At the operational level, the LVC Secretariat, based in Jakarta, Indonesia, does the day-to-day work of coordinating actions and implementing the conference agreements. Ten issue-based International Working Commissions augment the coordination work of the ICC. Each commission, with one male and one female peasant leader as elected representatives from each of the nine regions, coordinates the work of La Via Campesina on each issue group. The following are the issues of the current working groups:

- Agrarian reform
- Food sovereignty and trade
- Biodiversity and genetic resources
- Climate change and peasant agriculture
- Sustainable peasant agriculture
- Human rights
- Migration and farm workers
- Women and gender parity
- Education and training
- Youth

In addition to these working groups there are four active campaigns:

- Global Campaign for Agrarian Reform
- Seeds: Heritage of Rural Peoples in the Service of Humanity
- The Campaign to End All Forms of Violence Against Women
- The Campaign for an International Charter of Peasant Rights

The methods for building the LVC movement are rooted in three major values:

- **Autonomy.** Each LVC member organization has a constituency, a membership to which it is accountable. Respect for the autonomy of each member is a key value. This does not mean there are no contesting of points of view. Indeed, members commonly lobby others to support particular positions. Each member brings to the table the particular concerns of its base, with the objective of taking part in dialogue to reach a common position, which leads to the second value.

- **Consensus.** The decision-making process is grounded in deliberation and a commitment to seek consensus. This takes time, much more time than is often accorded such discussion in NGOs. Peasant organizations do not respond quickly, and sometimes complete agreement may not be possible. Nevertheless, the results in terms of trust, and thus capacity for collective action and minimizing of internal splits, has created a solid base from which to push back against the dominant model and contend for an alternative food system.
- **Pride.** This system of deliberation is imbued, at all its different levels, with a core strategy focused on strengthening members' pride in being peasants, farmers, and workers of the land. Cohesion is reinforced through the powerful use of symbols and rituals involving seeds, soil, fire, and water, which capture the grounded elements that bind members to their common covenant of commitment to protecting and serving humanity through their struggle for food sovereignty. This combination of reflection, analysis, deliberation, action, and integration of symbols and rituals allows an incredible diversity of people attached to various religions, political creeds, and languages to achieve a remarkable unity.

Current Priorities

LVC's current internal priorities are to strengthen the base of leadership at local and regional levels. By 2004 there were 300 people who understood fully the global terrain of the peasant and family farmer struggle and who had come to know each other, a remarkable achievement in just 10 years. Now the aim is to strengthen the internal capacity for mobilization at the local and regional levels as well. Extending the reach of the training schools, the women's training centers, and the political education already in place is one focus. This effort is linked to the drive to establish regional secretariats across the globe and to strengthen some member organizations that are still weak in several areas.

LVC has established a university that offers training to increase the knowledge, skills, and capacity of the sons and daughters of peasant farmers so they can accelerate the transition from fossil-fuel-intensive forms of agriculture to ecological and organic methods and organizing skills. Practical in its orientation, the university is also viewed as a critical factor in advancing LVC's political differentiation of food sovereignty from the dominant model.

Seventeen years on, LVC encompasses 148 organizations and networks that represent some 500 million families. The empowerment that these people have achieved through La Via Campesina is a hopeful sign for all who fear the growing uncertainty, instability, and inequality of the 21st century.

Transition Factors

More starkly than any of the foregoing examples, La Via Campesina confronts us with the political dimension of transition. Its advances cannot be understood without acknowledging LVC's capacity to aggressively oppose, resist, and challenge the established power structure, which has been organized by capital to advance the interests underlying free-market ideology. Neither can they be understood in the absence of LVC's propositions to build a food system based on a decentralized, democratic basis, in which markets are shaped by principles of fair price, fair trade, and ecological sustainability.

"Resist and Build" is perhaps one way to describe the broad strategic orientation needed for transition, or so it would seem based on the experience of La Via Campesina. How can one expect to construct local sustainable food systems if trade agreements favoring global exports and national governments converge legally and powerfully to constrain the placing of social and environmental governors on the market place? How can sustainable agriculture — aimed at feeding local, regional, and national markets — compete on a level playing field in a so-called free-market system that is enabling global and sovereign nations (including China and the Persian Gulf oil states) to buy up millions of acres of farmland in Africa and on other continents? To ignore such trends, on the basis of a "local only ideology," and hope for the best is naïve, to say the least.

On the other hand, without vigorously advancing propositions and policies that support the kind of food system being pioneered by the likes of Seikatsu, how can we expect to stem the destructive consequences of the neoliberal model? Doing the hard work of connecting the dots of finance, agro-ecological methods of farming, affordable land tenures, succession strategies, and ethical market construction must be part of the mix. Opposition and proposition, resist and build: are not these the guiding mantras for 21st-century leadership?

This dialectic, held in tension over time, has been central to building a movement with the growing potential to SECURE the change being sought. The dynamic, deliberative approach builds a common analysis that underpins political actions and developmental strategies. This process has enabled La Via Campesina to continuously clarify how it SEES the world and has sustained its efforts to SEEK strategic pathways forward. The gender-balanced approach to governance is structured to hold the tension. Dialogue and consultation allow the movement to discern the priority interests of its respective constituencies. Representatives of member networks and organizations enter a robust and animated exchange that in turn leads to intentional, focused action. Might not this nuanced, robust approach to ongoing learning, action, reflection, and synthesis point a way to what one might call a transition culture, a way of being, deciding, and acting that could help us navigate the difficult challenges we face on the planet?

Finally, integrated into the cultural shift and embodied in this movement is another dimension often either overlooked or set aside. The compelling historical conjuncture of people and planet we have arrived at is fraught with difficulties, struggles, ambiguities, and contradictions. For peasants and farmers to maintain a focused, intentional, and long-term struggle to transform food production from a commodity-based, for-profit system to a sustainable and ecological source of livelihood requires a formidable commitment to inspired grinding. The integration of symbols and ritual into the life of LVC reveals the importance of spiritual and emotional touchstones to carrying on the work.

Transition has many levels, from the individual to the systemic. But if change is to take place at all, at any level, people must step up to the plate. Individuals must decide for themselves if they are going to participate or not, if they are going to embrace citizenship or retreat to the ease of living in the stupor of individualistic consumerism. The public use of symbols and rituals points to a profound recognition that the process of shaping change resides not just in the systemic but also in the interior life of individuals. Consciousness of the deep interconnection we have with each other as stewards of our common planetary heritage, and of the wondrous miracle of life, is fed by integrating meaning into the shared task of transition. Reinventing symbols and rituals that keep people grounded and connected is part of La Via Campesina's reclaiming of the cultural strength to persist in the transition struggle.

Resilience Reflections

La Via Campesina was born out of a struggle to find ways to reverse the cultural, ecological, and economic homogenization of commodity-based, fossil-fuel-intensive agro-business. *Its goals; its decentralized but overlapping layers of governance;* its elevation of the moral dimensions of our relationship to food, land, water, and forests; and its empowerment of millions to have an effective voice in international rule-making institutions reflect the resilience principles of *diversity, modularity (autonomy but connectedness), and well-calibrated feedback loops.*

The strength of these principles has been reinforced by a deliberative process that builds trust and respect and forges commitment to common action. The *social capital,* mobilized and sustained in a wide variety of ways and under a diversity of leadership, continues to be deliberately broadened and strengthened.

Innovation is fed by an integrated process of *learning and experimentation* with autonomously created rules and a deliberate focus on building and unleashing leadership, which opens up the space for creative adaptation. These characteristics, when combined with LVC's autonomous but intertwined bottom-up organizations, networks, and ever-evolving institutions, create a *flexible, messy, but cohesive governance system.*

Lastly, the LVC values, philosophy, politics, and practices reflect a respect for the services the earth provides humanity. LVC's *singular rejection of a profit-only relationship to the use of land, water, and forests, an ideology that externalizes the cost to people and the environment,* is strident and persistent. Perhaps this is why LVC has resonated so powerfully with such a diverse array of the human family in the short time it has existed.

Federating to Advance Fair-Trade Finance: A Transition Challenge

In Chapter 8 we ended our survey of the emerging ecology of finance with what remains an unanswered challenge: how do we bring the diverse models and networks of finance into a relationship with each other in order to expand aggressively the capital available to address social and ecological purposes? It is a difficult but urgent issue.

The Chantier, by federating many different networks, has created a powerful voice and a capacity to mobilize and focus a blend of financial and other resources to expand the social economy in Quebec. La Via Campesina has powerfully federated networks across the globe to change the rules that thwart food sovereignty and transition to a sustainable and more self-reliant food system. Might there be a sufficient base of alternative financial institutions, organizations, and networks — local and regional, national and international — that through federating them could build a powerful voice and more effective capacity to influence the rules of the game and capture capital for transition? Might we have what it takes to build a fair-trade finance movement?

Certainly, on the face of it, there appears to be a wonderful opportunity for the world's broad array of credit unions, building societies, microfinance institutions, community development loan funds, community banks, and other social and ecological banks to be given a serious look-in by policy makers and governments. Why is this not happening? There are many reasons, many of which have already been explained in this book's coverage of deregulation of the finance and investment industry. However, some reasons lie in the lack of federating action in the sector itself.

- Many community and social finance organizations are invisible to each other and thus have little sense of what might be accomplished if they were connected in common purpose with others of similar ilk. Nor do they appear to have any idea of the significant aggregate size and scope of the sector.
- Where there is some recognition of connection, the public image is typically weak — at best, "non-full service," but in some cases viewed as old-fashioned or inefficient, or regarded as marginalized and banks for the poor.
- While there are multiple trade bodies, there is no strategic unity; indeed, the propensity is to compete rather than cooperate, making it impossible for the sector to be taken seriously as an alternative, let alone a vibrant movement.
- Many of the building societies and credit unions originally built to address unmet financial needs in their communities have an identity crisis. Because they are focused on competing with the banks for market share, many have become disconnected from their roots and are out of touch with their members. While innovations are emerging in several credit unions, most just keep their heads down and "stick to their knitting," competing with banks for personal, mortgage, and commercial lending business.* On this basis, they have little chance to rebuild their historical market share. A different approach is needed, one that connects them with the substantive challenges we face.

---

* An example of one area where credit unions' competition with the banks has not turned out so well is mutual funds. Canadian credit unions entered this market almost 20 years ago, branding their offering "ethical funds." Clearly, credit unions in Canada were well positioned to attract investment from the millions of people who are their owners. And they have done so, but so far these members have realized little in the way of return — an average compounded rate of 1.055 percent between 1994 and 2008. However, if credit unions invested members' resources more creatively and directly in the community, supporting some of the innovations we have highlighted in this book, they would secure better financial *and* community returns.

In contrast to this unnerving picture of the current state, there is a large potential for innovative and cooperative leadership to step forward. By 2007 there were 3,300 microfinance institutions in developing countries, with over 665 million members. Thousands of similar institutions exist in "developed" countries, offering microfinance, community development loan funds, social banks, and community development venture capital funds. For example, in Canada there are about 250 community futures development corporations in rural areas and several hundred aboriginal development corporations that together are involved in financing of various kinds amounting to hundreds of millions of dollars annually. In the UK, about 70 community development finance institutions (CDFIs) have been established over the last 10 years.

The International Association of Investors in the Social Economy (INAISE) is a trade body for some of the most innovative practitioners. Initially mainly a European organization, INAISE is increasingly attracting members from other continents and includes both social banks and other cooperatively owned social finance organizations. A number of the larger CDFIs in Canada and the UK are members of INAISE, and there are members from Africa, Australia , Asia, and Latin America

The 800 CDFIs in America have grown impressively in the first decade of the 21st century, pursuing a market the banks ignore: affordable loans and low-yield equity products to meet the needs of low- and moderate-income households and businesses. A review by the US Social Investment Forum in 2010 reveals that they fall into four main CDFI categories and each has experienced the following rates of growth over ten years:

- Community development loan funds from $1.7 billion to $11.9 billion
- Community development credit unions from $610 million to $11.1 billion
- Community development venture capital funds from $150 million to $2 billion
- Community development banks from $2.9 billion to $17.3 billion.

In the past two years, disgust with the banks, and the solid reputation of CDFIs, has, under the Move Your Money campaign, led to the opening of some 650,000 new credit union accounts since September 2011.

This impressive growth in the United States pales in comparison to the assets of cooperatively owned financial institutions, which Alan Robb, J.H. Smith, and Tom Webb estimate to be around $2.5 trillion internationally. However, the focus of many of these institutions on solidarity economic objectives is muted. Many rarely finance other cooperatives. When they do, they provide little support in the form of equity, and the loan terms are seldom different than those provided by conventional lenders. Few provide the kind of integrated approach to relationship and knowledge banking illustrated by the many smaller organizations highlighted in Chapters 7 and 8.

It appears that the idea of uniting finance and social purpose is strong in the innovative and emerging part of the sector, while those with the most resources are the least innovative — perhaps too distant from the cooperative principles they espouse or too blind to the potential. Nevertheless, the number of people looking for less exploitative and more stable places to invest is growing. Robb, Smith, and Webb note that, after the financial meltdown of September 2008, "millions found their retirement savings decimated and their faith in capital-centered investments eroded. Co-operative financial institutions experienced significant growth as people looked for ethical and more responsible investment opportunities. There was also an increase of interest in ideas like 'slow capital' that both fosters stable development and does not seek rapid windfall gains."

The urgency of transition is clear. The success of the innovators is clear. There is a sound track record. The need is growing. New cooperatives and old mutuals need each other to leverage the resources of the sector and to learn from each other. More and more people want their money to contribute social and ecological justice where they live rather than being used in an out-of-control, self-interested casino economy based on the "virtue of greed." Might more people in this nascent sector SEE the possibilities and start federating to gain visibility? Could they be inspired by the strong voice and resilient unity La Via Campesina has achieved? Are they capable of rediscovering democratic mutualism focused on addressing unmet needs? Could they then step beyond this to use convivial banking innovations to mobilize cooperative forms of capital to secure SEE change in the 21st century, locally, regionally and across the planet?

These are core strategic questions that urgently need to be addressed. The early adopters are showing the ways forward, and the roadmap is becoming clearer. We need the mighty international cooperative finance institutions to replicate the work of the pathfinders or to invest in them through creative partnerships. The time has come. La Via Financiera is a path we must build if we are serious about navigating the Great Transition.

CHAPTER **10**

Economic Democracy and Cooperative Capital

Co-operation is the seed.

— Father Jose Maria Arizmendi

*Capitalism has made of work a purely commercial activity,
a soulless and joyless thing. But substitute the national service of the
Guilds for the profiteering of the few; substitute self-government and
decentralisation for the bureaucracy and demoralising hugeness of the
modern State and the modern joint stock company; and then it may
just be once more to speak of a "joy in labour" and once more to hope
that men may be proud of quality and not only of quantity in work.*

— National Guilds League pamphlet,
quoted by Bertrand Russell in *Roads to Freedom*

BERTRAND RUSSELL AND R.H. TAWNEY ARGUED in the 1920s that guild socialism was practical if methods and systems could be introduced for ending
usury and making capital the servant and no longer the master. The major
barriers were not just political and economic ones. There were also deep psychological factors at work. Already in the 1920s an increasingly sophisticated
media was beginning to manufacture consent, using advertising that cleverly
played on people's fears and insecurity, promoting what Erich Fromm characterized as the value of "having" rather than "being," and what Tawney called
the "acquisitive society." Russell's "road to freedom" was obscured by a cultural
fog that impeded the journey toward social justice, peace, and mutual liberty.

In setting out his "principles for social reconstruction," Russell argued
that this shifting cultural orientation, reinforced by an increasing volume
of advertising designed to create the desire to have more, was an extension
of the ongoing process of enclosure. The powerful lure of acquiring and

consuming a widening array of goods lulled citizens who were already inse-cure, dependent, and competitive into a false sense of freedom, one that served to dull inherent human desires to be truly free.

Fromm explored this further in his 1941 book *Fear of Freedom*. In the darkest period of World War II, he tried to understand the factors propelling the fearsome rise of totalitarianism, which crushed the cooperative movement, enslaved whole countries, and instigated genocide. He posited that there are two kinds of freedom: "positive freedom," which is "freedom to" — freedom to build toward the realization of a "cooperative commonwealth," akin to Russell's freedom road and Mill's vision of "mutual liberty"; and "negative freedom" or "freedom from," which is freedom from government restriction in order to free markets, free trade, free the movement of capital, and free cor-porations to maximize private profit and offer free choice for consumers. This is similar to the classical liberal perspective of laissez faire (to leave alone). Unfortunately, embedded in this twisted matrix of "negative freedom" is the idea of individual freedom. Twist the whole insidious logic one more notch and we arrive at Ayn Rand arguing the "virtue of greed," which can only be guaranteed by protecting individuals' right to maximize their own gain.

In contrast, positive freedom is a mutually shared, existential freedom that can enable people and social organizations to chart their own course and fulfill their own cultural and economic potential. Key to securing posi-tive freedom, Fromm suggested, are structures that could unite personal actualization to achieve "solidarity with all men." Fortunately, as we have seen, there are growing numbers of people managing to clear away the fog and choose "positive freedom" as the authentic "road to freedom." Resistance and outright opposition to those who would privatize the entire planet are growing. Concrete transformative propositions are not only being made but are also being put into practice and showing themselves to be robust. They demonstrate the efficacy, effectiveness, and efficiency of reintegrating fair-ness and equity into the economic equation. Conscious striving and efforts by those feeling "blessed unrest" to recalibrate our economic activities to ecological realities are becoming stronger. People and organizations are wel-coming, and becoming actively engaged in, the creative tension that comes from strategic efforts to reunite the "I" with the "We." The impressive array of decentralized and shared ownership models reveals an organic acceptance of the resilience imperative. It is as if the immune system of the human fam-ily recognizes there are a host of dangerous bacteria that need to be fought.

Outwitting Enclosure: The Mondragon Formula to Equity

J.W. Smith (in *The World's Wasted Wealth*) and other economic democracy experts have pointed to the success of the Mondragon cooperative system of worker control and job ownership as a modern and very effective form of the guilds, particularly with respect to its harnessing of collaborative social relations and fair price systems as core features of the system. In Chapter 2 we described how the medieval guilds were made up of local enterprises of the same type — stone masons, woodworkers, and ironsmiths, for example. In the case of Mondragon, it was not crafts but business units that were the organizing fulcrum — manufacture of refrigerators or sports equipment, or food retailing, for example. All units are federated into a co-op of co-ops, a structure not unlike the guild of guilds.

Mondragon was born in the mixed industrial and agricultural economy of the Basque country within Spain, which under the dictatorship of General Francisco Franco suffered from lack of investment. The region had been a Republican stronghold during the Spanish Civil War and was never a fan of the monarchy. In the late 1940s it was racked by poverty and decline, an unlikely place for the evolution of what has become the largest complex of worker cooperatives in the world.

Father Jose Maria Arizmendi, a rural priest, was the founding visionary and architect. The values and principles that motivated his work came from the encyclical "Rights and Duties of Capital and Labour," issued by Pope Leo XIII on 15 May 1891. The pope's central concern was the need for some amelioration of "the misery and wretchedness pressing so unjustly on the majority of the working class," and he supported the rights of labor to form unions, while rejecting communism and unrestricted capitalism. This foundation of social justice eventually led Arizmendi to formulate three interdependent institutions — a technical training school, a social services cooperative, and a regional cooperative development bank — that still remain the core of the Mondragon cooperative development system (see Figure 10.1).

- **School.** The technical training school's first graduating class contained only five students. They became the worker-owners of the first manufacturing business, which made paraffin heaters. From that beginning, the cooperative has gone on to become, according to the Mondragon website, "the foremost Basque business group and the seventh largest in Spain." Today, Mondragon offers cooperative education, technical training, and education focused on the management of democratically owned businesses.
- **Social Services.** Arizmendi first approached the central government for assistance to set up a system to provide social and health security services for workers and their families. The government refused because it viewed the workers as self-employed. Out of this

Democratic Control Network of Mondragón Activities

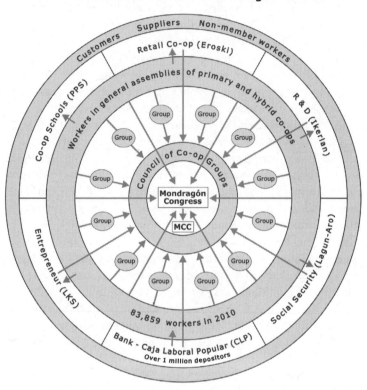

Fig. 10.1: *The Mondragon cooperative system is democratic, financially profitable, and internally capable of generating talent and capital. It generates equality among its workers and a range of benefits to the Basque region and Spain as a whole. Complex yet capable of great focus, Mondragon is a leader in social and economic innovation.* Source: Dr. Shann Turnbull (updated with permission).

rejection was born a social services cooperative to ensure the needs of workers could be met securely. Today this co-op has become a hugely successful mutual insurance group that operates across Spain.

- **Bank.** The third organization was born from the need for access to investment capital to finance the expansion of existing enterprises and to start up new worker co-ops. The Caja Laboral Popular began as a credit union and became a regional cooperative development bank. It has been central to designing and implementing ways to fill the equity gap.

Together, technical education, social insurance services, and patient capital provision make up the cornerstones of a dynamic and integrated core infrastructure that in 2010 was a democratically owned and governed complex of 256 enterprises employing 83,859 workers and generating $20 billion in annual revenues.

Since it was established in 1959, the Caja Laboral Popular (CLP) has been the strategic fulcrum of the system. It has been described as the heart of the cooperative movement, pumping a diverse blend of capital through the system to where it is needed. By linking patient capital, research and development, and solid technical and professional assistance capacity, the entrepreneurial ingenuity of worker-owners is systematically unleashed.

Employing originally a methodology known as "group self-employment," the CLP leveraged what today we refer to as social capital. The criterion for support from the CLP was an equity investment from a group of three or more workers in a similar trade. The sum required was at least one year's salary per worker-owner. This could be raised from savings, families, or friends. The initial equity investments of the founding workers needed to total at least one-third of the sum required to capitalize the business. They could borrow the remaining two-thirds from the CLP once the venture was deemed investment ready. This is an example of the economic principle of reciprocity.

Consider, for example, the reciprocity at work in Mondragon's collective equity accounts. Profits after tax are allocated in three ways:

- Ten percent is distributed to local charitable organizations and other nonprofit services. This rule reflects the obligation of the enterprises to their members and other residents in the communities where they operate.
- Forty percent is invested in the reserves Mondragon aggregates for ongoing research and product development. Ongoing reinvestment is essential to continue updating and expanding the business model for the benefit of present and future workers.
- The other 50 percent of profit goes to individual worker accounts to ensure worker-owners have adequate pensions. These funds have no voting rights and are only available when members retire, whereupon they receive whatever their final salary levels were. Until they are drawn, these worker accounts are a pool that can be used as collateral to raise loan funds from the CLP at very low rates. The result is that workers enjoy the fruits of their labor in a manner that balances the interests of the individual in a fully funded pension with the interests of the collective.

The guild concept of "just price" is enshrined in the Mondragon approach to fair wage scales. The disparity found in the large global corporations does not exist. Compensation is set within a framework of minimum and maximum salaries. Originally this ratio was 3:1 between the highest-paid and lowest-paid workers in the co-op. Today the ratio is 9:1, still vastly lower than the 400:1 ratio between US Fortune 500 CEOs and their lowest-paid employees. Overall, the Mondragon salary levels are high, underpinned as they are by consistently high rates of productivity and profitability. Per capita income levels in the valleys surrounding the town of Mondragon are the highest in Europe, and the income gap between rich and poor households is the lowest.

From 1969 to 1991 the Empresarial (entrepreneurial) Division was at the heart of the CLP. This division was designed to act as the "collective intelligence" of the Mondragon development system. It included specialist staff working on research and development in several areas of business, including industrial products, agriculture, and food and service industries. Technical assistance was also available through this division for both new co-op formation and mentorship for the management of a new enterprise during its early years. When a co-op was experiencing business problems, specialist staff would intervene. Many methods are employed: interest on loans for a firm could be suspended, additional capital could be made available, or specialist managers could be brought in to turn a business around. The results speak for themselves. In over 50 years, only one Mondragon co-op has failed. In 1991 the Empresarial Division was established as a separate management consultancy, one step removed from the bank. It is not surprising that researchers point to the crucial role of the Empresarial staff in securing the success of Mondragon in its dramatic years of growth. (During these years the CLP would evaluate start-up proposals for 12 to 16 new co-ops a year, of which three or four would be selected for patient capital investment. Frequently the CLP would conclude that although the idea was good and there was a market for the products, the worker-owner group did not have the managerial expertise to make it a success. In these cases, the investment would be contingent on the group recruiting a manager to a specification agreed with the CLP.)

The Mondragon movement has shown that a combination of equity raised from worker-owners, the availability of low-cost credit for business start-ups, plus a rich matrix of training, technical assistance, and marketing expertise can produce secure, stable, equitable, and democratic enterprises that are sustainable over the long term. The Mondragon system of collective equity accounts enables patient capital to be recycled and limits the need for debt finance.

Mondragon has been cited as a unique and non-replicable system. However, there are strong similarities to the strategic approaches and the mobilization of technical assistance, social capital, democratic governance, and patient equity finance that have been core to the success of many initiatives covered in this book. Additionally, the sector and targeting strategies employed by many of the social banks emerging in Europe (see the section on Triodos in Chapter 8) also have a growing impact through their long-term financing of social and environmental enterprises.

Driven by a business model based on its principles of "People and the Sovereignty of Labour," Mondragon has demonstrated that it is possible to develop highly participative companies rooted in solidarity, with a strong social dimension, and still achieve outstanding business excellence. Its example has inspired inventive cooperative action in other areas of Europe, including the economically democratic solutions at the regional and local economy level in both Italy and Denmark that we look at next.

Democratizing Social Care in Italy

Italy has a rich cooperative tradition. However, 40 years ago the scope and size of the sector was not much different than that in other European countries. Since 1970 it has taken off in a virtual renaissance that has expanded the scope, diversity, and size of the cooperative movement to make it one of the largest in the world. In 1971, cooperatives accounted for 2.3 percent of the large-business sector (that is, firms with more than 500 employees). By 2001 they represented 8.3 percent of large businesses in Italy. Even more impressive, by the 1990s the co-op sector alone accounted for 25 percent of the growth of Italian employment.

The roots of success can be traced back to a cooperative networking strategy in the early 1970s, augmented by a strategy from 1976 onward to build collaborative partnerships with local authorities. The breakthrough came when co-ops applied cluster theory. The idea was to stay small (most have from 5 to 50 workers), network the businesses, emphasize local and regional connections, and support them with appropriate communication and technical assistance services. The result: innovation is increased, market penetration grows, and cost competitiveness increases.

Emilia-Romagna, with a population of 4 million, is a province in northern Italy whose social entrepreneurs have dramatically expanded and extended the cooperative model across diverse social and economic sectors, including health and social services. It is now both a productive agricultural region and the leading manufacturing center of Italy. Worker and consumer cooperatives have been key in this transformation, but so too has been the growth in mutual aid and cooperation between a wide range of local, family-owned businesses. Six in ten residents in Bologna, the largest city in Emilia-Romagna, are members of one or more cooperatives; 10 percent work in one. In Imola, a town of 100,000, 115 local co-ops account for 60 percent of local economic output. Equally striking is the fact that 55 percent of citizens actively invest capital into these firms.

A key organizing feature of this renaissance has been the way the cooperative spirit was marshalled to create a mutual aid frame of mind across the region. Winning over "heads and hearts" began in 1976 when regional government was introduced across Italy. To address a trend of rising unemployment, Emilia-Romagna developed a regional resilience strategy, the result of dialogue brokered between the regional government, municipalities, business leaders, trade unions, and the co-op sector. To implement this new strategy, the various sectors formed a partnership with two main roles: to operate as a think tank to strengthen the regional economy; and to play a role as a diagnostic/research and development agency. ERVET, as the partnership is known, eventually broadened its base to include provincial universities and technical colleges.

Local Service Centers

With this capacity in place, the first step was to map the local and regional economy to find out who was doing what with whom and where. Teams of researchers analyzed the results and helped define, among other things, 100 industrial districts, which became the geographical base for engaging many local partners in the design of local area action plans. Local service centers (LSC) were then created and became crucial for supporting the health and growth of local firms. Each LSC receives a combination of public sector funds and fees from their membership and is run by a board made up of elected members who monitor staff, budgets, and results and report back to the general membership regularly. The result is social and economic networking, and exchange between the enterprises in each district, that builds the synergy, cooperation, and nimbleness needed to respond to rapidly evolving and changing opportunities.

Jane Jacobs showed in *Cities and the Wealth of Nations* that the LSC concept was well founded. From medieval to modern times, artisans and small businesses in similar trades have commonly been located in the same quarters of a town or city. Deliberately encouraging geographical clustering enables small businesses to expand their reach by working together to leverage the sum of their parts. The theory is that closer contact and greater density will accelerate the exchange of knowledge, ideas, methods, and market information. A concentration of firms involved in similar trades also attracts skilled labor and facilitates social networking. This helps develop trust, an essential ingredient for developing associations to buy materials in bulk or to negotiate capital investment and credit on better terms.

Consortia

The Italian co-op sector has three national federations, which are supported in particular sectors by specialist consortia — some operating provincially, others locally. These consortia provide a modern guild-like structure through which smaller member firms can collaborate to reduce risk, decrease fixed overheads, and access specialized goods and services. For example, in 1978 there were three small local consortia supporting the construction co-ops in different cities within Emilia-Romagna, each working in relative isolation from the others. Analysis and dialogue between the three led to a merger. The resulting Consorzio Cooperative Costruzione (CCC) soon produced several benefits: the construction co-ops were able to negotiate larger building contracts; backroom legal, financial, and adminstrative tasks were done more efficiently; and legislative and environmental issues important to member firms could be monitored more effectively at lower cost. Today the CCC is the leading construction organization in Italy with 230 co-op firms and 20,000 worker owners.

Since 1980 the consortia methods have been applied across diverse sectors, including agriculture, food processing, wine production, construction, machine production, retail, transport, housing management, and social services. Wider access to low-cost patient capital is a key success of the consortia model. Development finance has been advanced through mutual guarantee funds that enable investors to pool risk, avoiding the need for worker-owner members to provide personal guarantees on bank loans or for small-business members to put up their homes for security. The consortia then use the mutual guarantees to leverage credit at discounted rates from Italy's regional cooperative banks. By 1986, local and regional guarantee funds were pooled nationally into the CGM Finance Consortium, which further increased their flexibility and leveraged their influence.

Members of consortia commit to work in solidarity by pledging time and money to help other members improve their business performance and quality. As John Restakis from the British Columbia Co-operative Federation has observed, this system builds mutual aid but also a healthy form of competition for all members to up their game.

Social Solidarity Cooperatives

Some of the most prominent innovations of the last 20 years have been in the area of social care, particularly in services for health, addiction, elderly people, disabled people, and the unemployed and marginalized. The genesis of a new model for care was the late 1970s, a period of rapidly rising unemployment in Italy. Public services were slashed, which affected access to care. The crisis triggered a movement led by families and care workers to examine what practical steps they might take to stem the tide. The vision that emerged was of care organizations actively supported and governed by the stakeholders — that is, the users of services, the families of people receiving care, the paid staff, and the volunteers. Social solidarity cooperatives were born.

Such an approach represented a big change. In theory, Italian public bodies were expected to provide social services. Indeed, as Paul Gosling has noted in *Social Co-Operatives in Italy*, charitable and private social care organizations were taken over and integrated into public bodies under legislation dating back to 1890. Local authorities were at the core of education, health, and social services. However, social services for the aged, the disabled, and the addicted were always the lowest priority; extended families were expected to be the core care providers in these cases. The result was a growing gap in services to many in need, exacerbated by falling tax revenues and a high level of tax avoidance — estimated in the 1970s to be 14 to 20 percent of GDP.

Ironically, this combination of factors forged the crucible of need that fed the explosion of social cooperatives. The tradition of mutual aid within families and, more broadly, in the community, coupled with the growing gap between need and organized capacity to provide adequate care, created a space for innovation. Throughout the 1980s a campaign to enable non-profit foundations and the voluntary sector to operate independently but with government financial support grew. In 1988 it succeeded. However, the solution was not a fit for the rapidly growing number of social cooperatives (there were already 650 across northern Italy by 1985, and 1,800 by 1990). Instead, they mobilized broad grassroots support and three years later secured the passage of social cooperative legislation.

The new law defined the mission of social cooperatives to pursue the general interest of the community and to achieve the social integration of citizens by managing social, health, and educational services. The culture of solidarity from which these co-ops grew was recognized. So, too, was their role in securing employment for disadvantaged people through industrial, agricultural, commercial, and service activities. The law allowed for two forms of social cooperative:

- **Type A** solidarity cooperatives deliver social, health, and educational services, mainly for local authorities. Workers and volunteers make up to 50 percent of the primary members. Public sector bodies are enabled under the law to preferentially contract for Type A services.
- **Type B** solidarity cooperatives focus on integrating disadvantaged people into the labor market. At least 30 percent of the cooperative's workforce must be disadvantaged. Members include workers, volunteers (up to 50 percent), and family members.

Approximately 59 percent of the co-ops are Type A, 33 percent are Type B, and 8 percent are mixed. Type A cooperatives provide services primarily to public authorities but also offer a mix of direct services to nonprofit organizations, companies, and households. Under the law, the "disadvantaged people" that Type B cooperatives serve include people with disabilities or with drug and alcohol addictions, and offenders serving noncustodial sentences. In practice, they often serve the homeless, the long-term unemployed, lone parents, and refugees. The average size of a social cooperative is about 30 workers.

To secure contracts with public bodies, a cooperative with more than 50 workers must, by law, have persons with disabilities making up at least 7 percent of its staff. Type B cooperatives have used this legal requirement to extend their job-development role through specialized services to train their clients and then secure jobs for them in both the private sector and with local authorities.

Four guiding principles reflect the core of their approach to structuring cooperation and solidarity:

- Clients and family members participate in the design, content, and delivery of services.
- Membership in a social cooperative is limited to 100 members to facilitate building and maintaining strong social ties within the organization.
- Managers are accountable to members.
- Services are delivered within a defined geographical area.

In his evaluation of the model, Restakis points to the emphasis on "relational goods" as being of core importance to the co-ops' success:

> Unlike conventional goods, relational goods cannot be enjoyed by an individual alone but only jointly with others. Examples include the collective joy of an audience experiencing a musical performance, the generalized laughter at a comic film or the surge of energy that explodes when one's team scores a goal...Friendship and care are relational goods and they are their own reward. They are things whose sale would destroy their worth...Co-operative structures, in which power is shared between provider and user, make this possible.

Beyond this social glue, which is dramatically increasing the quality of care, the 1991 legislation set out measures to support the expansion of social cooperatives. Key among these is a series of tax measures (described by Gosling in his study of social cooperatives):

- Social cooperatives pay a lower rate of corporation tax than other companies.
- Type B co-ops are exempt from paying a national insurance tax contribution for welfare services for disadvantaged employees.
- VAT (value added, sales tax) rate on service contracts for social cooperatives is only 4 percent compared to a national rate of 20 percent.
- Funders who make grants and donations to social cooperatives are eligible for tax relief.
- Social investors buying "solidarity bonds" issued to fund social cooperatives are also eligible for tax relief.
- Surplus trading income is not taxed if it is placed in the capital reserves of the cooperative.

The sector has its own cooperative consortia, similar in role and function to others in Italy. They provide market and back-office services, technical assistance and training, and pooling of resources to improve contracting capacity and access to lower-cost finance. The scope and range of financing that has evolved, beyond the tax measures and consortia pooling, is a remarkable ecosystem of interrelated tools. Patient capital from member shares, "financing members" (typically local authorities), and solidarity bonds are different components. Co-ops can also access working capital at below-market rates through mutual loan guarantees from social banks like Banca Etica Popolare and other regional cooperative banks. The Marconi Fund, to which all Italian cooperatives are expected to contribute 3 percent of their annual income, is another significant source of solidarity finance.

Italia Lavoro, a publically funded agency, provides another unique set of supports. Specializing in the development of niche markets in such areas as cultural heritage, the environment, multimedia, and training services, Italia Lavoro links its knowledge of these sectors to an exciting and productive social venture investment program. It makes equity investment available to eligible co-ops for a three-year period; after that time it can be converted into loans. This financing method secures a stable source of blended capital that helps social cooperatives start up, grow, and thrive.

Together, these layered and interrelated supports have fueled an ongoing expansion. After the birth of the idea in the late 1970s, some 1,800 social cooperatives were trading by the time the new legislation was passed in 1991. Sector growth since then has been robust. By 1996 there were 3,857 registered. By 2005 over 7,000 were operational, employing over 280,000 people and representing 23 percent of the nonprofit workforce. Today the number of enterprises is between 12,000 and 14,000. Moreover, social cooperatives have spread beyond Italy, and replication or an adapted form of social cooperative is developing in other European countries, especially Belgium and Poland.

Cooperative Energy Services: Mobilizing Green Economic Actors

Denmark is the most energy-secure country in Europe. Why? Simply because residents decided decades ago to travel on an unconventional road. The enviable success of the Danes stems from a unique set of policy decisions that were made about 30 years ago to decentralize and locally distribute their energy supply system.

In the wake of the OPEC oil crisis of 1973–74, many countries strategically reviewed their national energy policies. The UK was fortunate to be able to tap into its huge, newly discovered reserves of North Sea oil and gas. France invested in a rapid expansion of nuclear power. With no fossil fuels, Denmark foresaw the future potential of renewable sources. Offshore and onshore wind power, and district heating systems fed by waste heat and biogas were the main energy resources in their 1980 plan. Feed-in tariffs that paid a higher price for renewable sources were a strategically important component. The other key feature relates to ownership. Denmark explicitly set out to broaden its utility ownership system. As a result, cooperative, municipal, and various joint-venture forms of ownership have evolved into a diverse, decentralized, democratic system generating not just energy but also cash for reinvestment at the local level.

As innovative as the Danish approach is, it is not without precedent. Indeed, during the Great Depression a cooperative strategy was employed with significant effect in the United States. Many rural areas across America had no access to electricity, unemployment was huge, and it appeared that joblessness was not about to be tackled by free enterprise. President Franklin Roosevelt needed solutions, so he sent a task force to Scandinavia to study the rural electricity co-ops that were thriving there. The task force members were impressed. As a result, and as part of the 1935 New Deal, the US government set up a joint venture between itself and a still-to-be-established network of rural electricity co-ops. Access to low-cost finance was vital to making the scheme happen. The initial low-interest loans were extended in 1944 for a further 25 years at a fixed rate of 2 percent.

Patient capital focused on unmet needs led to an explosion of rural power supply. Today over 900 mainly rural energy co-ops own 40 percent of national power lines in the United States and provide light and power to 42 million people in 47 states. Eleven percent of the power supplied is from renewable sources. In 1998 most of the energy co-ops came together to form Touchstone Energy, which is now asking a divided Congress for a collaborative strategy that would make renewables and carbon reduction part of a Green New Deal — an obvious necessity that is getting nowhere fast as legislators fight about the national debt, service cuts, and ideology.

Without cooperation, low-cost finance, proper pricing, and intentional focus, the high capital costs of renewable energy will stymie progress. In the meantime, though, as we have seen in the historic example of US rural electrification and in places such as Kristianstad, local authorities can play a key role in creating cooperative solutions that, given sufficient understanding and vision, will mobilize resources to get on with the job. In 2004, Co-operatives UK and the UK's Department of Trade and Industry (DTI) collaborated to research the success of the energy co-ops sector in Denmark and Sweden. The resulting report, *Co-Operative Energy: Lessons from Denmark and Sweden*, highlighted the importance of several factors:

- Support to communities from technical advisors and practitioners who transferred know-how
- Commitment of government and local authorities to community involvement and ownership models and to a cooperative approach with many small units of delivery
- Education and information to promote public familiarity with the range of cooperative structures and energy services
- Multiple-bottom-line perspective to develop a public consensus that the price of energy should not be the only driver of energy policy

Denmark's 1979 Heat Supply Act was key to setting targets, providing incentives, and mobilizing investment to develop local heat grids and what has become a highly resilient distributed-energy system. Also essential was government support for direct engagement of communities in ways that informed, educated, and supported households, small businesses, farmers, and local authorities to promote collaboration between various interests. Another critical factor was incentive schemes. Feed-in tariffs were key as they provided payments to the producers of renewable energy. For example, if a household installed a solar array, the electrical utility would pay to purchase its surplus power. Similarly, if a cooperative of farmers installed wind power, they would be provided a relatively high price for generating electricity. The price incentives are typically high initially, with the idea being to create a market for innovation; as the cost of technology comes down, so too does the price of the feed-in tariff, which at some point is removed altogether. Also important was access to low-cost, patient sources of capital, which were attracted by creative underwriting and by the financial backing provided by local authorities.

In their report *Collective Power: Changing the Way We Consume Energy*, Robbie Erbmann, Hugh Goulbourne, and Piya Malik describe what can be achieved with a focused approach and a 25-year strategic energy plan that mobilizes joint action at local and regional levels:

- **Combined heat and power (CHP) and district heating:** 60 percent of Danish space heating is provided from these sources, which frequently use municipal and local waste sources for fuel. Of the 400 district heating networks, 300 are consumer owned; in the bigger cities, most are municipally owned.
- **Wind farms:** 23 percent of the country's wind capacity, and over 3,200 turbines, are owned by local citizens through investor cooperatives with over 100,000 members. For the largest wind farms, the local authority ownership stake is also significant.
- **Biomass fuel:** Farmers and cooperatives manage this fuel supply chain and own the majority of the 120 wood- and straw-fed district heating plants. Local authorities have enabled these rural district heating networks to be developed; they have also facilitated access to low-cost finance by providing guarantees and underwriting support.
- **Anaerobic digestion:** Farmers and cooperatives own more than 20 large digester plants. Local authorities have been key partners in developing this waste management infrastructure and in underwriting investments.

The Danish experience demonstrates an inherent business advantage for a cooperative approach. While gas and electricity are regulated supply services, heat in most countries is unregulated. To trap and recycle it requires close collaboration with local authorities to install heat grids under streets and on other public land. This creates a natural monopoly, like water services. In such circumstances, democratic accountability is the obvious solution to limit exploitation and provide transparency. Such accountability can be achieved through consumer-owned businesses or multi-stakeholder mutuals developed as joint ventures with local government bodies.

The successful development of CHP and district heating services across Denmark over the past 30 years has confirmed that community cooperatives and local authority partnerships are key to success. Thus, the importance of an enabling government policy framework cannot be ignored. Also amply demonstrated by the foregoing is the importance of access to low-cost, long-term capital. Along with the example of the Roosevelt New Deal financing of rural electrification, there is the 20-year post-war period in Europe to illustrate this point. In *The Green New Deal*, Andrew Simms, Ann Pettifor and new economics foundation researchers describe how Keynesian-inspired controls on the banks' base interest rates kept inflation low and capital costs for major investments under 2.5 percent during this period. Without this international and rigorous control of the banks, it would not have been possible to develop welfare-state programs after 1945 like affordable housing, hospitals, public transport, and other public facilities needed as part of reconstruction and modernization.

Transition Factors

A central challenge of transition for communities and regions reinventing their economies is the extent to which most of us have become entangled in the global financial system. Increasingly, concentrated wealth and capital coupled with weak regulation has led to the dominance of dysfunctional global capital markets. As a result, we must figure out how to repatriate control of our money from Polanyi's big "M" Market so we can apply it to projects, businesses, and infrastructure investments explicitly focused on navigating a triple-bottom-line transition. If we cannot shake our lethargic response to an unaccountable financial system that insidiously picks our pockets and colonizes our minds, we cannot expect to forge adequate solutions.

The three examples in this chapter show a way forward. Each organizes and applies capital resources to ends that relegate finance to a servant role, a lubricant that eases the way for other values to be manifest.

Mondragon has created a democratic system of raising and applying low-cost capital. The rules under which capital is mobilized and leveraged have fostered a dramatic level of equality compared to that in the global corporate sector and have secured for workers decent incomes and high-quality benefits, including secure pensions. In business terms, profitability and productivity are among the highest in Europe. In community and regional terms, the accumulated impacts of decades of social innovation have transformed a declining European region into a thriving complex of mutual innovation that enjoys a cultural conviviality attractive to people from around the globe.

Worker cooperatives contribute two forms of investment: their labor and their capital. As the success of Mondragon has demonstrated, the effective stewardship of cooperative capital demands forms of trusteeship that limit their vulnerability to being taken over by outsiders. To maintain this strength requires an effective, transparent, and equitable system that will steward the productive capital and allow it to be reproduced and organically grown year on year. The Mondragon innovation of internal capital accounts for worker members has been a key to solving this problem.

This is very different than the situation in some other co-ops, where worker ownership is denominated in shares rather than clearly vested in the rights and responsibilities of worker-owners and their active participation in governance and management. The American Plywood co-ops in the northwestern United States, for example, were very successful enterprises for decades but ended up being sold off by an aging workforce that held shares so valuable that no younger people could afford to buy in. Unable to steward the capital in a way that reproduced itself year on year, and with all the value attached to individual shares, the co-ops ended up selling off their holdings to large private companies.

George Benello summarizes the relevant lessons:

> The lesson of employee ownership is clear: when control is vested in shares and is not a right of working members, this control can easily be separated from worker members. Managers can easily acquire more shares with higher salaries, and, just as important, the idea that workers have a right of control of their workplace does not exist...workers have gradually come to realise that share ownership should have been accompanied by the right of control, but the realisation has come too late. The possibility of control had passed from their hands.

Another feature of these examples is that the capital created is retained within the region. It is genuine cooperative capital. Returns are, by definition, limited, and benefits are explicitly and precisely distributed based on principled and fair criteria. This hallmark is also reflected in Emilia-Romagna and the 30-year transition of Denmark to a conservation-based, low-carbon energy system. In both instances the capital mobilized within the region is encouraged and rewarded. A blend of pricing, regulatory, and tax measures has been critically important in structuring the evolution of social care and energy provision from highly centralized systems to decentralized, higher quality, more sustainable modes of production. Meanwhile, in Mondragon, the Caja Laboral Popular has grown into a development institution that manages 13.9 billion euros and has allowed people in the Basque region to invest in their own future, well away from speculative, nontransparent derivatives marketed for profit in the casino economy.

Furthermore, each of these European forms of economic democracy is framed by a process of ethical development that explicitly distributes the economic and social benefits of ownership among various stakeholders who control the enterprise mutually. In Italy it is not just the workers in the social co-operatives who are stakeholders but also the users of the services. Moreover, both are required to operate within a mandate that secures the public benefit of a higher quality of service and outcome. In Denmark, a wide range of different stakeholders are involved as energy producers — municipalities, farmers, citizens, and others operate in a variety of nested economic relationships based on shared geography and the specific type of energy conservation and distributed, locally based production they are involved with.

Cooperation between cooperatives is another key feature. A single enterprise or a small group of isolated enterprises using the cooperative system is not sufficient to realize the potential of cooperative capital and ownership. Of the examples in this chapter, each gives systematic and ongoing strategic attention to transmitting knowledge and providing the technical support necessary to shape the mindset of local stakeholders. Getting this process right is essential if a co-op is successful to transfer the know-how needed to succeed. It is difficult to imagine how the scale of success described here could have been achieved without the jigsaw pieces being fitted together carefully and strategically.

Resilience Reflections

Capital close to home (*modularity*), ownership that is democratic (*tightened feedback loops*), nested relationships that are functional (*social capital*) and tied to specific geographies, associational linkages that support and reinforce knowledge transmission, and innovation over space and time — these all reflect the resilience principles.

The need for *social capital*, the connections and relationships that foster trust, is self-evident. So too is the importance of the connective tissue that continuously builds and renews *trust*. Democratic enterprises must be nourished in a supportive institutional web of capital, knowledge sharing, and technical assistance focused on *innovation and problem solving.*

The emphasis on *learning, experimentation, local development rules,* and *adaptation to change* are hallmarks of the *innovation* that characterizes *resilience*.

Also impressive is the plethora of *overlapping mixes of governing structures* that weave various interests into a dense web of cooperation and solidarity. In particular, the way these co-ops reclaim capital from the grip of the market dominated by profit provides an inspiring and practical testimony that we can bring capital home from the global market.

In *The Great Transformation*, Polanyi describes the casualty of enclosure this way: "Whereas previously the market had been an adjunct to society, tragically society became an adjunct to the market." Just as the community land trust movement is a contemporary manifestation of the struggle to reclaim the commons of land, each of the economic democracy pathfinders in this chapter manifests the powerful potential to reclaim the commons of capital.

To foster the *innovation* required to move in this direction does require forging new patterns of market, *governance*, and social relationships. Central to the change is a profound paradigm shift to cooperative and horizontally collaborative approaches to *social learning*. These in turn must be applied to transforming the institutional and organizational processes through which we organize our social, economic, and cultural lives. Increased levels of consciousness, coupled with animating and mobilizing resources into collective transition efforts, are vital.

The critical importance of these observations are reinforced in Chapter 11. The depth of the challenge involved in transforming the financial system will become ever more apparent. So too will be the need to draw upon and bring together the ingenuity of the many who have been working, advocating, and successfully experimenting with ways to break out of the box we are kept in by the global financial system and corporate concentration.

CHAPTER 11

Ownership Transfer: Accelerating Transition

Ye shall know the truth and the truth shall make you mad.

— Aldous Huxley

Read what Plato said; that you must not let any one man
be too poor, and you must not let any one man be too rich; that
the same mill that grinds out the extra rich is the mill that will grind
out the extra poor, because in order that the extra rich can become
so affluent, they must necessarily take more of what ordinarily
would belong to the average man.

— Huey P. Long, from the "Every Man a King" speech

T HE IMPORTANCE OF CLOSING THE EQUITY GAP and the crucial role of low-cost finance have been central to the cooperative innovations we have featured in this book. In micro-ways they roll back the forces of enclosure and unite money, land, and ownership with social purpose. From a transition perspective, they put in place the democratic ownership by which they distribute benefits more fairly and through which they can reinvest. Without a means to invest, more self-reliant and low-carbon economies cannot be secured and sustained. In this chapter we delve more deeply into this process and explain how restructuring ownership can be advanced more systematically.

Our challenge is to scale up these innovations in a context where the enclosure of land, buildings, firms, and money dominates, boxing financial and human capacity into undemocratic profit-maximizing organizations. The power and influence of these organizations skew perceptions of what is real and what is considered to be realistic. However, as we SEE things differently and are exposed to other ways of thinking, doing, and being, our capacity to offset destructive low-road capitalism grows. Expanding democratic ownership is a key counterweight to the low-road, anything-goes-that-makes-a-profit economy, and a key strategy for building a high-road, low-carbon economy.

However, we are where we are. Ownership is concentrated, and the 500 corporations that dominate the global economy are largely unaccountable. We have to find ways of transforming ownership to multi-stakeholder hybrids grounded in social purpose and ecological reality. To advance such an ambitious agenda requires a solid analysis of what is and what can become a framework for ownership transfer that enables people to take action, practically and politically.

We therefore spend time at the beginning of this chapter fostering a deeper analysis of what is. If we are to accelerate the rate and scope of change, we must understand more profoundly the systemic drivers of the usurious and predatory behaviors embedded in the financial system. We then explore the democratic trusteeship corporation, an ownership framework that indicates the concrete possibilities for root-and-branch change. The contrast between what is and what is already being done presents the fertile ground on which regional networks can collaborate across the public, social economy, and private sectors to adapt, scale up, and improve the results being achieved.

Structural Dysfunction of the Global Investment Industry

Since 2008 volatility in the global financial system has grown. The long-term impact of the latest and deepest crisis since the Great Depression has provoked considerable debate and discussion about how to prevent the need for another colossal taxpayer bailout of the banking industry. Adair Turner, chairman of the Financial Services Authority (the UK banking regulator), caused a furor by suggesting that parts of the financial services industry were "socially useless" and that the industry had "grown beyond a reasonable size."

Many others agree. Indeed, they go further. Paul Woolley, a former IMF economist and fund manager, now at the London School of Economics, unabashedly states that global financial markets are dysfunctional and destructive. He provides evidence that shows how the investment industry manages to skim the "croupier's take" from the casino operations of global banks and other collective fund managers by charging unreasonably high fees in investment transactions. Common wisdom has it that the average stock portfolio will achieve a real return of 5 to 6 percent a year over the long term. According to Woolley's analysis, common wisdom is not reflected in reality. For small retail investors the actual net return is closer to 1 percent. Their investment earnings are squeezed by a succession of fees, levies, kickbacks, and taxes, including the following:

- 1 percent is lost to payments to investment fund managers and corporate executives for their award of share options.
- 0.5 percent is lost to the fees paid to investment banks that make their money from encouraging mergers and acquisitions.
- 1 percent is lost to the commissions paid to brokers and the stock exchange for trades.
- 2 percent is lost by small retail investors who pay additional management fees to managers of mutual funds, insurance funds, pension funds, etc.
- 0.5 percent goes to taxes related to stock purchases in the UK or taxes on mutual fund profits in the United States.

Woolley concludes that this "croupier's take" of up to 80 percent of earnings is the reason private pensions and returns to small investors are so poor. And where does the money go? Just consider the "performance" bonuses executives award themselves, described by John Gapper in a *New York* magazine article in April 2011:

> Two and a half years after the crash, Wall Street ought to be feeling pleased. It lost billions of dollars, devastating the world's economy in the process, the federal government had to put up $700 billion of taxpayers' money to prevent an even worse disaster, and otherwise reasonable politicians began using epithets like "fat cats" and "robber barons" for the first time in decades. And yet now the financiers are firmly back in business. Bonuses are flowing again — JP Morgan Chase CEO Jamie Dimon got a 51 percent raise in 2010, to $23 million — and Bernie Madoff is the only chief executive to end up in jail. It's almost as if nothing had happened.

The average bonus across the lower ranks, however, dropped to a meager $128,500. In the UK, some bank chief executives are retiring on pensions of £700,000 a year, while the average pension has fallen to £8,000.

To overcome the erosion of earnings on retail funds, professional fund managers have turned to hedge funds and private equity funds in search of higher returns. But this has turned into a zero-sum game and simply increased the volatility of the global financial markets. For hedge funds, even where returns may be higher, Woolley shows that average fees are twice what they are for other fund managers; the take has just become higher.

The aggregated impact from churning transactions on global financial markets at an ever-accelerating rate is destroying investment value of all manner of collective investments, including pension funds, unit trusts, and investment trusts. The adverse impact on funds the general public has entrusted to the financial markets is cumulative, and the results are devastating.

The scale of the global banking collapse is a concern, but it is just one symptom of the underlying socially and ecologically damaging dysfunction that is both a structural and systemic problem. The system must be radically reformed, a conclusion further confirmed by Richard Murphy and Colin Hines, whose 2010 analysis *Making Pensions Work* provided further evidence of the systemic nature of the "croupier's take" in private sector pensions. Total pensions paid out in 2007–8 in the UK were £117.6 billion. Of this total, £57.6 billion was paid out of the national income-tax-funded state retirement scheme, a further £25 billion from the public sector pension scheme, and the balance (£35 billion) from private sector pension schemes. What Murphy and Hines found was that the tax relief for the private sector pension industry in 2007–8 was £37.6 billion, £2.6 billion more than what was paid out. As the report sums up, "every single penny of the cost of UK [private sector] pension payments in 2007/08 was paid by the UK government." The finance industry added nothing at all; instead, that industry consumed all investment returns in fees and charges. This is a colossal sum of squandered public money — equivalent to the current UK defense budget and approximately 25 percent of the British fiscal deficit in 2010–11.

However dramatic the implications of the "croupier's take" presented by these studies, they still do not fully explain why the top one percent of Americans, and their counterparts internationally, are getting richer and richer while the vast majority of citizens in most developed countries (leaving aside those in developing countries) are struggling just to stay afloat.

A Corporate Tax System that Enriches the Few and Imprisons the Many

The "third" world debt crisis led to structural adjustment in the "South." The "first" world debt crisis is now leading to similar adjustment in the "North." Across large swaths of the "North," citizens are suffering the impact of governments' bank-induced higher debt load. Higher taxes, reduced access to secure jobs, reductions in private and public pensions, massive cuts in public services, and further privatization of health and social care are all underway.

But there is more to this story of how we are getting boxed in. The global enclosure of finance is inextricably tied to the growing concentration of corporate power. Access to finance for the majority has decreased, and inequality of global wealth and income has skyrocketed. Over the past 40 years in the UK, the share of national wealth of the top one percent of households has doubled, while the share of the bottom 50 percent of households has fallen by a quarter. The concept of "trickle up" has been working exceedingly well since globalization began.

In the 1950s, Louis Kelso, an American corporate lawyer, analyzed the growing problem of inequitable distribution of income due to rapid technological change and what he pointed out as a growing inequality in ownership of productive assets. As we have noted elsewhere, most households in developed economies have seen a drop in real incomes since the 1970s. This is why it is necessary for a household to have two breadwinners when previously just one was enough.

In simple terms, technology has been accelerating the productivity of business assets. A better machine increases the number of widgets that can be produced in an hour, thus reducing costs and increasing profit. If you have the money to invest and buy the machine, this increased productivity will reward you. The problem for workers is that they cannot compete with machines. Therefore, machines replace labor, enriching the wealthy even more, while rendering the average citizen's hold on a livelihood more tenuous.

Kelso recognized that any investment that increases productivity is intrinsically self-financing. For example, if you invest $1 million into a business to buy technology that doubles production without increasing costs, the profits generated will be enormous. If you don't have a spare million in the piggy bank, you will need credit to keep everything together until the machinery pays for itself. Kelso's insight leads to an obvious conclusion: the goal of more democratic ownership of productive assets depends on democratizing access to finance, a subject we will return to shortly.

The Closed-Loop System: The Dynamic of Modern Enclosure

Jeff Gates, as legal counsel to Senator Russell Long, drafted the US tax laws in 1974 that included incentives to encourage the widespread adoption of self-financing Employee Share Ownership Plans (ESOPs) introduced by Kelso. In 1998, Gates wrote *The Ownership Solution*, which built on the insights of Kelso and his Australian supporter Shann Turnbull, who had dedicated his 1975 book, *Democratising the Wealth of Nations*, to Kelso.

Referring to G.K. Chesterton's arguments in favor of distributing business assets widely amongst citizens, Gates shows that modern "capitalism is not structured to create more capitalists; rather it is designed to invisibly finance the concentration of more and more capital and wealth to existing capitalists." Chesterton pointed out this absurdity in the 1920s. Indeed, the separation of business assets from local and regional business owners is a trend that can be traced back to before World War I, and the socially unjust impact has been getting worse every decade with the expanding hegemony of increasingly large global corporations.

This problem is of little concern to economists because ever since Adam Smith wrote about the wealth of nations, they have considered wealth to be income rather than ownership. In *The Ownership Solution*, Gates drew back the curtain to reveal netherworlds of corporate financing few comprehend, including economists. In particular, he showed how the taxation privileges of global corporations produce a closed-loop system that propels the inexorable trend to deepening inequality.

Gates stresses the need to recognize that there are two sources of internal funds held within large corporations. First, there are after-tax profits ("retained earnings" in accounting parlance). They are kept within the company for reinvestment. Then there is cash created by depreciation allowances. Originating from ancient accounting practices that established sinking funds (i.e., cash reserves) to purchase new assets as the old wore out, their use today is hardly so laudable. Depreciation significantly reduces reported profits, which, in turn, significantly reduces taxes. The large cash pools created are used as the basis for investment funds to be recovered, tax free!

There are also two external sources of funds that a corporation can access. Money is borrowed from a variety of sources and must be repaid by the company. This method of raising money creates a liability on the company balance sheet, but the interest costs are tax deductible. Dividends paid on shares are more expensive, and share issues are more expensive. Shares are typically issued either directly to high-net-worth individuals or indirectly via collective investments to the general public (who are kept outside the closed-loop system).

Not all these sources of funds are of the same relative importance to large corporations. Internal sources commonly make up 75 percent of funds used and are the most important. Of the 25 percent remaining, debt typically accounts for 19 to 22 percent; new equity, raised through share issues, only accounts for 3 to 5 percent of new money. In some years, net money raised by all publicly traded corporations is negative as they buy back their shares and issue bigger dividends to their already wealthy owners.

The most important point to understand is that depreciation is by far the largest source of funds — typically 90 percent of internal sources and roughly 67 percent of the total from all sources, internal and external (Figure 11.1).

So what does this mean to the vast army of retail investors who make funds available to a large corporation? They are investing in good faith in what they think will yield them a higher return than other options, but they

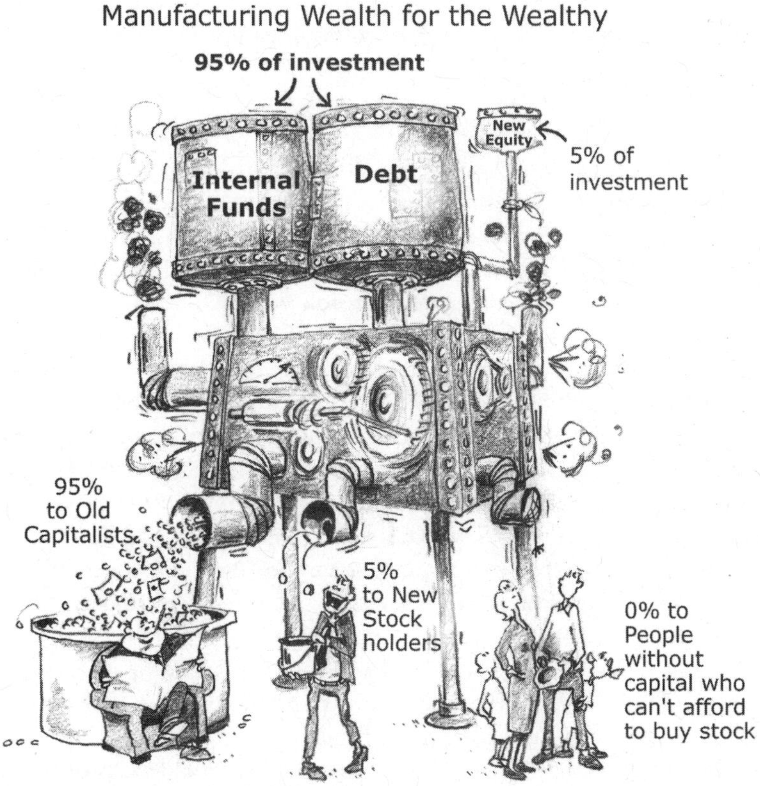

Manufacturing Wealth for the Wealthy

95% of investment

Internal Funds

Debt

New Equity

5% of investment

95% to Old Capitalists

5% to New Stock holders

0% to People without capital who can't afford to buy stock

Fig. 11.1: *In large corporations, capital and money flow through what is virtually a closed-loop system, the major beneficiaries of which are the wealthiest.*

have no influence over what happens with 95 percent or more of the funds that corporations have access to.

Once one starts putting all the pieces together, a stunning picture emerges. First, as already noted, depreciation allows corporate owners to get back all the funds they invested on a tax-free basis. They are no longer exposed to the risk of investment loss. Second, corporate owners retain control of all their sources of income, even after getting back the value of their original investment. Third, because corporate owners retain ownership, they can use it to raise more finance to acquire more income-earning investments in perpetuity.

None of this is fair or just. Why should investors get their money back, tax free, and keep it hidden from view as a point of leverage that allows them to continue making money out of money? Why should they not be required to incrementally relinquish their ownership to other worker-citizen-stake-holders who, through the government allowances, financed the corporation's tax deductions?

Shadow Bankers: Predation at Work

As indicated earlier, Paul Woolley notes that more investors, especially larger pools such as pension funds, are investing in hedge funds. The crash of 2008 revealed the invisible and unregulated shadow banking industry, which operates in offshore tax havens and works closely with global banks and investment banks. This corporate collusion was unknown to most politicians before 2007.

Hedge funds are at the heart of the casino economy, which specializes in making high-risk investments with rich people's money. When the Glass-Steagall Act, which disallowed the integration of commercial banks, investment banks, and insurance companies, was repealed in 1999, it paved the way for financial speculation that escaped public scrutiny. As a result, Alan Rappeport was reporting that by 2001, $531 billion had been invested in hedge funds. By 2007 that amount soared to $2 trillion, mostly through the unregulated investment of shadow banks and credit creation by commercial banks. The seriously rich and the global banking sector had found a way to leverage other people's money and pensions for expanding private gain.

Using an obscure system of financial transfers that do not show up on the balance sheets of investors, hedge funds are akin to an invisible conduit through which money flows to a few super-rich shareholders, unbeknownst to retail depositors and regulators — a perfect system for investment banks, pension funds, and commercial banks that want to quietly hedge their risks, whilst offering the scope for much larger returns using other people's money.

A few key points about hedge fund investment:

- Hedge funds specialize in derivative trading and seldom act alone; they collaborate with private equity companies and with the global investment banks and commercial banks.
- Hedge funds charge fees to their rich clients of 1 to 2 percent and additionally take 20 percent of the profits of their speculative trades in shares, bonds, futures, and currencies.
- Hedge funds introduce huge instability into the global financial system. Mega-profits for a hedge fund come at the expense of huge losses for those investors on the wrong side of a trade.
- Investor funds commonly arrive from offshore tax havens, which is crucial to completing their transactions cost-effectively.

- Hedge funds are gambling syndicates for the rich. To be accredited investors, individual clients of hedge funds need to be worth at least $1 million and in many funds the minimum investment is $1 million. So no open door for the 99 percent.

These points make it clear that such investment benefits, and is accessible to, only the already wealthy.

The shadow banking industry is a key provider of finance for private equity companies. In *The Future of Money*, Mary Mellor points out that most private equity firms are not listed on the stock exchange, are unregulated, and many operate in a predatory manner. They do so by extracting equity from a company's balance sheet and replacing this with excessive levels of debt.

Here is how the system works: Private equity fund managers target companies that have been undervalued by stock markets because of hidden asset values and/or ineffective managers. Once they have a company in their sights, they bring their investors' finance into play and hunt for more money from global banks and, increasingly, pension funds. Typically, private equity managers leverage the money they have in hand 15 to 20 times — in other words, they can turn $20 million from a group of investors into up to $400 million. With a well-stocked treasury, private equity firm managers maneuver to gain control of the company. When that goal is achieved, they often repay their creditors by seeking to sell the company on for a higher share price or by breaking up the company and selling off the parts, realizing a much higher share price from the sale of the pieces than they could ever achieve by selling off the company as a single entity. The returns can be colossal.

Welcome to the world of the leveraged buyout. As they are unregulated, private equity investors can readily convert the equity and retained earnings (after-tax profits), cash, and unreported windfall gains of otherwise healthy companies into a mountain of debt that can seriously weaken company capacity. What remains after the banquet is a debt-ridden company and an even richer group of investors on the hunt for another unsuspecting prey.

Mellor cites a 2009 report by Ernst and Young that revealed an average return of 330 percent on the transactions of the private equity industry and also showed that the health of companies subject to such sharp dealing was significantly eroded. On average, their debt levels were more than three times those of companies not subject to private equity takeovers.

The intense concentration of assets among the richest one percent, and the machinations of the unregulated shadow banking system resulting from these shenanigans, is condemned roundly by economist David Korten in *Agenda for a New Economy*: "Wall Street has been engaged in class warfare pure and simple [through]...debt bondage." The societal implications of this debt bondage, and the reckless behavior that has created it, are profound. Steve Keen, an Australian economist, has compared the levels of debt amassed in the Great Depression with the much higher global debt load of today. In 2010 he predicted a long period of deflation far worse than that of the 1930s (Figure 11.2).

> Rising debt...augments demand during a boom; but falling debt subtracts from it during a slump...During the 1990s and 2000s...the annual increase in debt accounted for 20 percent or more of aggregate demand...twice as much as it had ever contributed during the Roaring Twenties...The reduction in aggregate demand to date hasn't reached the levels we experienced in the Great Depression — a mere 10 percent reduction, versus the over 20 percent reduction during the dark days of 1931–33. But since debt today is so much larger (relative to

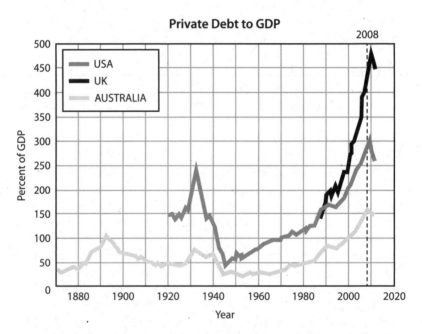

Fig. 11.2: *Personal debt has increased steadily over the last 70 years. Has it peaked? Look at the downward curve in 1930 and the beginning trend down in 2008. How long will today's decline in debt last and how steep will be the decline? And what does this mean with respect to transition to a steady state economy?* Source: Steve Keen, "Economics in the Age of Deleveraging," Steve Keen's Debtwatch, 28 January 2012, accessed 1 February 2012 from www.debtdeflation.com/blogs/2012/01/28/economics-in-the-age-of-deleveraging.

Fig. 11.3: *Class warfare.* Source: © Nikiya Palombi | Dreamstime.com.

GDP) than it was at the start of the Great Depression, the dangers are either that the fall in demand could be steeper, or that the decline could be much more drawn out than in the 1930s.

Little wonder the Occupy movement has resonated with so many ordinary folks. Enclosure, debt bondage, and inequality seem to go together these days.

Trusteeship: A Way out of the Enclosure

The impressive array of decentralized and shared-ownership models described in earlier chapters reveals an organic acceptance of the resilience imperative. It is as if the immune system of the human family recognizes that there are a host of dangerous bacteria which need to be fought.

For the immune system to win, we need many things, but economic democracy is a cornerstone. It seeks to shift the power of ownership from shareholders to stakeholders, from a small elite group of asset owners to a matrix of participants in the production process — workers, investors, consumers, regular suppliers, local authorities, civil society organizations — some or all of which may possess an ownership interest, depending on the nature of the business. The diverse forms of stakeholder democracy that will evolve as we craft ownership forms that account for varied interests and circumstances are all strategic pathways to Fromm's vision of "positive freedom" and what Mill called "mutual liberty."

Yet the transition to economic democracy is daunting because property rights in our economies foster restricted and exclusive forms of ownership and weak structures of accountability. The shareholder corporation is the norm, and it is supported by public sector institutions that have become accustomed to and captured by a dysfunctional paradigm. This must change. A brief detour into history helps us explain why more clearly.

Economic Depressions: The Ownership Link

In 1819, Jean Charles de Sismondi, a Swiss economist, was trying to solve a not-so-simple question: Why do economies go into depression? The Napoleonic wars had ended in 1815, and the economies of western Europe went into the first industrial-age slump from 1816 to 1819. As 300,000 soldiers returned to Britain, and as the expanding factory system threw more and more weavers out of work, unemployment rose, leading to dire poverty and spreading social unrest. Income was dropping and so was demand. Sismondi noted that employers had every incentive to ratchet up investment in machinery and ratchet down wages, thus decreasing the cost of production and prices, but while this increased their short-term competitiveness, it also meant the overall purchasing power of workers plummeted.

In his *New Principles of Political Economy*, Sismondi argued that it was absurd for industrialists to have the freedom to use machinery as a weapon against society when the cost of the unemployment they were causing was paid for socially, not by the factory owners. Unless the issue of underconsumption (due to lack of demand from poorly paid producers) was solved, economies would be prone to recurrent depressions. What was required was a system to spread the wealth that the machinery was generating by spreading the ownership of the enterprises.

Sismondi's analysis preceded that of Keynes by a full century. Moreover, his forecast was accurate. There followed a second slump from 1825 to 1831, and a third even deeper one from 1839 to 1842. To stabilize the economy, he suggested a two-pronged "social economics" strategy to share wealth equitably. First, industrialists should be taxed to force them to pay for the social costs they generated, thereby curtailing their practice of foisting all the costs onto society. A second necessary and linked reform was to ensure equity ownership for all the workers. Sismondi proposed a 50-50 share so that workers "after a probationary period would come to possess a right of ownership in the business to which he gives his sweat."

The first measure was proposed as a stick to encourage the implementation of the second, the worker equity stake. The result would be a dual-income system for workers, who would earn wages plus a fair share of profits. Sismondi argued that this would dampen economic volatility by balancing demand and supply and advancing social justice. He expected that as technology improved, a stable balance between demand and supply could be maintained by moving to a shorter workweek and an increased equity share of profit income to compensate for lost wages.

However, Sismondi saw that if short-term profit remained the primary motivation of investors, breaking the back of the boom-and-bust cycle through rigid or marginal shared ownership would not be sufficient. The pattern would continue just as it does today, with taxpayers forced to pick up the tab, governments mired in debt, natural resources ransacked, and workers left with too little income to spend.

Sismondi, and those who have followed his lead since, continue to be ignored. Short-term profits dominate, volatility continues, peaks slide relentlessly into troughs, and growing the economy faster to make up the losses is the only solution. The stability that Sismondi recommended is still not seen as a humane and ecological strategy to aim for. Only by redesigning ownership rights and getting the big boys to take a longer-term view can an economy be set on a steadier trajectory.

John Stuart Mill studied Sismondi's ideas in Paris in the early 1830s. When a severe depression hit in the "hungry 40s," his propositions for worker ownership drew from Sismondi's analysis, which ultimately shaped his views on how the cooperative commonwealth could be built and how in due course a "stationary state" economy might be achieved. In his *Principles of Political Economy*, Mill was clear that worker ownership and economic democracy were fundamental reforms required to correct the social defects of capitalism:

> The form of association, however, which if mankind continue to improve, must be expected in the end to predominate, is not that which can exist between a capitalist as chief, and work-people without a voice in the management, but the association of the labourers themselves on terms of equality, collectively owning the capital with which they carry on their operations, and working under managers elected and removable by themselves.

As we know, Mill's ideas were either ignored or actively resisted. Indeed, all through the latter half of the 19th century, legislation was enacted that went in precisely the opposite direction; corporations were legally freed from any restriction but one: to maximize profit for their shareholders. Is it any wonder, then, that the Bourses du Travail in France and the Knights of Labor foundered? Is it a surprise that the guild socialist movement was stymied because of its failure to solve the finance problem? The need for economic democracy should be even more self-evident today, as the increasingly powerful forces of enclosure in the 21st century persist in their attempts to expand their freedom to have more. Yet the core ideas that fed opposition to enclosure, and the propositions for a different way of "being" in the world, have not been expunged.

Huey Long: Sharing the Wealth

The light continued to shine, even as Wall Street crashed in 1929 from the weight of corporate greed. The Great Depression was the deepest ever; by 1934, half of all Americans were in poverty and the slump was becoming intractable. Huey Long, a maverick social reformer, became governor of Louisiana in 1928 and set out to tackle poverty by insisting that Standard Oil pay unprecedented extraction charges for oil. These charges were used to fund public infrastructure and job-creation programs. Long's success inspired many of the public investment policies taken up by President Roosevelt's New Deal.

Long became a US senator in 1931. Inspired by Plato's view of a maximum 5:1 wealth ratio between citizens, and the Bible's injunction to celebrate a jubilee of land reform and debt forgiveness twice a century, he launched a radical Share the Wealth program in February 1934. Born in a farming community, Long compared wealth to manure, saying that it stinks unless it is well spread, and when it is spread it can do a lot of good. Long proposed not just the first US national minimum wage but also a maximum annual salary and a ceiling beyond which wealth could not be accumulated; personal fortunes would be capped at $50 million (about $600 million today), inheritance at $5 million (about $60 million today), and income at $1 million per year (about $12 million today). The money for his plan was to come from increasing wealth taxes on both the rich and corporations, and the funds raised would provide every family a guaranteed income of $2,000 (about $24,000 today), one-third the national average. A lot of Americans thought his plan sounded more than reasonable.

A year after the program launch there were 27,000 local Share Our Wealth societies across the United States, 3 million members, and 60,000 letters of support arriving on Senator Long's desk each week. Tragically, he was assassinated in 1935. Four decades later, his son Russell Long, a US senator from Louisiana, took up the torch by providing tax incentives to spread the adoption of Kelso plans. The incentives introduced for ESOPs sought to advance what Sismondi had advocated 150 years earlier: a means by which workers could become owners and thus share the wealth.

Gandhi and Trusteeship

While Huey Long was launching his Share the Wealth platform, Mahatma Gandhi was leading the struggle to force the British to leave India and go back where they belonged. He also advocated a nonviolent redistribution of land and corporations, which were under the concentrated ownership of a tiny elite. Inspired by the writings and action of John Ruskin and Henry George (see Chapter 2), Gandhi saw citizen responsibility, community service, and economic democracy as the equitable path between privatization and nationalization. He called this third way "socialization," and he named his model of ownership "trusteeship."

Gandhi regarded trusteeship as an intergenerational system for the stewardship of productive assets. "What I expect of you," he explained to the industrialists and landowners supportive of the expanding Indian National Congress, "is that you should hold all your riches as a trust to be used solely in the interest of those who sweat for you...I want to make the laborers co-partners in your wealth." Bhikhu Parekh describes Gandhi's common-sense proposition in *Gandhi's Political Philosophy*:

> Concerning the form of ownership, Gandhi proposed his well-known theory of trusteeship...The theory was intended to avoid the evils and combine the advantages of both capitalism and communism, and to socialize property without nationalizing it. As he imagined it, every industrialist employing more than a certain number of workers was to look upon his industry not as property but as a social trust. He was to work with his employees, take no more than was needed for a moderately comfortable life, and look on them as "members of his family" and jointly responsible with them for the management of industry, and to provide healthy working conditions and welfare schemes for them...Both he and the workers were to regard themselves as trustees of the consumers, and to take care not to produce shoddy goods or charge exorbitant prices. Part of the moderate profit they made was to be devoted to the welfare of the community, and the rest to the improvement of industry.

Gandhi's idea of trusteeship ultimately led to the Bhoodan ("land gift") and later Gramdan ("village land gift") movements, which resulted in millions of acres of land either being gifted to poor tenant farmers or entrusted to villages between the 1950s and the 1970s.

John Lewis Partnership: Ownership Transfer Put into Action

As is the case today, Gandhi was not alone in his thinking; others could see that the boom-and-bust system was producing social and economic devastation and circumscribing freedom. In the heart of the British empire, John Lewis, son of a London department store owner, was not just thinking these thoughts but actually putting them into practice the year before the Great Depression — two years before Gandhi began developing his own concept of trusteeship.

John Spedan Lewis came into his father's business during the First World War at the age of 19. Arthur Penty's 1906 call to reinvent the guild system (described in Chapter 9) inspired him to begin experimenting in one of the company's stores, inviting workers to participate in management and share in profits. The results were astonishing. Under his leadership, this store became the most profitable of the 100 properties his father owned. When his father died in 1928, the young Lewis set out to design a trusteeship company in which all employees would have a say in management and production and would be entitled to an annual share of the profits.

His first step was to set up a trust to endow the assets of the business for the benefit of the entire workforce. Under the trust deed, all employees became partners in the business. Lewis sold the business to the trust in 1929 for a sum of £1 million and provided the trust an interest-free loan so it could repay family members out of the profits over an extended period — a simple self-financing and tax-efficient method of ownership transfer that Kelso demonstrated could be widely replicated.

This was an extraordinary decision. The normal exit route for such a hugely successful family business would be to convert it to a shareholder corporation, take it to the market, and sell it for a whole lot more than a million quid. Ignoring this cashing-out option, Lewis set out to design a system based on the principles of the guild. He was convinced from his early experiments as manager of one store that a system of self-governance would do much better in the marketplace. But there were deeper considerations than just the success of the business.

Ethically, Lewis had come to view as unjust the fact that he and his siblings, year on year, collected such a disproportionate share of the profits that were transparently being generated by the workers. His decision to pursue what he called "industrial democracy" resulted from his arrival at the "sweet spot," where conscience, context, consciousness, and commitment to make a difference in the world converge. (A similar convergence of circumstances saw the ownership of the Scott-Bader manufacturing company in the UK transferred to its employees from 1951 to create a highly successful trusteeship company, the Scott Bader Commonwealth.)

In *Jobs and Fairness*, Robert Oakeshott cites the expressed motivation of John Spedan Lewis himself to transfer ownership of the family's highly successful firm to the workers:

> The more I considered all this the more utterly unreasonable did it seem to me. There on the one side was my father and on the other side his staff — my father with over a hundred separate pieces of property that he never saw and that were nothing but a bother to him, and with an income so far larger than the cost of his very comfortable way of living that the surplus was constantly obliging him to make more and more of those investments: the staff with an employment that was extremely insecure and that gave them a living so meager that they were far less happy than they perfectly well could have been, a happiness that would have increased very greatly both the soundness of the business and the real happiness of my father's own life.

Since 1929, the John Lewis Partnership has never lost this "sweet spot." It is the largest worker-owned firm and the third-largest private business in the UK with almost 70,000 partners. Business expansion has been continuous. The workforce grew from 1,500 in 1928 to 28,000 in 1978 and to 41,000 in 1996. A national supermarket chain was added in the 1930s, along with a few manufacturing supply businesses and a farm. All workers in every business unit are full partners. Moreover, the firm has consistently outperformed other major retailers in every category.

This trusteeship model has three components that evolved from what John Lewis learned in early experiments: share the gains, share the knowledge, and share the power. (The Mondragon cooperatives independently developed the same components).

- **Sharing the gains** relates to the wages and salaries of partners. These are regularly and independently compared with those of other shareholder-owned companies and are consistently rated good or better. Unlike a shareholder corporation, and in line with the advocacy of John Stuart Mill and many others, a core feature of the John Lewis Partnership is the provision of an ownership share that generates a substantial secondary income for all the partners.

This is paid as an annual fixed-percentage cash bonus that has ranged for decades from 9 percent to 20 percent of partner salaries. The average yearly bonus has been about 16 percent, equivalent to two extra months of income (over a 40-year period of employment, this works out to more than five years of wages). In addition, the company pension is superior to that of other major retailers in the country.

- **Sharing the knowledge** is facilitated by full transparency and accountability. The weekly partner newspaper, the *Gazette*, sets out the previous week's business performance data. Partners are encouraged to write in to suggest changes or make complaints. Managers are obliged to reply within three weeks. The partners can choose to sign or not sign their letters, and the managers must treat all such letters equally and deal with them conscientiously. Non-managerial staff elect Committees of Communication at each branch to represent the shop-floor views. Minutes of the meetings are prepared and widely circulated to all partners, but the identity of who said what is not disclosed.

- **Sharing the power** is achieved through a federated system of councils, reminiscent of the guilds. There are branch store forums and divisional councils, which are responsible for the noncommercial aspects of the business, including social policy, community involvement, and support for nonprofit organizations. The partners also elect 80 percent of the 82 representatives to the Partnership Council (the guild of guilds), which keeps all the businesses of the John Lewis Partnership under review. The Partnership Council elects five directors to the main partnership board of the company. The chair appoints five more directors who, with the five elected directors and the vice-chair, make up the commercial board. Wisely, the chair can be removed from this post by a weighted majority vote of the partners.

Like Mondragon, the company has secured its growth and stability through self-financing, avoiding exposure to casino speculators who do their hunting on the public stock exchanges.

The robust proof of democratic corporate trusteeship is in the John Lewis Partnership track record. The fact that the company has not been driven to maximize shareholder value has led to a continuous growth in the number of business outlets and the number of partners. Since the 2008 crash, which led to a massive layoff of staff by other corporations, the partnership has continued to expand and do well, with annual bonuses of 15 percent in 2008 and 2010, and 14 percent in 2011. While every one of the top 100 corporations on the London stock exchange have ended their final salary pension arrangements, the John Lewis Partnership pension scheme remains strong — so much so that each partner is entitled to a fully paid sabbatical for six months after completing 25 years of service.

Not only partners benefit; so too do customers, who receive high-quality service at a fair price, backed up by the firm's policy of "never knowingly undersold". Any customer who after a purchase finds the same goods at a lower price in another retail store will be refunded the difference by John Lewis Partnership (the policy does not apply to products sold over the internet). This policy has been in place and honored since the 1920s and is a nationally recognized hallmark of the firm's unrivalled consumer service.

Evolution of the Trusteeship Model: Toward a Framework for Ownership Transfer

Fritz Schumacher was a co-developer (with John Maynard Keynes) of the British welfare state in the 1940s and a senior economist of the UK Coal Board from 1950 to 1970. Best known as the author of *Small Is Beautiful*, he was inspired by the transformative social change invocation of Gandhi: "You must be the change you want to see in this world." He was also shaped by the tumult of the history he was born into. In 1968, with the world seemingly going to hell during the Vietnam War, Schumacher picked up on the idea of "trusteeship" as a route to reform. With his awareness of the problems that befell many nationalized industries and large private corporations, he sought a mechanism that would steward wealth fairly, in a manner that respected all contributions of key stakeholders.

He took up this idea from a unique vantage point. His senior management experience in the corporate sector had taught him the games played by big business, the taxes companies avoided, and the hidden subsidies large corporations enjoyed that were unwittingly supported by the general public. In the final chapter of *Small Is Beautiful*, his solution was to get rid of the taxation of large corporations in exchange for non-tradable shares that would be held in a dispersed way in the districts where the corporations traded. Through his proposed reform, a tax rate of 35 percent would be transformed into a 35 percent equity share.

To manage this ownership interest, he proposed that local social councils be established, made up of employee, community, and professional stakeholders. Along with a local government observer, this multi-stakeholder area board would decide on how this substantial new source of equity income should be spent or invested. Social council representatives would also be at the company board table, with suspended voting rights that could be activated if they deemed that the corporation was not acting in the public interest. Here, in one insightful fell swoop, was the outline of an option that had the potential for diversifying, distributing, democratizing, and decentralizing corporate ownership — in the process equipping local people with a means to influence their own future.

Employee Stock Ownership Plans

In 1973, the same year Schumacher and Turnbull were independently setting out their corporate reform proposals, Louis Kelso, Jeff Gates, and Norman Kurland were working with Senator Russell Long, the son of Huey Long, on legislation to create employee stock ownership trusts. Kelso had launched the first employee stock ownership plan (ESOP) 17 years earlier in California as a way to enable the three owners of Peninsula Newspapers to sell 72 percent of the firm's stock to their employees and then retire. The idea demonstrated Kelso's insight that any viable business must pay for itself and be intrinsically self-financing. Like the arrangement introduced by John Spedan Lewis, the deal required the owners therefore to accept annual payments for the value of their shares, guaranteed by IOUs issued by the new owners. Employee-owners used their share of annual profits to make good on the IOU, which an employee ownership trust could then use as a tax deduction. Voila! Creativity and trust enabled profit-sharing with employees, a win for them; and the employees were given the golden opportunity to progressively buy out the former owners, a win for the three happy retirees.

Russell Long's legislative reform work was inspired both by his father's campaign against a structurally unjust system of corporate ownership and by Kelso's practical success. As Gates put it in *The Ownership Solution*:

> An economy which makes it easier for John Paul Getty to get a third of a billion dollars than it does for two-thirds of the families in the country to get $500 ahead of their debts is buying a lot of hogwash about the value of John Paul Getty. The aggregate motivation in the millions of individuals that is destroyed and frustrated by such an insane arrangement is infinitely more productive than anything that one individual could contribute, irrespective of what that may be.

The Kelso plan was another method of ownership transfer. Like the proposals of Sismondi, Mill, and Gandhi, it transformed workers into owners, working for their wages and benefiting from a second income that flowed from the surplus generated by the business. This combination of wages and dividends to increase aggregate income and wealth sharing for all citizens is now known as "binary economics." Kelso's tax-efficient ESOP cleverly applied corporate financing techniques to distribute ownership of businesses without necessarily spreading control, power, and benefits. According to Robert Ashford of the College of Law at Syracuse University, "Binary economic principles...assert that one widely overlooked way to empower economically poor and working people in market economy is to universalize the right to acquire capital with the earnings of capital. This right is presently largely concentrated, as a practical matter, in less than 5% of the population."

The first prerequisite for a successful ESOP is to secure mutual collaboration between the company, its owners, its employees, and a lender. The second requirement is to ensure access to low-cost finance to grease the wheels for the transaction to happen over time. Kelso accomplished this by using trust law and pension-plan tax shelters. Later, Russell Long, with the help of Jeff Gates, established four linked tax incentives, each designed to secure the ownership transfer objective.

- Tax relief on interest earned by bankers financing share plans
- Tax relief related to the expense of repaying the loan principal
- Tax deductions for the employer for dividends paid on worker shares
- Tax exemption for the profits from selling shares to workers

ESOPs and the latent potential of Daily Democracy

Since Kelso died in 1991, ESOPs have developed significantly in the United States. Today, according to the National Center for Employee Ownership, 13 million out of 120 million nongovernment employees are involved with an ESOP. Broadly, these plans fall into five types:

- those that rescue a business from failure, using a worker and/or management buyout
- those that are used as a low-cost and tax-efficient way for private firms to raise equity without becoming publicly traded;
- those used as a profit-related incentive scheme
- those that are a defense mechanism for publicly traded corporations to limit hostile takeover bids
- those used as a mechanism for ownership transfer to employee stakeholders.

In fact, Kelso rarely had an incentive to promote power sharing with new employee-owners because the client base of the merchant bank he established, Kelso and Company, was made up of existing corporation owners who mostly wished to retain power as residual owners and arrange for any vendor loans to be repaid. *

Some problems with ESOPs have surfaced in the intervening decades:

- Corporations have taken up ESOPs as a tax-efficient method of raising new equity rather than as a means to introduce meaningful sharing of control with employees and/or other stakeholders (eg. consumers and suppliers).
- Executives exploit the substantial tax advantages to establish special "Top Hat" plans for themselves, involving all other workers in a far less generous plan only in order to legitimize their own elite arrangements when shareholder approval may be required.
- Voting shares are held in trust and are controlled by trustees or a trust board, typically nominated by the owners and/or managers, which does not advance economic democracy.
- Governance in most ESOPS is based on voting shares rather than on the principle of each working member of the firm having a vote; thus, cooperative and democratic principles of trusteeship have been advanced in only a minority of cases.

The encouraging news is that more than one in ten ESOPs have been developed to achieve either worker control or a multi-stakeholder corporation. Massachusetts, Vermont, and 14 other American states have secured changes in state law to establish these democratic corporations as "for Benefit corporations" (or B Corporations). For example, Chapter 157A of the Massachusetts General Laws includes provisions that allow the setup of a Mondragon-style worker cooperative with internal redeemable ownership accounts.

These organizations would have pleased John Stuart Mill. He would have described them as enablers of "mutual liberty," which he regarded as being at the heart of a system of governance that facilitated more united action to create commonwealth (community benefit). He would also have viewed them as a platform for practicing daily democracy, a cornerstone, along

---

* Kelso also developed Consumer Stock Ownership Plans (CSOPs), which involved external stakeholders as co-owners. He helped small farmers in California set up Valley Nitrogen Producers (a fertilizer business) as a CSOP in 1958 in the face of strong opposition from the oil industry. The farmer consumer-owners reaped a double benefit, the large dividends from their company self-financed their loans, and their fertilizer costs plummeted. Ironically, Kelso and Company, established in 1971 as a merchant bank in San Francisco, has grown since Kelso's death to become one of the top 50 private equity firms in the world.

with intensive cooperative education, for his vision of a future cooperative economy.

A century after Mill died, George Benello made the case for daily democracy through a radical transformation of work and power relations that involved the expansion of bona fide worker cooperatives. Moreover, he viewed this movement toward economic democracy as intimately linked to the strengthening of political democracy and based on active citizenship, first and foremost at the workplace.

> The principle of voluntary membership, understandable in non-worker cooperatives, must be significantly modified in the case of worker cooperatives. A worker cooperative is like a mini-republic, with a constitution, administrative, legislative, and judicial functions, and a citizen's rights and responsibilites. Entering members must be willing to accept the laws of the republic as well as be qualified for the position which they see.

The need for continued expansion of more democratic stakeholder corporations has been highlighted by the abject failure of the privatization agenda initiated by Thatcher and Reagan in 1980. Whether one looks at care homes for the elderly, bus services, or refuse collection, the results in the UK show who benefits from privatization. In *Jobs and Fairness*, Oakeshott cites the privatization of 72 municipal bus companies in the UK to illustrate this outcome. While 70 bus services were acquired by leveraged management buyouts, 2 were bought by a partnership between managers and workers. The management buyouts typically involved only a small handful of people. In all those cases, the companies were taken over by two large stock market corporations within a couple of years. Each manager walked away with between £1 million and £3.5 million. It was a different story for the other two companies, where employees resisted for eight years before they sold out. The distribution of gains involved all the workers and was radically more equitable, with between £16,000 and £33,000 going to each worker.

Oakeshott shows that the privatization programs promoted by western advisers in Eastern Europe were even more catastrophic. Data indicate that in Russia and almost all former communist companies, managers or communist party top brass dominated the buyouts and paid minuscule prices.

Despite this, trusteeship solutions have developed; indeed some 12 percent of ESOP companies in the United States now have a strong democratic ownership model that addresses the weaknesses noted above. Research by the National Center for Employee Ownership shows that ESOPs with employees involved in management and governance outperform other non-ESOP companies by 8 percent to 11 percent.

ESOPs in the Small and Medium-Sized Business Sector: Allied Plymouth

More than eight in ten ESOPs are in the small and medium-sized business sector, where they are increasingly used as an ownership succession strategy and/or as a means to raise new equity without the need to become publicly traded. The tax exemption for owners selling shares to employees helps ward off takeovers by large companies, while increasing the competitiveness of more democratic and generative options for workers and for owners seeking to retire. Allied Plymouth, a Virginia-based company, illustrates why this is so.

The Sanders family, which founded Allied Plymouth as a small building supply business in Akron, Ohio, struggled in the first few years of trading. Ed Sanders, the manager, researched building activity levels in US cities in the early 1950s and found Alexandria, Virginia, to be at the top of the list. He and his wife relocated the business there and began to prosper.

In a few years, Sanders began to experiment with profit sharing, thinking it could help grow the company. Workers were given the option of staying on salary or joining the profit-sharing scheme, which offered a 20 percent lower base rate of pay in return for a 30 percent share of profits. Daily financial performance data was shared so workers could see the results of their efforts. This open-book transparency worked like a charm. All employees joined the profit-sharing scheme, and turnover increased superbly. To improve performance even more, Sanders introduced an additional annual cash profit share. This was based on a number of weighted criteria, including the days worked in the year, the employee's length of service, and a peer assessment of the worker's performance by his colleagues. The results were outstanding and extraordinarily equitable. In all years the employee share of profits exceeded their 20 percent discounted wages; the average was a phenomenal 40 percent and 58 percent of their basic salary.

By 1977 Sanders was looking to retire. By then Allied Plymouth had 20 employees, and he decided an ESOP was a good option for them. He and his wife sold 12 percent of the company to their senior manager to ensure effective leadership of the firm beyond their retirement. They also committed to allocate annual profits to the Employee Stock Ownership Trust on behalf of their employees for five years or until 50 percent of the stock was in employee hands. Midway through this five-year period, the profits brought the amount to the 50 percent level, sufficient for the trust to secure a bank loan to finance the balance.

In the next decade the company established six new outlets, the workforce increased to 124, and sales increased from $6.2 million to $30.2 million.

By 1996 the company turnover had doubled to over $60 million, there were 14 outlets across five states, and the number of employees had reached 180.

The tax efficiency that Russell Long, and Kelso designed into the ESOP legislation created another substantial benefit. After the bank loan was paid off, the company was able to pay up to the maximum of 25 percent of payroll into the trust each month for every worker's pension. In this American case, key aspects of Gandhi's "socialization" model of trusteeship emerged. The public sector can get more taxes from higher wages in the process, and workers can look forward to a decent pension.

Transforming Property Rights: A Solution in Search of a Home

Shann Turnbull had an epiphany during a summer break from his MBA studies in 1962 while working as a financial analyst for Standard Oil in New York City. He was looking at proposals for refineries, chemical plants, ships, and the like, which came in to Standard from around the world, supported with 20- to 30-year cash-flow projections. What amazed Turnbull was that these long-term projections did not affect the decision to approve a project. Instead, approval hinged on the likelihood that the invested funds could be fully recovered with a competitive profit in ten years or less, depending on the country. Any profits arising beyond that horizon were "surplus" to the incentive to invest, even if they were double or triple the original investment.

Turnbull had a second epiphany a few years later when he was back in Australia. As a partner in a private equity firm, he was hunting for undervalued companies to take over, break up, and sell off at a big profit. When he looked at the financial statements of hundreds of firms listed on Australian stock exchanges, he discovered that most of the equity value of firms arose from the property they owned, not what they produced. The initial money invested in the business, and reinvested profits, were but a small fraction of their net asset value. A far greater portion derived from the rising value of the land owned by the business. To take just one example from Turnbull's seminal 1973 article "Time Limited Corporations," (in which he proposed changing the property rights of corporations to make them time limited), he describes a site owned by General Motors in a Melbourne suburb. After discounting for inflation, GM had had its original site investment repaid in real terms by more than 100 times in 47 years. Turnbull found that few firms included the full extent of these windfall gains on their balance sheets.

Turnbull came to the conclusion that this approach, in which corporations sat on their haunches and collected unearned wealth, was inefficient and inequitable. It was the people who lived in the area that created the potential for the huge gains, and they were getting nothing.

Accountants do not identify and report the "surplus profits" that Turnbull identified in his first epiphany. Nor are accountants required to identify and report the windfall gains from owning land that provided the second epiphany for Turnbull. Investors typically want only to recover all their money plus a tidy profit as quickly as possibly, preferably within ten years. This desire shapes their decisions. Time plus profit potential within this truncated time horizon can be thought of as the "incentive" to invest. In contrast, private owners, managers, and workers in companies like the John Lewis Partnership — or in cooperatives like Mondragon — see their working lives as the relevant time horizon.

Unfortunately, there was not then, nor is there now, any mechanism for capturing the public benefit of either surplus profits or windfall gains. Little wonder that the Fortune 500 global shares have continued to claim more and more of global net worth.

So Turnbull turned his mind to figuring out a way to redirect these unrecognized and unreported sources of wealth at source. Like the American revolutionaries who kicked out the British and exercised citizen powers to define and enforce corporate charters (described in Chapter 2), Turnbull seeks to revolutionize the definition of property rights.

Who Creates Value and How to Capture the Unearned Increment?

Traditionally, property owners have enjoyed a timeless claim to the wealth associated with a piece of land, regardless of what they do with it. That is one of the secrets to the concentration of wealth, which we have witnessed over generations. This situation is especially inefficient and inequitable in cities because the value of the entire land base is determined so heavily by public investments in roads, schools, sewerage, transport, and the like. Why should the private owners of urban land or buildings realize windfall gains from value they did not create?

Turnbull's bold idea was to separate the ownership of the urban land base from the ownership of buildings on the land. He proposed that all the land belong to a community or cooperative land bank (CLB), with shares in the bank distributed to residents based on the area occupied by their dwelling (e.g., one share per square meter). Ownership in a dwelling or commercial or industrial building would take the form of a transferable lease from the CLB. Whereas the leases on dwellings are perpetual (what some jurisdictions call a "strata" title), those for commercial or industrial buildings are time-limited. The CLB thereby captures all the uplift in land values created by public investment in infrastructure. Ownership and all its benefits go to those who create value by buying or renting dwellings.

To understand how this works, consider what happened in England when taxpayers invested £3.5 billion in the 1990s to extend the London Underground. Following the completion of the Jubilee Line, property values within 1,000 yards of each of the eleven new stations jumped 3.7 times, to £13 billion. Who benefited from this windfall? Not average folks in the borough of Southwark, that's for sure. The spike in property values — and the rise in rents they justified — all went to landlords, most of them absentee corporate owners. The wealth created by the investment of taxpayers' money in the Underground was sucked out of the community, right into the pockets of the wealthiest. To make matters worse, depreciation allowances allowed those property owners to recover, tax free, whatever money they invested in their properties. They might even have chosen to borrow against their property in order to invest and acquire more money. These are a couple of the ways in which, year by year, exclusive forms of ownership concentrate wealth in the hands of a few at the expense of the many. Meanwhile, the public debt load rises and private citizens suffer the consequences: higher taxes, reduced pensions, and massive cuts in public services and state subsidies for affordable housing, among many others.

If, instead, all the land within 1,000 yards of those new subway stations had been owned by a CLB, the outcome would have been much different. The CLB would be the beneficiary of the uplift in property values — and those higher property values would not prompt the landlord to jack up residential rents. Instead, tenants and the lessees of offices, stores, and factories would pay higher rent-rates to the CLB. These would enable the CLB to service whatever debt it had incurred as a partner in the original development. Surplus profits and profits from the sale of CLB shares would be additional sources of income with which the CLB could subsidize sustainable, affordable housing and invest in other important community priorities and services. In this way the CLB would become self-financing, and all residents, as co-op shareholders, would draw benefit from community improvements (see Figure 11.4). Note that CLB residents would share in these benefits whether they own their dwelling or rent it. Indeed, since rented homes and apartments only have value insofar as they are occupied, Turnbull proposes that tenants acquire co-ownership rights in their dwellings over time.

This separation of building ownership from ownership of the community's land base significantly enhances the political power of residents. With the shares comes the right to vote in CLB deliberations. Voting shares are not issued to the lessees of office buildings, supermarkets, and factories. This reallocation of ownership and political power ensures profits and rents stop leaking out of the community. Residents gain equity in the entire site, not just the area occupied by their dwelling. Tenants, progressively increase their

Fig. 11.4:

Cooperative Land Bank (CLB)*

approximate area | 10% | 40% | 40% | 10%

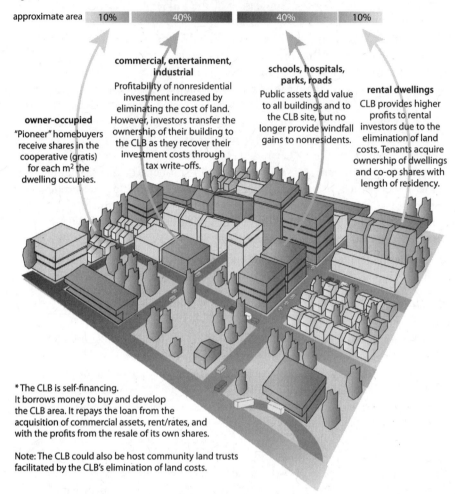

owner-occupied
"Pioneer" homebuyers receive shares in the cooperative (gratis) for each m² the dwelling occupies.

commercial, entertainment, industrial
Profitability of nonresidential investment increased by eliminating the cost of land. However, investors transfer the ownership of their building to the CLB as they recover their investment costs through tax write-offs.

schools, hospitals, parks, roads
Public assets add value to all buildings and to the CLB site, but no longer provide windfall gains to nonresidents.

rental dwellings
CLB provides higher profits to rental investors due to the elimination of land costs. Tenants acquire ownership of dwellings and co-op shares with length of residency.

* The CLB is self-financing. It borrows money to buy and develop the CLB area. It repays the loan from the acquisition of commercial assets, rent/rates, and with the profits from the resale of its own shares.

Note: The CLB could also be host community land trusts facilitated by the CLB's elimination of land costs.

ownership share as long as they rent and thus are encouraged to maintain and improve them. Those who create value by buying or renting dwellings gain ownership and all its benefits. Commercial and industrial investors retain ownership only until they recover their investments (with the opportunity to obtain a competitive profit). Incentive for entrepreneurship is preserved, while the system which progressively enriches the few and marginalizes the many is discarded.

This countercultural, yet simple, reconceptualization of how value is created and how property rights can be redistributed has many fascinating implications. But before exploring them, it is useful to see how Turnbull proposes to put a CLB in place.

Establishing a Cooperative Land Bank

Although it has not been tested since Turnbull hatched the idea 40 years ago, the CLB model can be applied as readily to the construction of a new community of up to 100,000 residents as it can be to the redevelopment of an impoverished inner-city neighborhood of 5,000. Whichever the case, several steps apply.

First, a company is registered for the purpose of operating the CLB. It is thus able to issue preferred shares. However, organizationally speaking, it operates under cooperative principles — one vote per resident citizen, no matter the number of shares they may hold.

The CLB then obtains an option to purchase a large parcel of land for development or redevelopment at existing use value. It must also obtain approval to rezone the land. It is expected that rezoning will create an uplift in the value of the site, just as it does when a private developer wins a rezoning permit. The increased value is captured by the CLB, thus enhancing its ability to raise loans for development.

The acquired land is mortgaged. This puts money in the hands of the CLB to finance subdivision development or, in the case of a blighted neighborhood, redevelopment. It also finances operating costs during the early stages. As in private property development, this stage increases the value of the land too.

At this point the CLB issues leases and shares. The perpetual leases for dwellings include terms and conditions that allow the land and buildings to be mortgaged. The first ("pioneer") homebuyers are issued their shares gratis. Later buyers purchase dwellings from the previous owner and purchase the requisite number of shares for the dwelling in question from the CLB.

The CLB also issues time-limited leases for commercial and industrial investors. The terms of these leases mimic the annual deductions that businesses are allowed to make for the depreciation of their investments in the property — for instance, constructing a new building. Here, however, the mechanism serves as a way to gradually transfer ownership to the CLB. For example, a new shopping center might be depreciated over 25 years, with a tax deduction of 4 percent per year. For the $80-million building (no land costs apply), the leaseholder would be able to write off $3,200,000 annually until the building was paid for. The CLB would obtain co-ownership of these nonresidential developments as they are written off for tax purposes. The rights to income would remain with the commercial operator.

In residential developments — for example, an apartment block — equity in the building would be transferred in a similar fashion but in this case to the tenants, who also receive shares from the CLB. In short, landlords "write off" ownership while they write off the costs of investment.

The accounting profits of commercial and industrial investors would not change as ownership is written off; the bottom line remains the same. At the end of the 25 years, however, all shopping centers, office blocks, factories, entertainment facilities, and other nonresidential developments would be wholly owned by the CLB. This puts a cap on the surplus profits — those that did not affect the private owner's decision to make an investment in the first place. (Likewise, windfall gains from the long-term uplift in the value of the land would accrue to the CLB, not to the investor.) The owner could then lease the building back, or the CLB could lease it to others or redevelop it.

Residents buy their homes by mortgaging their perpetual lease. If they rent their home out, the incoming tenant becomes a co-owner at 4 percent per year, just as the CLB becomes an owner in commercial properties by mimicking the depreciation rate. This provides an incentive for leaseholders to sell rather than become landlords. Why lose 4 percent ownership of their house each year to a tenant?

Revenue flows to the CLB from several sources: residential rents and charges for services; commercial and industrial rate/rents; and the surplus profits. In addition, the CLB builds up its equity from the windfall gains associated with CLB-owned buildings, and from trading in the CLB's own shares.

This latter revenue source is a bit complicated. To illustrate, consider what happens when people sell their homes in a CLB. Two types of equity change hands. Vendors sell their lease to the dwelling to buyers. The vendors also redeem their co-op shares from the CLB. And the CLB sells the co-op shares to new buyers. Only a portion of the receipts are paid to the vendors, however. Say there are 100 shares associated with a dwelling, which the vendor (a pioneer homeowner) has occupied for ten years. In the current market, the 100 shares the vendor got for free are worth $1,000 each. The homebuyer would pay $100,000 to acquire the shares from the CLB. However, the vendor would only get $40,000 of that (10 x 4 percent of $100,000); the CLB retains the remaining $60,000. The difference between $60,000 and the price at which the shares were originally issued ($0, in this case) is profit to the CLB. Transient homeowners thus get less for their homes, and extract less from the community, while the CLB shares in some of the capital gain.

What Benefits Would a CLB Generate?

The first major benefit is that a CLB would eliminate the cost of the land for pioneer homebuyers and for commercial developers, new or old. CLBs could also jump-start community land trusts and mutual home ownership cooperatives, as the CLB can provide them with sites at no cost, eliminating the need for CLTs or MHOSs to obtain a grant or gift, and accelerating their development and expansion.

Second, a CLB can reduce, and possibly remove, the need for taxpayer support for affordable housing. Because they eliminate the cost of land, which typically represents half the cost of a house, CLBs provide half-cost housing. At the same time, their revenue- and equity-building features allow CLBs to become self-financing.

Third, a CLB captures, for community benefit, the value created by public investments in schools, hospitals, transportation, etc. This is only fair, as without the residents these assets would have little value. It remains to work out how uplifts in value (like those experienced around the London subway) would be shared with public authorities in order to recognize the contribution of taxpayers to such large investments. This is not only fair but is also more economically efficient and appropriate. For example, a good school can have an effect on the market, drawing people to compete for housing in a particular neighborhood so they can send their children to that school.

Fourth, a CLB eliminates speculative real-estate investment by commercial interests and considerably reduces the influence of developers on local and other governments, which is often applied to increase the value of existing private assets. This changes the developers' role from buying/owning/selling to acting as an agent in the establishment or redevelopment of democratic communities, a change that substantially reduces the funding and business risks for developers.

Fifth, CLBs make it more difficult for companies to sit on property for speculative purposes. This would end the tradition of private developers capturing windfall unearned profits by riding the upswing in urban markets. Similarly, companies would have less opportunity to misrepresent their assets to shareholders by hiding unearned values from land holdings. Accountability would be enhanced, and the value of what is actually produced by firms would become more transparent. This backdoor corporate reform facilitated by the CLB tenure system could help make market economies more efficient, equitable, and sustainable. (The CLB would also offset any steep decline in local land values — due to rezoning, for example — with gains in value elsewhere.)

Sixth, pioneer homebuyers and all residential tenants would obtain, without cost, equity in their dwelling and the CLB shares associated with the dwelling. Because this equity cannot be cashed out until their dwelling has been sold or has been fully written off, at a rate of 4 percent per year, this means that all tenants eventually receive a "nest egg" that could contribute to their pension. In mature CLBs, both homeowners and tenants could obtain dividends from the CLB shares, which thus provide a way to reduce welfare dependency and costs and assure dignified retirement incomes, reducing the burden on governments.

Finally, by halving the cost of buying a home, a CLB attracts other developers to the housing market. Commercial investors would provide more rental housing. Nonprofit investors would set up CLTs and MHOS to provide sustainable, affordable housing.

Implications for Reweaving Local Economies and Navigating Transition

The fact that the model has not yet been translated into a test site is not surprising; it turns the dominant paradigm on its head. Nevertheless, as more people understand how property rights feed inequality and unsustainable cities, interest in the CLB model grows. In the UK, the Garden City of Letchworth (with a population of 33,000), pioneered in the early part of the last century, is the only precedent for a CLB we know of, and it is now inspiring discussion about the prospects of a new Garden City movement for ecological towns and cities. There are several reasons for this.

First, as CLBs acquire ownership of land and the built environment, wealth will be shared, as Spence, Mill and Howard said it would. If CLBs

S 6396   SOLLERSHOTT E. LETCHWORTH GARDEN CITY

Fig. 11.5: *A postcard depiction of Sollershott East, Letchworth, Hertfordshire in 1910.*
Source: Kingsway Real Photo Series. Margaret Pierce

are widely adopted, they will introduce a "third" way to distribute wealth. The distribution of surplus profits as dividends to CLB members reduces the need for governments to raise taxes, pay pensions, and provide social assistance. This would reduce the size and cost of government bureaucracy. It would also reduce the constant pressure to grow the economy any which way in order to create jobs so tax revenue can be increased to pay for these public expenditures.

The time-limited commercial and industrial leases also minimize the private retention of surplus profits. Enterprises can still make profits, even excessive profits, but only for a limited time. Windfall gains are eliminated. Speculation is also eliminated and replaced with a positive and structured incentive to invest in productive businesses, made stronger because the cost of financing urban sites/land has been removed. The surplus value captured by the CLB is thus freed up for investment in the transition to a steady-state economy.

By capturing rising property values and surpluses, CLBs pool assets that could be applied to the various investment-starved transition challenges that need to be addressed at the local level, such as combined heat and power, retrofitting for energy efficiency, and renewable energy production. Given their larger scale, CLBs could issue their own bonds and even establish their own local or regional currency and credit system tied to a locally created unit of value (such as the electricity generated from renewable sources).

In short, CLBs could help steer us in the direction of a more democratic, steady-state economy. Turnbull argues that no public decisions regarding major infrastructure investments or any major rezoning decisions should take place without the adoption of a CLB.

Norm Kurland of the Center for Social and Economic Justice in the United States has argued that it may not be as difficult to get CLBs going as one might expect. Local authorities could transform the public land banks they create for urban renewal into CLBs. This land assembly is currently supported with national government funds and works hand-in-glove with private developers in public-private partnerships. Kurland says:

> Publicly owned land could...be donated to the CLB for development, keeping local land in the hands of local voters. (This is based on the principle that anything owned by government can and should whenever possible be owned by the citizens that government is supposed to serve.) Public condemnation powers [used for urban renewal clearance] could also be delegated by government to the CLB to enable local voters to acquire land for CLB development projects.

Robin Murray of the London School of Economics has suggested something along the lines of a public-social partnership. For example, in a city like Irvine or Chicago, where city-wide CLTs have been set up, a partnership between the municipality and the CLT could leverage private developer involvement while securing windfall gains for community benefit. Another option where large CLTs exist could be to morph them into a CLB by creating shares for residents under a mandate to specifically steward the land and secure the local benefits for residents, the local authority, local small businesses, and local community organizations.

Apart from these various methods, a CLB could be established anywhere a majority of residents agree to exchange their existing property rights for equivalently valued property rights in a CLB.

One can see the transformative potential such a creative and dynamic transfer of ownership could generate. True, there is much more detailed work to be done. But the CLB flowing from Turnbull's epiphanies almost half a century ago is much more than a vision. Indeed, the precedent of Letchworth Garden City, though not a fully fledged CLB, does show it is possible to capture unearned income for community benefit. Turnbull's modern version provides practical steps to reverse enclosure and advance a steady-state economy.

Transition Factors

Progressively restructuring property rights and accelerating ownership transfer to "trusteeship" companies is a vital part of fostering more competitive and responsible businesses and a more stable economy. Sharing the wealth makes economic sense, is fairer, and, importantly, revitalizes, extends, and deepens democracy. Through trusteeship companies and CLBs, local democracy can literally become a vibrant, daily, and active verb for all workers, tenant-owners, and other stakeholders.

From the perspective of transition, capturing the unearned income from speculation and surplus profits has the potential to liberate hundreds of billions of dollars/pounds/euros for reinvestment in the countless projects required to achieve a low-carbon, steady-state economy.

Resilience Reflections

We have argued that if we are to have some chance of successfully navigating the challenge of transition, democratic, decentralized, diversified, and distributive solutions are imperative. Our way of living must adjust to the ecological limits that none of us can transcend. Economic growth can no longer be our mantra. The Resilience Imperative is at the heart of the movement we need to strengthen and the people we need to become.

Consider the facts that:

- We live in a world where many corporations have a greater turn-over than the GDP of most countries.
- Of the 100 largest economies in the world, 52 are corporations and 48 are countries, and these corporations have sales figures between $51 billion and $247 billion.
- Seventy percent of world trade is controlled by just 500 of the largest industrial corporations; in 2002, the top 200 had combined sales equivalent to 28 percent of world GDP. However, these 200 corporations employed less than 1 percent of the global workforce.
- In the United States, 98 percent of all companies account for only 25 percent of business activity, leaving the remaining 2 percent to account for 75 percent.
- The top 500 industrial corporations, which represent only one-tenth of one percent of all US companies, control over two-thirds of the business resources in the United States and collect over 70 percent of all US profits.

What is resilient about this picture? Decreasing *diversity*, increasing centralization, more and more power and wealth in the hands of fewer and fewer people who continuously drive their corporate ships to grow; this portrait is a caricature of resilience, a malicious system out of control and headed for disaster. It is completely untenable to depend on the current model of global capitalism, where two-thirds of global GDP is controlled by 500 corporations that create less than one percent of global employment. Neither the majority of human beings nor the planet can sustain it.

It need not be this way. We have seen visionary and practical pathways toward ownership transfer. In this chapter, we have introduced the theoretical, political, economic, and practical basis to proclaim "enough is enough"; the dominant assumptions that are fueling economic growth and corporate concentration of wealth and ownership are the wrong ones for the people of the 21st century.

Resilience means *diversifying* and decentralizing ownership (*increasing modularity*). Resilience means bringing the economy home from the market, tightening the *feedback loops* between our social, ecological, and economic existences. Without such a SEE change, we will not be able to live within our *ecological limits*.

Moreover, the outpouring of *social capital, experimentation, and innovation* exemplified by the cases presented in this chapter convincingly demonstrates that increasing equality through *shared* ownership and democratic *participation in enterprise governance* yields sterling economic results.

So we have this stark challenge. We know change is possible. Likewise, we know the current unprecedented corporate concentration of wealth and power produces economic growth that breeds inequality and unsustainable exploitation of the natural world.

The resilience imperative demands we repatriate ownership and regain influence over the enterprises that affect the communities and regions we live. We cannot navigate transition unless we have much greater control of our own economic resources.

The resilience imperative demands we shape our consumption to support transition, which means taking our purchasing to local, regional, and ethical companies. This is part of reshaping the markets.

The resilience imperative means organizing politically to take up Huey Long's clarion call to "share the wealth." We need not accomplish this only through the State, although political organizing in support of policies that encourage, rather than thwart, resilience and transition is critical. Indeed, without breakthroughs on the political level, the challenges of transition will be much greater.

The probability that humans will meet the demands that flow from the resilience imperative remains to be seen. In the next chapter we take up the most murky and opaque factors that will ultimately shape the answer: our cultural patterns, within which the meaning of our lives is ultimately derived and mediated.

CHAPTER 12

From Cultural Captivity to Focused Intention

*We in America built more and more stores, to sell more and more
stuff, made in more and more Chinese factories, powered by more and
more coal, and all those sales produced more and more dollars, which
China used to buy more and more Treasury bills, which allowed the
Federal Reserve to extend more and more easy credit to more and more
banks, consumers and businesses so that more and more Americans
could purchase more and more homes, and all those sales drove
home prices higher and higher, which made more and more money
to buy more and more stuff and more and more Chinese factories
powered by more and more coal which...*
— Thomas Friedman, *Hot, Flat, and Crowded*

*It is perhaps not too much to say that, in the first decade of
the new millennium, humanity has entered into a condition that
is in some sense more globally united and interconnected, more
sensitized to the experiences and suffering of others, in certain respects
more spiritually awakened, more conscious of future possibilities and
ideals, more capable of collective healing and compassion, and, aided by
technological advances in communication media, more able to think,
feel and respond together in a spiritually evolved manner to the world's
swiftly changing realities than has ever before been possible.*
— Richard Tarnas, *Cosmos and Psyche: Intimations of a New World View*

*How is one to live a moral and compassionate existence when one is
fully aware of the blood, the horror inherent in life, when one finds
darkness not only in one's culture but within oneself? If there is a
stage at which an individual life becomes truly adult, it must be when*

*one grasps the irony in its unfolding and accepts responsibility for a
life lived in the midst of such paradox. One must live in the middle of
contradiction...There are simply no answers to some of the most pressing
questions. You continue to live them out, making your life a worthy
expression of leaning into the light.*

— Barry Lopez, *Arctic Dreams*

We have met the enemy and he is us.

— Walt Kelly, Pogo comic strip, 1970

T HE MOST FAMOUS LINE IN THE LEGENDARY POGO COMIC STRIP was inspired
by the experience of Pogo and his pal wading through a desecrated landscape. Pogo, gazing back from whence they had come, lamented, "We have
met the enemy and he is us."

Yet is this really true? Are we the enemy? Or might we be in the midst of
a re-evolution, as suggested by Richard Tarnas? The first Earth Day was held
in 1970, just days after Pogo uttered his provocative declaration; 20 million
Americans showed up. Forty years later, according to the Wikipedia entry on
Earth Day, 500 million people showed up in 175 countries.

How does this promise fit in the context of 40 years of growing volatility on a global merry-go-round, powered by a hyper-drive, that we don't
seem to know how to jump off of? We are so interconnected that if Western
shoppers stopped going to Walmart to get more on the cheap, the Chinese
economy might falter, putting at risk the financing of American debt and
throwing Chinese workers out of work. Walmart aside, in 2008, fueled by
$147-per-barrel oil and a rampant subprime mortgage crisis, Friedman
reported that "thousands of factories went dark and whole Chinese villages
found themselves unemployed."

"How is one to live a moral and compassionate existence...in the midst
of such contradictions?" Barry Lopez asks. Given our cultural patterns, can
we hold the tension, remain hopeful, muster the courage and focused intention to untangle our addiction to "having," and consciously move to "being"
humans who live within our means? Or are we destined to desecrate the
only earth we have by recklessly stumbling around, enveloped in a growth-
addicted cultural stupor that we are either unable or unwilling to shake off?

There are reasons to be hopeful. There are also reasons to despair. Both
exist in our midst. While a "blessed unrest" is growing, so too is the concentration of unaccountable wealth powerful enough to devour and destroy
the planet we depend on. The project of writing this book is testimony to
the contradictions we exist within. We have felt them, deeply. Pogo may be
right; we may well be our own worst enemies. But this does not mean we are

not evolving. The testimony in this book reveals our capacity to transition toward the resilience imperative. But is it probable? Or can we know at this juncture what the future holds for our evolution as a species?

Beyond Eden: Our Disconnect from Nature

Current estimates of the rate of species extinction caused by humans affecting the health of ecological systems is 13,000 each year. The realization of the magnitude of our impact on nature is muted but growing. Yet resistance and denial continue to be dominant, or so it seems.

Ecopsychology, a rapidly expanding field that tries to understand our disconnection from nature, its consequences, and its causes, suggests that denial is rooted in the repression of this reality. It feels unbearable. To know, even unconsciously, that we are primarily responsible for this assault on other creatures that have evolved over millions of years is too much to take in. Despair, denial, discounting, and resistance are common avoidance behaviors. And if the ecopsychologists are right, "the primary responsibility for this catastrophe lies with human psychology, culture, values and lifestyle."

The discipline of psychology has long been captivated by what many in the field have come to see as a misguided project. In a nutshell, the profession has put human beings at the center to the exclusion of other creatures and our relationship with the natural environment. The sources of this self-absorbed perspective are several and possess a long lineage. Some would argue that the Judeo-Christian heritage with its founding Creation story, in which humans are sent forth to hold dominion over God's creation, is at the root. Others point to earlier times, to the advent of agriculture's ascendancy over the hunter-gatherers and the subsequent birth of cities, as an even deeper root. While these threads may be debated, more recent conceptions of nature are less contentious, perhaps. From Descartes to Isaac Newton, the philosophies and discoveries underpinning 20th-century science have variously depicted nature as being subject to mechanical laws, a force to be dominated and tamed, and/or an inert mass of resources to serve human needs.

These perspectives also shaped Sigmund Freud, the father of modern psychology. When seen in the light of the zeitgeist of the industrial revolution, the distortion of Darwin's "survival of the fittest," and the "progress" of modernity, nature was more often than not demonized. According to psychologist Will W. Adams, "Presuming that the 'human community' needs to 'defend' against 'the dreaded external world,' Freud advocated an 'attack against nature and subjecting *her* to the human will'" (emphasis added).

Other branches of psychology also uncritically elevated humans over the rest of nature. Fortunately, with the growth of transpersonal psychology, environmental psychology, and ecopsychology, the discipline has begun to reintegrate humans with nonhuman nature. In the words of Will Adams: "We are thus deepening our understanding of how it may be useful to *differentiate humankind from the rest of nature without deeming ourselves separate from or above nature.* Appreciating our kinship, identity, and intimacy with non-human nature, along with our differences, is enabling us to begin realizing that human kind is actually a manifestation of nature, one with quite distinctive ways of being" (emphasis in original).

This is, of course, not a foreign view to most indigenous cultures, where interdependence and kinship with nature was embedded in a world view that the likes of Francis Bacon and others, right up to the present, variously considered either savage, exotic, or mere obstacles to progress.

The analysis emerging from ecopsychology is critically important to absorb and internalize as we prepare to deal with the 21st-century crises we face. Three insights are particularly poignant:

- We identify exclusively as (supposedly) separate, autonomous, individualistic, skin-bounded, ego-bound subjects.
- We presume a dualistic separation (or dissociation) of self from the broader world, of our humanity from nature.
- Our ideologies, values, and practices are exclusively human-centered.

"These interrelated phenomena reveal that we are terribly confused about who we are, what the natural world is, and what really matters," Adams suggests. They are what Jung would call "'the shadow side' of the great emancipatory achievements of modernity. This alienation [from the natural world], the result of a long cultural–historical process, is now taken as 'natural,' inevitable, just 'the way things are and have to be.' Captivated by these views, values, and ways of being, we exist in a state of impoverishment," in a fog about what is most important. We have evolved into creatures of habit, isolated from the wholeness and aliveness of Gaia, the living earth. We think of nature as ours to consume in a myriad of ways designed to satisfy us. In so doing we reduce ourselves and nature. Both become viewed as commodities to be used, hired, and manipulated for personal gain. Perhaps this is the historical legacy of enclosure.

Psychologists are beginning to refer to our psychic disconnection from nature as a pathology, the elements of which are self-reinforcing. "Pathology in the psychological, sociocultural, and spiritual realms generates pathology in the ecological realm (diminished biodiversity, habitat destruction, environmental toxicity, global warming, etc.)," writes Adams. "And this ecopathology generates further individual and sociocultural pathology." Ecologist Robert Michael Pyle suggests that "the most dangerous idea in

"I say, bring it on! With global warming Global
Food Corp can produce year around!!"

the world is that humans are separate from the rest of nature. The greatest
enormities against the Earth stem from such delusions, just as us-and-them
thinking justifies our inhumanity toward one another."

Transition: An Inner and Outer Journey

For the growing number of citizens across the globe willing to grapple
with the facts as we are coming to understand them, the result can be psychologically devastating. Deep cultural change is likely to be painful. Clive
Hamilton, in his book *Requiem for a Species*, put it this way:

> Climate disruption's assault on all we believed — endless prog-
> ress, a stable future, our capacity to control the natural world
> with science and technology — will corrode the pillars that
> hold up the psyche of modern humanity. It will be psychologi-
> cally destabilizing in a way exceeded in human history perhaps
> only by the shift to agriculture and the rise of industrial society.

Yet as we have seen in this book, people are shaping strategic pathways
that give concrete proof that change is possible. These people are conscious,
persistent, and organized. The reality of crisis has motivated them to rethink
the ways they live, individually and collectively, and then act. They are
already on the path of transition. Is it not logical to conclude that they will
be better prepared, emotionally and psychologically, to cope with the formidable challenges ahead? That because they are organized and connected in a
common purpose, they are likely to face far less danger of becoming psychi-
cally isolated and immobilized as the crisis deepens? Solidarity is a resource
in itself, unleashing energy that feeds resilience and adaptive capacity.

Wendell Berry, a long-time advocate of grassroots change and place-shaping activity that starts at home, suggests there are eight basic principles that point to some important aspects of the cultural shift we need to contemplate. Staying rooted where we are planted is his sage advice. He describes a mindset that could help prepare us for the psychological, emotional, and spiritual difficulties we will encounter this century.

> The hummingbird successfully crossing the Gulf of Mexico is adapted mile by mile to the distance. It does not exceed its own physical and mental capacities and it makes the trip exactly like pre-industrial human migrants, on contemporary energy.
>
> For humans, local adaptation is not work for a few financiers and a few intellectual and political hotshots. This is work for everybody, requiring everybody's intelligence. It is work inherently democratic.
>
> What must we do?

- We must not work or think on a heroic scale. In our age of global industrialism, heroes too likely risk the lives of places and things they do not see.
- We must work on a scale proper to our limited abilities. We must not break things we cannot fix. There is no justification ever for permanent ecological damage. If this imposes the verdict of guilt upon us all, so be it.
- We must abandon the homeopathic delusion that the damages done by industrialization can be corrected by more industrialization.
- We must quit solving our problems by moving on. We must try to stay put and to learn where we are — geographically, historically and ecologically.
- We must learn, if we can, the sources and costs of our own economic lives.
- We must give up the notion that we are too good to do our own work and clean up our own messes. It is not acceptable for this work to be done for us by wage slavery or by enslaving nature.
- By way of correction, we must make local, locally adapted economies based on local nature, local sunlight, local intelligence and local work.
- We must understand that these measures are radical. They go to the root of our problem. They cannot be performed for us by any expert, political leader or corporation.

This is an agenda that may be undertaken by ordinary citizens at any time on their own initiative. In fact it describes an effort already undertaken all over the world by many people. It defines also the expectation that citizens who by their gifts are exceptional will not shirk the most humble service.

Contemplating living by such principles may characterize the millions trying to discern pathways to transition. Others may be aware of the growing crisis but choose to carry on business as usual, believing there is really nothing they can do. Still others are captured by the deadening rhythm of consumer culture; they remain in denial or in silent dread. Some just do not care, even though they have the means to contribute. More are so burdened they have neither the time nor the resources to devote to contemplating a future when their present is so precarious.

Carolyn Baker is a psychologist who focuses her practice on assisting people in various psychological and emotional states related to the big issues of our time. In her book *Navigating the Coming Chaos*, her depiction of people trying to come to terms with peak oil and climate change is instructive:

> Perhaps you have been preparing logistically for the collapse of industrial civilization for some time. You may have attended to food and water storage, energy supply, herbal medicines, organic gardens, and sustainable shelter. Perhaps you are exquisitely prepared for what James Howard Kunstler calls The Long Emergency and you have every base of logistical preparation covered, but some part of you feels queasy when you contemplate living in a chaotic world during or following the collapse of most or all of the systems of civilization which at this moment in history we take for granted, and have all of our lives.
>
> Perhaps you have envisioned possible scenarios of that world or read books or seen movies suggesting similar or worse scenarios. As you sit with them you notice an eddy of emotions that churn and spin like whirlpools of molten lava throughout your body. One moment you feel fear, the next sorrow, and in another, disorientation as you imagine events, landscapes, situations, and behavior that in present time are scarcely fathomable.
>
> Many options for responding to those feelings present themselves to you. You may choose to reach for a stiff drink, a comforting dessert, a hug from a loved one, the furry snuggle

of a household pet, a mindless TV series — or you may just choose to go to sleep and forget about what you're feeling. Yet some part of you knows that sooner or later, you are likely to be faced not only with one of the disturbing scenarios you imagine or one like it, but even more poignantly, the feelings that such an event will activate in you.

Still another part of you hopes that everything you've read or imagined about the future is false. Perhaps all the prognosticators are wrong, and the diehard champions of "technology will eventually save us" are right. Perhaps the future isn't so bright that you "need to wear shades," as the eighties rock hit boasts, but perhaps it really won't be as bleak as the "doomers" say it will be.

In fact, even now as you read these words, you may fear or resent me for writing them. You may argue that I shouldn't be scaring people. Yet after a decade of studying the state of the planet in depth and after witnessing that the majority of the human species is still unwilling to acknowledge its plight, I cannot in good conscience report to you "good news" that does not exist.

If there is no good news, or if there is not enough of it, the process of accompanying people toward a path more akin to Berry's principles will be a major task. How do we deal with the insecurity and loss of meaning as we discover our belief in "endless progress, a stable future and our capacity to control the natural world with science and technology" is founded on crumbling assumptions?

"Yes, I feel it too. It's a sort of synchronicity that we all share. Aren't anti-depressants marvelous?"

William Bridges, a psychologist and organizational consultant whose 1980 book *Transitions: Making Sense of Life's Changes* was a bestseller, suggests that the first painful step in transition is letting go of the false assumptions to which we have attached our identities. Despair often accompanies this initial stage. The second step is an in-between period of living in what he calls the neutral zone. Think about it as a therapeutic takeoff on the Beatles song: "He's a real nowhere man, sitting in his nowhere land." This is a state of groundlessness, a space after something has ended and before something new takes its place. Teri Dillion, a psychotherapist, has described it as "a fertile time that could be used to make the internal shifts necessary for a new beginning to be, well, *new* — more than simply a recapitulation of old ways of operating, dressed up in a new costume."

Perhaps drawing on Bridges' idea of transition stages, Transition Towns, a growing movement around the world, also encourages members to take both inner and outer journeys. Born in the town of Totnes, England, this community animation and development strategy attempts to strengthen community resilience in the age of climate change and peak oil. It helps members creatively navigate energy descent, increase self-reliance to meet basic needs, and shape more convivial and cooperative community cultures.

While Transition Towns are all about taking concrete action where people live, its founders make a point of emphasizing that the transition process is not just about action out in the community and larger society. It is also about people undergoing an inner process of change. This suggestion that an inner realignment of body, mind, and spirit is a necessary component of transition — that we need to become in our inner life the change we are seeking outwardly — is one of the distinguishing features of the movement. Many Transition Towns have "heart and soul" groups that explicitly focus on accompanying people on the inward journey. Not surprisingly, they have adapted the 12-step program for overcoming addiction. Why not? Did not George Bush himself say we are addicted to oil? As Teri Dillion wrote:

> To truly "recover" from an addiction one must go through the transition of recognizing first that one's way of life is not working — the compulsion with the behavior or substance is getting in the way of one's relationships, health, future well-being, and growth. In other words, one recognizes their desire to consume is insatiable and destructive, and a change is needed. Once this realization happens, there comes the need to wander in the unknown, not having answers for what to "do" about it..."How

exactly do I get from this destructive way of life to something healthy and useful — a way of living that doesn't hurt me or others? How must I change my thinking and acting in order to step into this wholly different way of life?" The answers to these questions are not easily won; oftentimes, people find they need to find some personal sense of spirituality or meaning in order to find answers.

Though no panacea, the inner dimension of change recognized by Transition Towns is strategically important. Change is hugely taxing and difficult. Sustaining leadership for the long haul requires inner strength. Rediscovering and reinventing what it means to be fully human is at the heart of the deep cultural evolution we require. In the process we may rediscover the depth of John Ruskin's declaration that "Wealth Is Life."

In our time, letting go of the egocentric presumption that we are the center of all that is important is one step. A second is finding ways of becoming reconnected to the pulsating, wondrous, at-risk creation we inhabit. This is not some romantic sideshow. Rather, it is a radical departure from the emotional poverty embedded in the mindless mantra "more is better." To move to a culture of sufficiency characterized by vibrant and active connections with each other, where we have the skills and time to become more self-reliant in our households and communities, where trust can be nourished and diverse expressions respected — is this not a path to a richer way of living? This is the positive vision elevated within the Transition Town philosophy, all the while trying to do what one can, where one lives, on our crisis-ridden planet.

Breaking the Armor of our Cultural Captivity

There is a crack in everything
That's how the light gets in.

— Leonard Cohen, "Anthem"

Much of this book has been about bridging the gap between present and emerging global realities and how we might advance the transition by strengthening resilience at the household, organizational, and institutional level. The innovations we have described indicate that change is possible.

Yet it is naïve to assume the increasing plethora of inspired examples will by themselves overwhelm the growth-driven mania. Recall from Chapter 2 the maniacal rush for natural gas known as fracking — literally blowing up rock underground — that is, among other things, poisoning our groundwater. Consider the geopolitical posturing aimed at capturing the economic benefits from Arctic drilling and eventual oil production. As the Northwest

Passage melts, a modern caricature of humankind emerges. Competing to dominate a new industrial rush for spoils enabled by the rapidly warming Arctic, we will spend billions upon billions to produce more of the stuff we will then sell and burn, contributing even more to the sea-level rise that within 90 years will drive hundreds of million inhabitants from any seaside abodes that are not at least 1.7 meters above current sea levels.

More and more of us see can see the contradictions. The clash between the human titans of economic growth and the planetary imperative for restoring resilience is creating an unprecedented period of cultural dissonance filled with denial, confusion, guilt, apathy, ideological and religious fervor, promises of quick fixes, fear, and sorrow. It is a growing cacophony of dissonance, varied and layered. It is in this deepening gap between reality and illusion that cultural change is brewing.

Jeremy Leggett is the executive chairman of Solar Century, a successful solar firm in the UK. His varied career as an oil industry geologist and climate change negotiator for Greenpeace gives him a unique vantage point from which to probe for cracks in the institutional armor of the oil industry. The cultural challenge is, in his view, perhaps the most significant obstacle thwarting change in the ranks of oil executives and economists. In 2009 he gave an interview to Dave Bowden and Steve Andrews of the Association for the Study of Peak Oil-USA, in which he answered the following questions:

> **Question:** When did you first learn about the peak oil issue?
>
> **Leggett:** I came late to the peak oil issue. I read the original Campbell-Laherrere paper in Scientific American in 1998 and I think, like many creatures of the geological community, I was vaguely concerned by it but then I thought with great acuity that this can't possibly be right and with the benefit of hind sight, that was the limit of my scientific analysis at the time. It was the Shell reserves fiasco in 2004 that gave me a mental slap around the face, and I thought "there is a chance, son, that you are not paying attention here. Why don't you do a bit of homework on this issue," and that's when I started digging and that's when I went through the process of having my peak oil moments. And I think there's an important point here; I think cultures are very, very big in the issue. In the geological community many just don't want to accept this. There is a real denial, a cultural resistance to it. I see it in my former friends. I have lots of friends and former contemporaries in the oil industry, some of them in impossibly senior positions and

when I talk to them about this issue, that's what I see. I see a process of denial and I think it's quasi institutionalized.

Question: But since some know, why aren't more people in the oil industry talking about the peak oil issue?

Leggett: I think there's a cultural problem in the oil industry at the top tables. There is just simply a social silence. It's what the anthropologists studying the financial crunch have called a social silence that was erected around the bonus system. They discouraged, institutionally in individual conversations right through to institutional behavior, any discussion of the risk of these financial issues. In the same way, the leadership in the oil industry really frowns, in most cases, on any sensible discussion about peak oil. Former colleagues in BP tell me that it's almost like an act of treason to talk about peak oil in that company. And so I think that's a real issue.

That said, I had a debate with a former chief geologist of BP at a major oil industry conference here in London a few months ago. We debated the issue of whether or not peak oil had gone away as a problem. He argued, yes it has gone away as a problem — that was the motion. I argued against it and I expected to be roundly defeated. There were 500 or so practicing oil men in the room and more than two-thirds of them voted against the motion. So there is an understanding in the industry that there's a problem and I think ultimately that will come to the help of the whistle blowers. We could imagine a tipping point where there'll actually be so much pressure from within the industry for a fair and accurate portrayal of the situation that the leadership has to get in. In the same way as they had to get in, in BP and Shell, on climate change. They gave in on arguing the costs over global warming simply because of the guilt and disgust of their own membership, their own workers as it was described to me in both companies, and I think it ultimately will be the same with peak oil.

Question: Now when it comes to the economists and the peak oil story...

Leggett: I think it's entirely appropriate for the entire economics community, with the notable exception of the very few economists who saw the financial crash coming, to go back to the drawing board. I mean they got that whole thing catastrophically, systemically wrong. And I was shocked but pleased to see on British television news the other night the head of the economics faculty at the University of Chicago saying, when asked, what are the implications of the financial crash? He said, we have to go right back to the drawing board, I'm paraphrasing, but he was as strong in his wording as this. "We got everything wrong at a systemic level. We should be full of humility...Our whole discipline has been operating on flawed assumptions." And that's what they have to break.

We hear this from the economists now about peak oil: that the price mechanism works, that simply when oil prices go up, they'll go out and they'll find more oil; it's there under the ground isn't it? Economics will find the oil. Wrong, wrong, wrong. And we know this. But they have to take some of the humility that is absolutely required of them as a result of the financial crisis and bring it to a re-examination of what they're saying about peak oil.

Question: As a leader in the renewables industry, what do you see as the pros and cons of this plateauing of world oil production for both the renewables industries and the oil industry?

Leggett: I think it would be a mistake for renewables advocates to in any way celebrate what peak oil is going to do for the renewables industries because the bigger issue is that our economies are going to be gravely stressed, right down to the challenge of keeping social cohesion together, and this is a huge challenge. That said, there's no doubt that when we get off the peak, or mini plateau or whatever it is, and we go down the descent, and the shock hits the system, we're going to have to mobilize clean tech, energy efficiency and renewable technologies as fast as we mobilized tanks and aircraft and all the rest in the run up to World War II, and faster if we can. And the good news here is that at that point, people who work with these technologies day-to-day, like myself, feel very strongly that they can be mobilized faster than most supposed energy pundits would suggest. That'll be the good news.

The bad news is there's no scenario I think where they can be mobilized fast enough to make the difference. So there's going to have to be behavioral change, structural change in society to wrestle with that problem. But then when we get going, provided that people don't make a suite of stupid decisions and go to the longer flash-to-bang time technologies like coal to liquids, tar sands, nuclear power and really zero in on where Silicon Valley is putting its money today, which is clean tech, then who knows. Maybe we have a chance then of engineering a real renaissance in society, because you get all the rolling fringe benefits of renewables then — the local production, the local economies, the enhanced security, the air quality, the whole suite of things that just happen to spring from the innate characteristics of renewables. And that's an upside that I describe in *Half Gone*. I'm not going to say it's going to happen, but I do believe it could happen. And frankly, that's one of the things that gets me out of bed every morning.

Perhaps, as poet Leonard Cohen suggests, cracks are appearing everywhere. If even the illusory assurances from the heights of economics and big oil are being questioned from within, perhaps there is hope. But, as Leggett points out, there are no guarantees; even if we manage to put the brakes on the "flash to bang" technologies of carbon sequestration, tar sands, and liquid coal and move fully toward renewable energy options, we cannot bridge the gap quickly enough. Thus the importance of changing the way we think and behave. And so we return to the conundrum we started this book with — the challenge of SEEing our world differently, of replacing the dominant imperative of growth with the planet's nonnegotiable demand for resilience.

The "Price" of Transition: Are We Willing to Pay Our Way?

"Few challenges facing America — and the world — are more urgent than combating climate change," Obama said in November 2008, two months before being sworn in. "My presidency will mark a new chapter in America's leadership on climate change that will strengthen our security and create millions of new jobs."

Rousing as such a message may have been, it has been relegated to footnote status within Obama's current policy focus. Just 18 months after he assumed the presidency, green jobs and reducing carbon emissions got a single line, about 10 seconds, in the 45-minute speech he gave at Milwaukee Laborfest on Labor Day, 2010. With 14 million Americans out of work, the Labor Day message, tailored to workers and the unemployed, picked up on his central campaign message — "yes we can." Yes we can restore economic growth. Yes we can mobilize our people's capacity for work and American ingenuity and return our country to its former glory. Yes we can pull out of our economic slump, and we will do it so competitively that "made in the USA" will once again be a testimony across the globe to our resilience, to our capacity as a people.

What a rude awakening; so much for Obama being a global spokesperson for inconvenient truths. Economic growth was front and center, just as

Fig. 12.3: *Obama*. Source: © Evan Meyer | Dreamstime.com.

it has been for every other president in the last 40 years. Even "green growth" language was evaporating from the public discourse. The current crisis is what is important; the slow creep problem of peak oil and climate change cannot compete with 14 million unemployed Americans.

The diffidence and short attention span of political leaders are nothing new. Just three years after the first Earth Day, people around the globe woke up to a 400 percent rise in the price of oil. Arab countries, fed up with US military support to Israel, decided to fight back with the one weapon they could wield to hurt the United States — cutting off the oil supply. Within days there were frustrated lineups at the pumps. The government rationed fuel available to truckers, causing an angry, violent, nationwide strike. Truckers who kept working were attacked, even bombed.

You can bet the priority of energy skyrocketed. US determination to secure its energy supply became "the moral equivalent of war." Nothing was more important to the nation when President Jimmy Carter took to the airwaves in 1979:

> In little more than two decades we've gone from a position of energy independence to one in which almost half the oil we use comes from foreign countries, at prices that are going through the roof. Our excessive dependence on OPEC has already taken a tremendous toll on our economy and our people. This is the direct cause of the long lines which have made millions of you spend aggravating hours waiting for gasoline. It's a cause of the

increased inflation and unemployment that we now face. This intolerable dependence on foreign oil threatens our economic independence and the very security of our nation. The energy crisis is real. It is worldwide. It is a clear and present danger to our nation. These are facts and we simply must face them.

Increase coal production, radically increase auto fuel standards, and invest in renewable energy production; these were Carter's policies, all of which were gutted a year later by a new president, Ronald Reagan, whose free-market ideology precluded government interventions to shape the markets for energy. Strangely, it was George W. Bush, in his 2006 State of the Union address, who told Americans that "we have a serious problem: America is addicted to oil, which is often imported from unstable parts of the world." Increased spending on renewable energy, clean coal, nuclear power, and increased auto fuel efficiency were his solutions, reminiscent of Carter's solutions 30 years earlier. Both argued that government investment and regulation, joined up with the creativity and ingenuity of science and the private sector, would make it happen. Many leading scientists, businesspeople, and economists today argue that aggressive public intervention to shape markets is vital to ensure the transition to clean energy. Clear price and regulatory signals would drive investment, creativity, and ingenuity across America.

But clean energy motivated neither Carter nor Bush; their goal was to secure American independence from foreign oil and maintain economic growth. Neither contemplated that consumer expectations might need to be recalibrated — quite the opposite, in fact. When media asked White House press secretary Ari Fleischer if Americans needed to reduce their energy consumption, Fleischer responded, "That's a big no. The president believes...it should be the goal of policymakers to protect the American way of life. The American way of life is a blessed one."

Even among those advocating aggressive greening of the economy, many of whom guffaw at such self-absorbed American blessedness, economic growth is seldom questioned as a goal. Consider the bizarre and confused language embedded in the website of Green Growth, a policy of the UN Economic and Social Commission for Asia and Pacific:

> Green Growth is a globally relevant approach to sustainable economic growth that was developed in Asia. It is imperative that countries in the Asia and Pacific region continue their economic growth to alleviate poverty and to achieve social progress. However, increased environmental degradation, climate change and diminishing natural resources require an

unconventional approach to support the export-driven economic activities of the region.

Bizarre perhaps. Confused for sure. But as a policy statement it emphasizes an important political rationale with wide acceptance: economic growth is the route to social progress and poverty reduction. Economic growth is vital; we just need unconventional approaches to keep it going.

And what might those unconventional approaches be? The most obvious and immediate solution is clear to many: we must lower the energy input needed to create one unit of production. Greening global supply chains is a key priority requiring aggressive and focused policy implementation. It is the most immediate intervention that can yield big gains. But, as we pointed out in Chapter 1, and as Tim Jackson argues in *Prosperity Without Growth*, nowhere is it evident that this is happening. Even when one doubles energy efficiency and triples production, more energy is used.

None of this is to say that energy efficiency and a wide range of other technological innovations should be ignored. In his book *Hot, Flat, and Crowded*, Thomas Friedman advances a compelling and well-researched argument: if America radically increased the price of carbon, maintained it at a stable level, and put in place an intelligent regulatory regime, it would unleash a tsunami of innovation and investment that could sustain economic growth...maybe.

Friedman's big "maybe" parallels the conclusions and the big question embedded in the 2007 report of the Intergovernmental Panel on Climate Change. While 70 percent of the carbon-reduction target set for 2050 could be achieved by systematic and broad-based investment in existing technologies, they are not being deployed quickly enough. As for the other 30 percent, nobody knows; there is only the hope that spontaneous technological innovations will be invented and deployed quickly enough to keep atmospheric carbon under the maximum 450 parts per million needed to avoid catastrophic climate change.

This is a radical assumption — politically compelling, perhaps, but a leap of faith nonetheless. As Clive Hamilton says in *Requiem for a Species*, "Yes we can" is an assertion that, "like the future economic growth that depends on it, is incontrovertible only because of the faith placed in it," which "must be accepted without proof or verification." The problem is that failure is a very real option in the "real" world, and ignoring this fact only exacerbates the risks. It is as if we prefer to camouflage reality in order to save ourselves from psychological anguish and cultural dissonance. We want concrete reasons to hope more and worry less, as well as routes to avoid despair altogether. Belief that technology will save us "just in time" can serve this function.

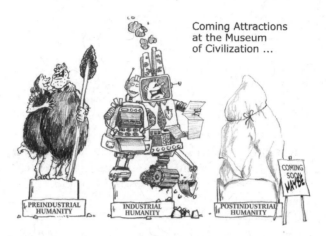

Coming Attractions
at the Museum
of Civilization ...

PREINDUSTRIAL HUMANITY

INDUSTRIAL HUMANITY

POSTINDUSTRIAL HUMANITY

COMING SOON MAYBE

Technical salvation is not the only way we shield ourselves from the complexity of our circumstances. The re-localization movement, which is gaining momentum around the globe, can also foster attitudes and espouse simplistic solutions almost as naïve as those which assert economic growth is the only way forward. Insulating ourselves by limiting our peripheral vision so it fits nicely within our comfort levels is not uncommon among a wide range of us who hold diverse views on how to navigate into the future

What we can say without self-deception is that moving from the growth imperative to the resilience imperative requires recalibration at many levels of human society. We cannot wish it into existence. Focused intention, building on what is being learned, federating allies to change the discourse and the rules of the global growth game, continuing the work of reweaving our economies locally and regionally, decoupling ourselves from narcissistic and self-destructive behaviors — all are part of the transition to a steady-state economy.

Blessed unrest is bubbling up across the globe. Powerful forces addicted to growth persist. There is no purity. We are all caught, to a varying extent, in the contradictions of where we are as a species on this planet. Our most basic decision is whether we are going to "lean into the light" or not, whether we are going to commit to building a "high road" based on solidarity, cooperation, and sufficiency or mindlessly remain captive to a widening "low road" economy propelling us toward an ecological and social precipice.

There is one political choice we can organize around that, if successful, could mobilize action across a broad swath of political and economic perspectives. Ecological economics holds the answer. To position transition from the "maybe possible" to the "possibly probable," the single most powerful lever we have is price. If we priced the ecological and social costs of producing and distributing a plastic doll, an SUV, or a fast-food hamburger, the low-road growth economy would contract and the high-road transition to steady-state economy would expand. Ironically, it is price, the central driver of commerce, that may be our most powerful ally in growing a resilient steady-state economy. To unleash innovation and deploy solutions, we must price the social damage we are causing ourselves and the ecological damage we are inflicting on the planet.

It is a path full of trials. Businesses and jobs that cannot adjust will wither. Dislocations will likely increase before adjustments can be navigated. As Huey Long pointed out in the 1930s, the errant rich should not be allowed to take unearned wealth that belongs to the people. They will have to be shamed, taxed, regulated, and compelled as necessary to bring back the "people's capital." They must not be allowed to stand in the way of social change and fundamental reforms that are necessary.

> We have been praying to the Almighty to send us to a feast. We have knelt on our knees morning and nighttime. The Lord has answered the prayer. He has called the barbecue. "Come to my feast," He said to 125 million American people. But Morgan and Rockefeller and Mellon...have walked up and took 85 percent of the victuals off the table!
>
> Now, how are you going to feed the balance of the people? What's Morgan...and Rockefeller and Mellon going to do with all that grub? They can't eat it, they can't wear the clothes, they can't live in the houses.
>
> Giv'em a yacht! Giv'em a Palace! Send 'em to Reno and give them a new wife when they want it, if that's what they want. But when they've got everything on God's loving earth that they can eat and they can wear and they can live in, and all that their children can live in and wear and eat, and all of their children's children can use, then we've got to call Mr. Morgan and Mr. Mellon and Mr. Rockefeller back and say, come back here, put that stuff back on this table here that you took away from here that you don't need. Leave something else for the American people to consume. And that's the program.

For those who squander natural wealth, overconsumption must become very costly and the meeting of basic needs less so. It is going to be a bumpy ride if we can get to the starting line. The question is whether a bumpy ride is more desirable than no chance to ride at all. Acting locally and federating globally to assert a "fair price" that pays for the full externalized costs of our lifestyle is a political choice that we can embrace or ignore. We will either share the pain coming our way now or reap the despair we will experience later as a planet weary of our excesses hits the tipping point and closes down our options for survival.

Even with proper pricing of greenhouse gases, the outcomes are uncertain. We cannot merely take heart from orators with the skill and conviction of Obama, who proclaim that "failure is not an option." Unquestioning faith in the impossibility of failure obscures very real threats and dulls the senses. Generating false hope is irresponsible, as is counselling despair. The issue is whether we have the courage and foresight to pay our way.

Weaving the Strands into a Resilient Fabric: Possible?

Perhaps the one fact we can proclaim that is unlikely to provoke much debate is that none of us can escape: We are where we are. The past is past and the present is the space within which we make decisions that will shape our future, whether individually, in our households, in our communities, our nations, or our planet. Our attitudes, values, and choices will determine whether the cracks in our cultural armor are allowed to widen enough to let in more light, or whether we continue to fill them with epoxy, trying yet again for a temporary fix. We make the choices every day.

As we move to the conclusion of this book we want to revisit some of our basic propositions. The first is the basic SEE Change method we advanced in Chapter 1. We suggested that as we begin to SEE the predicament of our planetary home and our place upon it more clearly, as our peripheral vision is extended, we have the possibility of SEEKing solutions more in sync with reality. As we SHARE what we SEE, we discover fellow travelers oriented to changing the status quo. As we SEEK pathways to a make a difference, we are drawn into acting where we can. As we act we learn more and connect in more ways with fellow seekers. Individually and collectively, we are extending our learning and our potential for creating positive impacts. Building the cooperative road as we go, our peripheral vision expands. We start seeing the linkages. Seeking and doing builds our analysis. We see federating with others as a way to create change. As a result, we begin meeting the preconditions to SECURE the changes we seek — not an easy struggle in the rough and tumble of a volatile world. Contention is to be expected. Many neither share nor like the implications of such a SEE Change agenda.

One of the things we learn more deeply is that our way of seeing the world and how it works is socially constructed, an evolutionary product that reflects from whence we have come. Our existing institutions, practices, behaviors, and systems are the result of contested ideas and the power of those who won the terrain. The last 500 years of history have been particularly powerful. Those who came to dominate the march of history shaped and enforced the ascendency of the big "M" Market. Now, as we arrive at an unprecedented conjuncture of human history, spinning from the rapidity of change in the last 60 years, we are living for the first time in what one might call a global culture. Increasingly homogeneous, yet paradoxically fracturing, we are experiencing, in breathtaking ways, what Clive Hamilton termed the most psychologically destabilizing period in human history. More than the relatively slow-moving agricultural revolution, and with greater rapidity than the industrial revolution, we are in for a century of collective turning and twisting to absorb change and adapt to new realities.

Living generations are the beneficiaries of an unprecedented period of cultural change. The extraordinary extension of power unleashed by fossil fuels has carved the contours of contemporary local and global cultures. We are the inheritors of a crazy glue of accreted expectations and material abundance unimaginable to our forebears. And, much to our consternation, we have an unprecedented awareness that we are responsible for the welfare of future generations, whether we accept it not. Indeed, our decisions will shape the contours of human life for many more generations into the future than the 200,000 years *Homo sapiens* have existed thus far.

At the beginning of the Great Depression, John Maynard Keynes embraced the steady-state vision of John Stuart Mill in his essay "Economic Possibilities for our Grandchildren." Mill's and Keynes's thoughts on moving beyond growth to secure "the art of living" provides a worthy vision for our perilous time. Keynes foresaw that usury would be recognised as a psycho-pathology:

> When the accumulation of wealth is no longer of high social importance, there will be great changes in the code of morals...The love of money, as a possession...will be recognized for what it is, a somewhat disgusting morbidity, one of those semi-criminal, semi-pathological propensities which one hands over with a shudder to the specialists in mental disease. All kinds of social customs and economic practices...which we now maintain because they are tremendously useful in promoting the accumulation of capital, we shall then be free, at last, to discard.

Rescuing Main Street from Wall Street

Working on Wall Street was financially rewarding for Ralph Borsodi, but by 1920 he was disillusioned. The assumption that big corporations were more efficient and thus necessary to modern commerce was sticking in his craw. It was his work as a business analyst for Macy's, the largest department store in Manhattan, that helped him define what was wrong with the Wall Street line of reasoning. His findings are insightful: in most circumstances, when they grew beyond a certain size, and when the distance to markets extended beyond a regional area, the large companies became more inefficient than smaller ones.

True, there are economies of scale. When production rates increased, unit costs went down by more than 20 percent, according to Borsodi's analysis of the previous 50 years' data. However, the costs of distributing units went up 300 percent, representing up to 66 percent of the production cost. He went on to show that between 50 and 66 percent of the goods examined could be produced and distributed locally and regionally at lower costs. Other research backed this conclusion. For example, a Twentieth Century Fund study of profitability in 1919 showed that "the largest corporations earned less than the average of all corporations...and the earnings declined almost uninterruptedly, with increasing size."

In Borsodi's view, the economic and cultural implications of this flaw in Wall Street's bigger-is-better philosophy were significant:

- The amount of waste in long supply chains was huge.
- More and more people were spending more and more time moving more and more goods farther and farther away. In the process, they were becoming more and more disconnected and estranged from the meaning of their work.
- The steady erosion of economic self-reliance and growing levels of personal insecurity were rapidly destroying the resilience of America's communities and the skills of their citizens to make and grow what they needed.
- Increasingly divorced from meaningful work, more and more people were becoming more and more susceptible to redefining meaning and their status in the community by what they were able to consume.

Borsodi, versed as he was in big business culture, saw that this was a key corporate strategy in the 1920s. The American "Roaring 20s" were fed by the frenzy of rapid growth driven by corporate greed and excessive consumer spending by the newly established middle class. Economic growth required market expansion, and it went hand in glove with promulgating a new superculture of consumption. National brands designed on Madison Avenue and reinforced by an increasingly sophisticated advertising industry were luring people to desire possession, and conflating ownership of consumer goods with what mattered, what constituted status — in short, with what was deemed meaningful. When the bubble burst, Wall Street crashed, unemployment skyrocketed, and the flow of people to the city was reversed; people headed back to the countryside.

With land costs plummeting in rural areas, Borsodi initiated what became a series of CLT-like rural land-reform experiments. Convinced that a more decentralized economy must be rebuilt, he set out to test his emerging ideas in rural New York and New England. Over the next few years he bought parcels of land and converted them into a communal leasehold tenure system, where individual homesteaders could own their own homes, farm the land, and set up enterprises for local and regional markets. Through a series of advances and setbacks, Borsodi came to two central conclusions:

- Participative democracy was a key to success; thus cooperative education was a vital necessity.
- To increase the success of cooperative homesteaders, it was crucial to have low-cost development finance for leasehold tenures based on common ownership.

To advance the educational prerequisite, he and his wife set up the School for Living on the first homestead. The school attracted many people from the the eastern United States and quickly became a national beacon for a growing range of "back to the land" groups. The diversified food-growing methods the school promoted became a major influence on the development of American organic farming. The cluster of cultural, agricultural, and land-reform innovations Borsodi advanced under the concept of "Trusterty" — a social form of "property" — became for him a profound truth. He believed that to secure our well-being and peace, we must steward the earth's treasures (the land, water, sky, and natural resources) in perpetuity, but they should never be possessed.

Borsodi continued to collect data that challenged conventional economists' ignorance of household economics, in particular the enormous economic value of home production. This analysis led him to distinguish between monetary income, which flowed from the market, and the imputed income of household caring, repairing, cooking, and growing food. The latter production might not have a dollar figure attached to it, but it was just as real, and Borsodi argued that its contribution to local production, and its reduction in waste due to shorter supply lines, should be counted properly. He also argued that reorganizing production and distribution on a more local and regional basis was key to rebuilding self-reliance, reconnecting people to the meaning of their work, and creating a cultural life based on enhancing the well-being of people and the natural environment.

Almost 40 years after the onset of his disillusionment with the sterility of Wall Street, Borsodi crafted a distillation of his research and applied experimentation. His 1958 "Decentralist Manifesto" set out the key measures he believed could revitalize and mobilize the latent cultural desire for meaning into a social renaissance that would enable work, meaning, community, and common-sense economics to come together in ways that would advance a measure of social justice and fulfilling livelihoods. The action points in his call for democratic decentralism summarize neatly many of the themes of both his forebears and those who continue to work for SEE Change.

- **Academic and educational autonomy:** Overcome dependence on government and develop an independent and inspiring system of instruction to cultivate artistic, cultural, scientific, and practical learning with strong links to crafts, vocations, and higher learning for all and the cultivation of a deep understanding of moral economy systems.
- **Regionalism:** Develop regional self-reliant economies that would become interdependent with those of other self-reliant regions.
- **Participative democracy:** Devolve power to citizens at the local level, and invert the hierarchy by maximizing decision making at the local and regional level.
- **Co-operative development:** Replace unaccountable corporations over a period of time, bring democracy to workers and consumers, and secure economic justice.
- **Just prices:** Develop a fraternal system of competition that utilizes markets but develops between buyers and sellers a price system that is equitable.
- **Mutualization:** Mutualize all natural monopolies, including rail services, water and energy companies, telephone and communication services, irrigation systems, and pipelines.
- **Cooperative banks and stable currency:** Remove from commercial banks the right to create money as debt, and create a noninflationary and stable cooperative money system.
- **Land reform and abolition of wage slavery:** Give citizens free access to land for housing and productive purposes in order to secure regional self-reliance, but hold land and natural resources in trust, outside the market, so they cannot be privately appropriated.
- **Tax reform:** Replace conventional taxes steadily with land value taxes and other resource rents to capture the unearned increment and corporate windfall gains to meet community needs.

The Crucible of Home: Revisiting Household Economics

We now return to where we are in 2011, with blessed unrest all about, trying to find ways to weave the pieces together in the neutral zone, where many still hold on to the old, and the new is accelerating its struggle to make it down the birth canal. One of the most important venues in which we will live out this struggle is our own households, alongside the circle of people we are most intimately connected to. The crucible of "home" and friendship shapes us, imbues life with meaning, supports and challenges us. In its absence we suffer. Love, security, belonging, becoming the best we can be — all are at risk without the home crèche. Our experience of the daily round of life reveals the truth of this.

What many of us may not know is the extent to which households contribute to the carbon conundrum. We were startled to come upon European Union research claiming 40 percent of all carbon emissions are traceable to the household. Household size, fuel sources, energy efficiency, heat and air-conditioning use, furnishings, and waste all help define our home's carbon footprint. And while increasing energy efficiency is one important strategy to reduce carbon, if it simply leads to increased demand for other energy-intensive products (if cheaper heating helps pay for more air travel, for instance), it will not have the intended carbon-reduction impact. If we would permanently reduce energy consumption, it must become a way of life.

It is thus self-evident that the household is an essential cornerstone of the multilevel transition strategy required to move us toward a steady-state economy. Sounds smart, but when the embedded costs of the household are already incurred, debt taken on, and operating costs are steadily rising, many householders find themselves running harder just to keep up. However, a deeper look at some of the numbers helps us put some of the big pieces of the puzzle together. We use Canadian statistics here, but the pattern in many countries is similar.

In April 2011 the value of an average house in Vancouver, BC, home of the 2010 Olympics, was $786,311. Offshore money flowing in from China was driving a speculative boom in the city. Toronto homes were only $456,147 and Calgary's $398,836, just a bit over the $371,000 average across Canada. In 1980 the average cost of a North American house was $68,700, just 18 percent of what it is today. You might think the rise in wages over the last 30 years would keep the buying power at a similar level, but that is nowhere near the case. The average wage in 1980 was $19,700, almost 29 percent the cost of a house. The average wage today is $39,449, only 11 percent of the average home cost in Canada — and only 5 percent of the average cost in Vancouver. The reality is that in today's dollars the 1980 wage was $51,000, 28 percent higher than the wage of the average Canadian living in 2011.

Just 65 years ago the average house size in Canada was 800 square feet. In 1975 it was 1,075 square feet, and by 2003 it had reached 1,800 square feet in Canada and 2,330 in the United States. A larger house means more carpets, more wood, more drywall, more flooring, more concrete — all of which mean higher costs, more embedded carbon, and more energy to operate the expanded space. Ironically, while houses almost tripled in size, the number of people inhabiting them has shrunk from 3.9 persons per household in 1961 to 2.6 in 2011. Add escalating land and construction costs, interest payments, tax assessments, and energy costs, and a bit more of the picture becomes clear. True, energy efficiency has improved, but residential energy use increased in Canada by 3.7 percent between 1990 and 2001. So too has our overall carbon footprint per person. At 16.4 tonnes per capita, Canada is the 15th-largest carbon emitter in the world.

Little wonder average Canadian families must have at least two incomes to scrape by. Little wonder single people living alone have affordability challenges. You need 2.5 average incomes per household to achieve par with one income 30 years ago. Add to this the cost of child care, which ranges from $650 to $1,200 per month (except in Quebec where it is $7 per day per child), and you get a vivid picture of why so many people are going into debt and feeling their lives are out of control.

The carbon conundrum for a Canadian householder is indeed a tangled web. True, some of the cost drivers are the result of choices made by the individual consumer. The numbers paint a picture of how our choices over time have, perhaps unwittingly, shaped lifestyles beyond our economic and ecological means to sustain. However, it is equally clear that systemic factors also drive the cost treadmill. Deregulation of the financial system costs householders dearly. The unearned profits that, year after year, have benefitted householders in rising property markets have driven housing costs so high that average wage earners in many countries cannot obtain affordable shelter. Energy costs can be reduced with appropriate investment, but many do not have the cash to do so, and financing on terms that might allow them to take up carbon-reducing measures is seldom available. So we keep running faster to keep from falling off a treadmill we just can't slow down. And if we do fall off, we are likely to be blamed by a society still enamoured of the "I" and still too ignorant of the "We" required for navigating transition.

Revisiting the Hartwicks

Scattered throughout this book we have explored some solutions that allow people to begin slowing down the treadmill. They are not the whole answer by any means. Indeed, macro issues and solutions involving banking, currency, corporate, pension, and basic income reforms are part of the puzzle that must be solved. They have not received the attention they deserve — a subject we return to briefly in the epilogue.

Yet even the modest solutions we have highlighted are greeted by counterarguments. We must expect resistance to innovations that run counter to cultural norms shaped by the historical and ongoing dynamic of enclosure. Consider a few caricatures of the attitudes you will likely encounter when you share the stories of this book.

ON LAND TRUSTS

✓ *Take land out of the market? Why would people want to have their house in a land trust when the return they could get from owning the whole shebang is so much higher?*

✓ *Why should I or my children give up on the dream of owning our own land with a house on it we can call our own?*

✓ *Holding land collectively just does not sit right with me; it feels like a ruse to restrict individual rights and freedom.*

ON COMPOUND INTEREST VERSUS FEE-BASED FINANCING

✓ *The whole financial system is built around compound interest and would fall apart if we messed with it.*

✓ *The JAK Bank is a collectivist Swedish aberration; it's interesting but impossible to contemplate here.*

✓ *I am going to remain in control of where I put my money and under what terms. I am happy to play the margins between the interest I pay on my mortgage and where I invest my savings.*

✓ *2.5 percent? What's the big deal? I am only paying 2.75 percent on my five-year mortgage now. Interest rates are low. Why would I want to have to save as much as my mortgage costs every month when I can invest it in the stock market for a profit?*

ON PRICING RENEWABLE ENERGY

✓ *Forget about these crazy ideas of feed-in tariffs for renewable energy that are putting the price of electricity through the roof. Governments should not be meddling in the market.*

✓ *Why should I as a consumer pay such premiums to subsidize an industry that cannot make it on its own?*

ON FOOD SYSTEMS

✓ *Oh yes, Seikatsu is a very interesting story. Those Japanese are remarkable. They are so different culturally; it could never happen here in North America.*

✓ *You will never get people here to build a system that takes so much effort to build and maintain when the superstore at the mall is only a 10-minute drive away.*

As we engaged a wide variety of people, we have heard all these arguments from Stockholm to Vancouver. We have also had the opportunity to hear from people who are just treading water, trying to pay their rent and keep food on the table, or worried about the debt they are accumulating to go to school.

As we wrote this book, a few things have happened. First, we have learned more than we ever imagined. Second, we were constantly pressing our foreheads, trying to figure out how the basic needs sectors we selected — food, finance, shelter, and energy — were connected to each other. Third, we struggled with the fact that though we were focusing on reweaving economies on a more local and regional basis, the importance of macro-economic factors could not be ignored. Last but certainly not least, we had to figure out some way to bring the implications home in ways that even a high school student might understand. If people and families could see the impacts on their lives and those they were closest to, perhaps we might break through the cultural assumptions that block comprehension of alternative pathways or, if they are understood, lead to their rejection because they seem too unrealistic.

Thus the Hartwicks, the mythical family we followed through Chapters 3 to 6, were invented to explore how joined-up solutions might shift the economics of an average household in Europe or North America. Returning to the Hartwick family reminds us of the economic and resilience gains that are possible at the household level, gains we can forge if we are conscious, organized, and persistent enough.

In Table 12.1 we have reconfigured the numbers around the $371,000 cost of the average Canadian house with a loan term of 25 years. The down payment is 10 percent ($37,500), yielding a mortgage of $333,500. The cost of land as a portion of the house purchase is set at 40 percent. The savings from energy conservation over this period (in 2011 dollars) are conservative and are based on the savings yielded by only one efficiency investment — cavity insulation ($364 per year, based on Kirklees; see Chapter 5). We have not adjusted this for increased costs of energy over time.

The higher mortgage rates in this version highlight the dramatic economic impact on the household. Savings are $11,479 per year. The Hartwicks each earn a net of $15 per hour. Together their household income is $225 per day, $112.50 each. The cumulative savings is equivalent to 1275 days. At 240 days of work per year, this is an astonishing 5.3 years of work for each of the two Hartwick parents. The $74,875 extra in food costs that one would

Table 12.1: Hartwicks Summary				
Comparison of JAK Bank and conventional mortgage costs	Bank mortgage (8.05%)	JAK fee-based system for loan	Savings $	Savings in hours life energy
25-year mortgage of $333,500	433,290	125,546	$307,744	
Impact of land trust on financing costs mortgage (40% of 371,000 = 148,400 – mortgage becomes $222,600	289,206	83,872	$205,344	
Actual capital cost saving of land to the householder under land trust model **$148,400 one-time saving not included**				
Kirklees conservation savings over 25 years			$ 9,100	
Net Savings by combining Models – JAK, CLT, Kirklees			**$522,188**	
Subtract increase in food costs			Minus 74,875	
OVERALL NET SAVINGS OVER 25 YEARS			447,313	14,910

add in to pay for organic food at a fair price to farmers seems like chump change, at about 20 percent of the savings. And when one considers the life energy that could be redirected to other activities, the potential for creative conviviality is increased substantially. However, if the Hartwicks decided to blow all the extra cash on carbon-emitting consumption, not much would be gained.

Once people see the household impact, their interest in exploring these alternatives rises dramatically. It is as if a panorama of unconsidered and hidden life options might be contemplated for the first time. People also begin to glimpse the broader implications: if this is the impact on the household, just imagine what the aggregated benefits could be in the community and for society as a whole. The reader will recall the research of German analyst Margrit Kennedy, which suggested that the exponential impacts of compound interest embedded in the economy may make up close to 35 percent of the hidden cost structure. Every supplier in every sector's supply chain is paying compound interest, money that is flowing directly into the banks from money they manufacture out of nothing and then charge us interest on.

That there are practical means to advance change widens the cracks in the cultural armor. More light gets through. We can begin to imagine a way through the murkiness. As the culturally induced fog lifts a bit, we can begin to SEE from which direction the light is coming and can lean into it. Murkiness gives way to the perception of a landscape that, though challenging and treacherous, just might be navigable. Maybe it is possible that the economy can serve human ends in a way that respects the earth. Maybe humans don't have to serve economic ends in a way that destroys Earth's capacity for human life.

There is another method available to each of us unless we are already out on the street; one that will seem to many a radical step, especially for most North American and European householders. Nevertheless, it is a present and real opportunity for many of us to reduce carbon and the adverse economic impact of our households.

When the children of one of the authors moved out of the family home, the energy and carbon efficiency of the household declined. The woodstove and backup electricity were no longer providing warmth for five individuals but only two. The per capita carbon footprint went up; efficiency went down. However, when the empty nesters, the oldest daughter, her husband, and three grandchildren decided to move in together, the carbon footprint per capita became lower, energy efficiency higher, and child care less challenging and expensive. Managing household resources for the benefit of all may have become a bit more complex, but the shared space meant lower costs for both sets of parents.

All was not pure. The author concerned wryly congratulated himself on how he had so deftly reduced his carbon footprint and his share of household expenses in one fell swoop. He also used to joke that he did not feel so bad flying around the countryside now that he had reduced his own contribution to household emissions by half to only 14 percent.

Joking aside, imagine the impact on carbon, household economics, community, and culture if we began to increase the number of people living in the average 1,800-square-foot house. If we could just adjust our attitudes and calibrate our values a bit, we could increase the average 2.6 per household to the 3.9 inhabitants of our grandparents and still have much more living space per person than the author's parents managed with. As well, we would cut personal carbon emissions, decrease affordability problems, and potentially lead a much more connected and convivial life.

These are practical choices for many of us. Thinking and feeling through such a choice may help us characterize the road to transition as an inner journey as well as one that that engages the outer reaches of systems change. After all, we will not succeed in navigating the SEE change our species must somehow accomplish unless we accept its most basic premises: we are all connected to the earth and to each other. There is nowhere else to go. We are the living in whose hands our future rests, whether we like it or not.

Epilogue: The Great Transition

*Production originates from know-how...similar to the processes
of evolution based on genetic information. The chicken egg never
produces a hippotamus. It doesn't have the know-how, it only has
the know-how to produce a chicken...The ongoing processes of
evolution, of which economic development is merely a recent
example, are limited by the evolutionary potential of the system.
The development of evolutionary potential never produces
exponential growth. It produces a pattern of growth,
maturity, stability, and eventually death.*

— Kenneth Boulding

*Even the values of the nation-state and private property have outlived
their period of greatest service to mankind. Superficial measures of
economic or political readjustment will not suffice: the remedy demands
a change of the contemporary mentality and a fundamental transfoma-
tion of our values and the profoundest modification of our conduct.*

— Pitirim Sorokin

THE TAKE-HOME MESSAGE from the Boulding quotation is that we are acting like a bunch of chickens who keep trying to hatch hippopotami,
dazedly ignoring the limits of our evolutionary potential. Unaccepting of
inherent limits, we plan to continue growing exponentially; after all, we are
an ingenious species. We have proved it is possible at least since the first oil

was discovered in 1858 by James Miller Williams near his asphalt plant at Oil Springs, Ontario.

"We make our tools and then they shape us," Boulding surmised. We have created plenty of tools in the last 150 years, amazing technologies that have permeated the globe. In the process they have shaped our perception of ourselves and our planet. It's no wonder we have trouble contemplating transition to a low-carbon economy is so tough; most of our contemporary tools remain dependent on fossil fuels.

Perhaps the most powerful meta-tool that has led us to our present confused state is free-market economics. We are only just beginning to realize what Boulding pointed out decades ago: "There is no such thing as economics, only social science applied to economic problems." And once he did apply his scientific and social science lenses, which just happen to include the bald assumption that the earth is a living, dynamic, but closed system, he came to the obvious conclusion: "Anyone who believes that economic growth can go on forever is either a madman or an economist."

Yet our decision making continues to be dominated by economic assumptions that largely exclude the ecological economy of the earth as a living system. Put in resilience terms, our desire to continue business as usual is due to faulty feedback loops that limit our capacity to absorb 90 percent of the important information necessary to make intelligent decisions. The grossly inequitable super-culture that has emerged as a result threatens our survival, especially since globalization took off in the 1970s. As Boulding wrote in *Ecodynamics* in 1978:

> A quarter, perhaps a third, of the human race has moved toward a kind of world super-culture of skyscrapers, automobiles, airplanes, and inter-continental hotels. The rest of the human race still remains close to subsistence...The development of the super-culture is the result of the knowledge explosion, which led not only to new theories and processes, but to new discoveries, especially of fossil fuels and rich ores. In 1859 the human race discovered a huge treasure chest in its basement. This was oil and gas, a fantastically cheap and easily available source of energy. We did, or at least some of us did what anybody does who discovers a treasure in the basement — live it up and we have been spending this treasure with great enjoyment.

Our mindset and our tools are designed to maximize economic throughput, as if the earth was a limitless frontier. Now, as reality wakes some of us up to the foggy cultural stupor that has kept us from acknowledging our home planet has limits, we better SEE that we have been living in a relation-less wet dream, a product of our lively imaginations. We have no choice: we must transition from our conception of Earth as an open-ended treasure chest that is "ours" to enjoy to a conception of the planet as a unique precious spaceship that we must steward with wonder and care.

Fortunately, the millions of people represented in this book, seers and contemporaries alike, bear witness to our capacity to shake our heads, say no, and forge generative pathways that lead us closer to resilient solutions. Across the globe, millions are shaking the images of the past that have rendered us captives. We are beginning to SEE the world and our place on the planet differently and seeking out new ways of adapting. This is the new "cooperative capital" in formation — knowledge born of an awareness derived from a mix of science and awakening spirituality that situates humankind as part of creation rather than its master.

In 1964, in *The Meaning of the Twentieth Century*, Boulding described the required root-and-branch evolutionary transformation we must make from the economic growth paradigm to a steady-state paradigm. He called it "the Great Transition," and we are now in the midst of it. Our modest contribution in this book is to attempt to connect a few more of the dots. As we do so, and as we expand our knowledge and join it up with wide and diverse nodes of thinking and action, new knowledge will continue to emerge and our "cultural know-how system" will advance.

Boulding indicates that this cultural know-how system, or the "noo-sphere," is most easily understood as an evolving image. The Image is the knowledge that individuals believe to be trustworthy; it is made up of sub-images based on past experiences, new experiences, and adjustments to the Image. In this sense, knowledge is a moving picture. It is affected and modified by new information from the family, from the media, from school, from daily life, etc. Images are constantly updated and revised as new information is received. SEE Change, as a fresh approach to fundamental transformation and the Great Transition, requires an entirely different Image predicated on a radically new set of assumptions.

Imagination can work wonders if the creative Image is grounded in practical innovations like those we have featured throughout this book. Yet there remains this difficult question: Can our cultural system advance quickly enough for our species to successfully navigate the Great Transition? We cannot know, but the signs are both encouraging and deeply disturbing — and, without a doubt, intriguing.

Since January 2011 we have seen powerful expressions of the desire for change in diverse parts of the globe. Paul Mason surveys much of "everywhere" in his new book *Why It's Kicking Off Everywhere: The New Global*

Revolutions. Of Egypt, for example, he notes how deep frustration with society, coupled with the inspiration emanating from Tunisia and the instantaneous communications of social media, created the basis for a hastily forged coalition of "slum-dwellers, union activists, unemployed graduates, faith groups, and even football hooligans that drove Mubarak from power." These uprisings spread quickly across North Africa and the Middle East. It was as if Tunisia was a giant fertilized egg that rapidly divided into cells that became actively resistant to elite corruption, thwarted democracy, and unfairly appropriated and distributed wealth.

Likewise, as the European debt crisis took shape, people found their way into the streets every day for weeks on end. They no longer accepted that average taxpayers should pay for a crisis manufactured by the banks. Who were the governments responsible to, anyway?

David Stockman, former Republican congressman, budget director for Ronald Reagan, and investment banker on Wall Street, gave his answer to the question of who the American government is responsible to in an interview with Bill Moyers on 20 January 2012:

> During a few weeks in September and October 2008, American political democracy was fatally corrupted by a resounding display of expediency and raw power. Henceforth, the door would be wide open for the entire legion of Washington's K Street lobbies, reinforced by the campaign libations prodigiously dispensed by their affiliated political action committees to relentlessly plunder the public purse.

Stockman's soaring but accurate rhetoric echoes the utterances of many Occupy protesters on Wall Street and at 1,900 Occupy sites around the globe. This is both ironic and encouraging; it is also hopeful. The Great Transition requires a broad range of citizens, from civil society groups to small businesspeople and from farmers to trade unionists to find common ground and see the mutual attractiveness of a SEE Change. What is discouraging is that Stockman sees no change coming out of the crisis of 2008. He believes a similar crisis will happen again and, indeed, that such a crisis must be bigger and deeper if Americans are to be woken up sufficiently to mobilize the political forces needed to overcome corporate America's undemocratic assault on freedom.

In *Tools for Conviviality*, Ivan Illich prophetically described the existential and culturally repressive trap we are in as a form of industrial serfdom in which global corporations have become overlords of a prison with invisible bars. He argued that they exert a radical monopoly that restricts autonomous activity by citizens and limits civic freedom due to the corporations' vast and expanding power over the media, institutions, and markets. Perhaps the bars are not so invisible anymore. Even Stockman, who engineered the infamous Reagan tax cuts, sees that the "free markets" he once fervently upheld no longer exist; they have been rendered irrelevant by a bloated and arrogant financial industry that has become too big to fail and that fully expects to be rescued by governments and taxpayers when it is tripped up by its greed. Moreover, the titans of the financial industry, who according to Stockman spend $600 million per year on campaign contributions and lobbyists in Washington, are not suddenly going to desist because they are good hearted and really do want the public interest to be served.

Such depressing shenanigans in the world of finance seem very distant from the character and focus featured in the innovations we have described. Nevertheless, those innovations are also uprisings of a kind. One can think of them as manifestations of the "slow protest" movement, uprisings fed by the yeast of focused intention, the search for practical pathways to enduring change, and the commitment to put democracy into daily action. And though the nexus of our featured innovations are mostly local and regional, we know (perhaps most vividly in the case of La Via Campesina) that local innovation, political advocacy, and protest can and should be linked up.

Clearly we need to change the rules of the game; this is why La Via Campesina militantly agitates for change in WTO, IMF, and World Bank rules. But this is not the whole game. We all have to answer the question "After the revolution, who is going to deliver the milk?"

This is not a theoretical issue. It is an issue in Egypt, where the military controls and owns large sectors of the economy. It is an issue in Tunisia, where after decades of dictatorship they are actively trying to discern how to build economies that are locally rooted and regionally relevant, that can meet the basic needs closer to home. They know that building a political democracy must extend to the economic sphere. If that does not happen, the space for freedom will be stunted. Stockman notes the same statistics advanced earlier in this book: namely, that the profits of the financial sector have increased from 14 percent to almost 40 percent of all corporate profits in America. In the process, democratic culture and practice has been radically twisted and compromised.

Counter to this discouraging picture, we have witnessed a glimmer of what is possible when daily democracy is extended into the economic realm: fee-based finance; alternative land tenures; action to reshape markets, democratize ownership, and restructure relations between consumers and producers in the basic needs areas of food, fuel, and finance; these encompass all manner of experiments to extend financing to those without access.

The lessons being learned in these creative and generative spaces are fueling a movement to conserve our planet and advance fairness and equity among all people.

This movement reveals the charade of individualistic ideologies that cloak elite malfeasance to be self-serving, economically inefficient, and disconnected from the real world. By making the bars of corporate enclosure visible, we can see more clearly how limited and weak our political representation is, and how culturally limited our passive consumption and dependent mindset render us.

This recognition is absolutely critical to addressing the resilience imperative. Moreover, unless we can glimpse more broadly and deeply why and how ownership, governance, and social finance are central to navigating transition, the promising innovations we have highlighted will lack the environment that will make it easy for us to adapt them and scale them up in diverse contexts. In short, we need to strengthen the practice of daily democracy and equity in all the domains of our lives. This is all about being the change we must incarnate. Democracy must shift from being a valuable but rationed civil right to a pattern of daily life. If we seize economic democracy as activist consumers, producers, social investors, and engaged citizen stakeholders, we will open the door to mutual liberty and positive freedom.

We are talking about a cultural shift of history-changing proportions. In *Social and Cultural Dynamics*, Pitirim Sorokin, the founder of the Department of Sociology at Harvard, described a cyclical pattern of cultural transformation that appears to recur every 300 to 400 years. He analysed these shifts, going back a few thousand years, and found that cultural values underpin linked political, economic, and technological systems. His analysis notes a waxing and waning between three historic patterns: ideational (religious absolute standards of justice, truth, and beauty), sensate (materialistic, where nothing exists beyond the sensory) and idealistic (an intermediate stage in which the spiritual and the sensory coexist). The sensate culture has been dominant since the emergence of empirical philosophy with Thomas Hobbes at the time of the English Revolution in the mid-1600s.

In the late 1930s, Sorokin forecast a growing decadence of the industrial mentality based on materialistic values. He predicted the next shift would propel us to a radically new "cultural mentality" based on more spiritual values and ideals. We are again nearing a cultural turning point. Is something big cooking?

It may be that one of the revered spokespeople of the anti-apartheid movement in South Africa, Archbishop Desmond Tutu, a Protestant pastor in an anti-colonial struggle far from the rarefied halls of Harvard, has captured the essence of the next cultural shift: "We are not made for an exclusive self-sufficiency, but for interdependence, and we break the law of our own being at our own peril."

This is the essence of the cultural shift we are struggling through in these early years of the 21st century, transitioning from cultural notions of independence and individualism to interdependence and mutualism, a reuniting of the "I" with the "We" as Martin Luther King prophesied. Perhaps a Declaration of Interdependence would concentrate our heads and hearts in ways that could crystalize the essence of the massive cultural shift we are in the midst of, and which we must organize and leverage in a big way if human kind is to survive with any dignity.

If interdependence is the essence, resilience and cooperation are the cornerstones. Linked up, the seven principles of resilience and the seven

| Table 13.1 Principles of Resilience and Cooperation ||
Seven Resilience Principles	Seven Cooperative Principles
1. Promote and sustain social, economic, and biological **diversity**.	1. **Member economic participation.** Members contribute to and democratically control the capital of their cooperative but receive no or limited compensation.
2. Maintain **modularity**. Connect but avoid dependency, and ensure there are independent means to modify and adapt.	2. Each cooperative is **autonomous** and **independent**; external relations, financing, and federating are democratic decisions.
3. Tighten the communication **feedback loops** to ensure awareness of what is happening and avoid crossing critical thresholds.	3. There is **cooperation among cooperatives** at local, regional, national, and international levels.
4. Build **social capital** of strong networks, trust in relationships, and capable leadership that enables collective action.	4. Cooperatives have **voluntary, open,** and **inclusive** membership.
5. Focus on learning, experimentation, building local rules, and change-oriented **innovation**.	5. Cooperatives provide **education, training,** and **information** to their members, elected representatives, and all staff. They also reach out to the public at large to educate about the nature and benefits of cooperation.
6. Design **overlap** and redundancy into governance systems and blend common and private property rights.	6. **Democratic governance** means a cooperative is accountable to its membership — one member, one vote.
7. Value and price all **ecosystem services**.	7. Cooperatives work for **community benefit**. (The amendment of this principle to include **respect for the environment** is now formally under discussion.)

cooperative principles (see Table 13.1) provide a robust, transdisiplinary foundation from which we can act creatively where we live and join together effectively across time and space to press for the political, legislative, and policy changes needed to facilitate, rather than thwart, transition to a low-carbon, democratic, and steady-state economy.

The time we have is short, perhaps too short, to bend the curve of history sufficiently so as to avoid our demise. We cannot know. What we can do is make deliberate choices to affirm life, to seize positive freedom, and to propel ourselves onto the path of transition.

The SEE Change agenda has to mobilize a broad front of stakeholders to embrace the evolutionary opportunities spelled out by Boulding. As we have seen, these include citizens in all guises: tenants and homeowners, small businesses and trade unionists, environmentalists and social justice campaigners, social finance providers and local government, civil servants and enlightened business leaders, preachers and politicians, the old and the young, the rich and the poor, those in the North and those in the South.

The choice fundamentally is about Your Money or Your Life. Our consumerist addiction blinds us to the latent democratic power in our own hands. R.H. Tawney described economic democracy as democracy for real — the genuine article because it requires us going the distance to secure it.

John Stuart Mill set out his stationary state vision in this vein as a positive opportunity for all citizens to aim for and secure — most importantly the chance to get off the treadmill to pursue right livelihoods.

> "A stationary condition of capital and population implies no stationary state of human improvement. There would be as much scope as ever for all kinds of mental culture, moral and social progress; as much room for improving the ART of living.....when minds cease to be engrossed in the art of getting on."

All the answers are there. It is up to us to organize within and between sectors and with our communities and region to make this vision become a steadily evolving reality. While there is no quick fix, there are many interconnected avenues to travel together that can incubate the synergies we need to accelerate the process of transition.

Between now and 2050 we can choose to expand our investment in green infrastructure year on year. Jobs will be lost in the transition from fossil fuels. But there are millions of jobs to be had as we redirect our time, talent and resource. We must merely decide it is important, raise the price of carbon year on year and unleash the resilience of our species in a more realistic direction.

Between now and 2050 we can grease the wheels for green infrastructure and many other transition pathways by choosing to implement options for radically reducing the financial, human and planetary costs of compound interest. According to the evidence we have cited, Germans pay 33% of household costs in interest and 35% of business expenses is created by compound interest. Is it any wonder so-called progress is miring us in deeper and deeper levels of poverty and growing joblessness? Follow the money trail. We know that usury can be overcome. We have made the case for public banking, cooperative money and fee-based lending options to slash the growth-inducing cancer of compound interest and release life energy and investment resources to transition towards the Green ART of Living.

Between now and 2050 we can definitely choose to implement broad land reforms that ensure both affordable housing for all and fairness, and justice in the distribution of benefits that flow from the fruits of the earth, thus equipping ourselves collectively for the ongoing investment in transition.

Between now and 2050 as we phase in land reform and lending reform and phase out usurious charges for land and capital, we will reclaim our lives from the moneylenders and speculative developers. We can then take back power steadily from the Market and be able to reduce our working time one percent per year. Long-term unemployment can simultaneously be addressed through sharing paid work and releasing our "life energy" for what William Morris and Fritz Schumacher called *Good Work* — growing food, looking after each other, pursuing the arts, playing music, and engaging in a widening panoply of restorative investments of our time, talent, and resource.

Between now and 2050 we can choose to stabilize citizen incomes substantially through ensuring people share ownership under a diversity of Trusteeship companies and CLBs, thus accessing a "binary" income — both wages from our work and a share of the profits from democratic enterprises. Working hours may go down but if profits are shared, income stability can be enhanced, performance improved, and the transition to a steady state economy can be progressively achieved.

The agenda of the Great Transition also encompasses three major dimensions of change. Think of them as the 3 Ps: the personal, practical, and political. Simplistic silver-bullet solutions, and sound bites spun for culturally stunted attention spans, will not do. Consciously acting to link up the three Ps with a multi-level agenda guided by the resilience imperative and cooperative transitions is complex. Balkanized movements cannot contend with the scale of the problems and challenges we face, nor the powerful forces that must be resisted and restrained. All kinds of constituencies must be engaged — unions, regionally based small and medium-sized businesses, all manner of community and cooperative enterprises and intermediaries, farmers, credit unions and progressive financial institutions, arts and culture organizations, faith organizations, environmental groups, politicians, and academics. We can also work with large companies, though caution and principled shrewdness is necessary. Companies occupying the low-road/high-carbon economy have too much power, are unaccountable, and are so addicted to the capitalist logic of growth that they represent a real and present danger to all of us. However, there are other companies that are committed to building a high-road/low-carbon economy, and we need their know-how and partnership if we are to navigate the Great Transition without violence.

So there we have it — we are challenged to work consciously from local to global across sectors, engage creatively multiple constituencies, while all the while paying attention simultaneously to the macro and micro features of the transition challenge. Isn't life interesting?

We have been acutely conscious, while writing this book, that our concentration has been on the micro side of the transition challenge, though we have attempted to keep the macro side consciously in play as a kind of counterpoint tension. We hope we have shown how crucial change at the macro policy and systems level is for facilitating and easing transition to a low-carbon, more democratic, and fair economy. Indeed, there are a number of key policy questions that we have raised directly or indicated in passing. These evident and practical possibilities can be summarized as:

- **100 percent debt-free money:** Why not move step by step toward governments issuing democratic currency free of interest and, indeed, removing from banks the power to freely issue money as high-cost debt?
- **Green quantitative easing :** Why is printing money (i.e., quantitative easing) justifiable for refinancing the banks and not for financing the Great Transition? Why not use the power of government to issue interest-free bonds to pay for the green infrastructure needed in the 21st century, just as Henry Ford advocated for building needed economic infrastructure in the 1920s?
- **JAK banking and anti-usury:** Why not replace unregulated compound interest with fee-based financing and strictly regulate interest rates (with a ceiling of 5 percent) as Adam Smith and John Maynard Keynes recommended?
- **Negative-interest money:** Why not introduce Gesellian currencies, like those that helped communities in Depression-era Austria,

Germany, Denmark, and the United States revive local economies until they were banned, despite the vociferous backing of Irving Fisher, then the world's leading economist on monetary theory and practice?

- **Price on carbon:** Why not price carbon appropriately in order to accelerate, broaden, and focus the drive to bring the human species into balance with the limits of what nature can absorb?
- **Trusteeship, citizens' charters, and ownership transfer:** Why not put in place legislative and policy frameworks to democratize the ownership of corporations and revive citizens' charters, with time limits for renewal, binary income and governed by public and ecological accountability?
- **Tobin tax:** Why not institute a transaction tax that will be paid every time a currency trader buys or sells a currency for short-term profits? Known as the Tobin tax (named after Nobel Prize winner James Tobin), even a small tax on the $4 trillion of daily currency transactions (2010 statistics) would slow the flow of speculation that contributes to instability. Such a levy could become a social-financing mechanism for creating a fairer and greener planet.

As we move to implement effective means to address these strategic policy options, we are encouraged by the growing work of many others who are focusing their knowledge and creativity on helping all of us connect more of the dots. We hope our contribution can join with theirs, and together we can successfully mobilize more clearly and powerfully to make the Great Transition.

There are abundant opportunities for doing so, surely more than we know. For our part, we are interested in weaving closer ties with the innovative work on macro-economic modelling to map more clearly the routes for the transition to a steady-state economy. Here the work of the new economics foundation and the related work of Tim Jackson and Peter Victor is groundbreaking.

The tasks of transition are many. The challenges are daunting. The outcomes are uncertain. Our courage remains untested. But we are a resilient species. We are not alone; there is "blessed unrest" all about. If we but open our eyes, we will SEE change is possible. If we act in ways that recognize we are interdependent, we will continue to innovate cooperative transitions to the steady-state economy.

There is one personal question we need to ask ourselves: What stories will we be able to tell our loved ones about what we did to advance the Great Transition?

Notes

These notes give source information for quotations, statistics, and details included in the text. Full publication details for books mentioned in the text or in the notes are listed in the Bibliography. Reports and journal articles cited in the notes below are also included in the Bibliography, but newspaper articles and brochures, websites, and short reports or summaries are only listed below.

Chapter 1: Resilience: The 21st-Century Imperative
Fossil Fuels and Climate Change

For a summary of the AAMP report, see Tibi Puiu, "Sea level rise of up to 1.6 meters projected for 2100," ZME Science website, www.zmescience.com/ecology/ environmental-issues/sea-level-rise-of-up-to-1-6-meters-projected-for-2100/.

James Hansen, along with several co-authors, made his suggestion about the ideal ratio of carbon in the atmosphere in "Target Atmospheric CO_2: Where Should Humanity Aim?" *Open Atmospheric Science Journal* 2 (2008): 217–31.

The US Energy Information Administration's "International Energy Outlook 2011," 19 September 2011, is at www.eia.doe.gov/oiaf/ieo/index.html.

Information on the International Energy Agency's projections, rising and falling emissions, world reliance on oil, and declining oil reserves is from:

John Vidal, "Carbon Emissions Will Fall 3% Due to Recession, Say World Energy Analysts," *The Guardian*, 6 October 2009, www.guardian.co.uk/ environment/2009/oct/06/carbon-cuts-recession-iea.

"Global carbon emissions hit record high in 2010," SustainableBusiness.com News, www.sustainablebusiness.com/index.cfm/go/news.display/id/22476.

Kevin K. Tsui, "More Oil, Less Democracy: Evidence from Worldwide Crude Oil Discoveries," *Economic Journal* 121 (March 2010), 89–115, www.res.org.uk/economic/freearticles/2011/march2011.pdf.

The Godard research is written up by P. Kharecha and J. Hansen in "Implications of 'Peak Oil' for Atmospheric CO2 and Climate," *Global Biogeochemical Cycles* 22 (2008), doi:10.1029/2007GB003142; and Casey Kazan and Rebecca Sato "NASA Asks: How Will Global Peak Oil Impact Climate?" Daily Galaxy website, 15 April 2009, www.dailygalaxy.com/my_weblog/2009/04/nasa-study-illu.html.

Fossil Fuels and Global Finance

J. Porritt wrote about oil prices and food riots in "The Three 'Rs'," *Resurgence*, November/December 2009.

Two websites that are particularly good on the subject of peak oil and its relationship to finance are those of the American Post Carbon Institute (www.postcarbon.org) and Feasta, the Foundation for the Economics of Sustainability (www.feasta.org/), which is based in Ireland.

Money and Meltdowns

The financial sector's growing size was described in D.M. Kotz, "Neoliberalism and Financialisation" (conference paper, Political Economy Research Institute, University of Massachusetts Amherst, 2008).

Progress and Growth: Navigating through the Rearview Mirror

For a graphic view of the population explosion, see the World Population Growth History Chart at www.vaughns-1-pagers.com/history/world-population-growth.htm.

You can read Alan Greenspan's 23 October 2008, testimony to the Committee of Government Oversight and Reform on the PBS Newshour website, www.pbs.org/newshour/bb/business/july-dec08/crisishearing_10-23.html

Resilience: Strengthening Our Capacity to Adapt

The definition of "resilience" came from Brian Walker's *Resilience Thinking: Sustaining Ecosystems and People in a Changing World.*

The Stockholm Resilience Centre (www.stockholmresilience.org) is an international center that advances transdisciplinary research for governance of social-ecological systems with a special emphasis on resilience — the ability to deal with change and continue to develop. The center has played a key role in the international network of scholars known as the Resilience Alliance (www.resalliance.org/).

Reclaiming the Commons

Nicholas Hildyard asks whether the enclosure of the commons is putting us all at risk in his essay "Whose Common Future: Reclaiming the Commons," *The Ecologist* 6, no. 1 (1994): 127.

The story of the Pakistani Fisherfolk Forum comes from Raj Patel's *Value of Nothing*. Patel summarizes the work of a 2007 report by ActionAid International in "Taking the Fish — Fishing Communities Lose out to Big Trawlers in Pakistan."

Patel drew the statistics on marine by-catch from R.W.D. Davies et al., "Defining and Estimating Global Marine Fisheries Bycatch," *Marine Policy* 33 (2009).

Elinor Ostrom's comments on self-governing forms of collective action come from an interview by P.D. Aligica of the Mercatus Center, George Mason University, in 2003, "Rethinking Governance Systems and Challenging Disciplinary Boundaries – Interview with Elinor Ostrom."

Reinventing Democracy

Much of the description of what associative democracy could look like comes from Paul Hirst's discussion in *Associative Democracy: New Forms of Economic and Social Governance.*

Constructing a Social Solidarity Economy

The idea of co-producers building a "high road" economy came from Mike Lewis and Dan Swinney, "Social Economy? Solidarity Economy? Exploring the Implications of Conceptual Nuance for Acting in a Volatile World."

Pricing As If People and the Planet Mattered

Malte Faber's description of ecological economics comes from his article "How to Be an Ecological Economist," *Ecological Economics* 66, no. 1 (2008):1-7. For more on ecological economics see Ken Boulding's essay "The Economics of the Coming Spaceship Earth," N. Georgescu-Roegen's *The Entropy Law and the Economic Process*, and H. Daly's *Steady-State Economics.*

The National Academy of Sciences study cited is U. Thara Srinivasan et al., "The Debt of Nations and the Distribution of Ecological Impacts from Human Activities," *Proceedings of the National Academy of Sciences* 105, no. 5 (2008).

Chapter 2: Wealth versus Commonwealth

Details of Polanyi's body of work on the informal economy in Africa can be found in *Trade and Markets in Early Empires* and *Dahomey and the Slave Trade.*

For an introduction to some of the other social economists, see, for example, the work of anthropologist Keith Hart and his 1973 article "Informal Income Opportunities and Urban Employment in Ghana," which led the way to define the informal economy. See also the work of Ivan Illich at the Mexican Center for Intercultural Documentation (1964–76) and his book *Shadow Work* (1981), and Marshall Sahlins and his book *Culture and Practical Reason* (1976).

Heilbroner discussed Adam Smith's assertion of the inherent "human propensity to barter, truck and exchange" in Chapter 2 of *The Worldly Philosophers.*

Small "m" Markets at Work

S. Turnbull discusses the City of London charter in "The Limitations in Corporate Governance Best Practices," Chapter 25 of *Handbook of Corporate Governance*, ed. C. Clarke and D. Branson.

J. Farr writes about the struggles of local artisanal groups and the organization of guild tables and federations in *Artisans in Europe, 1300–1914*. He describes how artisans in Cambrai in Flanders fought from 907 to 1076 to secure their town charter. In 1107 the charter was repealed; it was regained in 1127, repealed again in 1138, and finally secured in 1180.

G. Goyder explains the meanings of *con pagus* and *con panis* in *The Just Enterprise*. He also described how the guild officials managed the local market. He points out that the original English word for "ownership" was "owership," which was used in England to indicate possession until the 17th century. People would say, "I oweth this book [or this house or this land]." In other words, personal possession and assets had social obligations.

Tristram Hunt wrote about Joseph Chamberlain and the influence of Mill and Ruskin in *Building Jerusalem: The Rise and Fall of the Victorian City*.

Evolution of the Big "M" Market I: The Struggle for Land Reform

You can read some of Winstanley's work in *Gerard Winstanley: Selected Writings*.

In Britain and North America, the influence of Ruskin's ideas and practices can be found in the Garden City movement, the guild socialist movement, the preservation of historic buildings, the development of national parks, and in conservation and environmental land trusts. In part inspired by Ruskin, Octavia Hill and two others set up Britain's National Trust (whose full name is National Trust for Places of Historic Interest or Natural Beauty). Ruskin's trusteeship model was also a key inspiration for Gandhi. The Bhoodan land gift movement and its successor Gramdan movement brought over four million acres of land into community ownership across India during the 1950s and 1960s, a truly remarkable achievement.

For information on the Land Value Tax in Hong Kong see Neville Bennett, "Opinion: The Merits of Land Value Tax; Lessons from Hong Kong," on the interest.co.nz website, May 22, 2009, www.interest.co.nz/news/44914/opinion-merits-land-value-tax-lessons-hong-kong. He states that 38 percent of the Hong Kong tax base now comes from the Land Value Tax.

Evolution of the Big "M" Market II: The Ascendancy of the Corporation

Much of the information on company charters in early America is from R. Grossman and F. Adams, *Taking Care of Business: Citizenship and the Charter of Incorporations*.

The list of conditions states put on charters that were granted comes from Reclaim Democracy's "Our Hidden History of Corporations in the United States," February 2000, reclaimdemocracy.org/corporate_accountability/history_corporations_us.html.

Details on the situation in the United Kingdom are from T. Johnston and G. Edgar, *Law and Practice of Company Accounting in New Zealand* and G. Goyder's *The Just Enterprise*.

Statistics on corporations in the 21st century are from the Key Facts on Corporations page of the Share the World's Resources website (www.stwr.org/multinational-corporations/key-facts.html). The UN estimate regarding unfair trade is from the Trade Liberalisation page of the World Trade Organization website (www.gatt.org/trastat_e.html).

The Halliburton loophole was described in a *New York Times* editorial on 2 November 2009, www.nytimes.com/2009/11/03/opinion/03tue3.html. A particularly useful summary of shale drilling is provided in a Youtube video (www. youtube.com/watch?v=PO2Hhs3DeG8), which also includes a shot of flames enveloping the sink of a fracking victim.

Evolution of the Big "M" Market III: Banking Masters and Debtor Slaves

The quotation opening this section comes from a public address in Central Hall, Westminster, London, in 1937.

Details of the history of banking and money come from M. Mellor's *The Future of Money.*

The statistic about the amount of money circulating as bills and coins comes from the Money Reform Party's website, which also gives a good summary of the different types of money today: www.moneyreformparty.org.uk/money/about_ money/index.php.

The information on credit cards in 2007 came from Paul Mason's book *Meltdown: The End of the Age of Greed.*

Details of usury and interest rates in the 19th and 20th centuries came from J. Persky, "Retrospectives: From Usury to Interest," *Journal of Economic Perspectives,* 21, no. 1 (Winter 2007): 231–33.

Recent UK interest rates were exposed by B. Carter, whose findings were reported on the BBC's *Money Box* program on 3 December 2011.

Alternatives to the Modern Banking System 1: Public Banks

E. Brown discussed the Bank of North Dakota in "The Global Debt Crisis: How We Got In and How to Get Out?" *Global Research* 6 (June 2011).

The information on the rate of return from UK government bonds is from the UK Pensions Commission (UK). *Pensions, Challenges and Choices: The First Report of the Pensions Commission* (Pensions Commission, 2004), 55–63.

Richard Priestman and Connie Fogel wrote about the Bank of Canada in, respectively, "Is There Hope for All Canadians?" and "How the Debt-Based Monetary System Functions in Canada," published in *COMER, The Journal of the Committee on Monetary and Economic Reform* 23, no. 9 (September 2011). Information on the long-term interest rates on Canadian government debt came from the International Monetary Fund's *World Economic Outlook* report of April 1985.

The information on KfW is from Gudrun Gumb and Rudolf Hennes of KfW, 'Financing Energy Efficiency in Buildings — the German Experience', paper presented at the International Workshop on Financing Energy Efficiency in Building on 16–17 February 2012, Frankfurt, Germany

Alternatives to the Modern Banking System 2: Cooperative Finance and Alternative Currencies

J. Birchall wrote about building societies in *Building Communities the Co-operative Way.* This pub-concocted experiment inspired many others, including the Starr-Bowkett societies.

B. Lietaer told the stories of the WÄRA Exchange Society and the free schillings of Wörgl, Austria, in *The Future of Money.*

S. Turnbull of the International Institute for Self-Governance wrote about the American experiment with stamp scrip in "Options for Rebuilding the Economy and the Financial System." R. Douthwaite wrote about the end of the experiment in *Short Circuit.*

M. Anielski wrote about JAK in "The JAK Members Bank Sweden — An Assessment of Sweden's No-interest Bank" (report prepared by Anielski Management Inc. for Van City Capital Corporation, 17 October 2006).

J. Palmer and P. Collinson wrote about the Chiemgauer in "Goodbye Euro, Hello Chiemgauer," *Guardian Money,* 24 September 2011.

Alternatives to the Modern Banking System 3: 100 Percent Money (Debt-Free)

The Henry Ford quotation is from D. Boyle, *The Money Changers: Currency Reform from Aristotle to e-cash.*

Irving Fisher set out his plan in "100% Money and the Public Debt," *Economic Forum,* April-June 1936, pp. 406–20. In 1939, Fisher and several other noted economists (Paul H. Douglas, Frank D. Graham, Earl J. Hamilton, Willford I. King, and Charles R. Whittlesey) wrote an expanded "Program for Monetary Reform," which can be seen in full on Wikipedia at en.wikipedia.org/wiki/A_Program_for_Monetary_Reform.

James Robertson included comments on the Positive Money campaign in Chapter 3, "Managing the National Money Supply," of his forthcoming book, *Future Money: Breakdown or Breakthrough,* to be published by Green Books in March 2012. Robertson released a draft version of the chapter in July 2011.

The Economics of Sufficiency: Living within the Planetary Commons

For more on a future economy without growth see Tim Jackson's *Prosperity without Growth?* mentioned in Chapter 1. A book by Canadian academic Peter Victor, *Managing without Growth,* is also receiving worldwide interest.

For more on Herman Daly's views, see his books *Beyond Growth* and *Steady-State Economics.* He drew the connection between compound interest and the exponential growth of debt, unemployment, inflation, and environmental degradation in "The Economic Thought of Frederick Soddy," an essay in *Beyond Growth.*

The All About Science website explains the second law of thermodynamics here www.allaboutscience.org/second-law-of-thermodynamics.htm.

Chapter 3: A Path beyond Debt: Interest-Free Lending at Work

For more on dominant revenue, see William Krehm, *Towards a Non-Autistic Economy: A Place at the Table for Society.*

Margrit Kennedy published her findings in *Interest and Inflation Free Money.* Helmut Creutz described his findings in "Tumorartige Selbstvermehrung der Geldvermögen," *Zeitschrift Humane Wirtschaft* 1 (2009): 30–31. Kennedy's estimate of the money flowing from the bottom 80 percent to the top 10 percent is in *A Changing Money System: The Economy of Ecology.*

The data on household debt in the United States and personal bankruptcies in the UK come, respectively, from Mark Jickling, "Consumer Bankruptcy and Household Debt, updated 21 March 2005," Congressional Research Service, 14 March 2010, www.bna.com/webwatch/bankruptcycrs3.pdf, and KPMG, "Bankruptcy Levels Reach Record High as Recession Grips Britain," *Business Weekly: East of England Business News,* 15 May 2009, www.businessweekly. co.uk/2009051534937/kpmg/bankruptcy-levels-reach-record-high-as-recession-grips-britain.html.

Key Points in the JAK Philosophy and Analysis

Much of the information on Sweden's JAK Bank throughout this chapter comes from Mark Anielski's "The JAK Members Bank Sweden — An Assessment of Sweden's No-interest Bank" (report prepared by Anielski Management Inc. for Van City Capital Corporation, 17 October 2006.)

How the System Works

The explanation of the equity deposit is from Mark Burton's dissertation *Unravelling Debt: The Economy, Banking and the Case of JAK.*

Impacts on the Household Economy: The Hartwick Family

For more on the ups and downs of mortgage rates, see the rate history (1980 to 2011) at www.erate.com/mortgage_rates_history.htm.

Chapter 4: Uniting the "I" and the "We": Affordable Housing in Perpetuity

Hilary Osborne wrote about the average age of homebuyers in the UK, and compared the costs of renting and mortgages in "Special Report: The Rent Crisis," *The Guardian,* Money section, 12 November 2011.

The Community Land Trust Model in the United States

Much of the information in this section comes from International Independence Institute, *The Community Land Trust: A Guide to a New Model for Land Tenure in America,* cited in Julie F. Curtin and Lance Bocarsly, "CLTs: A Growing Trend in Affordable Home Ownership," *Journal of Affordable Housing and Community Development Law* 17, no. 4 (2008): 367–394; and a good Wikipedia article on CLTs, en.wikipedia.org/wiki/Community_land_trust.

Susan Witt mentioned the ideas and thinkers who inspired Bob Swann and Slater King in "A New Peace" (comments made at the Global Dialogue for Peace Gathering 17–21 September 2001, Ashdown Park, Forest Row, Sussex, England), neweconomicsinstitute.org/publications/authors/witt/susan/anewpeace.

The Champlain Housing Trust: Restoring the Commons — An Affordable Solution

The amount of income renters and homeowners in Vermont pay for their housing is from M. Colins, "Between a Rock and a Hard Place: Housing and Wages in Vermont," 2011 update (Vermont Housing Finance Agency, 2011), www.vhfa. org/documents/housing-wages-2011.pdf.

Diane Diacon, Richard Clarke, and Silvia Guimarães wrote about the Champlain Housing Trust in *Redefining the Commons: Locking in Value through Community Land Trusts.*

The 2003 study of the Champlain Housing Trust was by Burlington Associates (John Emmeus Davis and Amy Demetrowitz), *Permanently Affordable Homeownership: Does the Community Land Trust Deliver on Its Promises?* www.burlingtonassociates.com; the 2009 study was John Emmeus Davis and Alice Stokes, *Lands in Trust, Homes That Last: A Performance Evaluation of Champlain Housing Trust.*

Rebecca Baran-Rees, Nathaniel Decker, Kevin Dowd, Tom Knipe, C.J. Randall, and Janani Rajbhandari Thapa looked at CLTs in hot and cold markets in their report "Community Land Trusts: An Analysis of CLTs in Three Housing Markets," prepared for Professor Mildred Warner's graduate course in the Department of City and Regional Planning, Cornell University, May 2011, government.cce.cornell. edu/doc/pdf/BaranRees_CLT.pdf.

Scaling up CLTs in the Cities: Irvine, California

For more on the Irvine plan, see CivicStone Inc., *City of Irvine Housing Strategy and Implementation Plan*, 14 March 2006, on the city's website, www.cityofirvine. org/civica/filebank/blobdload.asp?BlobID=8842.

Community Land Trusts in Britain: Rekindling Land Reform in the 21st Century

For further information on the expansion of CLT formation and development in England and Wales see Bob Paterson and Karl Dayson, *Proof of Concept: Community Land Trusts*, which can be downloaded from www.community finance.salford.ac.uk/.

The Mutual Homeownership Model: Scaling up Urban Affordability

For more on MHOS and its inspirations, see P. Conaty, J. Birchall, S. Bendle, and R. Foggitt, *Common Ground — For Mutual Home Ownership*, and D. Rodgers, "New Foundations—Unlocking the Potential for Affordable Homes." Rodgers wrote about MHOS funding in "Mutually Beneficial," a section in *Ground Breaking — New Ideas on Housing Delivery.*

For more on the LILAC (Low Impact Living Affordable Community) Ecovillage in Leeds, visit the website at www.lilac.coop/.

Transition Factors

For more on Population Health, see the Canadian Institute for Health Information website at www.cihi.ca.

Chapter 5: Seeking Strategic Pathways to Energy Sufficiency

The new economics foundation briefing paper, from July 2009, was "Decarbonizing Local Economies: A Local Green New Deal Supporting Local Community Action on Energy."

The National Round Table on the Environment and the Economy quotation and analysis come from "Advice on a Long-Term Strategy on Energy and Climate Change," June 2006. The Round Table's analysis was based on "Stabilization Wedges: Solving the Climate Problem for the Next Fifty Years with Current Technology," *Science* 305, no. 13 (August 2004): 968–72.

The statistics on UK carbon emissions come from the Department of Energy and Climate Change, "UK Climate Change Sustainable Development Indicator: 2009 Greenhouse Gas Emissions, Provisional Figures, and 2008 Greenhouse Gas Emissions, Final Figures by Fuel Type and End-User" (DECC/ONS, 2010).

The statistic on fuel poverty in the UK is from a BBC report, "Tax Plan to Tackle Fuel Poverty," 9 June 2009, news.bbc.co.uk/2/hi/business/8091917.stm.

YES to Conserving Energy: Yorkshire Energy Services at Work

Many of the details on the Kirklees project were drawn from "Local Energy Action: EU Good Practices" (European Commission, 2004), 7–8, www.managenergy. net/download/gp0410.pdf; and from Helen Eveleigh, *The Future Is Local: Empowering Communities to Improve Their Neighbourhoods*, p. 29, www.sd-commission.org.uk/data/files/publications/SDC_TFiL_report_w.pdf.

Details of the Warm Zone program are from "Fantastic Finish for Warm Zone," www2.kirklees.gov.uk/news/onlinenews//newsdesk/fullstory.aspx?id=2471; and "Free Home Insulation Still Available in Kirklees," www2.kirklees.gov.uk/news/onlinenews//newsdesk/fullstory.aspx?id=3046, both from Kirklees Council Online News, 17 July 2010, and 12 December 2010, respectively; "Kirklees Warm Zone — Case Study," a report from Kirklees Council, January 2010, www.kirklees.gov.uk/community/environment/green/pdf/WZ CaseStudyWithJanuaryFigures.pdf; and "Hampshire-Wide Climate Change Vision and Strategy: Collaborative Measures" a report from the Hampshire-Wide Partnership, December 2010, Section 1, p. 6, www3.hants.gov.uk/vision_and_strategy_decision_making_papers.pdf.

Fossil-Fuel-Free Kristianstad

Much of the information on Kristianstad came from "Fossil Fuel Free Kristianstad: Municipality of Kristianstad, Sweden," Case Study 254 (European Commission Directorate-General for Energy and Transport, January 2011), www.managenergy.net/download/nr254.pdf; and from Nora Godsteing, "Kristianstad on Track to meet Fossil Fuel-Free Goals," *BioCycle* 52, no. 4 (April 2011), www.jgpress.com/archives/_free/002319.html; and "Fossil Fuel Free: Kristianstad (SE) (Projet MEELS – IEA)" (case study prepared by Svekom as part of Task 9 of the International Energy Agency DSM Implementing Agreement, Municipalities and Energy Efficiency in a Liberalised System, 30 January 2011), www.energie-cites.eu/db/kristianstad_566_en.pdf.

The Impact on the Household and Community Economy

The carbon price of $84 (€60) from 2013 onward is derived from EU carbon market traders surveyed by the International Emissions Trading Association's (IETA) sixth annual GHG market sentiment survey. Rebecca Hampson, "Carbon

Price of €60/Ton Needed to Hit Targets Say Traders," *Energy Risk,* 8 June 2011, www.risk.net/energy-risk/news/2076993/carbon-brokers-carbon-price-eur60-ton-reduce-emissions#ixzz1U1jManrE.

Chapter 6: Seeking Pathways to Sustainable Food

The second opening quotation is an extract from the "Declaration for Living Change," presented by the Laureates of the Right Livelihood Award (the alternative Nobel prize), Bonn, Germany, 16 September 2010, www.ifoam.org/press/positions/pdfs/IFOAM-Declaration_EN_web.pdf.

We got the statistic about food production on Vancouver Island from members of the Van Island Heritage Food Co-op, who have been working on local food issues on the island for the past ten years. The statistics on farming worldwide come from International Assessment of Agricultural Knowledge, Science and Technology for Development (IAASTD), *Agriculture at a Crossroads,* p. 2. Those on the situation in the United States are from the US Department of Agriculture website, www.csrees.usda.gov/qlinks/extension.html.

Cheap Food and Its Price

Luis de Sousa explains how he calculated the human equivalent of a barrel of oil in "What Is a Human Being Worth (in Terms of Energy)?" *The Oil Drum: Europe,* 20 July 2008, europe.theoildrum.com/pdf/theoildrum_4315.pdf.

Agricultural Emissions — Greenhouse Gases and Nitrogen

The calculation of the amount of energy used to feed an American is from J. Hendrickson, *Energy Use in the U.S. Food System: A Summary of Existing Research and Analysis.* (Reference taken from Jay Tomczak, "Implications of Fossil Fuel Dependence for the Food System," www.energybulletin.net/node/17036.)

Information on natural gas and fertilizer is from V. Smil, "Population Growth and Nitrogen: An Exploration of a Critical Existential Link," *Population and Development Review* 17 (1991): 569–601. Cited in IAASTD. For more on nitrogen's effects in rivers and oceans see Ian Parnell, "Agriculture Impacts Oceans," Geology/Ecology @ Suite 101, 25 August 2008, ian-parnell.suite101.com/agriculture-impacts-oceans-a66089#ixzz0Wa64SlXv.

Data on GHG emissions from livestock are from *Livestock's Long Shadow* as well as an FAO press release from 29 November 2006, "Livestock a Major Threat to Environment," that announced the report (www.fao.org/newsroom/en/news/2006/1000448/index.html). Information is also taken from a New Zealand Ministry of Agriculture technical PowerPoint file that charts the percentage of GHG emissions from livestock. Harry Clark, "New Zealand's Methane and Nitrous Oxide Inventory Methodologies for Agriculture," AgResearch, 2007, www.maf.govt.nz/Portals/0/Documents/environment/climate-change/tools/inventory-methodologies.pdf.

Felicity Lawrence's *Guardian* article was "A Never-Ending Love Affair — The Case for Cutting Meat Consumption Has Never Been More Compelling," 10 September 2011.

Corporate Concentration and the Price of Food

Statistics on food spending are from the US Department of Agriculture, www.
ers.usda.gov/briefing/cpifoodandexpenditures/data/Expenditures_tables/table7.
htm; and "Americans Spend Less Than 10 Percent of Disposable Income on
Food," www.salem-news.com, 19 July 2006, www.salem-news.com/articles/
july192006/food_prices_71906.php (based on USDA research).

Information on the amount of the food dollar that goes to farmers is from Don
Hofstrand, "Energy Agriculture — Food versus Fuel," *Ag Decision Maker*, October
2007, www.extension.iastate.edu/agdm/articles/hof/HofOct07.html.

Canadian farm statistics are from National Farmers Union, "NFU Participates in
'Agriculture 2020' Consultations: Tells AAFC to Stop Distorting Farm Income
Figures," press release, 26 May 2010. (AAFC is Agriculture and Agri-Food Canada,
the federal agriculture ministry.) Details of corporate concentration in Canadian
agriculture are from "Empowering Canadian Farmers in the Marketplace," a
2005 report by Wayne Easter, MP for Malpeque, prepared for the minister of
Agriculture and Agri-Food, www.agr.gc.ca/farmincome_e.phtml; and from the
National Farmers Union, *Understanding the Farm Crisis*.

David Pimentel, an ecologist at Cornell University, calculated the amount of water
needed to produce a kilogram of beef. According to Pimentel, "The data we had
indicated that a beef animal consumed 100 kg of hay and 4 kg of grain per 1 kg
of beef produced. Using the basic rule that it takes about 1,000 liters of water
to produce 1 kg of hay and grain, thus about 100,000 liters were required to
produce the 1 kg of beef." See en.wikipedia.org/wiki/Environmental_impact_
of_meat_production and also "US Could Feed 800 Million People with Grain
that Livestock Eat," press release from Cornell University, 7 August 1997, www.
news.cornell.edu/releases/aug97/livestock.hrs.html.

Climate Change

Details of the drought of 2009 can be found in Matthew Craze, "Argentina
Drought May Halt Wheat Exports for 1st Time," Bloomberg, 29 June 2009,
www.bloomberg.com/apps/news?pid=20601086&sid=acXLbbY1XcxE; and Eric
deCarbonnel, "Catastrophic Fall in 2009 Global Forecast," Global Research.ca,
10 February 2009, www.globalresearch.ca/index.php?context=va&aid=12252.
The latter provides a map and an annotated listing of all the food-production
impacts in countries where drought is a serious problem.

For more on water resources see the page of statistics from the Stockholm
International Water Institute, www.siwi.org/sa/node.asp?node=159.

For more on the Ogallala Aquifer see the *Water Encyclopedia*, www.water
encyclopedia.com/Oc-Po/Ogallala-Aquifer.html.

Seikatsu: "Living People" Transforming their Relationship to Food and Each Other

John Restakis wrote about the formation of the Japanese Consumer Cooperative
Union in *Humanizing the Economy: Co-operatives in the Age of Capital*. There
is also information on the Cooperative Union, and Seikatsu, in Jet Hermida,

"The Seikatsu Club Consumers Cooperative: A Unique Producer-Consumer Relationship in Japan," in *Initiatives on Pro-Small Farmer Trade*, and in Robyn Van En, "Eating for Your Community: A Report from the Founder of Community Supported Agriculture," *In Context: A Quarterly of Human Sustainable Culture*, 1995, www.context.org/ICLIB/IC42/VanEn.htm.

For more information on Seikatsu, including some of the policy changes arising from the group's activities, see "Outline of the Seikatsu Club Consumers' Co-operative Union," on the Seikatsu website, www.seikatsuclub.coop/english/.

Transition Factors: Transforming the Value Chain

The description of the free market as a place of atomization, isolation, and competition among people is from M. Arruda, ed., *Exchanging Visions of a Responsible, Plural, Solidarity Economy*.

Who Will Grow Our Food? The Problem of Succession

The average age of the Canadian farmer is from "Trends in Canadian Agriculture Continue," press release from the Canadian Farmers Association, 16 May 2007, www.cfa-fca.ca/media-centre/news-releases/2007/trends-canadian-agriculture-continue.

Restoring Salmon: Restoring the Commons in Alaska

Much of the historical information on Alaska is from D.F. Amend, "Alaska's Regional Aquaculture Associations Co-Management of Salmon in Southern Southeast Alaska," in *Co-Operative Management of Local Fisheries: New Directions for Improved Management and Community Development*, ed. E. Pinkerton.

Impacts on the Household Economy: The Hartwick Family

Again, statistics on food spending are from the US Department of Agriculture, www.ers.usda.gov/briefing/cpifoodandexpenditures/data/Expenditures_tables/table7.htm.

The San Francisco–based urban farmer is described in an article by Justin Clark, "Back(yard) to the Land," *San Francisco Chronicle*, 22 July 2006, www.sfgate.com/cgi-bin/article.cgi?f=/c/a/2006/07/22/HOGTMK219B1.DTL (excerpted from *Natural Home Magazine*).

Chapter 7: Reweaving Our Economies Close to Home

The Norbert Rost quotation is drawn from his paper "Regional Economy Systems as a Complement to Globalization," which can be found at www.regional entwicklung.de/regionales-wirtschaften/uebersetzungen-translation/regional-economy-systems-as-complement-to-globalisation/.

The quote on the 2004 Internal Revenue Service Report is from G. William Domhoff's essay "Wealth, Income and Power," posted on his website *Who Rules America?* in September 2005 (updated January 2011) see sociology.ucsc.edu/whorulesamerica/power/wealth.html. It cites David Cay Johnston's 28 November 2006 article in the *New York Times*, "04 Income in U.S. Was Below 2000 Level."

For more on the Chantier de l'Economie Sociale, see www.chantier.qc.ca/. English documentation is available at www.chantier.qc.ca/?module=document&uid =1059.

Weaving the Strands Together: Constructing Local Development Systems

Lizbeth Schorr describes the US research on inner cities in *Common Purpose: Strengthening Families and Neighbourhoods to Rebuild America.*

The list of key functions performed by outsiders is from Mike Lewis, "Ecology of Success," *Making Waves* 10, no. 1 (1999), communityrenewal.ca/sites/all/files/ resource/MW100112.pdf. This article is a summary of the key conclusions in Lizbeth Schorr's *Common Purpose.*

The Canadian research referred to was done by Mike Lewis and Stewart Perry and presented in *Reinventing the Local Economy: What Ten Canadian Initiatives Can Teach Us About Building Creative, Inclusive, Sustainable Communities.* Available from the Canadian Centre for Community Renewal, www.communityrenewal. ca.

Coastal Enterprises Inc. — Community Development Finance in Rural Maine

Ron Phillips told his story and outlined his mission in "Faith Based Collaboration: Connections That Work for Communities," *Making Waves* 12 no. 3 (2001).

Many of CEI's projects are described in Keith Bisson, "The Triple Bottom Line and Community Development Finance," *Making Waves* 20 (Winter 2009). Much of the Triple Bottom Line Collaborative (TBLC) material later in this section is also from Bisson's article.

CEI's Sector Approach

Carla Dickstein lists the tools CEI uses in its sector strategies in "Crafting Sustainable Development: A Case Study of Maine's Coastal Enterprises Inc.," *Making Waves* 10 no. 2 (1999).

Transition Factors

Paul Hirst wrote about the doctrine of subsidiarity and the control of "the great bulk" of social and economic affairs in *Associative Democracy: New Forms of Economic and Social Governance.*

Resilience Reflections

The definition of resilience comes from Brian Walker,*Resilience Thinking: Sustaining Ecosystems and People in a Changing World.*

Chapter 8: Convivial Banking Innovations: Seeds for Transitions

Christopher Le Coq wrote about the special branches the big banks set up for elites in "Experts Say Smaller Businesses Need Traditional Banking," *Egypt Daily News,* 26 October 2010.

US Credit Union Innovations: Federating Solutions

See the Neighborhood Trust Federal Credit Union and CWCID website at www. cwcid.org/whatwedo.htm.

Statistics on the US credit union movement are from the National Credit Union Administration, *2010 Annual Report, "Resilience and the Road Ahead,"* and the Credit Union National Association website, www.cuna.org/public/press/credit-union-basics.

The history of the Latino Community Credit Union is described in "Latino Com munity Credit Union Brings Full Service Banking to Latino Immigrants in North Carolina" on the National Immigration Forum website at www.immigration forum.org/resources/success/home-ownership-finances?. See also the credit union's own website at www.latinoccu.org/en/social-investment.

Organizing the Self-Employed

A. Bibby has written about trade unions organizing the self-employed in "Opening the Doors Wide to the Self-Employed," a report for UNI Global Union, October 2005 (available on his website, www.andrewbibby.com/socialpartners.html), and "Organizing Self-Employed Workers," *World of Work* 46 (March 2003).

Mutual for the Self-Employed

Information for this section came from London Business School, *Global Entrepreneurship Monitor: The Definitive Study of Entrepreneurship in 2006*; UK Women's Enterprise Task Force, "Key Women's Enterprise Statistics and Trends," www.womensenterprise.co.uk/stats_wetf.asp; and P. Conaty, R. Foggitt, R. Tarusenga, and S. Bendle, *Self-Help and Mutual Aid: A Mutual for the Self-Employed to Underpin Local Economies across Britain.*

Cooperative Capital in the UK: Withdrawable and Transferable Shares

Information on Industrial and Provident Societies came from J. Birchall, *The Co-Op: The People's Business*, p. 77; and the Social Enterprise Coalition, *Unlocking the Potential: A Guide to Finance for Social Enterprises.*

For more on Shared Interest see the website at www.shared-interest.com. For more on the Phone Co-op see www.thephone.coop/the-difference/investments. For more on Energy4All see www.energy4all.co.uk/energy_home.asp.

Relationship Banking from a Distance

J. Freedland wrote about Zopa in "Don't Just Howl with Rage. Try an Idea That Does Away with Banks Altogether," *The Guardian*, 19 August 2009.

For more information on Kiva, see the website at www.kiva.org/app.php?page= businesses.

Low Interest-High Impact Lending for Vulnerable Homeowners

P. Conaty wrote about community development loan funds in 2011 in "Community Development Finance and Home Improvement Partnerships," an unpublished report for the Fit for Living Network, a national task force on home improvement established by the Housing Associations Charitable Trust. For more information on Wessex Home Improvement Loans see the website at www.wessexhil.co.uk/.

Revolving Loan Funds for Affordable Housing: Risk Pooling
There is a good profile of Habitat for Humanity at Wikipedia, en.wikipedia.org/wiki/Habitat_for_Humanity.

Social and Ecological Banks: Investing in the Unconventional
Steiner's philosophy of social economy is explained in Rudolf Steiner, *Economics: The World as One Economy*. Minsky's comments are from "The Financial Instability Hypothesis," mentioned in Chapter 1.

Triodos
For more on Triodos Bank, see the website at www.triodos.co.uk/en/about-triodos/ We also drew information from the 2010–11 annual report "Welcome to Sustainable Banking: Your Inspiring Change 2010/11."

Caisse d'economie solidaire Desjardins
For more on Caisse d'economie solidaire Desjardins, see the website and annual report information (in French) at www.caissesolidaire.coop/. We also drew information from an unpublished paper by Y. Poirier, "Caisse d'economie solidaire Desjardins — A unique financial institution."

Transition Factors
The Kenneth Boulding quotation is from his essay "Economic Development as an Evolutionary System."

Chapter 9: Federating the Change Agents: Securing the Gains
The Louis Kelso quotation is from Bill Moyers, "Louis Kelso, Capitalist," in *A World of Ideas II*, ed. A. Tucher.

Reinventing the Guilds: A Way Forward?
The New Age was a weekly magazine of political and social policy commentary, which also included debates on the arts and culture. Edited by A.R. Orage, it enjoyed a wide circulation in the UK for over 30 years.

Background
C. Bryant discussed the papal encyclical in his book *Possible Dreams: A Personal History of the British Christian Socialists*.

Federating a Development System to Build the Social (Solidarity) Economy
Statistics on the social economy in Quebec are from the Chantier de l'économie sociale website, www.chantier.qc.ca.

Credit
Margie Mendell and Rocio Nogales wrote about the Fiducie in "Social Enterprise in OECD Countries: What Are the Financial Streams?" in *The Changing Boundaries of Social Enterprises*, ed. Antonella Noya.
The equity gap in Quebec was analyzed by Michael Lewis in "Common Ground: CED and the Social Economy: Sorting Out the Basics," *Making Waves* 15, no. 1 (Spring 2004): 7–11.

Equity

The Nova Scotia case study involving federal tax credits was in Lena Soots, "Supporting Innovative Co-operative Development: The Case of the Nova Scotia Co-operative Development System — Research Report," BALTA, March 2007, pp. 13-14, auspace.athabascau.ca/handle/2149/2805.

Stewart E. Perry and Garry Loewen, "Equity Tax Credits As a Tool of CED: A Comparison of Two Local Investment Incentive Programs," *Making Waves* 20, no. 3 (Autumn 2009): 21–25.

Transition Factors

The full text of the 2006 Declaration is available on the Chantier website at www.chantier.qc.ca/userImgs/documents/CLevesque/sitechantierdocuments/declarationsommetang2006.pdf.

La Via Campesina: Building a Global Movement for Food Sovereignty

Much of this section is a synthesis of an excellent journal article by M.E. Martinez-Torres and P.M. Rosset, "La Via Campesina: The Evolution of a Transnational Movement," *Journal of Peasant Studies* (February 2010), www.stwr.org/food-security-agriculture/la-via-campesina-the-birth-and-evolution-of-a-transnational-social-movement.html.

Statistics on the size and makeup of La Via Campesina come from A.A. Desmarais's PhD thesis, *The Via Campesina: Peasants Resisting Globalization.*

On the World Scene

The gap between production costs and the price of dumped food was analyzed by M. Ritchie, S. Murphy, and M.B. Lake in "United States Dumping on World Agricultural Markets," Cancun Series paper no. 1.

Structure

P. Rosset and M.E. Martinez-Torres wrote about the structure of LVC in *Participatory Evaluation of La Via Campesina: Public Version.*

Federating to Advance Fair-Trade Finance: A Transition Challenge

The information on microfinance institutions in 2007 is from R.P. Christen, R. Rosenberg, and V. Jayadeva, "Financial Institutions with a Double-Bottom Line: Implications for the Future of Microfinance," and from the Microcredit Summit Campaign's *State of the Microcredit Summit Campaign Report 2007.*

For the 2010 review by Social Investment Forum see L. Anderson, "Experts: As Traditional Banks Fail to Meet More and More Local Needs, Community Investing Poised to Break through to the Mainstream in 2011." Press release from Green America, 13 April 2011, www.greenamerica.org/about/newsroom/releases/2011-04-13.cfm.

Chapter 10: Economic Democracy and Cooperative Capital

Works mentioned or quoted from in the introductory section are Bertrand Russell, *Roads to Freedom*; R.H. Tawney, *The Acquisitive Society*; Bertrand Russell,

Principles of Social Reconstruction; Erich Fromm, *The Fear of Freedom*; John Stuart Mill, *Principles of Political Economy, On Liberty*, and *Utilitarianism*; and Thomas Wilson, *A Discourse on Usury*.

Outwitting Enclosure: The Mondragon Formula to Equity

The Mondragon English-language website is at www.mondragon-corporation. com/ENG.aspx?language=en-US.

Information on Mondragon's fair wage scales is from A. Robb, J. Smith, and J. Webb, "Co-Operative Capital: What It Is and Why Our World Needs It" (paper presented to the conference on Financial Co-operative Approaches to Local Development, Trento, Italy, 10–11 June 2010).

Information on the Empresarial Division is from R. Oakeshott, *Jobs and Fairness: The Logic and Experience of Employee Ownership.*

Democratizing Social Care in Italy

Much of the material on Emilia Romagna is from J. Restakis, *Humanizing the Economy: Co-operatives in the Age of Capital.*

Consortia

V. Zamagni wrote about the Consorzio Cooperative Costruzione in an unpublished paper from 2006, "Italy's Co-Operatives: From Marginality to Success."

Cooperative Energy Services: Mobilizing Green Economic Actors

See an analysis of New Deal rural regeneration objectives in P. Hall, *Cities of Tomorrow.* For more on the history of the joint venture see "History of Rural Electric Coops," Coop Litigation News website, at coop-litigation.com/rechistory.aspx. And for details on the situation today visit the National Rural Electric Co-operative Association website at www.ncreca.org.

Transition Factors

The George Benello quote is from "Worker-Managed Enterprises: Legal Shells, Structures, and Financing," a chapter in C. George Benello, Robert S. Swann, Ward Morehouse, and Shann Turnbull, *Building Sustainable Communities: Tools and Concepts for Self-Reliant Economic Change.*

Murray Fulton and Brent Hueth noted the current size of the Caja Laboral Popular in "Cooperative Conversions, Failures and Restructurings: An Overview," *Journal of Co-operatives* 23 (2009): i–xi.

Chapter 11: Ownership Transfer: Accelerating Transition

US senator Huey P. Long's "Every Man a King" speech was broadcast on the National Broadcasting Corporation's radio network to launch his national Share Our Wealth program on 23 February 1934.

Structural Dysfunction of the Global Investment Industry

Adair Turner's comments were reported in B. Semple, "Prospect's Adair Turner Interview Sparks Debate across the World," *Prospect Magazine*, 28 August 2009.

Paul Woolley's comments are in J. Ford, "A Greedy Giant out of Control," *Prospect Magazine*, 23 November 2008.

The average Wall Street bonus was reported by Joan Gralla and Clare Baldwin for Reuters in "Average 2010 Wall St Cash Bonus Fell to $128,530," 23 February 2011, www.reuters.com/article/2011/02/23/us-wallstreet-bonuses-idUSTRE71M68 420110223. The UK information comes from P. Inman, "Executives Switch Pension Pots to Cash to Avoid Clampdown," *Guardian*, 15 September 2009.

Erosion by Shadow Bankers

Alan Rappeport wrote about hedge funds in "A Short History of Hedge Funds," CFO.com, 27 March 2007, www.cfo.com/article.cfm/8914091/1/c_2984367.

Sismondi and Economic Depression

M. Lutz summarizes Sismondi's philosophy in *Economics for the Common Good: Two Centuries of Social Economic Thought in the Humanistic Tradition*.

Gandhi and Trusteeship

S. Ghosh included Gandhi's quote about making laborers co-partners in wealth in his article "Trusteeship in Industry: Gandhiji's Dream and Contemporary Reality," *Indian Journal of Industrial Relations* 25, no. 1 (July 1989).

John Lewis Partnership: Trusteeship Put into Action

For more on corporate pension schemes in the UK, see J. Dunkly, "Shell Closes Last FTSE 100 Final Salary Pension Scheme," *Daily Telegraph*, 5 January 2012.

Evolution of the Trusteeship Model: Toward a Framework for Ownership Transfer

A.K. Dasgupta drew comparisons between Gandhi and Schumacher in *Gandhi's Economic Thought*.

Employee Stock Ownership Plans

Jeff Gates described Kelso's work on ESOPs in *The Ownership Solution*, pages 50–56.

The Robert Ashford quotation is from "Binary Economics — An Overview," a 2010 paper available at papers.ssrn.com/sol3/papers.cfm?abstract_id=928752.

ESOPs Today

The National Center for Employee Ownership website is at www.nceo.org.

Regarding B Corporations, it appears that the earliest "for benefit corporation" was the Port of London Authority, established in 1908 by a separate act of Parliament to operate as a public trust in perpetuity. The idea was that it would trade like a corporation, become viable and self-financing, but operate for the benefit of the public. In other words, it would not operate as a "nonprofit" but as a "for benefit." The Quakers in Business group in the UK are working to more widely develop "for benefit" corporations on the Gandhian model of trusteeship. They have called these democratic stakeholder corporations for the 21st century, "Benefit Corporations."

The George Benello quotation comes from "Worker-Managed Enterprises: Legal Shells, Structures, and Financing," a chapter in *Building Sustainable Communities: Tools and Concepts for Self-Reliant Economic Change.*

Transforming Property Rights: A Solution in Search of a Home
Turnbull described the Standard Oil epiphany in "Grounding Economics in Commercial Reality: A Cash-Flow Paradigm," in *Essays in Heterodox Economics*, ed. P. Kreisler, M. Johnson, and J. Lodewijks, pp. 438-61, ssrn.com/abstract=946033. Details of the windfall gains and dividends paid to General Motors are provided in S. Turnbull, "Time Limited Corporations," *Abacus: A Journal of Business and Accounting Studies* 9, no. 1 (1973): 28–43, onlinelibrary.wiley.com/doi/10.1111/j.1467-6281.1973.tb00173.x/abstract.

Who Creates Value?
Turnbull's idea of a cooperative or community land bank was based in part on the community land trust (CLT) idea of Bob Swann and Slater King (see Chapter 4). Swann and King showed that by setting up CLTs, communities were able to get rid of land speculation by taking land off the market and putting it into a local "trusteeship," decommodifying it.

What Benefits Would a CLB Generate?
S. Turnbull wrote about the sixth benefit in "Achieving Environmental Sustainable Prosperity" (paper presented to 13th Conference of the Association of Heterodox Economics, Nottingham Trent University, UK, 10 July 2011), available at ssrn.com/abstract=1769349.

Implications for Reweaving Local Economies and Navigating Transition
Turnbull reports that Kelso considered the traditional static, exclusive, and perpetual property rights as an unalienable right in the tradition of Locke, and so objected to any proposals to change them. However, to avoid competition between the different approaches, Norman Kurland, a leading supporter of Kelso's ideas, entered into an agreement of a "shared vision" with Turnbull in 2001. Their "Statement of Shared Vision: Toward a More Free and Just Global Economy" is posted at the Center for Economic and Social Justice website, www.cesj.org/about/programs/declarations/sharedvision.htm. Turnbull had always seen the different approaches for distributing ownership as complementary and included Kelso's ideas in his book *Democratising the Wealth of Nations,* which he had dedicated to Kelso. Turnbull invited Kelso to visit Australia in 1975 to introduce his ideas after retaining Kelso in 1974 to advise his private equity group on a US acquisition.

Another mechanism developed by Dr Shann Turnbull is Ownership Transfer Corporations, described in his 1975 book *Democratising the Wealth of Nations,* available at ssrn.com/abstract_id=1146062.

As an example of a local or regional currency and credit system tied to a locally created unit of value, locally generated renewable energy could provide an independent unit of value defined in kilowatt-hours (kWh) of locally produced electricity. The currency would be inflation resistant, because any improvement in generating sources and/or technology would increase rather than reduce its value. To remove the possibility that it might be used as a speculative asset or that its value might increase through interest payments, Turnbull has proposed that it carry a cost, as proposed by Gesell in *The Natural Economic Order*. However, instead of the cost being incurred through the purchase of stamps affixed to currency notes, Turnbull envisages the use of digital money stored and spent through smart cellphones that also automatically remit the carrying cost to the CLB. These seigniorage-like remittances could provide an important source of additional income for CLBs.

Regarding Norm Kurland's ideas on setting up CLBs, see the Center for Economic and Social Justice's description of the Citizens Land Co-operative, which has some similarity to Turnbull's Cooperative Land Bank, at www.cesj.org/homestead/creditvehicles/cha-cic.htm. The quotation from Kurland was part of an exchange of emails between Shann Turnbull and Norm Kurland on 6 November 2010.

Robin Murray's idea is from *Danger and Opportunity: Crisis and the New Social Economy*.

Resilience Reflections

The statistics on world and US corporations are from a UK NGO and think-tank called Share the World's Resources. See the "Key Facts" page on its website at www.stwr.org/multinational-corporations/key-facts.html.

Chapter 12: From Cultural Captivity to Focused Intention

Beyond Eden: Our Disconnect from Nature

The quote about "the primary responsibility for this catastrophe" is from Will W. Adams, "The Ivory-Billed Woodpecker, Ecopsychology, and the Crisis of Extinction: On Annihilating and Nurturing Other Beings, Relationships, and Ourselves," *The Humanistic Psychologist* 34, no. 2 (2006): 111–33, soulcraftwisdom. wordpress.com/2011/10/08/the-ivory-billed-woodpecker-ecopsychology-and-the-crisis-of-extinction-on-annihilating-and-nurturing-other-beings-relationships-and-ourselves/. Other material credited to Adams in this first section is from the same essay.

The three insights credited to ecopsychology are from Will Adams, "Ecopsychology and Phenomenology: Toward a Collaborative Engagement," *Existential Analysis* 16 (2005): 269–83.

The Pyle quotation is from "Cosmic Convergence," *Orion* 24, no. 3 (2005): 68–69.

Transition: An Inner and Outer Journey

Wendell Berry's eight principles are from a speech he gave at the Future of Food Conference, sponsored by the *Washington Post*, in May 2011. You can read it online at www.energybulletin.net/stories/2011-05-05/what-must-we-do.

The Teri Dillion quote comes from a post on Carolyn Baker's website in which she discusses Bridges' book, "Addiction and Recovery as a Partner for Transition," 9 March 2011, carolynbaker.net/2011/03/09/addiction-and-recovery-as-a-partner-for-transition-by-terri-dillion/.

For more on Transition Towns see the Transition Network website at www.transitionnetwork.org/.

Breaking the Armor of Our Cultural Captivity

Portions of the Jeremy Leggett interview are at www.energybulletin.net/node/50290.

The "Price" of Transition: Are We Willing to Pay Our Way?

David Frum wrote about the oil shortage in the 1970s in *How We Got Here: The 70's*, p. 320.

The full text of President Carter's speech is available on the PBS *American Experience* website at www.pbs.org/wgbh/amex/carter/filmmore/ps_crisis.html.

Stephen Koff describes the transition from Carter to Reagan in "Was Jimmy Carter Right?" *Cleveland Plain Dealer*, 1 October 2005; available online at www.energybulletin.net/node/9657.

The Fleischer quote was included in Eileen Claussen and Elliot Diringer "U.S. Exceptionalism and Climate Change (Part II)," 20 July 2007, www.pewclimate.org/press-center/articles/us-exceptionalism-and-climate-change-part-ii.

The Green Growth statement is from the UNESCAP website www.greengrowth.org/index.asp.

"We have been praying to the Almighty to send us to a feast..." is from Huey Long's Barbecue Speech, given in 1934. You can find the full text on the TeachingHistory.org website, teachinghistory.org/history-content/beyond-the-textbook/23919.

Weaving the Strands into a Resilient Fabric: Possible?

Keynes's "Economic Possibilities for Our Grandchildren" was collected in *Essays in Persuasion*.

From Wall Street to Resilience

Borsodi published his findings in *The Distribution Age*.

The comment about the Twentieth Century Fund study is from Kirkpatrick Sale, *Human Scale*. Sale also cited US business studies since World War II that confirm the pattern of a falling rate of profit that exists between large corporations and smaller businesses. Further, in an interview on the BBC *In Biz* program on 25 August 2011, Gary Hamel, a visiting professor at the London Business School, described his current review of 20 large American industries, which confirmed this pattern of a diseconomy of scale and declining rates of profit among large corporations in comparison to smaller businesses.

Borsodi's ideas about stewardship and "Trusterty" were included in his "The Posessional Problem," included in *The Community Land Trust Reader*.

The Crucible of Home: Revisiting Household Economics

The European Union research on household carbon emissions was on the Gilded website. See "Governance, Infrastructure, Lifestyle Dynamics and Energy Demand: European Post-Carbon Communities," www.gildedeu.org/infosheet.

The prices of Canadian homes in April 2011 are from "Will the Hammer Drop on House Prices?" an 18 April article by Rob Carrick in the *Globe and Mail*. The 1980 price was from "The People History" website, www.thepeoplehistory.com/1980.html.

According to wiki.answers.com (How much would 1 dollar in 1980 be worth in 2010 dollars?) $1 in 1980 would be worth $2.60 today.

Statistics on the changing average size of Canadian homes are from Darren Barefoot's website, www.darrenbarefoot.com/archives/2006/01/what-is-the-average-size-of-a-house-in-canada.html.

Canada's ranking as a carbon emitter is from a listing prepared by the US Department of Energy's Carbon Dioxide Information Analysis Center, based on 1990–2008 data collected from country agencies by the UN Statistics Division and posted on Wikipedia (en.wikipedia.org/wiki/List_of_countries_by_carbon_dioxide_emissions_per_capita).

Epilogue: The Great Transition

The opening quotation and other quotes from Kenneth Boulding in the first three paragraphs are drawn from an article in *IEEE Spectrum*, October 1978, that was quoted by Hazel Henderson in *Politics of the Solar Age: Alternatives to Economics.*

The opening quotation from Pitirim Sorokin is from his Lowell Lectures and was also included in Hazel Henderson's *Politics of the Solar Age.*

The David Stockman quote is from his work-in-progress, tentatively titled *The Triumph of Crony Capitalism*, and was included in his interview with Bill Moyers on *Moyers and Company*, 20 January 2012. The interview and a transcript are available on the program website, billmoyers.com/episode/crony-capitalism/.

The quote from John Stuart Mill is from his Principles of Political Economy, Book IV, Chapter 7 on the Stationary State.

Bibliography

Adams, W.W. "Ecopsychology and Phenomenology: Toward a Collaborative Engagement." *Existential Analysis* 16 (2005): 269–83.

———. "The Ivory-Billed Woodpecker, Ecopsychology, and the Crisis of Extinction: On Annihilating and Nurturing Other Beings, Relationships, and Ourselves." *The Humanistic Psychologist* 34, no. 2 (2006): 111–33, soulcraftwisdom.wordpress.com/2011/10/08/the-ivory-billed-woodpecker-ecopsychology-and-the-crisis-of-extinction-on-annihilating-and-nurturing-other-beings-relationships-and-our-selves/.

Alinsky, S. *Rules for Radicals.* Random House, 1971.

Amend, D.F. "Alaska's Regional Aquaculture Associations Co-Management of Salmon in Southern Southeast Alaska." In *Co-Operative Management of Local Fisheries: New Directions for Improved Management and Community Development,* ed. E. Pinkerton. UBC Press, 1989.

Arctic Assessment and Monitoring Program. (2011). *Climate Change and POPs: Predicting the Impacts. Report of the UNEP/AMAP Expert Group.* www.amap.no.

Arendt, H. *The Human Condition.* University of Chicao Press, 1958.

Arruda, M., ed. *Exchanging Visions of a Responsible, Plural, Solidarity Economy.* ALOE, 2008.

Baker, C. *Navigating the Coming Chaos: A Handbook for Inner Transition.* iUniverse, 2011, carolynbaker.net/2011/01/11/792/.

BC Healthy Living Alliance. *Healthy Futures for BC Families: Policy Recommendations for Improving the Health of British Columbians.* BC Healthy Living Alliance, 2009.

Benello, C.G., R.S. Swann and S. Turnbull. *Building Sustainable Communities: Tools and Concepts for Self-Reliant Economic Change.* Edited by W. Morehouse. Bootstrap Press, 1989.

Bentham, J. *Discourse on Usury.* 1787; repr., Routledge, 1992.

Berry, W. *The Unsettling of America: Culture & Agriculture.* Sierra Club Books, 1977.

Bibby, A. "Organizing Self-Employed Workers," *World of Work* 46 (March 2003).

Biello, D. "Oceanic Dead Zones Continue to Spread." *Scientific American*, 15 August 2008.

Birchall, J. *Building Communities the Co-operative Way.* Routledge & Kegan Paul, 1988.

———. *The Co-Op: The People's Business.* Manchester University Press, 1994.

Bisson, K. "The Triple Bottom Line and Community Development Finance." *Making Waves* 20 (Winter 2009).

Borsodi, R. "A Decentralist Manifesto." 1958; repr., School of Living, 1978, www.cooperativeindividualism.org/borsodi-ralph_a-decentralist-manifesto-1958.html.

———. *The Distribution Age.* D. Appleton and Company, 1929.

———. "The Posessional Problem." In *The Community Land Trust Reader,* ed. J.E. Davis. Lincoln Institute of Land Policy, 2010.

Boulding, K. *Ecodynamics: A New Theory of Societal Evolution.* Sage, 1978.

———. "The Economics of the Coming Spaceship Earth," 1966, at dieoff.org/page160.htm.

———. *The Meaning of the Twentieth Century: The Great Transition.* Harper & Row, 1964.

Bowles, S., and H. Gintis. *Democracy and Capitalism: Property, Community and the Contradictions of Modern Social Thought.* Basic Books, 1986.

Boyle, D. "Economic Thought in the Middle Ages." *The Idler* 42 (2009). Available from Idler Books.

———. *The Money Changers: Currency Reform from Aristotle to e-cash.* Earthscan, 2002.

Brennan, M. "The Positive Impacts of Affordable Housing on Education: A Research Summary." Center for Housing Policy and Enterprise Community Partners Inc., 2007.

Bridges, W. *Transitions: Making Sense of Life's Changes.* Da Capo Press, 1980.

Brown, E. "The Global Debt Crisis: How We Got In and How to Get Out?" *Global Research* 6 (June 2011).

———. *The Web of Debt.* Third Millenium Press, 2010.

Bryant, C. *Possible Dreams: A Personal History of the British Christian Socialists.* Hodder & Stoughton, 1997.

Burlington Associates (J.E. Davis and A. Demetrowitz). *Permanently Affordable Homeownership: Does the Community Land Trust Deliver on Its Promises?* Burlington Community Land Trust, 2003, www.burlingtonassociates.com.

Burton, Mark. *Unravelling Debt: The Economy, Banking and the Case of JAK.* Dissertation, Schumacher College and the University of Plymouth, August 2008.

Canada. Senate Subcommittee on Population Health. *Population Health Policy: Issues and Options.* 4th Report. Government of Canada, 2008.

Christen, R.P., R. Rosenberg, and V. Jayadeva. "Financial Institutions with a Double-Bottom Line: Implications for the Future of Microfinance." CGAP Occasional Paper, July 2004.

Cole, G.D.H. *Guild Socialism: A Plan for Economic Democracy.* Bibliolife, 1920.

Conaty, P., J. Birchall, S. Bendle, and R. Foggitt. *Common Ground — For Mutual Home Ownership.* new economics foundation, the Housing Corporation, and CDS Co-Operatives, 2003.

Conaty, P., R. Foggitt, R. Tarusenga, and S. Bendle. *Self-Help and Mutual Aid: A Mutual for the Self-Employed to Underpin Local Economies across Britain.* new economics foundation, 2008.

Creutz, H. "Tumorartige Selbstvermehrung der Geldvermögen." *Zeitsschrift Humane Wirtschaft* 1 (2009): 30–31.

Curtin, J.F., and L. Bocarsly. "CLTs: A Growing Trend in Affordable Home Ownership." *Journal of Affordable Housing and Community Development Law* 17, no. 4 (2008): 367–394.

Daly, H. *Beyond Growth.* Beacon Press, 1996.

———. *Steady-State Economics.* Earthscan, 1992.

Dasgupta, A.K. *Gandhi's Economic Thought.* Routledge, 1996.

Davis, J.E., and R. Jacobus. *The City-CLT Partnership: Municipal Support for Community Land Trusts.* Lincoln Institute of Land Policy, June 2008, www.ihtmv.org/PDF/City-CLTPolicyReport.pdf.

Davis, J.E., and A. Stokes. *Lands in Trust, Homes That Last: A Performance Evaluation of Champlain Housing Trust.* Champlain Housing Trust, 2009.

Department of Trade and Industry and *Co-Operatives UK. Co-Operative Energy: Lessons from Denmark and Sweden.* DTI, March 2005.

Desmarais, A.A. *The Via Campesina: Peasants Resisting Globalization.* PhD thesis, Department of Geography, University of Calgary, 2003.

Diacon, D., R. Clarke, and S. Guimarães. *Redefining the Commons: Locking in Value through Community Land Trusts.* Building and Social Housing Foundation, 2005.

Dickstein, C. "Crafting Sustainable Development: A Case Study of Maine's Coastal Enterprises Inc." *Making Waves* 10 no. 2 (1999).

Douglas, P.H., I. Fisher, F.D. Graham, E.J. Hamilton, W.I. King, and C.R. Whittlesey. *A Program for Monetary Reform.* 1939, en.wikipedia.org/wiki/A_Program_for_Monetary_Reform.

Douthwaite, R. *Short Circuit.* Lilliput Press, 1996.

Erbmann, R., H. Goulbourne, and P. Malik. *Collective Power: Changing the Way We Consume Energy.* The Co-operative Party, May 2009.

Eveleigh, H. *The Future Is Local: Empowering Communities to Improve Their Neighbourhoods.* Sustainable Development Commission, July 2010, www.sd-commission.org.uk/data/files/publications/SDC_TFiL_report_w.pdf.

Faber, M. "How To Be an Ecological Economist." *Ecological Economics* 66, no. 1 (2008): 1–7.

Farr, J. *Artisans in Europe, 1300–1914.* Cambridge University Press, 2000.

Fisher, I. "100% Money and the Public Debt." *Economic Forum*, April–June 1936, 406–20.

Fogel, C. "How the Debt-Based Monetary System Functions in Canada." *COMER, The Journal of the Committee on Monetary and Economic Reform* 23, no. 9 (September 2011).

Ford, J. "A Greedy Giant out of Control." *Prospect Magazine*, 23 November 2008.

Friedman, T. *Hot, Flat, and Crowded: Why We Need a Green Revolution — and How It Can Renew America*. Farrar, Straus and Giroux, 2008.

Fromm, E. *The Fear of Freedom*. Routledge & Kegan Paul, 1941.

Frum, D. *How We Got Here: The 70's*. Basic Books, 2000.

Fulton, M., and B. Hueth. "Cooperative Conversions, Failures and Restructurings: An Overview." *Journal of Co-operatives* 23 (2009): i–xi.

Gandhi, M.K. *An Autobiography, or The Story of My Experiments with Truth*. Penguin Books, 1982.

Gapper, J. "The Wall Street Mind: Anxious." *New York*, 10 April 2011, nymag.com/news/business/wallstreet/john-gapper-2011-4/.

Gates, J. *The Ownership Solution: Towards a Shared Capitalism for the Twenty-first Century*. Penguin Books, 1998.

George, H. *Progress and Poverty*. Robert Schalkenbach Foundation, 2010.

Georgescu-Roegen, N. *The Entropy Law and the Economic Process*. Harvard University Press, 1971.

Gesell, S. *The Natural Economic Order*. 1929; rev. ed. Peter Owen, 1958.

Ghosh, S. "Trusteeship in Industry: Gandhiji's Dream and Contemporary Reality." *Indian Journal of Industrial Relations* 25, no. 1 (July 1989).

Gosling, P. *Social Co-Operatives in Italy: Lessons for the UK*. Social Enterprise London, 2002.

Goyder, G. *The Just Enterprise*. Adamtine Press, 1993.

Grossman, R., and F. Adams. *Taking Care of Business: Citizenship and the Charter of Incorporations*. Earth Island Journal, 1993.

Gumb, G. and Hennes, R. 'Financing Energy Efficiency in Buildings — the German Experience', paper presented at the International Workshop on Financing Energy Efficiency in Building on 16-17 February 2012, KfW, Germany

Gunderson, L., and C.S. Holling. *Panarchy: Understanding Transformations in Systems of Humans and Nature*. Island Press, 2001.

Hall, P. *Cities of Tomorrow*. Blackwell, 1988.

Hamilton, C. *Requiem for a Species: Why We Resist the Truth about Climate Change*. Earthscan, 2010.

Hansen, J., M. Sato, P. Kharecha, D. Beerling, R. Berner, V. Masson-Delmotte, M. Pagani, M. Raymo, D.L. Royer, and J.C. Zachos. "Target Atmospheric CO_2: Where Should Humanity Aim?" *Open Atmospheric Science Journal* 2 (2008): 217–31, doi:10.2174/1874282300802010217.

Hardin, G. "The Tragedy of the Commons." *Science* 162, no. 3859 (1968).

Hart, K. "Informal Income Opportunities and Urban Employment in Ghana." Journal of Modern African Studies 1 , no. 1 (1973): 61-89.

Hawken, P. *Blessed Unrest.* Viking Penguin, 2007.

———. *The Ecology of Commerce.* Harper Collins 1994.

Heilbroner, R. *The Worldly Philosohers: The Lives, Times and Ideas of the Great Economic Thinkers.* Simon and Schuster, 1967.

Henderson, H. *Politics of the Solar Age: Alternatives to Economics.* Knowledge Systems Inc., 1988.

Hendrickson, J. *Energy Use in the U.S. Food System: A Summary of Existing Research and Analysis.* Center for Integrated Agricultural Systems, UW-Madison, 1996.

Hermida, J. "The Seikatsu Club Consumers Cooperative: A Unique Producer-Consumer Relationship in Japan." In *Initiatives on Pro-Small Farmer Trade.* AFA & AsiaDHRRA, 2006.

Hildyard, N. "Whose Common Future: Reclaiming the Commons." The Ecologist 6, no. 1 (1994).

Hirst, P. *Associative Democracy: New Forms of Economic and Social Governance.* Polity Press, 1994.

Homer-Dixon, T. *The Upside of Down: Catastrophe, Creativity, and the Renewal of Civilization.* Knopf Canada, 2006.

Hunt, T. *Building Jerusalem: The Rise and Fall of the Victorian City.* Orion Books, 2004.

Illich, I. *The Right to Useful Unemployment.* Marion Boyars, 1978.

———. *Shadow Work.* Marion Boyars, 1999.

———. *Tools for Conviviality.* Harper & Row, 1973.

International Assessment of Agricultural Knowledge, Science and Technology for Development (IAASTD). *Agriculture at a Crossroads.* Island Press, 2009.

International Independence Institute. *The Community Land Trust: A Guide to a New Model for Land Tenure in America.* Author, 1972.

Jackson, T. *Prosperity without Growth? The Transition to a Sustainable Economy.* Sustainable Development Commission, 2009, www.sd-commission.org. uk/file_download.php?target=/publications/downloads/Prosperity%20 without%20Growth.pdf .

Jacobs, J. *Cities and the Wealth of Nations.* New York: Vintage Books, 1985.

Johnston, T., and G. Edgar. *Law and Practice of Company Accounting in New Zealand.* Butterworths, 1963.

Keen, S. "Debtwatch No. 42: The Economic Case against Bernanke." Steve Keen's Debtwatch website, 24 January 2010, www.debtdeflation.com/blogs/2010/01/ 24/debtwatch-no-42-the-economic-case-against-bernanke/.

Kennedy, M. *A Changing Money System: The Economy of Ecology.* Permaculture Publications, 1991.

———. *Interest and Inflation Free Money.* Seva International, 1995.

Keynes, J.M. "Economic Possibilities for Our Grandchildren." In *Essays in Persuasion,* 358–73. WW Norton & Co, 1963.

————. *General Theory of Employment, Interest and Money.* Palgrave Macmillan, 1936.

Kharecha, P., and J. Hansen. "Implications of 'Peak Oil' for Atmospheric CO_2 and Climate." *Global Biogeochemical Cycles* 22 (2008) doi:10.1029/2007GB003142.

King, M.L. *Where Do We Go from Here: Chaos or Community?* Beacon Press, 1967.

Korten, D. *Agenda for a New Economy: From Phantom Wealth to Real Wealth.* Berrett Koehler, 2009.

Krehm, W. *Towards a Non-Autistic Economy: A Place at the Table for Society.* Comer, 2002.

Kunstler, J.H. *The Long Emergency: Surviving the Converging Catastrophes of the Twenty-First Century.* Grove/Atlantic, 2005.

Kurimoto, A. "Member Participation Revisited: From Han Groups to What?" Consumer Co-operative Institute of Japan, 2007.

Lappe, F.M. *Democracy's Edge: Choosing to Save Our Country by Bringing Democracy to Life.* Jossey-Bass, 2005.

Lewis, M. "Common Ground: CED and the Social Economy: Sorting Out the Basics." *Making Waves* 15,1 (Spring 2004), 7–11.

————. "Ecology of Success." *Making Waves* 10, no. 1 (1999), communityrenewal. ca/sites/all/files/resource/MW100112.pdf.

Lewis M., and S. Perry. *Reinventing the Local Economy: What Ten Canadian Initiatives Can Teach Us About Building Creative, Inclusive, Sustainable Communities.* Centre for Community Enterprise, 1994.

Lewis, M., and D. Swiney. "Social Economy? Solidarity Economy? Exploring the Implications of Conceptual Nuance for Acting in a Volatile World." BALTA Working Paper Series. Canadian Centre for Community Renewal, 2007, auspace. athabascau.ca:8080/dspace/bitstream/2149/2649/1/BALTA%20C6%20Paper%20 -%20SSE%20Frameworks%20Two.pdf.

Lietaer, B. *The Future of Money.* Century, 2001.

Lipset, S. *Agrarian Socialism: The Cooperative Commonwealth Federation in Saskatchewan, A Study in Political Sociology.* University of California Press, 1950.

Lopez, B. *Arctic Dreams.* Vintage, 2001.

Lovelock, J. *The Vanishing Face of Gaia: The Final Warning.* Penguin Books, 2009.

Lutz, M. *Economics for the Common Good: Two Centuries of Social Economic Thought in the Humanistic Tradition.* Routledge, 1990.

Martinez-Torres, M.E., and P.M. Rosset. "La Via Campesina: The Evolution of a Transnational Movement." *Journal of Peasant Studies* (February 2010), www.stwr. org/food-security-agriculture/la-via-campesina-the-birth-and-evolution-of-a-transnational-social-movement.html.

Mason, P. *Meltdown: The End of the Age of Greed.* Verso, 2009.

————. *Why It's Kicking Off Everywhere: The New Global Revolutions.* Verso, 2012.

Mees, R. *Money for a Better World.* Hawthorn Press, 1991.

Mellor, M. *The Future of Money: From Financial Crisis to Public Resource.* Pluto Press, 2009.

Mendell, M., and R. Nogales. "Social Enterprise in OECD Countries: What Are the Financial Streams?" In *The Changing Boundaries of Social Enterprises*, ed. Antonella Noya. OECD, 2009.

Mill, J.S. *On Liberty and Utilitarianism*. 1859 and 1863; repr. Augustus M. Kelley Publishers, 1993.

———. *Principles of Political Economy*. 1848; repr. Augustus M. Kelley Publishers, 1987.

Millennium Ecosystem Assessment. *Ecosystems and Human Well-being: Synthesis*. Island Press, 2005, www.maweb.org/documents/document.356.aspx.pdf.

Minsky, H. "The Financial Instability Hypothesis." Working Paper No. 74. Prepared for *Handbook of Radical Political Economy*, ed. Philip Arestis and Malcolm Sawyer. Edward Elgar, 1992, www.levy.org/pubs/wp74.pdf.

Moyers, B. "Louis Kelso, Capitalist." In *A World of Ideas II*, ed. A. Tucher. Doubleday, 1990.

Murphy, R., and C. Hines. *Making Pensions Work*. Finance for the Future, September 2010.

Murray, R. *Danger and Opportunity: Crisis and the New Social Economy*. NESTA/ Young Foundation, September 2009.

National Association of Credit Union Workers, new economics foundation, and Rebuilding Society Network. "Community Banking Partnership: The Joined-Up Solution for Financial Inclusion and Community Economic Development." NACUW, April 2009, www.varotherham.org.uk/financial-inclusion-news/1177-community-banking-partnership-prospectus-published.

National Credit Union Administration, *2010 Annual Report, "Resilience and the Road Ahead."* NCUA, 2011.

National Farmers Union. *Understanding the Farm Crisis*. NFU, 2005.

new economics foundation. *Profiting from Poverty*. nef, 2003.

Oakeshott, R. *Jobs and Fairness: The Logic and Experience of Employee Ownership*. Michael Russell Publishing, 2000.

Ostergaard, G. *The Tradition of Workers' Control*. Freedom Press, 1997.

Parekh, B. *Gandhi's Political Philosophy: A Critical Examination*. Macmillan, 1989.

Patel, R. *The Value of Nothing: Why Everything Costs Much More Than We Think*. Harper Collins, 2009.

Paterson, B., and K. Dayson. *Proof of Concept: Community Land Trusts*. University of Salford, 2011, www.communityfinance.salford.ac.uk/.

Pearce, J. *Social Enterprise in Anytown*. Calouste Gulbenkian Foundation, 2003.

Perry, S.E., and G. Loewen. "Equity Tax Credits As a Tool of CED: A Comparison of Two Local Investment Incentive Programs." *Making Waves* 20, no. 3 (Autumn 2009): 21–25.

Persky, J. (2007) "Retrospectives: From Usury to Interest." *Journal of Economic Perspectives* 21, no. 1 (Winter 2007): 231–33.

Phillips, R. "Faith Based Collaboration: Connections That Work for Communities." *Making Waves* 12 no. 3 (2001).

Polanyi, K. *Dahomey and the Slave Trade*. AMS Press, 1990.

———. *The Great Transformation: The Political and Economic Origins of Our Time*. Beacon Press, 1957.

———. *Trade and Markets in Early Empires*. Free Press, 1957.

Pretty, J., and R. Hine. *Reducing Food Poverty with Sustainable Agriculture: A Summary of New Evidence*. University of Essex, 2001, www.essex.ac.uk/ces/esu/occasionalpapers/SAFErepSUBHEADS.shtm.

Priestman, R. "Is There Hope for All Canadians?" *COMER, The Journal of the Committee on Monetary and Economic Reform* 23, no. 9 (September 2011).

Pyle, R.M. "Cosmic Convergence," *Orion* 24, no. 3 (2005): 68–69.

Restakis, J. *Humanizing the Economy: Co-operatives in the Age of Capital*. New Society Publishers, 2010.

Ritchie, M., S. Murphy, and M.B. Lake. "United States Dumping on World Agricultural Markets." Cancun Series paper no. 1. Institute for Agriculture and Trade Policy, 2004.

Robertson, J. *Future Money: Breakdown or Breakthrough*. Green Books, 2012.

Rodgers, D. "Mutually Beneficial." In *Ground Breaking: New Ideas on Housing Delivery*. Shelter, 2009.

———. "New Foundations — Unlocking the Potential for Affordable Homes." The Co-operative Party, 2009.

Rosset P.M. *Food Is Different: Why We Must Get the WTO Out of Agriculture*. Zed Books, 2006.

Rosset, P., and M.E. Martinez-Torres. *Participatory Evaluation of La Via Campesina: Public Version*. The Norwegian Development Fund and La Via Campesina, 2005.

Rousseau, J. J. *Discourse on Inequality*. Penguin Books, 1985.

Rubin, J. *Why Your World Is About to Get a Whole Lot Smaller: Oil and the End of Globalization*. Random House, 2009.

Russell, B. *Principles of Social Reconstruction*. Allen & Unwin, 1916.

———. *Roads to Freedom*. Allen & Unwin, 1918.

Sahlins, M. *Culture and Practical Reason*. University of Chicago Press, 1978.

Sale, K. *Human Scale*. Secker & Warburg, 1980.

Schlenker, W., and M.J. Roberts. "Nonlinear Temperature Effects Indicate Severe Damages to U.S. Crop Yields under Climate Change." *Proceedings of the National Academy of Sciences*, 24 August 2009.

Schorr, L. *Common Purpose: Strengthening Families and Neighbourhoods to Rebuild America*. Doubleday Anchor Books, 1997.

Schumacher, E.F. *Small Is Beautiful: Economics as if People Mattered*. Vintage Books, 1993.

Semple, B. "Prospect's Adair Turner Interview Sparks Debate across the World." *Prospect Magazine*, 28 August 2009.

Simms, A., A. Pettifor, C. Lucas, C. Secrett, C. Hines, J. Leggett, L. Elliott, T. Juniper, and R. Murphy. *The Green New Deal*. new economics foundation, 2008.

Sismondi, J.C.L. de. *New Principles of Political Economy*. Translated by R. Hyse. 1827; repr. Transaction Publishers, 1991.

Smil, V. "Population Growth and Nitrogen: An Exploration of a Critical Existential Link." *Population and Development Review* 17 (1991):569–601.

Smith, A. *The Wealth of Nations*. Volume 1. Modern Library, Random House, 1994.

Smith, J.W. *The World's Wasted Wealth*. The Institute for Economic Democracy, 1994.

Social Enterprise Coalition. *Unlocking the Potential: A Guide to Finance for Social Enterprises*. London, 2004.

Soddy, F. *Money Versus Man*. E.P. Dutton, 1933.

———. *Wealth, Virtual Wealth and Debt*. E.P. Dutton, 1933.

Sorokin, P. *Social and Cultural Dynamics*. 1957; repr. Transaction, 1970.

Srinivasan, U.T., et al. "The Debt of Nations and the Distribution of Ecological Impacts from Human Activities." *Proceedings of the National Academy of Sciences* 105, no. 5 (2008).

Steiner, R. *Economics: The World As One Economy*. Rudolf Steiner Archive Series. Edited by Christopher Houghton Budd. New Economy Publications, 1993.

Tarnas, R. *Cosmos and Psyche: Intimations of a New World View*. Penguin Viking, 2006.

Tawney, R.H. *The Acquisitive Society*. Collins, 1921.

Taylor, C. *Hegel*. Cambridge University Press, 1975.

Thompson, E.P. *Customs in Common*. Penguin Books, 1991.

Tily, G. *Keynes Betrayed: The General Theory, the Rate of Interest and "Keynesian" Economics*, Palgrave Macmillan, 2010.

Tocqueville. A. de. *Democracy in America*. Penguin, 2003.

Tomczak, J. "Implications of Fossil Fuel Dependence for the Food System." Tompkins Country Relocalization Project, 11 December 2005, www.energy bulletin.net/node/17036.

Tsui, K.K. "More Oil, Less Democracy: Evidence from Worldwide Crude Oil Discoveries." *Economic Journal* 121 (March 2010), 89–115, www.res.org.uk/economic/freearticles/2011/march2011.pdf.

Tucker, B. *Instead of a Book*. 1887 available for download at www.scribd.com/doc/36310810/Benjamin-Tucker-Instead-Of-A-Book-By-A-Man-Too-Busy-To-Write-One.

Tudge, C. *Feeding People Is Easy*. Pari Publishing, 2007.

Turnbull, S. "Achieving Environmental Sustainable Prosperity." Paper presented to 13th Conference of the Association of Heterodox Economics, Nottingham Trent University, UK, 10 July 2011, available at ssrn.com/abstract=1769349.

———. *Democratising the Wealth of Nations*. Social Science Research Network, 1975, ssrn.com/abstract_id=1146062.

———. "Grounding Economics in Commercial Reality: A Cash-Flow Paradigm." In *Essays in Heterodox Economics: Proceedings of the Fifth Conference of Heterodox Economics*, ed. P. Kreisler, M. Johnson, and J. Lodewijks. University of New South Wales, 2006.

———. "The Limitations in Corporate Governance Best Practices." Chapter 25 of *Handbook of Corporate Governance*, ed. C. Clarke and D. Branson. Sage Publications, 2005.

———. "Options for Rebuilding the Economy and the Financial System." 2009. Available at ssrn.com/abstract=1322210.

———. "Time Limited Corporations." *Abacus: A Journal of Business and Accounting Studies* 9, no. 1 (1973): 28–43, onlinelibrary.wiley.com/doi/10.1111/j.1467-6281. 1973.tb00173.x/abstract.

United Nations Food and Agriculture Organization. *Livestock's Long Shadow: Environmental Issues and Options.* UN FAO, 2006.

Van En, R. "Eating for Your Community: A Report from the Founder of Community Supported Agriculture." In *Context: A Quarterly of Human Sustainable Culture* (1995), www.context.org/ICLIB/IC42/VanEn.htm.

Victor, P. *Managing without Growth: Slower by Design, Not Disaster.* Edward Elgar, 2008.

Walker, B. *Resilience Thinking: Sustaining Ecosystems and People in a Changing World.* Island Press, 2006.

Wilson, T. *A Discourse on Usury*, ed. and introduced by R.H. Tawney. 1572; repr. G. Bell and Sons, 1925.

Winstanley, G. "New Year's Gift." In *Gerard Winstanley: Selected Writings.* Aporia Press, 1989.

World Water Assessment Programme. *United Nations World Water Development Report 3: Water in a Changing World.* UNESCO and Earthscan, 2009, www.uneS Co.org/water/wwap/wwdr/wwdr3/.

Yokota, K. *I Among Others: An Introspective Look at the Theory and Practice of the Seikatsu Club Movement.* Seikatsu Club Seikyo Kanagawa, 1991.

Index

About the Authors

Pat Conaty

PAT CONATY is a Californian working in England and Wales. He is a Fellow of new economics foundation and a research associate of Co-operatives UK. He specialises in action research on innovative forms of economic democracy and mutual enterprise. His work has been mainly in the fields of household debt solutions, community development finance and community land trusts.

Michael Lewis

At 25 Mike founded what is now known as the Canadian Centre for Community Renewal. Ever since he has been engaged community economic development (CED), development finance and the social and co-operative economy. He is a prolific author and a respected practitioner. From entrepreneurial development to building national networks, from strategic assistance to CED organizations in impoverished settings to designing tools and curriculum to strengthen community resilience, Mike has led hundreds of projects over the last 35 years. Drawing on this diverse experience, motivated by his grandchildren and increasingly conscious of the interplay of climate change, peak oil and the outrageous excesses of the global finance industry, Mike considers the issues and innovations outlined in 'The Resilience Imperative' as the core focus of his vocation.